A RESURGENT CHINA

A RESURGENT CHINA

South Asian Perspectives

Editors

S. D. Muni
Tan Tai Yong

Routledge
Taylor & Francis Group
LONDON NEW YORK NEW DELHI

First published 2012 in India
by Routledge
912 Tolstoy House, 15–17 Tolstoy Marg, Connaught Place, New Delhi 110 001

Simultaneously published in the UK
by Routledge
2 Park Square, Milton Park, Abingdon, Oxfordshire OX14 4RN

First issued in paperback 2015

Routledge is an imprint of the Taylor & Francis Group, an informa business

© 2012 S. D. Muni & Tan Tai Yong

Typeset by
Star Compugraphics Private Limited

British Library Cataloguing-in-Publication Data
A catalogue record of this book is available from the British Library

ISBN13: 978-1-138-66246-9 (pbk)
ISBN13: 978-0-415-50191-0 (hbk)

Contents

List of Tables and Figures

Tables

Figures

Preface

China's rise as a major Asian and world power has been acknowledged globally. The imports and impacts of this rise are, however, still in the process of being mapped out and grasped. Countries are looking at China's rise from their respective vantage points. There is admiration, expectation, anxiety and apprehension; in some cases, all of them together. The Institute of South Asian Studies (ISAS) decided to explore the perceptions of South Asian countries about China's rise. This study is an outcome of that attempt.

The best way to fathom the perceptions of the South Asian countries about China's rise was to go to the experts and policy analysts based in these countries. We prepared a concept note outlining the need for highlighting the country-perceptions, identifying the constituencies wherein these perceptions are rooted and articulated and looking at the projections of how they will unfold in the years to come. This concept note was sent to our country experts but it was made very clear that experts were free to go beyond the parameters of the concept note and bring out all the relevant aspects of the ways in which the respective countries are looking at China. Their contributions are presented for wider debate among academics, area experts and policy makers for a better understanding of our regional dynamics. The contributions of the country experts have been reinforced by relevant statistics on China's strategic and economic engagement with the South Asian countries prepared by the young researchers of the institute. We are thankful to both the country experts and the ISAS researchers for their valuable contributions.

Most of the leg (and finger) work in preparing this volume was done by our young colleague Tridivesh Singh Maini. He coordinated all the contributions meticulously; with hard work, dedication and a smile. We thank him for his endeavours. This project could not have been completed without the support of the institute's very able and committed administrative staff on a day-to-day basis. They also deserve our sincere thanks. We also owe our appreciation to the publishers for accepting this project and turning out an attractive product in a reasonable time span. This being the first volume of its kind, it is surely not free from gaps and lapses. We will learn about them through the comments and assessments of our readers and accordingly improve in the future.

S. D. Muni
Tan Tai Yong

Introduction

Tan Tai Yong

It is already a well-worn adage, attributed to Napoleon, that when China, a sickly, sleeping giant in the 19th century, eventually awakes from its long slumber, the whole world will tremble.[1] China has indeed awoken, and its rapid rise as a Superpower in the making is one of the most momentous developments in recent history. The position that it occupies today — it is probably (or potentially) the most significant power in the world after America — has fundamental ramifications for the international order. While American president Barack Obama seeks a more inclusive global order based on the participation of the G20, many observers hold the view that the new order will ultimately be predicated on the relationship between America, the incumbent Superpower, and China, the aspiring Superpower. In other words, it is not the G20, but the G2 that may eventually determine the framework of world affairs in the 21st century. The international community now needs little reminder that the Chinese factor will inevitably feature prominently in most major global issues today, from climate change to the global financial crisis.

China's rise in the past two decades has indeed been remarkable. The Chinese economy has been growing at breakneck speed since the late 1980s. Driven by the political need for performance-based legitimisation of the state, the Chinese authorities went on a path of economic development, with impressive results. For about twenty years, the Chinese economy grew at an average rate of 10 per cent annually, a trajectory that produced spectacular economic results, though not without inherent flaws.[2] The economic impact is driven by its formidable capacity as the factory of the world, producing more, cheaper and faster than any country in the world. The capacity shows no signs of abating and as long as demands are there, goods made in China will dominate the markets. At the rate that it is going, China will pull ahead of Europe, Japan, India and Russia in economic terms. Its unsurpassed economic growth has also been translated into a steady expansion of its diplomatic influence globally. The Chinese are now asserting themselves as they have never done before. The magnificent staging of the Olympics in 2008 was regarded as a coming-out party. In truly spectacular fashion, China has shown the world that it has arrived and is ready to claim its rightful place in the world. Even in the world of sports, the Chinese were determined to show that they were capable of outperforming everyone else by topping the medal tally table.

What are the implications of China's rise on the international system? How would China's pursuit of its national interests, strategic goals and its rightful position as an economic power-house affect the existing framework of the regional and international order? Will China's rise strengthen or disrupt the world order? Lee Kuan Yew, Singapore's elder statesman and an astute and long-term observer of China's rise, is of the opinion that the Chinese 'will not acquiesce to a *status quo* status indefinitely'. He feels that 'competition is inevitable, but conflict is not'.[3] In economic terms, the rise of China offers tremendous opportunities for some, concern for others. There are countries that view China's economic growth in a very positive perspective, as a source of opportunities and cooperation; while there are also countries that look at this growth as a source of threat and competition to their own growth and prosperity. Within Asia, for instance, reactions to the rise of China are a mixture of threat, competition and opportunity. Many of these countries, leveraging on the growth of China for their own economic development, have chosen to develop practical diplomatic and economic ties with China. But the relationships, driven by pragmatic considerations, have not always been easy. The size of the Chinese economy, its vast exporting capacity and inexorable demand for foreign direct investments make it a major competitor to the other major economies in the region, especially Japan, South Korea and India. As China's industrial might grows, its hunger for oil, fuel and raw materials will increase accordingly. National interests will spur China's search for and access to these resources and this may lead it to direct competition with other countries needing similar resources.

It is perhaps in the political and military spheres that the ascendency of a powerful China gives cause for consternation. Liberal opinion in western and Asian democracies views China's rise as ideologically discomforting and incompatible for a world system that has long embraced the western value system as its norm. As an Australian academic pointed out recently:

> In China the world confronts for the first time in many decades a more or less successful dictatorship. And this poses not merely a geo-strategic but also a political, even in a sense, an ethical challenge to those of us who believe that democracy does indeed represent a universal value.[4]

While the realists may see that post-Mao China is no longer operating out of an ideological straightjacket, the sudden rise of a country of the size of China, determined to raise the economic position of its massive population and in the process make its mark as the first ranked global power, will certainly have an impact on the global geopolitical and geo-economic landscape. Not surprisingly, China's unremitting modernisation of its armed forces is viewed with suspicion, generating uncertainty and apprehension about its future role and intent in Asian and world affairs. Small states in the region are still wary of the potential risks of a powerful China, and welcome the maintenance of balance in Asia, involving the Americans. Indeed, the interest in engaging China, through bilateral and multilateral forums, stems also from the belief that an involved China will be a key factor for regional stability and prosperity.

Aware that its spectacular rise is raising heckles among the major powers and in its neighbourhood, the Chinese have taken care to project their emergence as a 'peaceful rise' (*heping jueqi*). Premier Wen Jiabao put forward the thesis of China's peaceful rise on two separate occasions; in 2003, in an address at Harvard University and in 2004, during the Second Session of the 10th National People's Congress. In these speeches, he argued that China's development was dependent on world peace, and it would be self-defeating for China to threaten world order as it becomes a major player in world affairs. Indeed, it would be in China's interests to contribute to a peaceful order. He also assured the world that China would rely on its own resources and markets for its own development, which will take many generations to achieve, and that its main interest was economic growth, and that its growth 'will not be achieved at the expense of any particular country'.[5]

The Chinese leadership has therefore taken pains to remind the world that China has no intention of aggrandisement, consistently reassuring the major powers and its neighbours that there are no malicious intentions behind its modernisation programme, and that its purposes are entirely peaceful. To this end, China has embarked on a 'sophisticated military and defense diplomatic strategy', actively conducting diplomacy with its neighbours, projecting a 'good neighbour' policy in the Indian Ocean and Asia-Pacific region.[6] The main platform is trade, and the increasing volume of trade between China and its neighbours has, thus far, undergirded a strong and stable regional relationship. China has also sought regional cooperation to avoid conflict and through participation in confidence-building regional architecture, it seeks to assure its neighbours that it has no intention of upsetting the status quo. Chinese priorities at the moment will revolve around economic growth. This is needed to give political stability to the country whose population is now accustomed to, and expects, continuous growth and expansion of wealth. To do this, China knows that it would need markets for its exports. Trade will be essential and it would want an environment that is conducive for such activities. China has so far developed good economic ties with Japan, South Korea and India as well as a free trade agreement with the Association of South East Asian Nations (ASEAN). If they continue to do well economically, the Chinese can be assured they will become the greatest influence in the region.

China's interests have a direct bearing on the Indian Ocean region. In security terms, the Chinese are interested in becoming active stakeholders in a security architecture that affords it sea-lanes security, maritime support infrastructure and surveillance capabilities. In this regard, the Chinese navy has begun building relations with countries that rim the Indian Ocean, in the process consolidating its presence and expanding its engagement in the South Asian region. It has offered sale of military hardware at friendly prices to Indian Ocean littorals and has established footholds in key ports such as Chittagong in Bangladesh,

Hambantota in Sri Lanka and Gwadar in Pakistan.[7] China regards South Asia as a very important region, an integral part of its neighbourhood, and it hopes to create an impression that its intent in the region is benign and it desires to keep peace in the region, to have a stable South Asia. Yet, by projecting itself into a region that India, the other rising Asian power, regards as its strategic space, China will find itself not only confronting India, but also embroiled in the complex geopolitical dynamics of the South Asian region.

Chinese strategy in the Indian Ocean and its relations with South Asian countries are likely to be framed by its bilateral relationship with India. While Sino-Indian relations have improved significantly over the past decade, the positive outcomes in terms of a burgeoning bilateral trade are unfortunately matched by an enlarging 'trust deficit' between the two Asian giants. Alongside unresolved border disputes, China is uncomfortable that India continues to shelter the Dalai Lama, while India is suspicious of continuous Chinese support of its unfriendly neighbour, Pakistan.[8] Yet, both Beijing and New Delhi are making concerted efforts to further bilateral strategic cooperation for long-term gains. The key elements of China's policy, according to Chinese scholars, are to promote cooperation and manage potential conflicts, although in India, the mainstream view, while recognising China as a competitive power, calls for balanced engagement as a response.[9] As India sees itself as the primary power in South Asia, it will inadvertently view China's foray into the region with mixed feelings. China may view the South Asian region in terms of economic interests and goals, but these objectives cannot be separated from politics and security considerations.[10] India will perceive growing Chinese presence in South Asia (and naval presence in the Indian Ocean) as a challenge which, in turn, will influence its relationship with China on the one hand, and its South Asian neighbours on the other. In such a context, how China is viewed by India and the other South Asian countries, and the manner in which relationships are developed, bilaterally and multilaterally, will have significant impact on the political, security and economic dynamics of the region.

This volume will analyse in detail the perceptions of South Asian countries on both the economic and defence aspects of China's growth. Each country chapter has three broad sections.

In the first section, the country perspective on China's economic and defence growth will be identified and analysed. These chapters will not focus only on describing bilateral relations; rather they will examine how the policy makers in these countries look at China's economy, its defence modernisation, as well as its political and diplomatic role. In the second section, a careful and rigorous attempt is made to identify and examine the constituencies and stakeholders (such as business and industrial stakeholders, defence agencies, political parties and ideological groups, external interests, etc.), that contribute to the evolution and sustenance of the perceptions described in the first section. Each country would obviously have different stakeholders having both positive and negative perceptions of China's rise. The balance between them would be assessed on the bases of the strength, reach and potential of these constituencies/stakeholders. In the third section, the evolving and unfolding nature of these perceptions and the constituencies/stakeholders will be taken into account in a holistic manner to see what direction of future engagement between South Asian countries and China can be expected. Possibilities of changes in China's growth pattern, internal order and stability and foreign policy behaviour may also be factored into these analyses.

This volume will show that the rise of China will elicit different responses from the various countries in South Asia. These relationships will be determined by a matrix of factors, including threat perceptions, congruence of interests, policy options and the politics of international relations in a region where only national interests are permanent.

✳

Notes

1. This quote was attributed to Napoleon by Lord Amherst, British diplomat and ambassador extraordinary to the Ching Court in China in 1816, from William Safire's *New Political Dictionary*, New York: Random House, 1993.
2. Eswar S. Prasad, 'How to Sustain China's Growth Miracle', in Dali Y. Yang and Litao Zhao, *China's Reforms at 30: Challenges and Prospects*, Singapore: World Scientific, 2009, pp. 1–18.

3. Lee Kuan Yew, *The Fundamentals of Singapore's Foreign Policy: Then and Now*, S. Rajaratnam Lecture 2009, Singapore: MFA Diplomatic Academy, 2009, p. 11.
4. Greg Sheridan, 'Asian Democracy and Australia', in *The Asialink Essays*, August 2009, No. 6, University of Melbourne, p. 3.
5. See Zhang Guihong, 'China's Peaceful Rise and Sino-Indian Relations', *China Report*, vol. 41, no. 2, 2005 pp. 159–71, here p. 161.
6. Loro Horta, 'China Takes to the Sea', *Pacnet Newsletter*, no. 63, 18 September 2009.
7. Seminar presentation by Vijay Sakhuja, 'Maritime Multilateralism: China's Strategy for the Indian Ocean', at the Institute of Southeast Asian Studies, Singapore, 14 November 2009.
8. *The Sunday Times* published parts of a letter from AQ Khan on 20 September, detailing the help that China had given to establish nuclear weapons in Pakistan.
9. See Yuan Jing-dong, 'Sizing up the Elephant: Beijing's Perspectives on a Rising India', *East Asian Policy*, vol. 1, no. 4 (Oct.–Dec.), pp. 25–33. See Sumit Ganguly, 'Assessing India's Responses to the Rise of China: Fears and Misgivings', in Carolyn W. Pumphrey (ed.), *The Rise of China in Asia: Security Implications*, Carlisle Barracks: The Strategic Studies Institute, 2002, pp. 95–104, available at http://www.strategicstudiesinstitute.army.mil/pdffiles/PUB61.pdf.
10. Zhang Guihong, 'The Rise of China: India's Perceptions and Responses', *South Asian Survey*, vol. 13, no. 1, 2006, pp. 93–102, here p. 99.

1

Bangladesh
A Partner for Peace and Prosperity

C. M. SHAFI SAMI

'The world is experiencing one of the biggest revolutions in history, as economic power shifts from the developed world to China and other emerging giants', observes *The Economist*. The prestigious international weekly news magazine continues, 'Thanks to market reforms, emerging economies are growing much faster than developed ones. There is a widening gap between their growth rate and that of the sluggish developed world. . . . According to the IMF, this year they are growing almost four times as fast.'[1] An internationally recognised authority on contemporary Chinese affairs and international politics, Professor David Shambaugh believes that Asia is changing, and one of the primary catalysts of change in the region is the rise of China. He states:

> The structure of power and parameters of interactions that have characterized international relations in the Asian region over the last half century are being fundamentally affected by, among other factors, China's growing economic and military power, rising political influence, distinctive diplomatic voice, and increasing involvement in regional multilateral institutions.[2]

This rapid economic growth, global trading ties and expanding diplomatic cooperation have pushed China to the highest rank of nations.[3]

Napoleon Bonaparte had once observed, 'China is a sleeping giant. Let her sleep, for when she wakes she will shake the world.' China is fully awake today; only the future can tell if it will ultimately shake the world or not. Whether its entry on the global power stage will be confrontational and violent or conciliatory and peaceful will depend on a number of factors including how the existing global power structure braces up to it. But China's emergence as a major economic and political factor in the global power matrix is a reality that can no longer be ignored. With its ever increasing economic power and the resultant political clout, China appears set to realise the prediction of the world-famous historian Arnold Toynbee and the forecast of one of the most successful investors of the world, Warren Edward Buffet, that the 21st century would be the Chinese century.[4]

Rise of China

Growth Rate

For most of the recorded history of the past two millennia, China, which called itself the 'Middle Kingdom', was the world's largest and most advanced economy.[5] In the view of *The Economist*, 'China was not only the largest economy for much of recorded history, but until the end of the 15th century, it also had the highest income per capita and was the world's technological leader'.[6] According to the *Financial Times*, 'China has been the world's largest economy for 18 of the past 20 centuries'[7] As recently as 1820, China accounted for 33 per cent of the world's gross domestic product (GDP). Then it missed the Industrial Revolution of the 19th century and stagnated while Europe and America gained economic power. By the early 20th century, China accounted for only 9 per cent of the world's GDP.[8]

But the tables seem to be turning again. In the words of Professor Shambaugh, 'The tectonic plates that have characterized Asia for half a century are shifting, and China may be returning to its traditional role as the central actor in Asia'.[9] The largest developing country in the world, China, with a population of 1.3 billion, is experiencing an unprecedented growth rate since Deng Xiaoping initiated the reform process allowing market forces to play an increasingly important role in the existing stringent command economy of the country. China's role in the global economy has increased sharply in the past twenty-five years. During this period the Chinese economy has grown at an amazing rate of about 10 per cent per year, measured in GDP. In economic size China is the biggest economy in Asia after Japan and globally it is surpassed only by the US, Japan, Germany and France. Its share in global growth in 1995–2002 has been estimated at 25 per cent, compared to 20 per cent for the US.[10] With China's foreign exchange reserves of over $1 trillion, it enjoys the distinction of being the largest surplus country. Over the last decades the annual income per capita in China has risen tenfold from a bare $200 in 1978 to nearly $2,000 by 2007.[11] China is on the rise; to many Chinese people this signals a logical and rightful return of the country to the pre-eminent position it occupied for much of the past millennia.[12]

Foreign Direct Investment

Since China's modernisation and reform process started in 1978 foreign direct investment (FDI) became a fundamental instrument of growth for China. Foreign direct investment into the country increased from a bare $3 billion in 1990 to $52.7 billion in 2002, causing China's share of total FDI into the developing world to rise 32.5 per cent, and its share of FDI into Asia to soar to 55.5 per cent.[13] Today, China is second only to the US as a recipient of foreign direct investment and continues to be the largest recipient among developing countries in the world.[14] This trend is likely to gain further momentum as trade barriers in China continue to decline and infrastructural and communications facilities are improved. Furthermore, China's entry into the World Trade Organisation (WTO) is expected to give added impetus to its export, FDI and overall growth prospects.[15] China's growth rate since 1990 has surpassed the hitherto unbeatable 20th-century growth records of Japan and other East Asian 'miracle' economies like South Korea, Taiwan and Singapore.[16] Another remarkable feature is that the Chinese economy successfully isolated itself from the global economic meltdown in 2008 and registered a growth rate of 9.9 per cent in the first three quarters of 2008, and 11.9 per cent in the year 2007.[17]

Trade

Trade has been another critical instrument of China's economic growth. China has grown to be the third largest trading nation of the world following the US and Germany. It is also one of the largest traders with many Asian countries. Trade between China and the rest of Asia topped $495 billion in 2003, up 36.5 per cent over the figure of 2002.[18] Bilateral trade between the Association of South East Asian Nations (ASEAN) and China totalled $39.5 billion in 2002, growing at an annual average of slightly over 20 per cent since 1991 when overall trade amounted to only $7.9 billion.[19] In 2004 it surpassed $100 billion which is 100 times its value in 1978. At a global level China's foreign trade has expanded at an annual rate of 15 per cent since then. In 2004, China became South Korea's top trading partner with their bilateral trade growing at nearly 40 per cent to US$ 79 billion. That year China also became Japan's biggest trading partner, with their two-way trade reaching US$ 214 billion.[20] China–US trade was worth more than $260 billion in 2006 and is expected to rise to $300 billion by 2010.

Far beyond, China's trade relations have also expanded in Africa and Latin America. The 2006 Forum on China–Africa Cooperation set a target of $100 billion bilateral trade by 2010.[21] Trade with Latin America has increased from around $200 million in 1975 to $50.5 billion in 2005; the annual average growth between 2000 and 2005 was around 27 per cent.[22] China's trade has spread all over the globe.

Outward Foreign Direct Investment

China is not just trading; it is also becoming a significant investor with its Outward Foreign Direct Investment (OFDI) steadily rising. Recently it became one of the largest investors in Indonesia and has emerged as the largest source of foreign investment in some of the smaller economies in South East Asia like in Cambodia.[23] It is also spreading its investment around the globe — in Asia, Africa and in the backyard of the US in Latin America and even in the Western Hemisphere. According to statistics given by the Chinese Ministry of Commerce, Chinese companies invested a record $37 billion overseas in 2007, up 76 per cent over its investment in 2006. A staggering 85 per cent of China's total OFDI of roughly $128 billion (at the end of 2007) has been invested since 2001. This is projected to rise to over $70 billion by 2011.[24] In the years ahead, the newly launched China Investment Corporation with $200 billion in foreign exchange reserves at its disposal will play a significant role in boosting investment abroad. For countries in Asia and beyond, Chinese OFDI will offer an alternative source with enormous potential.

Military Strength

China's armed forces, the Peoples' Liberation Army (PLA), are the third largest military force of the world with about 2.25 million active members. In the early 1980s China had followed a policy of shrinking defence allocations so as to be able to increasingly devote its resources to economic development. Since 1985, however, it has pursued a policy of reform of the armed forces that focused on modernisation and adoption of high technology. The policy emphasised 'quality over quantity' and was aimed at making the PLA a world-class force.

In 1955, China decided to proceed with a nuclear weapons programme and subsequently conducted its first nuclear test, in 1964. China pledged no-first-use of nuclear weapons. It also pledged not to use nuclear weapons against non-nuclear states and nuclear-free zones. China continues to modernise its nuclear force and it has tested long-range submarine and launched missiles, capable of hitting the continental US from China's littoral waters. China is a signatory to the Non-proliferation Treaty (NPT) and has issued detailed nuclear export control regulations. China began implementing regulations establishing controls over nuclear-related dual-use items in 1998.

China is also developing cyber and space war capabilities. Doug Bandow, in 'China Rising: The Next Global Superpower' states that in January 2007 'China took a small but critical step to end American global dominance. Until now the US and Russia were the only two nations thought capable of making military use of space. But Beijing dramatically crashed this select club by using a ground-based ballistic missile to destroy an old weather satellite. Although America will remain the globe's military number one for decades, it must begin to contemplate a world in which it no longer stands alone.'[25] US defence secretary Robert Gates, testifying before the Senate Arms Services Committee in January 2009, also spoke of greater Chinese investments in military modernisation and its 'growing capabilities in cyber and anti-satellite warfare, anti-air and anti-ship weaponry, submarines and ballistic missiles' which he identified as a possible threat to the US. The Pentagon believes that China has the greatest potential to compete militarily with the United States and field disruptive military technologies that could offset traditional US military advantages.[26] Pentagon is also worried over the modernisation of China's nuclear force and fielding of intercontinental range ballistic missiles that enhances China's strategic strike capabilities and its increasing capabilities to enter into space and cyberspace domains from the traditional battlefields of land, air and sea dimensions.[27]

China is building up a strong navy with 'blue-water' capabilities and is pursuing a policy aimed at enhancement of early-warning systems, anti-missile defences and airstrike capabilities. In the words of President Hu Jintao, China 'should strive to build a powerful navy that adapts to the needs of our military's historical mission in this new century and at this new stage'.[28]

Evidently, China is becoming more capable and more assertive in military fields. Eventually, in the long run, it may emerge as a Superpower but it is still far from matching the military strength of the US in terms of strength and capacity. The United States' military capabilities remain unsurpassable for China for the present and shall remain so for the foreseeable future. Being a developing country, its ability to spend billions of dollars needed to bridge the huge gap between the capabilities of the two countries is also severely restricted. Undeniably, however, China's military strength and clout are increasing significantly. China may not become a Superpower in the immediate future but it is well on its way to emerging as a major power that sets in motion a process of bringing about multipolarity to the world order.

Foreign Relations

Since opening up, China has steadily expanded and strengthened its relations with neighbouring countries, with the developing countries all over the world and also with major western powers.

China's relations with its South East Asian neighbours have undergone a metamorphosis of sorts — from initial confrontational relations to those of cordiality. Its relations with South East Asian countries are robust in contrast to the situation a decade or two ago when China did not have full diplomatic relations with prominent regional countries like Indonesia, Singapore and South Korea.

In its immediate neighbourhood, China has succeeded in bringing about considerable improvements in its relations with

Japan. The two nations have agreed to develop a 'strategic and mutually reciprocal' relationship. The two countries are also mulling a five-point Chinese proposal to enhance mutual cooperation, expand cultural exchanges and strengthen mutual strategic trust.

With the developed world, China has followed a policy of building good relations tampered with a sense of pragmatism and flexibility and sought out common grounds for cooperation. The reversal of US–China bilateral ties from an adversarial relationship to a stable cooperation over the last four decades provides a typical example in which the growth of relations remained reasonably insulated from the negative impact of disputes. As the two nations concentrate on identifying common interests and on facing common challenges the level of their bilateral relationship has graduated to one of constructive cooperation.

China pursues the development of its relations with Arab and Middle East countries as well as African counties with a great deal of zeal. China has negotiated significant oil deals with Iran including a proposal to develop an oil field in that country. China's trade with the six Gulf Cooperation Council (GCC) countries is steadily increasing. It is actively engaged in developing relations with Latin America in which energy cooperation plays a pivotal role.

Multilateral Diplomacy

China has been active in international and regional multilateral diplomacy as 'both a participant and a sponsor'. China has increasingly assumed a constructive and responsible role in global political and economic issues. It has played an important role in dealing with the Asian financial crisis, nuclear arms race in South Asia, the Kosovo crisis, the post-9/11 anti-terror campaign, the Afghan war, the Iraq war and the Korean nuclear crisis among others.

China has deepened its engagement with the Association of South East Asian Nations at a multilateral level. It enjoys Summit partnership status with ASEAN as a member of ASEAN+4. China and ASEAN nations have agreed to form the largest free trade zone in the world by 2015. It is a significant development in promoting regionalism in Asia 'not only because it is the first such agreement that China has entered into after becoming a

WTO member, but also because it is going to be one of the largest FTAs ever negotiated, involving about 1.7 billion people, over $2 trillion in aggregate GDP and $1.2 billion in total trade spanning eleven diverse and heterogeneous economies, both in terms of their size and levels of development'.[29] China recently became the first non-ASEAN member state to join the Treaty of Amity and Cooperation in South East Asia that provides for the peaceful resolution of territorial disputes. China values the ASEAN Regional Forum (ARF) for its potential in establishing a regional cooperative security community and has deepened its participation in the organisation.

China has also developed its relations with the European Union (EU) which has come to consider China as a 'strategic partner' and has made developing relations with China a top EU foreign policy priority. The G8, consisting of Britain, Canada, France, Germany, Italy, Japan, Russia and the United States which plays an important role in world politics and economic affairs, is attaching greater importance to developing its relations with China.

Besides playing an important role in ASEAN, Asia-Pacific Economic Cooperation (APEC) and the Asia-Europe Meeting (ASEM) and forging ties with EU, China initiated the setting up of the Central Asian security grouping, the 'Shanghai Five', which was formalised as the Shanghai Cooperation Organisation (SCO). China's hosting of the six-party talks on the North Korean nuclear issue lends another important dimension to its active and constructive multilateral diplomatic profile.

An interesting aspect of China's diplomacy is its advocacy for a new just and reasonable international political and economic order to promote peace, development and multipolarisation as also regional economic and security cooperation in the world. China has continuously enhanced its role and participation in the United Nations and other international organisations and has taken a positive stand on UN reforms, its greater democratisation and on increasing the representation of developing countries in the UN Security Council. It seeks to make the UN and the Security Council the pivotal centres for addressing multilateral arms control and disarmament as well as combat terrorism and international conflict situations.

Over the past twenty years, China has become an active participant in UN peacekeeping. Moving away from its traditional adherence to the principles of non-intervention, it has evolved a pragmatic policy on international peacekeeping and has over 2,000 Peacekeepers serving in ten UN peacekeeping operations worldwide. Among the five permanent members of the UN Security Council (UNSC), it is the second largest provider of Peacekeepers.

Soft Power of Diplomacy

As its hard power of political, economic and military strength grows China is placing increasing importance on 'soft power' in the conduct of its foreign relations and is using the 'soft power' of culture and ideas to make friends all over the region.[30] China is providing higher education facilities to an increasing number of students from Asian nations; about 80 per cent of more than 78,000 foreign students studying in Chinese universities come from Asian countries.[31] China is sending cultural troupes and representatives of print and electronic media abroad. To promote respect for cultural diversity it also actively encourages cultural teams from friendly countries to visit China. At the official level Chinese people's friendship groups are visiting friendly countries in increasing numbers and also inviting such groups from these countries to visit China. Chinese think tanks are also increasingly engaging in bilateral and regional dialogues with their counterparts from abroad. As China's influence expands around the globe, China hopes to project its image through the use of 'soft power' by exporting its culture.[32]

China-South Asia Relations: Trends and Perceptions

South Asia–China relations are steeped in history dating back to the 3rd century. The southern branch of the famous silk route ran through the land mass of South Asia. It crossed the high mountains into northeast India via the ancient tea route and then travelled West along the mighty rivers, the Brahmaputra and the Ganges. Finally, it ran through Pakistan before joining the northern branch of the route over the Hindu Kush. It also had southward spurs connecting the maritime silk route that extended westward via ports on the coasts of India and Sri Lanka. The silk route not only provided a series of trade routes but these also served as arteries for cultural transmission and interaction by linking traders, merchants, pilgrims and citizens.[33] The linkages were extensive.

China is South Asia's next-door neighbour; it has traditionally accorded special importance to all countries of the region — big or small. Its relations with all the regional states are steadily growing with a strong underpinning on economic and trade relations.

China's relations with two South Asian countries — Pakistan and India — deserve special mention here. Pakistan is a major recipient of Chinese economic aid with large-scale infrastructure projects. Highways, electricity complexes, power plants and ports are being implemented with Chinese assistance. China has emerged as a major trading partner of Pakistan, accounting for nearly 11 per cent of Pakistan's imports in 2004. Trade between the two countries was worth $4.25 billion in 2005, a 40 per cent increase from the year before. The two countries are making efforts to improve their economic relations which, viewed in the context of their overall relationship, appear to be relatively underdeveloped.[34] China has installed a 325 megawatt nuclear power reactor in Pakistan and is engaged in installing a second power reactor of the same capacity.[35] A significant ongoing project between the two nations is the construction of a major port complex at the naval base of Gwadar on the Arabian Sea which will provide China strategic access to the Persian Gulf and a naval outpost on the Indian Ocean from which to protect its oil imports from West Asia.

The main stimulus to China–Pakistan relations was security consideration. However, the bilateral relations between the two countries progressively expanded to cover the entire gamut of relations — political, economic, cultural and strategic. Pakistan's relations with China blossomed as the latter's relations with India deteriorated after the 1962 India–China war. Deeply anchored in security and strategic considerations, the cornerstone of Pakistan's relations with China has been defence cooperation. Cooperation in the defence sector, including in setting up of defence industries, continues to be a very important component of China–Pakistan bilateral relations. The strategic relations of the two countries intensified as China provided unflinching support to Pakistan through war and peace. Today China has emerged as the most trusted ally of Pakistan.[36] Consequently, the ties between the two countries are characterised as an 'all-weather relationship' and 'time-tested friendship'.

Pakistan's dispute over Kashmir with India gave China a crucially important edge as it helped divert Indian troops and attention from the unresolved territorial dispute with China. The two countries supplemented each other in containing India's power. Pakistan also provides a bridge between Beijing and the Islamic world. Pakistan's role as a trustworthy go-between between the US and China during the late 1960s, leading to Chinese admission into the UN, further strengthened their friendship.

Building of closer ties with China has been the fulcrum of Pakistan's foreign policy for more than half a century now. Pakistan holds China as a valued, dependable and critically important strategic partner; it is believed that China gave Pakistan valuable assistance in the development of ballistic missiles and in its all important and highly prestigious security venture — nuclear weapons technology. 'For Pakistan, China is a high-value guarantor of security against India.'[37]

In recent times, however, a transition in China's policy is discernible. From the earlier position of total and absolute support to Pakistan, China appears to be shifting to a policy of 'equidistance diplomacy' vis-à-vis Pakistan and India. During his visit to India in November 2006, President Hu indicated that China did not wish to make any 'selfish gains' in South Asia and favoured the peace process between Pakistan and India.[38] The world's only Superpower, the United States, another long-time ally of Pakistan, also is moving towards a closer relationship with Pakistan's fiercest rival India. In response, a wary Pakistan is likely to gravitate towards a tighter embrace with China.[39]

China's relations with India, another rising power in Asia, are steadily growing. China and India are the two largest states in terms of population, each exceeding a billion people. They are also two of the world's fastest growing economies. India and China are placing increasing emphasis on trade and economic relations: Sino-Indian bilateral trade surpassed $10 billion in 2004 and set a new record at $18.71 billion in 2005, up nearly

38 per cent from the previous year and China became India's second largest trading partner after the United States. India's exports to China grew by more than 27 per cent in 2005. China's trade with India was projected to grow to nearly $50 billion in 2010. China has become India's largest trading partner and India has emerged as China's largest trading partner in South Asia. The two countries are also making efforts to enhance cooperation in high-tech industries and their mutual investments. In the sector of energy, driven by the need of their ever expanding economies, China and India are increasingly cooperating in the development and acquisition of petroleum resources in third countries like Iran, Syria and Sudan.[40] Significantly, they have agreed to strengthen cooperation in science and technology, including expansion of the civilian nuclear energy programme.[41] The growing economic muscle of the two countries has made them potential challengers and formidable contenders for power in Asia. At the same time there are positive factors that offer opportunities for fruitful and mutually beneficial cooperation. India's large middle class provides an attractive consumer market for Chinese goods. For resource-hungry China, India's large coal, manganese and iron ore reserves offer considerable scope for cooperation.[42]

Today India does not feel that its economic security is threatened by China's growing economic strength.[43] It has realised that both China and India will gain through cooperation as their development or competition is not a zero-sum game. It is also believed that the deepening investment links between them will improve the international competitiveness of the two countries by combining their comparative advantages. They also see similar opportunities for cooperation in the manufacturing and IT industries as well as in the service sector.[44] China and India also have an identical stance on the need for a 'multipolar world', and 'equitable' world trading system.

The Sino-Indian relationship has had its ups and downs going through the zenith of euphoric political cordiality and the nadir of military conflict and war. Recent developments in their relations indicate that they are determined to leave their mistrust behind and forge mutually beneficial ties. They have skillfully insulated their boundary dispute from the larger objective of expanding bilateral relations. China's softened stance on the Kashmir dispute is a strong indication that China would like to maintain equally close relations with both India and Pakistan.[45] China has also recognised Sikkim's integration with India as a quid pro quo for the latter's recognition of Tibet as a part of China.

The mutual security and strategic concerns between China and India with their emergence as dominant regional military powers with nuclear weapons and missile capability, large modernised armed forces and navy with blue water capability can not be wished away. Significantly, however, the two countries are making concerted efforts to develop closer strategic cooperation as they pursue confidence-building measures, such as direct air and road links and growing military-to-military exchanges. In 2005, India began a 'strategic dialogue' with China discussing terrorism, resource competition, and the US role in Asia. The signing of an agreement on 'India-China Strategic and Cooperative Partnership for Peace and Prosperity' during the Chinese prime minister's visit to India in April 2005 gave a new dimension and depth to the expanded Sino-Indian ties.[46] Later in 2006, the two countries further enhanced their cooperation by signing a 'Memorandum of Understanding between the Ministries of Defence of China and India Regarding Interaction and Cooperation in the Area of Defence'. Under this agreement, the two countries subsequently conducted a joint anti-terrorism exercise — 'Hand in Hand 2007' in Kunming.[47] All this indicates that the two countries are set to overcome mistrust and rivalry and are concentrating on building friendly and cooperative relations.

In the eyes of China, India has emerged as the predominant power in South Asia in the context of economic strength, diplomatic stature and military might. On its part, India is increasingly attaching importance to cooperation with China as an essential ingredient for building a peaceful regional environment. Notwithstanding India's threat perception from China and its reluctance to see other regional powers to have inroads into South Asia, India realises that cooperation between an emerging India and a rising China and the resultant synergy will greatly impact on the quality of progress, prosperity and peace not only in Asia but also in the world at large. The grave deficit of trust developed in the late 1950s that led to the 1962 war is being replaced by growing confidence in each other's peaceful and cooperative intentions in the present globalised political and economic reality. 'India is much more confident now in the field of National Security than it was forty or so years ago; and does not see any major military threat from China'.[48] The Indian prime minister believes that 'the world is large enough to accommodate the growth ambitions of India and China'.[49]

Multi-lateral Cooperation with South Asia

To deepen its traditional friendship and cooperation with South Asia at the multilateral level, China, since the end of the last century, has been seeking some form of association or observer status with the South Asian Association for Regional Cooperation (SAARC) — consisting of Bangladesh, Bhutan, India, Maldives, Nepal, Pakistan and Sri Lanka.[50] China stands for a peaceful, stable and prosperous South Asia and believes that a South Asia of harmony, cooperation and progress is as much in the interest of all countries in the region as it is in the interest of China. As a close neighbour, gaining of observer status in SAARC was a logical progression of China's policy of forging institutional linkage with regional organisations around the globe. On their part, SAARC member states are committed to build friendship and partnership within the region and beyond. They consider that the China–SAARC cooperation will promote peace, stability as also economic development and prosperity in the region. Cooperation with China will contribute to the strengthening of SAARC and will enable it to play a bigger role in regional and world affairs. It is no secret, however, that while most SAARC member states favoured externalisation of its relations to embrace China, India preferred SAARC to adopt a gradual, measured and unhurried approach in this respect. India's changing perception of China was critical in obtaining a unanimous SAARC decision on China. In 2005 China was accorded observer status in SAARC.[51]

China–Bangladesh: Ever Growing Relations

The historical contact between China and what is known as Bangladesh today, dates back to antiquity with Chinese traveller Fa Hien (Fa Xian) coming to Bengal in the 5th century and Huen Tsang (Xuan Zhang) during the first half of the 7th century. During the period of the Ming Dynasty, famous Chinese voyager Zheng He, in the course of his voyages in the Indian Ocean, frequently called at the port of Chittagong, as China's closest point of communications with South Asia. To commemorate the 600th anniversary of his voyages, the 'Envoy of Peace Exhibitions' were organised by China and Bangladesh recently. Atisha Dipankar Srijnana, an eminent scholar and monk from Vikrampur of Bangladesh is revered in China as a great god, Jobo Chhenpo, ranking second only to Gautama Buddha. He commenced his journey to Tibet in 1040 A.D. to preach Buddhism where he reformed Buddhism according to the Mahayana system, established the Buddhist Ka-dam (Ge-lug) sect and wielded considerable political and religious power. As a gesture of goodwill and tribute, his ashes were returned to Bangladesh in recent times. In commemoration of his great contributions to the Sino-Bangladesh friendship, the Chinese government built a Xing Yuan pavilion at his birthplace recently.

The liberation war of Bangladesh and its emergence as a sovereign independent state in 1971 came at a time when China–Pakistan relations were at their zenith. Pakistan's role in bringing about a China–US understanding had entered a crucially important stage that eventually led to the renouncing of official US opposition to the admission of the Peoples' Republic of China (PRC) to the United Nations and its acknowledgement that there was only one China, represented by the People's Republic of China. As a consequence of this, the PRC assumed the China seat in the UN was helping the PRC achieve worldwide official recognition as the one, only and true China. China assumed one of the five permanent seats in the Security Council with veto power. Understandably, the state of China–Pakistan bilateral relations impacted heavily on China's policy towards the newly emerged Bangladesh; China did not readily accord recognition to the new state. In 1974 it vetoed Bangladesh's bid to enter the United Nations.

In the backdrop of China's own bitter experience with colonialist and imperialist forces and its expressed support to liberation movements, there was some expectation that the Bangladesh liberation war might receive support from that country. That was not to be, primarily because of the state of China–Pakistan relations. Other issues that may have had a bearing on its policy include India's active support to the Bangladesh liberation war in contrast to its own cool state of relations with that country, following the 1962 war. China's apprehension that the dismemberment of Pakistan would tilt the balance of regional power in favour of a strengthened India may also have influenced the Chinese approach towards Bangladesh's liberation war. India's signing of a Friendship Treaty with the USSR in 1971, with whom China's relations were going through difficulties at that time, may have heightened that apprehension. China's adherence to the principles of sovereignty and non-interference may have been another determining factor. Its own internal preoccupation with similar issues like in Tibet and Xinjiang are believed to have played a decisive role in shaping the attitude of China towards the Bangladesh liberation war. It is, however, noteworthy that despite China's high-profile relationship with Pakistan it carefully steered clear of any direct military intervention in favour of Pakistan and was content with playing the role of a vocal advocate of Pakistan's integrity in the UN Security Council and supporting a political settlement.

An interesting detail of history is that the principal impetus to the growth of China–Pakistan relations in the 1950s came from what was then East Pakistan, which constitutes Bangladesh today. The leaders of progressive political parties and student organisations from the then East Pakistan played a vital role in sensitising public opinion for forging friendly ties with countries like China while the West Pakistan–based military bureaucratic establishment was more inclined to forging ties and developing alliances with the West, particularly the United States of America. The then East Pakistan provided the sheet anchor of popular support for building Pakistan's friendly ties with China. In the following years, while Islamabad served as the formal channel of official relations, Dhaka remained the hub of Chinese cultural ties with frequent sports events and visits of dance troupes and acrobatic teams. China also maintained a large diplomatic presence in their Dhaka consulate.

The new state of Bangladesh demonstrated remarkable maturity and pragmatism and undertook active initiatives to befriend China. It was a measure of the independent foreign policy of the newly emerged nation that these initiatives were taken at a time when on the one hand Bangladesh's bilateral relations with India and USSR were at its pinnacle and on the other hand the relations of China with India were at the lowest ebb and while China–USSR relations were also going through severe strains. Bangladesh continued to maintain the momentum of these initiatives even after China vetoed Bangladesh's admission to the United Nations. The historical background of pre-liberation ties also helped Bangladesh in pursuing this forward-looking policy towards China.

Since China's recognition of Bangladesh and establishment of diplomatic relations in 1975, the bilateral relations between the two countries have grown steadily. Political relations have grown and strengthened on similarity of ideas about the basic principles of inter-state relations based on sovereign equality and non-interference in the internal affairs of another state. The identity of views on many international political and economic issues that impinge on the interests of developing countries has also significantly contributed to the consolidation of understanding between these two countries. Bangladesh is an active participant in many international organisations and groups including UN, the non-aligned movement (NAM) and the Group of 77 and upholds these views forcefully. Pitted against some major powers on many such issues China finds a dependable ally in Bangladesh. In international forums Bangladesh has extended resolute support to China on issues ranging from human rights to its entry into the World Trade Organisation. On the question of Taiwan, Bangladesh has steadfastly supported China in the context of its 'One China Policy' and it considers Tibet as China's integral part.

In 1994, Prime Minister Li Peng of China had remarked that the relations between the two countries were notable for 'absence of any problem'. The state of bilateral relations is now being increasingly referred to as an 'all-weather friendship'. This close political understanding is nurtured by successive Bangladesh governments formed under different political parties and is sustained by frequent exchange of visits at the head of state/government level. There are also frequent exchanges of visits at foreign minister and other political and bureaucratic levels. Another noteworthy characteristic of the relations of the two countries is the recurrent exchange of visits by delegations from their friendship associations.

The Bangladesh–China bilateral friendship is anchored on some institutional frameworks. The two countries have set up an institutional arrangement of annual consultations between the two foreign ministries which is conducted at the level of foreign secretary of Bangladesh and vice foreign minister of China. The annual consultation sustains the momentum of relations and provides future direction to its development. It also serves as a steering wheel to keep overall relations on track. Another institutional framework, the Joint Economic Commission (JEC) identifies areas of economic and trade relations as well as scientific and technical cooperation. The JEC also develops projects and coordinates their implementation. Chinese economic assistance to Bangladesh is channeled through the JEC. Another significant aspect of the Bangladesh–China bilateral relations is defence cooperation. Bangladesh is placing increasing importance on foreign direct investment as one of the main drivers of its economic growth and Chinese investment has emerged as another important feature of their bilateral relations.

Bilateral Trade

Bilateral trade between the two countries is growing at a very fast pace. A number of trade agreements and protocols signed between the two countries have helped the trade volume increase significantly and its growth rate is rapidly increasing. According to figures of the Export Promotion Bureau of Bangladesh, the trade volume between the two countries in 2002–3 amounted to $1.085 billion rising from the figure of $661.03 million in the previous year, 2001–2, an increase of 64.21 per cent. During that period, the exports from China rose from $642.11 million to $1.066 billion and the exports from Bangladesh to China registered a rise from $18.92 million of the previous year to $19.50 million. Trade between the two countries reached a record level of $3.606 billion in 2007–8 having risen from $2.630 billion of the previous year growing at an impressive rate of 37.11 per cent, as the two countries continue to explore the potential to further expand trade. Bangladesh has now emerged as the third largest trading partner of China in South Asia. Bilateral trade between Bangladesh and China is expected to increase to $5 billion in 2010 from $4.58 billion in 2009.

There is, however, a serious asymmetry in the bilateral trade pattern, with Bangladesh suffering a huge deficit. This yawning trade gap between the two countries is causing considerable worry, more so as the gap continues to widen with the rising volume of bilateral trade. For example, China's exports during the last year grew from $2.5 billion to $3.5 billion while Bangladesh's exports to China rose from $92.99 to $106.95 million. China's exports are growing at a rate of 37.95 per cent while its imports from Bangladesh rose only at a rate of 15 per cent that year. Between the period of 2001–2 and 2007–8, China's exports to Bangladesh grew from $642.11 million to $3.50 billion and its imports from Bangladesh rose from $18.92 million to barely $106.95 million. During this period, the annual trade deficit of Bangladesh has increased from $623.19 million to $3.393 billion. The two countries are addressing the issue with great urgency as China has declared zero tariff access for some Bangladeshi export items and has granted them preferential access under the Asia Pacific Trade Agreement (Bangkok Agreement) since July 2006. For reducing the gap, the two countries are also exploring additional measures that would include widening China's import list from Bangladesh, enlarging the scope of zero tariff access and promoting massive Chinese investment in Bangladesh in sectors with export potential to China.

Another issue of considerable concern relates to the textile and readymade garments sector. Readymade garments are the single largest export earner for Bangladesh accounting for 77 per cent of national exports. This sector provides more than 60 per cent of the country's total employment in the manufacturing industry. The phasing out of the Multi-Fiber Agreement in 2005 ended textile export quotas for countries like Bangladesh. In a quota-free global market and with China's entry into the WTO the Bangladesh garments industry has been put in a situation of competition with China.[52]

To redress the situation and turn it into an opportunity, China is considering outsourcing textile jobs to Bangladesh with Chinese producers moving operations to Bangladesh. China is also reportedly seeking to set up an industrial park in Bangladesh including garment factories.[53] Bangladesh is encouraging Chinese investment in fabric production; joint ventures in this sector would benefit both the countries.

Taiwanese Hiccup

An unexpected strain appeared in the otherwise smooth relations between Bangladesh and China when in 2005 Bangladesh took a surprise decision to allow the opening of a Taiwanese trade representative office in Dhaka. Bangladesh became the second South Asian country to allow the setting up of such an office. Bangladesh's decision was apparently influenced by Taiwanese assurances of huge investment especially in the textile, electronics and ICT sectors, relocation of a large number of Taiwanese industries to Bangladesh and employment of its skilled, semi-skilled and unskilled manpower in Taiwan. The fact that Taiwan is one of the largest investors with a $100 billion investment in mainland China may have had an effect on Bangladesh's decision.[54] According to foreign ministry officials, influential political personalities of the then ruling party with strong interests in manpower export are believed to have played an important role in persuading the government to take that decision.[55] It provoked a sharp reaction from China. There was also resentment and anger in Bangladesh including in its civil and military bureaucracy as political analysts saw this decision running counter to Bangladesh's long and abiding adherence to the principle of the 'One China Policy'. In the face of such intense reaction the government decided to reverse its decision. The two countries, in a spirit of understanding, have decided to put this issue behind them.

Economic and Technical Assistance

China's economic and technical assistance to Bangladesh in sectors like power, communication, infrastructure development and telecommunications has been significant. Economic and technical assistance, interest-free loans, interest-subsidised preferential loans and grants constitute the basic elements of Chinese assistance to Bangladesh. Over the last decades China has become one of the important development partners of Bangladesh in the development of communications infrastructure. The construction of six major 'friendship bridges' in a country criss-crossed by mighty rivers has given a high-profile visibility to Chinese economic assistance. China has also assured cooperation in constructing two more bridges over two of the mightiest rivers, Meghna and Gomti. Proposals for the construction of other such bridges including a railway bridge over another major river, the Jamuna, as well as the construction of highways, are under consideration.[56]

The prestigious Bangladesh China Friendship International Conference Centre at Dhaka constructed with a Chinese grant lends high public visibility to the friendly relations of the two countries. The proposed Bangladesh China Friendship Exhibition Centre to be constructed with Chinese economic assistance to hold national, regional and international trade and industrial exhibitions will have a similar impact.

In the power and mineral resources sectors also the two countries have important collaborations. In power generation, considered a thrust sector in Bangladesh, China has provided assistance for the installation of two power plants of 210 MW capacity each in Chittagong. It has given substantial support for rural electrification through the Rural Electrification Board apart from funding projects for strengthening urban electrification in cities like Dhaka, Mymensingh, Sylhet, Comilla, Khulna and others.[57] Other important projects in this sector are also on the anvil.

A Chinese consortium led by the China Machinery Import & Export Corporation assisted in the development of a prestigious coal mining project with an annual production capacity of 1 million tons called Barapukuria Coal Mine Development Project with $109.238 million Supplier's Credit. China is also assisting in the development of Barapukuria Coal-fire Thermal Power Plant Project with a total capacity of 250 MW using coal extracted from the Barapukuria mine.

Foreign Direct Investment

Bangladesh considers foreign direct investment as a crucially important element of its economic growth strategy. While the industrialised West and the countries from South East Asia remain the principal source of FDI, the same from China in Bangladesh is also growing. The two countries have signed an Investment Promotion and Protection Agreement and an agreement on Avoidance of Double Taxation. To date, more than 150 direct and joint venture proposals from China have been registered with the Bangladesh Board of Investment with a total outlay of $291.26 million. The main areas of Chinese investments are in the agro-based, food, textiles, chemical, glass and ceramics, engineering and services industries.[58] China has agreed to actively encourage Chinese enterprises to expand investment in

Bangladesh, especially in the textile sector. The two countries are exploring possibilities of investments in small and medium ventures. China is also active with its investments in the Export Processing Zones of Bangladesh. The proposed investment in these zones is $475.89 million of which $241.55 million has already been made, creating substantial job opportunity for Bangladeshi nationals. With Chinese Official Foreign Direct Investment recording a sharp rise both in quantum and global spread, Bangladesh views China as an important potential source of FDI in the coming years.

Peaceful Use of Nuclear Power

The agreement signed in 2005 by China and Bangladesh on peaceful use of nuclear power lends new depth and dimension to the bilateral economic cooperation of these two countries. This agreement is basically designed for China to assist Bangladesh in installing nuclear power plants to meet the latter's growing energy needs. China will also help Bangladesh in exploring for nuclear minerals as well as the construction of a 600 MW nuclear power plant. It is expected that with this assistance, Bangladesh will succeed in making the Rooppur Nuclear Power Plant operational, which was conceived in pre-liberation days and has been lying dormant since then. China and Bangladesh also signed an agreement on peaceful uses of nuclear energy in the fields of medicine, agriculture and biotechnology.

Defence Cooperation

A salient feature of the China–Bangladesh bilateral relations is strong defence cooperation between the two countries that was initiated immediately after China accorded recognition to Bangladesh. The multi-dimensional cooperation in this sector includes training of personnel, material support, and production and upgradation of equipment and armaments. Bangladesh's army, navy and air force are predominantly equipped with Chinese military hardware including tanks and light tanks, frigates, patrol crafts and combat aircraft.[59] Over the years, the two countries have signed a number of protocols outlining cooperation in these areas. Consequently, China has emerged as the largest and most important provider of the latter's military hardware and training of Bangladesh's armed forces.[60] To collate the existing accords in the defence sector in one framework, China and Bangladesh signed a defence agreement in 2002. Cooperation in the defence sector is also underscored by the exchange of frequent high-level visits by leaders of the armed forces of both the countries.

Other Sectors

China's collaboration in the telecommunications sector is extensive; it is providing long-term concessional credits to set up and expand digital telephone networks in the country. Bangladesh and China have opened direct air communications between Dhaka and Beijing via Kunming which is boosting tourism between the two countries. Establishing the Kunming–Chittagong road link through Myanmar is also being explored. Other important areas of cooperation include diverse sectors like agriculture, science and technology, disaster management and environmental issues including training of personnel and development of manpower resources. China has also offered cooperation in the management of rivers and flood control in Bangladesh. The two countries have delineated a significant new area of cooperation; to ensure peace and stability in the region they have agreed to cooperate in fighting terrorism.

Education and Culture

Display of 'soft power' diplomacy is in evidence in the Bangladesh–China bilateral relations. There is regular exchange of cultural troupes between the two countries. Bangladeshi students in increasing numbers are studying in Chinese universities on scholarship. Likewise, Chinese students are also studying in Bangladesh. The two countries have forged cooperative linkages and there is regular and frequent exchange of visits by friendship groups between the two countries.

Boost to Bilateral Relations

The outcome of the visit of Bangladeshi prime minister Sheikh Hasina to China in March 2010 and the return visit to Bangladesh by Chinese vice president Xi Jinpeng paid in quick succession in June 2010 has imparted new depth and dimension to the existing bilateral relations. China agreed to help Bangladesh build a $8.7 billion deep-sea port in Chittagong. The planned port is a big and costly project and when completed in 2055, in three phases, it will have the capacity to handle 100 million tones of bulk cargo and 3 million 20 feet equivalent unit (TEU) containers annually. It is anticipated that several countries are likely to come up for financing the project. Bangladesh proposes to permit India, Nepal, Bhutan, Myanmar and China the use of the port which would generate revenue and would substantially promote the country's economic growth. This will provide an enormous boost for trade and economic cooperation not only with China but also with India and other neighbouring countries. In another significant development, China also agreed to exchange data about the Brahmaputra river that flows from Tibet to Bangladesh through India. Other important outcomes of these visits relate to China's assurance of assistance in installing Bangladesh's first space satellite and to develop connectivity between Kunming in the Yunnan province in China and Chittagong in Bangladesh by building road and rail links via Myanmar. Additionally, China will provide 40 million yuan ($5.8 million) as a grant to Bangladesh and has offered duty-free access to some 5,000 Bangladeshi products in a 'goodwill gesture'.

Perceptions and Way Forward

Promotion of its national interests, protection of national security, and ensuring of economic prosperity are critical elements of the foreign policy objectives of Bangladesh. In the course of human history, many countries in the world have achieved these objectives through aggression, war and exploitation while others have done so through peaceful cooperation with other nations. In the present-day world, national interests, security and prosperity are increasingly perceived in the context of human security and the economic well-being of the people. As a result, cooperation with other nations is progressively becoming the preferred option. Compared to China and India, Bangladesh is a small state with a relatively weaker economy and defence capabilities. For human security and the economic well-being of its people, Bangladesh also believes that peace and stability in the neighbourhood and beyond is an essential prerequisite. The pursuit of peaceful economic cooperation is thus a crucial element of Bangladesh's foreign policy. Bangladesh also believes that economic prosperity of the country is inextricably interlinked with that of the peoples of India, its immediate neighbour. Promoting friendship and peaceful economic cooperation with India is, naturally, a top priority for Bangladesh. A principal emotional factor that guides Bangladesh's attitude in this regard is the generous and all-out assistance that India gave to its liberation struggle. India's geographical location as its closest neighbour, its dominant presence in South Asia and rising economic and international political profile are also important considerations.

China recognised Bangladesh only after the end of the era of the Awami League and Bangabandhu Sheikh Mujibur Rahman, the founding father of the Bangladesh nation, in August 1975. The formal rapprochement between the two nations coincided with the deterioration of Bangladesh's relations with India and the Soviet Union. The new government of General Ziaur Rahman was seen as acting to counteract any undue dependence on India and moving Bangladesh away from the Indo-Soviet orbit of influence. As India's relations deteriorated with the new government, the new government felt that the country's strategic interests demanded overtures towards China against 'Indian expansionism and hegemony'.[61] In January 1977 China pledged its full support to Bangladesh in safeguarding its 'national independence and state sovereignty' and in resisting 'foreign interference'.[62] The statement did not name but clearly implied India as the foreign power. At the time of the formal commencement of Bangladesh–China relations, India, thus, factored prominently in the calculations. For China, the development of relations with Bangladesh was important to 'keep Bangladesh away from the Indo-Soviet orbit. For Bangladesh, it was imperative to checkmate the hegemony of its giant neighbour India.'[63]

It is interesting, however, to note that Bangladeshi attitude on building friendship with China predates the perceived move away from the 'Indo-Soviet orbit'. The policy was initiated and pursued by the post-liberation government of Bangladesh which had a high degree of commitment for friendship with both India and the Soviet Union. Immediately after the emergence of Bangladesh, the prime minister of the new nation, Tajuddin Ahmed, lauded China as a great nation with a tradition of fighting against imperialism and urged Chinese leaders to accord recognition to Bangladesh. Moulana Bhashani, the Bengali politician who served as the engine of popular movement, favouring development of Pakistan's friendly ties with China, wrote letters to Chairman Mao and Premier Zhou urging them to recognise Bangladesh.[64] As early as August 1972, Bangladesh's foreign minister Abdus Samad Azad made a formal statement extending 'hands of friendship towards China' and assured the Chinese leaders of 'profound goodwill and respect for them among the people of Bangladesh'.[65] Even after China vetoed its entry into the United Nations, Bangladesh, despite being discomforted, continued to cultivate Chinese diplomats all over the world. Though China recognised Bangladesh after the end of the Mujib era, its attitude towards the newly independent nation was gradually changing for some time. In 1974, during the Mujib era, China refrained from vetoing Bangladesh's entry into the UN, and in sharp contrast to its vitriolic statements of the past, the Chinese permanent representative in the UN expressed China's desire to establish good neighbourly relations with Bangladesh.

Geographically, Bangladesh is sandwiched between two rising Asian giants — India and China. India is the hugging neighbour and China is only 100 miles across the Himalayas.[66] India shares borders with almost all the countries of the region and no other country shares border with another. Bangladesh shares its borders with India from three sides making it almost 'India-locked'. This great geopolitical significance of India and its physical size, economic strength, military prowess as well as diplomatic standing make it crucially important for Bangladesh. 'Geopolitically, cultural as well as economic gravitational pull of India was the dominant trend in Bangladesh's perception. Relations with China provided a good opportunity to Bangladesh to offset perceived Indian dominance.'[67]

China also is strategically important for South Asia and a long-term foreign policy challenge for Bangladesh is to maintain 'a delicate balance of relations between China and India. If Bangladesh is perceived tilting to one, it may give misgivings on the other. Bangladesh cannot afford to have an imbalance of bilateral relations with two Asian giants as Bangladesh needs both of them.'[68] For Bangladesh, another challenge is how to maximise the benefits of its geopolitical situation, regionally and globally. From its view point, maintenance of good relations with China was partly to diversify its foreign relations.[69] While discussing the dynamics of regional economic cooperation Professor Rehman Sobhan makes an interesting point.

He says:

> For bigger countries such as India, there are also geo-strategic concerns which move them to forge ties outside the region. . . . Smaller countries such as Bangladesh seek to escape from being tied into local economic groupings where one country may acquire an overwhelming presence. . . . However at the end of the day, for all countries of South Asia, however much they seek to diversify their external links, the logic of geography and history drives them back to each other to cooperate in making the substantive investments needed to promote such cooperation.[70]

Some Indian political analysts have interpreted Chinese assistance to Bangladesh to develop the deep-sea port in the Bay of Bengal as Bangladesh 'offering the Chittagong port to the Chinese navy, providing it access to the Bay of Bengal and the Indian Ocean'. It has been portrayed by them as a sign of China's growing strategic inroads into South Asia. It has also been contended that Bangladesh was 'bending over backwards to please China, if only to thumb a strategic nose at India'. Some analysts in India also view Bangladesh's growing military cooperation with China as helping China's encirclement of India.[71] It has also been asserted that the China–Bangladesh military cooperation has the potential to exacerbate regional tensions and that New Delhi was anxious about Bangladesh's growing military contacts.[72] On its part Bangladesh firmly maintains that its defence cooperation with China is not directed against any country, far less India and that it would not affect Bangladesh's relations with its immediate friendly neighbour. The development of the deep-sea port and the enhanced connectivity through road and rail linkages are seen as tools of economic prosperity and are undertaken on purely trade and economic considerations; significantly, the ambit of cooperation embraces all regional countries including China and India. High-level foreign ministry officials in Bangladesh maintain that contrary to the claim by these analysts the government in New Delhi does not seem to harbour any such anxiety.

It is true that the formal relations with China were initiated by General Ziaur Rahman. These were nurtured and strengthened during his regime by the Bangladesh Nationalist Party. The same party, under his widow, Prime Minister Khaleda Zia, pursued the policy of strengthening the friendship with China during the two terms the party was in power from 1991 to 1996 and from 2001 to 2006.[73] President H. M. Ershad followed the same policy during the decade he and his Jatiya Party were in power in the 1980s. In 1996, the Awami League with Sheikh Hasina as prime minister came back to power and followed the same policy of consolidation and expansion of relations with China.[74] Sheikh Hasina visited China as leader of the opposition in 1993 and China was the first country she visited upon assuming the office of prime minister in 1996.[75] Awami League, Bangladesh Nationalist Party and the Jatiya Party are the three major mainstream political parties in Bangladesh. Thus, for decades, successive governments under all major political parties in Bangladesh have nurtured friendly relations with China. Between them, these political parties represent almost the entire spectrum of the public opinion of Bangladesh. Some of these parties are known to view India with circumspection and distrust while others are known for their attitude of friendly feelings towards that country. But all these political parties have been equally enthusiastic to develop relations with China.

The myriad cooperation points between Bangladesh and China embrace many sectors covering a wide breadth of relations including cultural, political, economic and defence fields, and bring into play both the hard and soft power of diplomacy. This cooperation involves an extensive group of people like politicians, intellectuals, civil and military bureaucrats and it impacts on big business — entrepreneurs, constructors and investors. It is significant that in a country remarkable for an acute absence of political consensus on many domestic and foreign policy issues, there is a universal consensus on forging friendly relations with China. In fact, there is an unmistakable emergence of a bipartisan approach that close relations with China will be a salient feature of Bangladesh's foreign policy, as they are seen to be in the best national interest of the country.[76] Guided by this perception Bangladesh believes in the promotion of friendship and peaceful economic cooperation with this important neighbour beyond the immediate region. China's rising economic stature and political clout at the global level also weigh heavily on this consideration. Bangladesh perceives that closer relations with a rising China will promote its economic interests.

Bangladesh admires China as a peace-loving, principled and responsible major power. Of particular importance to Bangladesh is that Chinese foreign policy eschews coercive diplomacy and emphasises win-win economic cooperation. It views with appreciation China's policy of building up friendship with neighbouring countries and creating trust and the confidence of smaller nations and weaker states for fostering amity, peace and prosperity. China's efforts in developing its ties with the countries in its immediate neighbourhood constitute a concrete evidence of this policy. As a comparatively small and weak state in South Asia, Bangladesh is fascinated by the Chinese foreign policy that emphasises — both in theory and practice — equality of all nations regardless of their size and strength. In the words of Bangladesh's foreign minister, 'Despite the transformations and shifts in global power politics, we see that China still maintains "peaceful co-existence" as the main principle in China–South Asia relations. The fundamentals of these principles are (i) mutual equality, (ii) non-interference in each other's internal affairs, (iii) mutual respect to territorial integrity, (iv) cooperation against hegemonic and power politics, and (v) mutual accommodation and benefit. This has instilled a healthy trust and confidence among all the South Asian countries to adopt policies that seek close and strategic partnerships with China.'[77]

Bangladesh also realises that China is making sustained efforts to bring about peace and stability in Asia and the world at large. This stands in sharp contrast to 'the earlier era of 1950s and 1960s, when China sought to destabilize regional governments by supporting armed insurgencies and exporting Maoism and had border disputes with virtually every contiguous country. . . . China is now exporter of goodwill and consumer durables instead of weapons and revolution.'[78] China has moved away from ideological warfare with countries having different socio-political systems. In its immediate neighbourhood and in Asia at large, it has developed strong and healthy relations while it continues to improve relations with all other countries of the world. With USA, European countries and the developed world, its relations have never before been better. All this is happening in the context of

China's belief in 'building up a harmonious world'.[79] But despite its great economic and political achievements, Bangladesh reckons that China is still a developing country; it still has a daunting task of alleviating poverty and providing better living conditions for its huge population. In the coming decades, China will continue to explore new horizons in its economic development with the completion of such mega-projects as the Three Gorges Dam and the Qinghai-Tibet railway.[80] But it will still have to traverse a long way before it achieves economic development commensurate with its emerging international standing. Bangladesh believes that China, thus, has a significant stake in peace and stability in the region and that Chinese national interest will impel it to adopt a course of 'peaceful development'; it will prefer to avoid any upheaval. During the Chinese president's visit to Europe in 2007, Hu emphasised, 'China is firmly committed to peaceful development. . . . It concentrates its efforts on development at home and endeavours to uphold world peace and common development internationally.'[81] Bangladesh sees China's continued rise as an economic power and its enhanced political and diplomatic prestige to be accompanied by a growing Chinese consciousness of the responsibility that devolves on it as a major power. Thus no political analyst in Bangladesh views China's rise as a military power with increasing political prestige and economic power as a threat to peace either to Bangladesh or to the region. All major political parties across the spectrum in the country subscribe to that perception.

China's advocacy for a new, just and reasonable international political and economic order and multipolarisation of the world's power structure also has considerable appeal to Bangladesh. Bangladesh believes that with the end of the cold war and the collapse of the erstwhile Soviet Union, China has emerged as the only country that has the potential to balance the existing unipolarity in global politics.[82] Bangladesh is also appreciative of China's efforts to make the UN and the Security Council the pivotal centres for addressing terrorism and international conflict situations. Bangladesh believes that friendly relations with a strong and prosperous China will help advance regional peace and stability and will promote economic prosperity for South Asia in general and Bangladesh in particular.

Bangladesh also believes that South Asia as a region and all SAARC member states individually need to look upon China as a partner in progress and not as an adversary as there is a strong convergence of economic interests. As South Asian countries move towards greater integration with the rest of Asia, they should stand to gain by forging cooperation with China. In addition, together they can form an effective partnership in strengthening multilateralism in international relations and in the establishment of a just international economic order that ensures equitable benefits to developing countries.

Bangladesh seeks to develop its relations with China but not at the expense of its relations with India; Bangladesh does not perceive its relations with China and India as a zero-sum game. India's own desire to strengthen its relations with China embracing the entire spectrum from trade and investment to defence and strategy is a vindication of Bangladesh's policy towards China. In its quest for economic prosperity Bangladesh is keen to develop its relations with both countries as the economic prowess of both these countries steadily increases and as both of them assume the attributes of major global powers.

Bangladesh does not perceive the rise of China as a threat and instead sees China's economic prosperity, its benign attitude towards friendly developing countries and its willingness to share the benefits of its economic growth with them as an opportunity. It appreciates China as a sympathetic and constructive partner in economic development. The scope for such cooperation is enormous in trade, in attracting Chinese FDI and in cooperating in the whole range of economic sectors from infrastructure development, telecommunications and transport to collaboration in the energy sector. Bangladesh perceives a high potential in the development of its relations with China as an opportunity to guarantee peace, stability and security as much as an opportunity for economic prosperity. Bangladesh is willing and eager to harness that potential.

❊

Notes

1. *The Economist*, 15 November 2007.
2. David Shambaugh, 'Return to the Middle Kingdom? China and Asia in the Early Twenty First Century', in David Shambaugh (ed.), *Power Shift —*

China and Asia's New Dynamics, Berkley: University of California Press, 2006, p. 1.

3. Doug Bandow, 'China Rising: The Next Global Superpower', available at http://original.antiwar.com/doug-bandow/2007/01/26/china-rising-the-next-global-superpower, www.Antiwar.com, 26 January 2007 (accessed 16 May 2009).

4. Dr John K. Chang, 'Striving Toward the Chinese Century', available at www.chsource.org/ Striving.htm (accessed 6 April 2009).

5. Ibid.

6. The Globalist, Globalist Factsheet, 'Global History. China in History — From 2000 to 2005', available at http://www.theglobalist.com/Search.aspx?txtSearch=China%20History (accessed 15 June 2009).

7. Forbes.com (accessed 19 June 2009).

8. Ibid.

9. Shambaugh, 'Return to the Middle Kingdom?', p. 23.

10. Carsten A. Holz, 'China's Economic Growth 1978–2025: What We Know Today about China's Economic Growth Tomorrow', available at ideas.repec.org/p/wpa/wuwpdc/0512002.html (accessed 27 March 2009).

11. Wang Jisi, 'China's Road to Peaceful Development and the USA', text of a lecture given at a meeting organised by Casa Asia and the Elcano Royal Institute on 18 July 2007 in Madrid, www.realinstitutoelcano.org/wps/ (accessed 10 May 2009).

12. Anthony Kuhn, 'China's Growing Influence', available at NPR.org, 31 March 2008 (accessed 19 June 2009).

13. Chin-Hong Puah, Jerome Swee-Hui Kueh and Evan Lau, 'The Implications of Emergence of China towards ASEAN-5: FDI-GDP Perspective', available at http://mpra.ub.uni-muenchen.de/4550/, Munich Personal RePEc Archive MPRA Paper No. 4550, posted 4 November 2007 (accessed 18 February 2009) and Wing Thye Woo, 'The Economic Impact of China's Emergence as a Major Trading Nation', available at www.econ.ucdavis.edu/ (accessed 10 May 2009).

14. Jisi, 'China's Road to Peaceful Development and the USA'.

15. Ramkishen Rajan, 'What does the Economic Ascendancy of China Imply for ASEAN?' available at http://www.freewebs.com/rrajan01/PRCASEAN-1.pdf (accessed 18 February 2009).

16. Albert Keidel, 'Assessing China's Economic Rise: Strengths, 2007, Weaknesses and Implications', available at www.carnegieendowment.org (accessed 8 April 2009).

17. Chen Xiulian, EconomyWatch.com (accessed 8 April 2009).

18. David Shambaugh, 'Rising Dragon and the American Eagle — Part I', online at YaleGlobal, 20 April 2005, Yale Centre for the Study

on Globalization, available at http://yaleglobal.yale.edu/content/rising-dragon-and-american-eagle-%E2%80%93-part-i (accessed 8 April 2009).

19. Rajan, 'What does the Economic Ascendancy of China Imply for ASEAN?'.

20. Christopher R. Hill, assistant secretary for East Asian and Pacific Affairs, Emergence of China in the Asia-Pacific: Economic and Security Consequences for the U.S., testimony before the Senate Foreign Relations Committee, Subcommittee on East Asian and Pacific Affairs, Washington, DC, 7 June 2005.

21. Report on Wilton Park Conference WP843, China's Growing International Security and Diplomatic Role, Thursday 15–Monday 19 March 2007.

22. Nicola Phillips, 'China: Is Development Space Disappearing for Latin America and the Caribbean?'. Working Paper No. 14, January 2007, available at www.cigionline.org (accessed 26 January 2007).

23. Hill, testimony before the Senate Foreign Relations Committee.

24. Clarence Kwan and Karl P. Sauvant, Ph.D., 'Chinese Direct Investment in the United States — The Challenges Ahead', available at http://www.cpii.columbia.edu/ (accessed 10 May 2009).

25. Bandow, 'China Rising'.

26. Ibid.

27. Doug Bandow, 'Turning China into the Next Big Enemy, Foreign Follies', available at www.antiwar.com/bandow/?articleid (accessed 18 May 2009).

28. Bandow, 'China Rising'.

29. Rajan, 'What does the Economic Ascendancy of China Imply for ASEAN?'.

30. Ibid.

31. Shambaugh, 'Rising Dragon and the American Eagle'.

32. Anthony Kuhn, 'China Tries to Export Culture as Influence Increases', China and the World, available at www.npr.org (accessed 7 April 2009).

33. C. M. Shafi Sami, 'Growth of SAARC and Prospects of SAARC-China Collaboration', paper presented at an international conference on China and SAARC: Towards a Partnership of Common Prosperity, organised by China Institute of International Studies (CIIS) and Bandaranaike Centre for International Studies (BCIS), 19–20 April 2008, Beijing, China.

34. Ibid.

35. CBS News, 15 June 2009, 12:12 a.m. EST.

36. Ibid.

37. Esther Pan, 'China and Pakistan: A Deepening Bond', available at http://www.cfr.org/publication/10070 (accessed 11 August 2009).

38. Mohan Guruswamy and Zorawar Daulet Singh, *India China Relations: The Border Issue and Beyond*, New Delhi: Viva Books, 2009.
39. Pan, 'China and Pakistan'.
40. *Asia Times Online*, available at www.atimes.com/atimes/South_Asia/HI26Df01.html (accessed 16 June 2009).
41. Report on Wilton Park Conference WP843.
42. Col R Hariharan (retd), 'China's Influence in India's Neighbourhood', Paper No. 2084, South Asia Analysis Group, available at www.southasiaanalysis.org (accessed 16 June 2009).
43. R. Swaminathan, 'India-China Relations in the Emerging Era', South Asia Analysis Group, available at www.saag.org/common/uploaded_files/paper2019.html (accessed on 12 August 2009).
44. Ibid.
45. Farooq Sobhan, 'South Asia, American Role in Asia: Asian Views', The Asia Foundation, California, USA.
46. Derek J. Mitchell and Chietigj Bajpaee, 'China and India', available at www.csis.org/media/csis/pubs/090212 (accessed 16 June 2009).
47. Kerry Dumbaugh, 'China's Foreign Policy: What Does It Mean for U.S. Global Interests?', CRS Report for Congress, 18 July 2008, RL34588.
48. Swaminathan, 'India-China Relations in the Emerging Era'.
49. Prime Minister Manmohan Singh of India addressing a high-level gathering of business leaders in London, *The Hindu*, 11 October 2006.
50. Subsequently, Afghanistan became a member of SAARC.
52. Dhaka Declaration, Thirteenth SAARC Summit,13 November 2005.
51. Urvashi Aneja, 'China-Bangladesh Relations: An Emerging Strategic Partnership?'. IPCS Special Report 3, Institute of Peace and Conflict Studies, New Delhi, India.
53. Ibid.
54. Anand Kumar, 'Changing Dynamics of Sino-Bangladesh Relations', available at www.saag.org/common/uploaded_files/paper1345.html (accessed 12 June 2009).
55. Bangladesh government sources declining to be identified.
56. Source: Economic Relations Division, Ministry of Finance, Bangladesh.
57. Source: Rural Electrification Board, Bangladesh.
Source: Power Development Board, Bangladesh.
58. Source: Board of Investment, Bangladesh.
59. Dr Subhash Kapila, 'Bangladesh-China Defence Cooperation Agreement's Strategic Implications: An Analysis', Paper no. 582, South Asia Analysis Group, available at www.southasiaanalysis.org/papers6/paper582.html (accessed 6 April 2009).
60. Aneja, 'China-Bangladesh Relations'.
61. Zaglul Haider, *The Changing Pattern of Bangladesh Foreign Policy*, Dhaka: University Press Limited, 2006.

62. Chinese vice premier Li Hsien-nien speaking at a welcome banquet given in Beijing in honour of General Ziaur Rahman, chief martial law administrator of Bangladesh.

63. Talukder Maniruzzaman, *The Bangladesh Revolution and its Aftermath*, Dhaka: Bangladesh Books International Limited, 1980 as quoted by Haider, *The Changing Pattern of Bangladesh Foreign Policy*.

64. Haider, *The Changing Pattern of Bangladesh Foreign Policy*.

65. *The Bangladesh Observer*, 27 August 1972.

66. Harun Ur Rashid, 'Bangladesh Foreign Policy: Realities & Challenges', *The Daily Star*, 5 January 2008.

67. Keshav Mishra, *Rapprochement across the Himalayas: Emerging India–China Relations in the Post Cold War Period (1947–2003)*, New Delhi: Kalpaz Publications, 2004, available at http://www.thedailystar.net/story.php?nid=17802.

68. Rashid, 'Bangladesh Foreign Policy'.

69. Mishra, *Rapprochement across the Himalayas*.

70. Rehman Sobhan, *Transforming Eastern South Asia, Building Growth Zones for Economic Cooperation*, Dhaka: The University Press Limited, 1999, available at http://www.sydneybashi-bangla.com/Articles/Harun_Bangladesh%20Foreign%20Policy%201.pdf.

71. Kapila, 'Bangladesh-China Defence Cooperation Agreements Strategic Implications'.

72. Vijay Sakhuja, 'China Bangladesh Relations and Potential for Regional Tensions', *China Brief*, vol. 9, no. 15, 23 July 2009, available at www.defence.pk (accessed 21 June 2010).

73. She is the widow of Gen. Ziaur Rahman.

74. She is the daughter of the leader of Bangladesh liberation struggle, Bangabandhu Sheikh Mujibur Rahman.

75. Mishra, *Rapprochement across the Himalayas*.

76. Ibid.

77. 'China and South Asia: The Emerging Relations and the role of Bangladesh', statement by foreign minister of Bangladesh at the Institute of Asia-Pacific Studies, Chinese Academy of Social Sciences, Beijing on 6 June 2006.

78. Shambaugh. 'Return to the Middle Kingdom?', p. 24.

79. Jisi, 'China's Road to Peaceful Development and the USA'.

80. Opinion, 'Economic Strength Sees Miraculous Changes in New China', *The People's Daily*, 19 June 2001, available at http://English.peopledaily.com.cm (accessed 31 March 2009).

81. Jisi, 'China's Road to Peaceful Development and the USA'.

82. 'China and South Asia', statement by foreign minister of Bangladesh at the Institute of Asia-Pacific Studies.

2

Bangladesh
Opportunities and Challenges

IFTEKHAR AHMED CHOWDHURY

China's rise has been a process rather than an event. While its pace has quickened in the immediate past decades, the richness of China's ancient civilisation provided a supportive matrix. Often this arduous journey has involved two steps forward, and one step backward. At times the reverse has also been true: two steps back, and only one step forward. Eventually the mix of a constellation of complex forces unleashed a kinetic energy that rendered the surge inexorable. Along the way the process involved, indeed derived impetus from, breaks with the past. The Revolution of 1949 was one such major break. But that event was a part of the broad sweep of history that has determined China's destiny.

Bangladesh's views of a 'rising' China were naturally shaped by its experiences and interactions with this large and powerful neighbour. Indeed in order to understand the present in this context, it is necessary to delve into the past. This is all the more so because, as we seek to demonstrate, there has been a consistency in the way China has been behaving with the rest of the world since its inception as a 'People's Republic'. This despite the many shifts in nuances and even tactics, all of those taking place within broad strategic parameters that have remained abiding.

China's very close links with Pakistan led it to oppose the birth of the new state of Bangladesh in December 1971. But once the independence of the new republic became an established fact and Pakistan itself recognised the reality in 1974, China moved rapidly to create a situation of an 'all-weather friendship' (the highest level of relationship in Chinese political and diplomatic parlance) with Bangladesh, as it had with Pakistan, thereby now having two distinct, separate and sovereign allies straddling the Indian heartland.

For Bangladesh this relationship opened up numerous opportunities. First, in many ways, this relationship helped close, to a degree, the enormous power-gap that existed between Bangladesh and India, the big neighbour whose territory virtually encircled Bangladesh. Indeed Bangladesh has always sought to build a web of extraregional linkages to bolster its sense of security. Second, China was an important supplier of cheap imports, much needed by Bangladeshi consumers. Third, Bangladesh inherited the military relationship that Pakistan enjoyed with China, and the latter became a key source of arms procurement for the Bangladeshi defence establishment. Finally, China became an important development partner, providing credits, though not always easy ones, for a number of projects, particularly in the infrastructural sector.

But ties with China provided many challenges as well. First there was always the need to carefully balance the relationship with that of India. However, though the treatment accorded to Bangladesh was similar vis-à-vis that given to Pakistan, Bangladesh was not Pakistan and had its own relationships within the region that it could not afford to unduly strain. Second, the close ties with China meant it was not always easy for Bangladesh to counter China in fora where global trading regimes were being negotiated as in the World Trade Organisation (WTO), in which Bangladesh's interests as a major exporter of readymade garments (Bangladesh's primary foreign exchange earner) may have at times run contrary to that of China's, a competitor in that trade. Third, the China links had potentials for drawing Bangladesh into 'big-power politics', given the complex Sino-American relations, something that Bangladesh has been chary of getting involved in. Finally, Beijing has been extremely sensitive to Bangladesh developing any lucrative connections with Taiwan, and Bangladesh has chosen to respect this sentiment.

This chapter focuses mainly on how Bangladesh and the elements within perceive the rise of China and deal with it. It will also entail a study of the relationship of China with a smaller neighbour, not necessarily central to its foreign policy concerns, yet important enough to be seen as a paradigm of how such links are subsumed within the broader world-view of this waking dragon of the east.[1]

The Dragon Wakes

Indeed, the awakening, or the reawakening of the Chinese dragon, considering the might it exuded at one time as the 'Middle Kingdom', coincided with the burst of the market reforms of the 1980s, within the parameters of wider communist values. The rise soon became inevitable. There ensued a debate within China whether the concept of a 'peaceful rise', or *heping juequi*, should constitute a major policy doctrine. Ultimately in late 2004, it was settled in favour of a less seemingly ambitious 'peaceful development'.[2] *This is to be placed within the framework of some broad strategic goals.*

The question must then be posed as to what are these broad policy goals? One analyst sees these as broadly threefold: First, preservation of the Chinese Communist Party (CCP) regime, despite remarkable changes in the governance principles; second, prosperity, mainly economic, which helps prop up the regime as with the loss of the communist rationale the CCP's legitimacy has become tied to performance. Finally, power, generally in the international realm, both in the 'hard' and 'soft' capabilities.[3] Another analyst holds that China's primary need is ensuring a peaceful environment to sustain its reform and modernisation programmes, which calls for a foreign policy which conforms to, rather than challenges, the existing international order.[4] A third views China as a champion of multipolarity, but which would like itself to be the only power in Asia to be able to stand up to the United States.[5]

The variety of opinions reflect specific observations of a policy framework which was laid down early by Chairman Mao Zedong, 'the great helmsman' himself. Mao analysed the globe as being divided into three worlds. He said: 'In my view the United states and the Soviet Union belong to the first world. The in-between — Japan, Europe and Canada — belong to the second world. Except Japan, Asia belongs to the third world. So does Africa and Latin America.'[6] These worlds were both mutually related as well as contradictory, and the two Superpowers were the sources of instability. Later, in April 1974,

Deng Xiaoping propounded that China, a socialist, developing, third world country, would join 'the oppressed peoples and nations' in their 'just struggle' against the 'oppressors'.[7] Since then, despite stylistic change, and its current rise notwithstanding, the bevaviour pattern of China has been derived from those 'original principles'.

China's Global Behaviour

Mao had once said to the American journalist Edgar Snow that China had no troops outside its own frontiers and had no intention to fight anybody unless its territory was attacked.[8] It is true that post-revolution China did not then, as it does not now, have troops beyond its borders, and its involvement in any wars and conflicts with outside powers such as with India in 1962 and along the Ussuri river with the Soviet Union in the 1960s was when Beijing perceived a threat to what it saw as its territory, or rather what it perceived to be its territory, the protection of which was obviously viewed by it as a 'core' interest.

Conversely, when its territory was not directly threatened, as during the Bangladesh War between India and Pakistan, it did not 'militarise' its strong verbal support, as we shall see later in this chapter, to its closest ally Pakistan. But can Mao's words be taken literally, especially when we have seen how subtle the Chinese can be both in terms of language and diplomacy?[9]

As for there being no Chinese troops outside its frontiers, this may not be an important factor as China will soon possess the capability of rapidly projecting military power beyond its borders. It is now focused on building a powerful navy.[10] This will enable it to transport men and material to far-flung corners of the world quickly, if need be. At a seminar in Singapore in 2008, a participant, Huang Jin, said that the People's Liberation Army Navy (PLAN) is the fastest growing force in the Chinese military.[11]

Since 2000, China has procured around twenty major surface vessels as destroyers and frigates, at least thirty-one new submarines and plans to build four to six aircraft carriers, commissioning the first by 2015.[12]

In addition, China does not need to have forces stationed outside the country to be able to strike at an enemy. It has an array of nuclear warheads, well over 400 in number and counting, deployed on long- and short-range missiles, capable of hitting targets near and far, from within Chinese territory.[13]A senior Chinese military officer has written:

> Our armed forces are now capable of striking back with nuclear weapons, which greatly strengthens our national defence and our international status. Additionally, it helps to weaken the nuclear monopoly of the superpowers, contain nuclear war, and safeguard world peace.[14]

In March 2009, China announced an increase of 15 per cent in its defence budget, raising it to US$ 70 billion, becoming the second largest defence spender in the world, after the United States, overtaking Russia, Japan, Britain and France.[15]

As for its territory, the conventional definition, as perhaps in Mao's days, meaning mainland China, including Tibet and now Hong Kong, with Taiwan as a province, may alter to include other strategic interests, such as economic assets in energy in Africa, as in Sudan and Central Asia, as also in Latin America. These could also be seen as *red lines* in Beijing. Any threats or attacks on these could also unleash Chinese retaliation in a variety of ways. We simply do not know for certain as yet.

With the dissolution of the Soviet Union, and the strategic decline of Europe on the global scene, the United States and China appear as the principal protagonists. The Harvard historian Niall Fergusson coined the term 'Chimerica' to describe the duo, and Professor Zbigniew Brzezinski floated the concept of the 'Group of Two' (G2). The Columbia University economist Jeffrey Sachs simply described China as 'the most successful development story in world history'.[16] By mid-July 2009, according to data released by the People's Bank of China, Beijing's forex reserves surpassed US$ 2 trillion for the first time, reinforcing the consensus that China is the dominant economic force on the global stage with the three other largest economies, the US, Japan and Germany, still struggling to resurface from the current global recession.[17]

Ironically, China's economic strength will directly assist the US with its growing fiscal deficit, and with it desperately needing foreign buyers, as China is, for its treasury issuance. It is evident that during the 2008–9 global financial crisis, China's ability to absorb the shocks has continued to grow, and its strong fundamentals have led the World Bank to predict that China would be the first country in the region to experience a 'rebound'.[18] Indeed, Goldman Sachs has predicted that by 2041 China would overtake the United States as the world's largest economy.[19]

The United States leadership has noted this burgeoning influence, and indeed, the power of China and the need to engage it. The US secretary of state, Hillary Clinton, then a presidential candidate, wrote in an article in 2008: 'Our relationship with China will be the most important bilateral relationship in the world in this century.'[20] The US president, Barack Obama, also a presidential candidate then, observed a touch more realistically perhaps, that, 'We will compete with China in some areas and cooperate in others. Our essential challenge is to build a relationship that broadens cooperation while strengthening our ability to compete.'[21]

At the London Summit of the G20 in April 2009, President Obama and the Chinese president Hu Jintao agreed to establish a new mechanism, the China–US Strategic and Economic Dialogue, that met in Washington in July. On that occasion Hillary Clinton acknowledged the importance of the role of China when she said: 'The US welcomes the *great achievements* of China in economic development and the *active efforts* of China to maintain peace and stability in the Asia Pacific Region.'[22]

The fact that China is not willing to play a second fiddle to the US, be it in the political or economic dimension, became abundantly clear in the recent dispute at the WTO. On 11 September 2009 President Obama levied tariffs up to 35 per cent on the import of tires from China. Despite the fact that this would have cost the Chinese tire industry only US$ 1 billion compared to the total export volume of US$ 252 billion annually to the US, China upped the trade-war ante by responding swiftly and sharply. Almost immediately China lodged a formal complaint with the WTO, and launched an anti-dumping probe into US exports of automotive parts and chicken meat. Niu Jun, a Sino-US expert of the Beijing University said: 'In the past the Chinese government would have merely protested and not taken any concrete measures.'[23] Clearly, no longer.

There have been apprehensions expressed by some American analysts of an aggressive 'string of pearls' policy whereby China would expand global influence by forging a linkage of ports and bases from the South China Sea through the Straits of Malacca, across the Indian Ocean and to the Arabian Gulf.[24] This would include countries such as Bangladesh, Myanmar, Sri Lanka and Pakistan. China has, however, denied that its attempts to build close links to these countries through helping them build port facilities have any hostile intent towards any one. Nevertheless, it does pose a challenge to countries like Bangladesh, who need the support, yet are required to emphasise its benign nature to others, in particular, to India and to the United States, in both of which Bangladesh, as well as others, have important stakes.

If China on the other hand was at times somewhat concerned about the negative implications on Chinese security of the growing ties between the United States and India, these were largely dispelled due to Washington's post-9/11 focus on 'terrorism' with which China, for its own reasons, had no quarrel.[25] As for the Indo-US nuclear deal of July 2005, New Delhi was initially apprehensive about Beijing's reactions, but China was sufficiently ambiguous in letting it pass without much ado.[26] In fact, China endeavoured to rope India into the Kunming Initiative aiming at improving communications, trade and investment links among Bangladesh, Myanmar, China and India.[27] The somewhat muted western reaction to the Chinese governmental actions in Xinjiang in the summer of 2009 points to western disinclination to annoy a rising China. However, the events in Urumqi and the issue with the Uighurs could have threatened to strain China's relationship with Muslim nations, of which Bangladesh is also one, but China took immediate diplomatic measures to ensure that is not the case by explaining its actions in the relevant capitals.

With China's rise, an accompanying feature would be China's aspirations to have a greater say in global economic policy making. In 1997, following the East Asian financial crisis, an idea was floated to create an Asian Monetary Fund (AMF), in order to finance required stimulus actions. With Japan and China as major contributors to this proposed AMF, they could have provided a real challenge to US leadership and control. According to Professor Joseph Stiglitz, it was this fear that drove the US Treasury department and the International Monetary Fund to squelch the idea.[28] The Chinese took note, as they often do in such situations, and learnt from it. So, when during the global financial crisis of 2008–9 there was talk of replacing the US dollar with some other currencies to be the major global reserve, the Chinese 'soft-floated' the candidacy of the Yuan (*renminbi*) and then took a restrained position. Thereafter Beijing ensued a process of taking steps to prepare its currency for such an eventual role over a long term by making it convertible and taking other relevant steps.[29] This is of importance to Bangladeshi fiscal policy makers who are challenged by how best to use its reserves which have surpassed US\$ 8 billion, and are growing.

At The United Nations

China is a key player at the United Nations. It is a permanent member of the all-powerful Security Council, wielding veto power on major questions of international peace and security. Its role at the UN also suggests circumspection and avoidance of unnecessary diplomatic conflicts. However, China does take a firm position against any attempt by any other power to oppose a stated Chinese posture. For instance, anything that resembles 'interference in internal affairs', such as in the case of Myanmar or Sudan, is not allowed to pass muster by Beijing in the Security Council, no doubt with China's own situation (Tibet?) in mind. This strong position is perceived favourably by weaker members of the UN such as Bangladesh.

China did not stand in the way of the adoption of the principle of 'Responsibility to Protect' by the Summit of Global leaders in New York in 2005 so as not to upset the apple-cart of consensus so carefully crafted around the concept.[30] According to this principle, also known as 'R2P', it is the responsibility of every state to protect its own citizens. Should any state be unable, or unwilling, to do so then the responsibility will devolve on the international community to execute it, but only operating through the UN Security Council, and that too only under four specific circumstances: genocide, war crimes, ethnic cleansing and crimes against humanity. Also the Chinese did not oppose the election in 2006 of the South Korean foreign minister Ban ki-Moon as the secretary general of the UN despite the fact of its close links with North Korea because Ban's election satisfied the main Chinese criterion that the next secretary general should be an Asian. Therefore, the characteristic behaviour pattern of China in the UN in general, and the Security Council in particular has been moderate rather than flashy. Bangladeshi diplomats assessed that in case of any threat to sovereignty to Bangladesh, Chinese support would be forthcoming at the UN in deliberations, but such support would not be 'militarised' as was not done by China even for its close ally Pakistan during the Bangladesh War in 1971.

As of now, though, the Chinese have relied more on Bangladesh's support in pursuance of its core policies at the UN rather than the other way round. This was evident in the discussions around the proposed membership of the UN for Taiwan. Whether the issue would be on the UN Agenda was decided by the General Committee which comprised chairs of various UN committees. Because of its active role at the UN, Bangladesh often sat in this Committee. Whenever that was the case, the Chinese Mission at the UN usually relied on Bangladesh to lead the opposition to the proposal which was often floated on behalf of Taiwan by a friendly African country such as Gambia. While this accorded Bangladesh the opportunity to be seen as doing Beijing a favour, it also placed that country in the eye of a diplomatic storm that it would have been happy to avoid. However, this situation might not recur as in September 2009 Taiwan announced that it would drop for the first time in seventeen years its annual bid to join the United Nations, widely seen as a move to mend fences with China.

Genesis of a Complex Relationship

How the Bangladeshi policy makers view China and its rise today is coloured by how their relationship began, and the twists and turns it experienced as it evolved. The beginnings of the Bangladesh–China relationship were fraught with great complexities. During the halcyon days of the Pakistan–China relationship, among the Bengalis there was a strong pro-China constituency comprising intellectuals and politicians. Prime Minister Zhou en-Lai had paid a very successful visit to Dhaka, the capital of East Pakistan in 1956. In the 1960s it was the Pakistan International Airlines flights linking Dhaka and Beijing that first connected China to the outside non-communist world. So the developing crisis in the subcontinent in early 1971, with the political movement for independence in the then East Pakistan, led by Sheikh Mujibur Rahman's Awami League, gaining momentum with New Delhi's moral support and Islamabad's fierce opposition, placed China between the devil and the deep blue sea.[31] For China, a united Pakistan, given the strategic bilateral relations at that time, would have been ideal.[32] It would also be acceptable to Beijing if the Awami League came into power at an all-Pakistan level in accordance with the results of the elections of December 1970, because individual Awami League leaders had a good rapport with Beijing.[33]

What was disturbing to China was a potential conflict within Pakistan between Mujib's Awami League and the Pakistan People's Party (PPP) led by Zulfikar Ali Bhutto, which had won a minority of seats nationwide in the 1970 parliamentary elections, though a majority in West Pakistan.[34] That could provide China's arch rival the Soviet Union, and to some extent India, a perceived source of threat to China ever since the Border War of 1962, an opportunity to exploit the situation by picking up clients from among the disputants. Zhou's concern was evident in the letters he wrote to both Bhutto and President General Mohammed Yahya Khan, who succeeded Ayub in 1969, urging them to come to satisfactory terms with the Awami League and Mujib.[35]

As the political crisis in Pakistan deepened after the 1970 elections, when the West Pakistani Yahya–Bhutto combination prevented the East Pakistani Mujib from assuming the prime ministership of Pakistan despite an Awami League majority in the National Parliament, two major pro-China political parties of then East Pakistan, Mowlana Abdul Hamid Khan Bhashani's National Awami Party (NAP-Bhashani) and the East Pakistan Communist Party (EPCP Marxist-Leninist), led by Mohammad Toaha and Abdul Huq, developed their own attitudes towards the issue of separation from Pakistan. Abdul Huq was stronger in his view that the separation would aid 'Indo-Soviet expansionism' than Toaha, who later initiated the concept of a 'two-way war' against both the Pakistani army and the Awami League.[36] There was a consequent split between Toaha and Huq.

The Huq line seems to have attracted Beijing's favour. His views along with similar ones held by Ashim Chatterjee of the Communist Party of India (Marxist-Leninist) were broadcast on 'Radio Peking' and 'Radio Tirana' in Albania.[37]Albania was a close ally of China during the phase of the Sino-Soviet dispute in the 1960s and 1970s. Bhashani, who enjoyed close personal ties with Mao and Zhou, also having visited Beijing, on the other hand, sent impassioned appeals to both Chinese leaders seeking assistance in the movement to separation.[38] Bhashani's urgings, however, failed to elicit the desired positive response.

China's Role During the 1971 Conflict

The first Chinese reaction following the Pakistani military crackdown in East Pakistan, that wreaked horrific havoc, came in a letter from Zhou to Yahya written on 11 April 1971. On the surface the letter appeared to express strong support for Pakistan:[39]

Your Excellency may rest assured that should the Indian expansionist dare to launch aggression against Pakistan the Chinese government and people will, as always, firmly support the Pakistan government and people in their just struggle to safeguard state sovereignty and National independence.

Such support was, however, confined to countering the potential threat from India, and seemed not to apply to any emanating in Pakistan domestically. On the domestic situation the letter was far more ambiguous:

'We believe that through the wise consultations and the efforts of Your Excellency and the *leaders of various quarters* (emphasis added) the situation in Pakistan will certainly return to normal.'

By exhorting negotiations with 'leaders of various quarters', Zhou was encouraging continuing engagement with the Awami League as well. However, support for a united Pakistan was expressed thus:

'In our opinion the unification of Pakistan and the unity of East and West Pakistan are basic guarantees for Pakistan to attain prosperity and strength.'

A Bengali foreign language expert in Beijing, who had translated the letter into Bengali for a 'Radio Peking' broadcast, said later that the published excerpts in the Pakistani media had left out what could be the most important sentence of the letter, in which Zhou had also said:[40]

'The question of East Pakistan should be settled according to the *wishes of the people of East Pakistan* (emphasis added).'

Three aspects of the Chinese stance emerge from this letter. First, China would support Pakistan in case of an external threat from India. Second, in China's calculations a united Pakistan was more desirable, obviously to be better able to stand up to India and the Soviet Union. Third, in its view, the way to normalcy was through negotiations with all political quarters, including the East Pakistani people. The third point indicated the disinclination of China to fully endorse Yahya's methods. With some deviation that was to remain, the Chinese position until that time was a definite veering in favour of Yahya in reaction to the perceived Indo-Soviet entente.

On a theoretical plane China believed the Bangladesh movement to be one of Bengali elite interests rather than a genuine grassroots peasant movement.[41] They saw no ideological motive, therefore, to support its cause. Although China would rather see the issue resolved peacefully between the disputants at this stage and therefore was hesitant to take sides in the domestic dispute in Pakistan, via-à-vis India Beijing was voicing strong verbal support to Islamabad. In April 1971 a *Renmin Ribao* commentator wrote:

> Of late, the Indian government has redoubled its efforts to interfere in Pakistan's internal affairs disregarding repeated stern protests of the Pakistan Government. The overbearing attitude of the Indian Government cannot but arouse the indignation of all justice upholding countries.[42]

While support was being accorded at one level against India, at another level the Chinese were urging negotiations. Zhou sent back a two-member Pakistani delegation comprising Foreign Secretary S. M. Khan and General Gul Hassan, a very senior military officer, with a request for political settlement.[43] China's opposition to Yahya's suppressive measures was indicated in an interview given later to a group of Australian National University scholars by Assistant Foreign Minister Chang-wang Chin. The Chinese apprehended deeper Indo-Soviet involvement if the situation deteriorated.

Even though Yahya paid little heed to Chinese counsels against the use of force and this is important in terms of Bangladeshi perceptions of the Chinese role, the Chinese may have calculated they would have little to lose whether Yahya successfully crushed the movement, in which case Pakistan would remain intact, or whether the movement transformed itself into a protracted war of liberation in which case there was the likelihood of its leadership passing into Maoist hands. The Chinese therefore chose to keep a low profile, till such time until India's intervention became imminent, negating the prospects of a prolonged struggle, and the emergence of Bangladesh under Indo-Soviet auspices became a distinct probability.

The Chinese decision to lie low was evident in the fact that it sent no arms to Pakistan until October, that is, until after the signing of the Indo-Soviet Treaty of Friendship in August.[44] If Pakistan was looking for more direct military support, the prospects were looking bleak. Bhutto's military mission to China in November 1971, by his own admission, was a failure. At a banquet in honour of the Pakistani leader who was sent to Beijing by Yahya, the acting foreign minister of China, Chi peng-Fei, urged that a *reasonable settlement* should be made by the *Pakistani people themselves*. Assurances were provided for the defence of Pakistan's state sovereignty and national independence, but any mention of support for *territorial integrity* was now conspicuously absent.[45] In the return banquet by Bhutto, which Premier Zhou also attended, the latter in his speech dwelt on Sino-Pakistan relations, but made no mention of any *external threats* to Pakistan. Bhutto was so disgusted that he later remarked to a journalist that 'Pakistan can hope for little help from China'.[46]

Chinese fears were, however, raised with the signing of the Indo-Soviet treaty of August 1971 as well as the support-seeking travels abroad of Indira Gandhi, the Indian prime minister. China, as a result, began to stiffen its pro-Pakistani posture on the international plane. On 24 November 1971, Zhou expressed his concern to the Pakistani ambassador over 'India's military provocations' along the borders with Pakistan.[47] Public assertions in support of Pakistan were made by Vice Premier Li hsien-Nien on 29 November on the occasion of the anniversary of the Albanian Liberation.[48]

China's hopes for a protracted struggle leading to a radical transformation of the character of the Bangladesh movement evaporated when actual hostilities between India and Pakistan broke out in early December 1971. At the UN, the Chinese chief delegate Huang Hua trenchantly criticised the Indo-Soviet 'song in a duet' and noted that the speech of the Soviet representative *Mister* (not *Comrade*) Malik had confirmed his suspicion that 'the Soviet social imperialists are carrying out aggression, interference, subversion, and expansion everywhere'.[49]

Indeed, Huang Hua conveyed to the US national security advisor Henry Kissinger, who had already visited China that year and with whom the Chinese had developed a close working relationship, his apprehensions that a 'precedence was being established by which other countries (China?) may be dismembered by Indo-Soviet collusion'.[50] In fact, Kissinger's own assessment was that the Soviets were encouraging India to exploit Pakistan's travails in part to deliver a blow to the US system of alliances, and 'even in greater measure to demonstrate Chinese impotence'.[51] On 6 December 1971, as fighting commenced on the subcontinent, Huang Hua compared the nascent Bangladeshi government to the 'puppet Manchukuo regime', and opposed the presence of the Bangladeshi representative at the UN Security Council.[52] What was alarming to the Chinese most was the extension of Soviet influence, particularly in the Indian Ocean region.

However, China's vigorous moral, political and diplomatic support to Pakistan was not translated into military action. Why? The reasons can be analysed as follows: First, there was the possibility of a Soviet counteraction and China was prudently mindful of the fact that it was not militarily strong enough to take on both India and the Soviet Union simultaneously, furthermore in a situation in which Chinese territory was not directly threatened. Second, China itself was passing through a political crisis that involved the purging of leaders like Lin Biao, Huang yang-Shem (chief of staff of the armed forces), Wu fa-Hsien (the air force commander) and forty other top military officers, that ruled out serious military engagement at that time.[53] Third, at a tactical level, winter was the most inconvenient season for military manoeuvrings in the Himalayas as the mountain passes were likely to remain snowed in, something that was also factored in by Indian planners in determining the time-frame for intervention. Finally, the Chinese may have simply given up on Yahya who had paid no heed to their counsels of moderation. Pragmatism obviously was a key determinant shaping China's behaviour.

However, there appeared to have been an understanding of the Chinese role among Bangladeshi policy makers in general. They included Awami Leaguers, some of whom later stated they would have contacted Beijing were it not for concerns about attracting Indian disapproval.[54] Officials of the Bangladesh government-in-exile noted the unconfirmed reports that the Pakistani ambassador in Beijing, K. M. Kaiser, a Bengali and a friend of Mujib, who was to later become the Bangladesh permanent representative to the UN, had been briefing Zhou sympathetically about Bangladesh.[55] Also important was the fact that China was avoiding direct criticism of the Bengali leadership, concentrating instead on India and the Soviet Union.[56] The door of future relations was thus kept wide open.

China, The Balancer

It took a while, though, for China to resume the role of a balancer in South Asia. Despite its circumspect role during the Bangladesh Liberation War, Pakistan's fierce opposition to the new republic and the latter's camaraderie with India and the Soviet Union precluded the possibilities of any close ties between Dhaka and Beijing. There was, however, a strong pro-China lobby within the Bangladeshi polity ready to swing into action at any given opportunity. Dhaka University, whose students always had a significant role in politics, had a strong left tradition. In the late 1960s the main left student body was the East Pakistan Students' Union (EPSU). It was split in two; a pro-Moscow faction led by Motia Chowdhury, and a pro-Beijing one led by Rashed Khan Menon.[57] While the Motia faction moved closer to the government, Menon remained an avid supporter of China. An influential weekly called the *Holiday* was the mouthpiece of the pro-China groups.[58]

Of the left-wing political parties, Muzaffer Ahmed's National Awami Party (NAP), as distinct from NAP-Bhashani, was deemed pro-Moscow and was so close to the government that he was accused of 'me-too-ism'.[59] The Communist Party of Bangladesh, led by Moni Singh, had a more autonomous existence, but less clout. The most influential left-wing politician remained Mowlana Bhashani. He always had Mujib's respect, but not necessarily his ears. He remained a friend of China consistently.

Mujib returned from Pakistani prison in January 1972 and assumed the reins of the government and the leadership of the ruling Awami League. On 5 March 1972, in the USSR, the second country he visited after India, he signed a Joint Declaration with Prime Minister Alexei Kosygin. The USSR also took upon itself the important task of clearing the Chittagong port of mines, to open up the new state to international commerce. Trade was mostly through barter with East European allies of the USSR, so the small business class in the socialistic economy of Bangladesh became dependent on Soviet allies. However, already the *Holiday* was publishing articles critical of the growing influence of the USSR, particularly in Chittagong.[60]

But Mujib was mindful of the need to diversify foreign interactions beyond both the USSR and its allies, and India. He visualised the potential importance of the role of China, not just as a regional balancer, but also as a global one. He declared as early as in March: 'we have great regard for the people of China. We admire their leaders and supported their revolution.'[61] His foreign minister Abdus Samad Azad, a one-time Marxist, echoed him: 'We have extended our hand of friendship towards China and we sincerely hope that this will be reciprocated by the Chinese leaders who, I am sure, will find profound goodwill and respect for them among the people of Bangladesh.'[62] The former Bengali Pakistani ambassador to Beijing, K. M. Kaiser, a friend of Mujib's, was sent as envoy to Rangoon, particularly tasked with monitoring relations with China.[63]

But it appeared that China was not in a position to reciprocate until Bangladesh–Pakistani fences were mended, a process that was ongoing. Meanwhile China blocked Bangladesh's application to join the UN. Its vice foreign minister Chiao kua-Hua said:

> The Chinese government holds that the question of admitting Bangladesh into the UN can be considered once the relevant resolutions of the General Assembly and the Security council are implemented without qualification. But this can be done only after the thorough implementation of the UN resolutions and not before.[64]

This position softened after the mutual recognition of Pakistan and Bangladesh in February 1974. On 7 July that year, the UN Security Council unanimously approved Bangladesh's membership. The Chinese delegate Chung-yen expressed gratification at the settlement of Bangladesh's dispute with Pakistan and on the tripartite agreement between the two countries and

India.[65] The stage was set for bilateral relations, starting in this case with economic cooperation. In May 1975 a three-member trade delegation was sent to China by the Bangladesh commerce ministry.[66] Kaiser also visited Beijing and met with the vice minister for foreign affairs, Han nien-Lung.[67]

The formal Chinese recognition of Bangladesh came on 31 August 1975, and the establishment of bilateral diplomatic ties was actually implemented in January 1976. With this the Chinese traditional role of according support to a smaller South Asian power vis-à-vis India was resumed. While attempts to mend fences between Beijing and New Delhi were in progress, and the Chinese dragon and the Indian elephant were happy to mutually coexist, the Chinese strategy was to continue to humour the other subcontinental actors like Pakistan, Nepal, Sri Lanka and now Bangladesh.

Following the brutal assassination of Sheikh Mujib and members of his family in Bangladesh on 15 August 1975, the only survivors being his two daughters, who were then in Europe, Sheikh Hasina Wazed, the current prime minister and Sheikh Rehana, in a coup by some junior army and ex-army officers, Khondakar Mushtaq Ahmed was briefly in power, but instability persisted till November when Major General Ziaur Rahman, later to be the founder of the Bangladesh Nationalist Party (BNP), emerged as the strongman.

Mutual Quid Pro Quos

A period of lows in terms of Bangladesh–India relations began with Mujib's assassination. Even when Zia assumed power, the issue of Farakka Barrage, whereby India was accused by Dhaka of seeking to divert the Ganges river water upstream, stood in the way of better Dhaka–New Delhi relations. Zia visited Beijing in January 1977 and in a banquet in his honour, Vice Premier Li hsien-Nien, in an obvious reference to Bangladesh's differences with India over the Farakka Barrage declared that 'China firmly supports the government and the people of Bangladesh in their just struggle to safeguard national independence and state sovereignty and resist foreign interference'.[68]

What the Chinese would have liked in return for their support, even though only verbal, was a clear Bangladeshi position against 'Soviet hegemonism'. This was obviously a clear challenge for

Bangladesh. Bangladesh was not able to oblige, because it was not yet in a position to alienate the USSR, still a Superpower, but with which bilateral relations had considerably cooled since 1975. Bangladesh's strong posture vis-à-vis Moscow only came about in the 1980s during the Soviet occupation of Afghanistan, but this was rendered easier by the strong backing of another Superpower, the US, and of the Muslim world. It appears that China understood Bangladesh's predicament, and its inability to a *quid pro quo* and remained content with such support as could be given when, at the Non-Aligned Summit Conference in Havana in September 1979, Bangladesh's foreign minister Shamsul Huq stressed the right of the Kampuchean people to 'freely choose a government without any *external interference or foreign military presence or intervention*' (emphasis added). The reference was to Vietnam with whom China had fallen out. This was designed to please China, who seemed quite happy to pick up any support, however indirect, that friends including Bangladesh could render. On the international stage, Bangladesh and China grew closer through common positions on such issues as the Soviet occupation of Afghanistan and the Vietnamese intervention in Cambodia.

Bangladesh had, by the 1980s, become a major procurer of Chinese military hardware. Therefore, obviously there was a close rapport between those Bangladeshi leaders with prominent military backgrounds, such as President General Ziaur Rahman, and after his assassination in May 1981, President General Hossain Mohammad Ershad. Ershad was very warmly received when he visited Beijing in July 1987. During the 1990s, Bangladeshi politics was dominated by the BNP led by Begum Zia, the widow of the slain president, and the Awami League led by Sheikh Hasina, Mujib's daughter; with both of them Beijing kept close ties. Indeed, it was when Prime Minister Begum Zia visited Beijing in December 2002 that the Defence Cooperation Agreement with China was signed. While Bangladeshis claimed it was merely formalising existing relations as in any case by then most of Bangladesh's weaponry, including tanks, naval frigates and combat aircraft were of Chinese origin, some Indian analysts saw this as reinforcing China's 'intrusiveness' in South Asia.[69] In April 2005, Chinese premier Wen Jiabao led a 102-member entourage to Bangladesh, signed nine agreements, and both countries declared 2005 as the 'Bangladesh–China Friendship Year'.[70]

The Chinese also went the extra mile to cultivate the caretaker government in Bangladesh that was in office between 2007 and 2009. The caretaker government was in need of international support and China indicated its endorsement through a visit to Dhaka by Foreign Minister Yang Jiechi on 24 and 25 April 2008, in course of which he described Bangladesh as an 'all-weather friend'.[71] Thereafter Beijing hosted the head of the caretaker government Dr Fakhruddin Ahmed from 15 to 18 September 2008. He was given a warm welcome by President Hu Jintao, Vice President Xi Jinping and Prime Minister Wen Jiabao.[72] Hu described Bangladesh–China relations being based on 'comprehensive partnership of cooperation', and 'appreciated' Bangladesh's support to China in 'successfully holding the Beijing Olympics 2008 and Paralympics Beijing 2008'.[73] During this time, Bangladesh championed China's observer status in the South Asian Association for Regional Cooperation (SAARC), and China, in return, backed Bangladesh's membership of the ASEAN Regional Forum (ARF), which focuses on security issues.

Bangladeshi policy makers found this relationship very useful when China played a constructive role in amicably resolving a spat between Bangladesh and Myanmar, China's close ally, in November 2008. It was when Myanmar had placed an oil-drilling rig within territorial waters claimed by Bangladesh in the Bay of Bengal. The author, then foreign advisor (foreign minister) of Bangladesh called in the Chinese ambassador in Dhaka, Zheng Qingdian, and requested Beijing's help to secure Myanmar's withdrawal of the rig. Immediately thereafter in Beijing, the foreign ministry invited the ambassadors of Myanmar and Bangladesh and urged calm. The Chinese foreign office spokesman Qin Gang issued a statement: 'We hope that the countries will settle it (the dispute) through equal and friendly negotiations and maintain a stable bilateral relationship and as their friend China will contribute in an appropriate manner.'[74] Myanmar withdrew the rig forthwith.

The current prime minister Sheikh Hasina maintained close contacts with Beijing even when she was out of power. As leader of the opposition, in November 2003 she paid a visit to Beijing as a guest of the Chinese Communist Party. Within thirteen months of assuming the office of prime minister in January 2009, she paid a visit to China in March 2010, two months after a trip to New Delhi. The Joint Statement that was issued referred to a '*Closer* Comprehensive Partnership of Cooperation', raising the perceived level of friendship a notch higher.[75] The visit was almost immediately reciprocated, with a speed uncommon in traditional diplomacy, by Vice President Xi Jinping, seen by many as a likely successor of President Hu Jintao, in three years, in June 2010.[76]

Stakeholders' Perceptions

Major stakeholders in relation with contemporary rising China in Bangladesh would be the two major political parties, the Awami League and the BNP. The leaders of both, respectively Sheikh Hasina and Begum Zia, place great store by their links with Beijing, partly because in their perception public opinion is in favour of such strengthened ties, but largely because of the dependence of the military on arms procurement from China. Chinese connections also offset Indian influence, though this is more likely to be a factor with the BNP than with the Awami League whose perceived relations with New Delhi are better. Ironically, though, the differences over Taiwan that put a temporary strain on the ties with Beijing occurred during the period of the BNP-led government. The far-left parties are mostly marginalised in Bangladesh. Earlier student leaders from the pro-Beijing factions of university bodies have found their way into both the mainstream parties.

Bangladesh has a very vibrant civil society. Many of its leaders are close to Beijing. The Bangladesh–China Friendship Association acts as a strong advocate of relations with Beijing. They also have the support of the Chinese embassy in Dhaka. A discussion programme on the fifty-ninth anniversary of the founding of the People's Republic in October 2008 was attended by the food advisor (minister) of the caretaker government, Dr A. M. M. Shawkat Ali, who said on that occasion that 'Bangladesh should learn from the Chinese model of development.'[77] In August 1999 a meeting was held in Yunnan, China, in which China, India, Bangladesh and Myanmar participated, which underscored the need for sub-regional cooperation. This led to the Kunming

Initiative, of which Professor Rehman Sobhan, a very prominent Bangladeshi economist, is an ardent advocate. Other members of the intelligentsia and thought-leaders supportive of close ties with the rising China include Faruq Ahmed Chowdhury, an author, and Farooq Sobhan, president of the Bangladesh Enterprise Institute, a think tank. Both are retired diplomats and authorities on China. Indeed retired ambassadors to China form an important pressure-group in this respect.

A more challenging environment in dealings with China is faced by the officials of the Economic Affairs Division (ERD), who negotiate external assistance. Since the establishment of diplomatic relations in 1975, China has provided Bangladesh US$ 1.5 billion in support, not a large quantum in terms of Bangladesh's needs, out of which US$ 978 have been in hard loans, whereas Bangladesh authorities had hoped for credit on softer terms.[78] For the future, at a meeting of the Joint Economic Commission (JEC) in Beijing, the Chinese side expressed interest in financing only five projects worth a little over US$ 1 billion, as opposed to the US$ 5.14 billion assistance sought by Bangladesh for twenty-eight projects.[79] When the Bangladesh side sought investment under a number of Public Private Project (PPP) initiatives they were reportedly told: 'Investment is market driven.'[80] For political reasons China prefers to fund 'landmark' iconic projects like 'friendship bridges', six of which have been financed and the seventh is under negotiation, and 'Friendship Conference Centres'. While not opposed to this, the Bangladeshi authorities would obviously prefer more diversification. However, there is one area where Chinese support is deemed critical by Bangladesh. To make up for energy shortage, Bangladesh has decided in principle to opt for nuclear power, and for this China has already been approached for a US$ 600 million credit for the Rooppur Nuclear Power project.[81] There is a perception among Bangladeshi aid officials, though, that despite the lack of obvious 'conditionalities' Chinese assistance does involve 'quid pro quo', on a case by case basis.[82]

According to the statistics provided by the International Monetary Fund (IMF) in 2008, Bangladesh's imports from China amounted to US$ 3.15 billion, and exports totaled only US$ 96 million. To offset this imbalance China granted tariff-free access to eighty-four Bangladeshi commodities within the framework of the Asia-Pacific Trade Agreement and expanded aid.[83] When this proved insufficient, at the July 2009 JEC meeting, Bangladesh sought duty-free market access for thirty-nine more products, but the Chinese side reportedly declined arguing that offering non-reciprocal facility is difficult under the current global economic turmoil, which is also affecting China.[84] Another concern of Bangladeshi businesses is competition with China in the area of 'readymade garments', Bangladesh's principal export. In the financial year 2008–9, Bangladeshi businesses exported a record US$ 12.35 billion, US$ 6.43 billion in knitwear and US$ 5.92 billion in woven apparel.[85] Bangladeshi trade diplomacy must be seriously geared to ensuring that Chinese items do not pose a threat to this commerce in the international arena.

Another challenge, a growing one, for the Bangladeshi environmentalists at present, though eventually it could assume a larger dimension, is the proposed diversion by China of the Brahmaputra river, flowing into India, and thereafter into Bangladesh. The river, with an average altitude of 4,000 metres is the highest in the world and runs 2,057 metres in Tibet before entering India. China is now reportedly contemplating divert-ing the water to the parched Yellow river. The idea has not been discussed much in public, but according to an Indian analyst, appears in an officially blessed book published in 2005 called *Tibet's Waters Will Save China*.[86] If the project goes through, the Indian analyst has said it will be tantamount to 'the declaration of a water war against India and Bangladesh'.[87] India would, however be pleased with the fact that Prime Minister Sheikh Hasina took the matter up with China and obtained their consent on the 'exchange of data'.[88] Bangladeshi observers like Barrister Harun ur Rashid are tracking the issue while they point to an irony between this and Indo-Bangladesh water disputes.[89]

However, the most significant constituency of China within the Bangladesh system would be the defence community. One of the accompanying features of the rise of China has been its reemergence — since the 1880s when, during the Iraq–Iran war it sold weapons to both sides — as a major player in the international arms market. It is now the world's fifth largest arms exporter, after such traditional suppliers as the US, Russia, France and the UK.[90] In 2007 China submitted a report on its weapons exports and imports to the UN Arms Transfer Register for the first time in a decade, having stopped providing this information ten years earlier because the US had mentioned Taiwan in its footnote explaining some of its exports.[91] According to its declaration, in the previous year China sold sixty-five large caliber artillery systems, sixteen combat aircraft and 114 missile and related equipment to Bangladesh, rendering it the prime purchaser of weapons made in China.[92]

The aggregations of the perceptions and interests of these groups and categories in Bangladesh, and their interplay, have a significant influence on the state's relations with this neighbour with burgeoning international clout. As the foregoing analysis demonstrates, while their views may vary, the weightage on the whole appears to be tilting in favour of close ties, and the government does indeed take this reading of public opinion. There are thus critical sectors in the Bangladeshi system where Chinese support would be seen as essential.

Conclusion

The pluralist political tradition of Bangladesh, the intellectual connections, the commercial and economic dependence, and the presence of the very large diaspora in those countries would normally dictate closer proximity of the country to the West, to the Middle East, to Europe and to the United States. But China breaks this pattern, and not just because it is seen as a counterpoise to a more powerful neighbour, India, but mostly because the average Bangladeshi sees China as a country to learn from. Indeed, as India is also rising with China, there is a prevailing sentiment in Bangladesh that the world is on the threshold of an Asian Age, and all Asians will benefit from it, in the fashion of the 'flying geese paradigm' with those more challenged benefitting from following those more privileged. Furthermore, Bangladeshi leadership views the Sino-Bangladesh amity as a new model of bilateral relations, not designed as a traditional 'balance of power' counterpoise to India, like the Sino-Pakistan strategic relationship; rather, the perception is that of a conduit or bridge connecting China with the other rising power in Asia, India.[93]

China on the 'rise' has also been cautious, prudent and circumspect. China no longer allows the ideological heart to dominate the pragmatic head. As Deng Xiaoping had famously remarked:

'it does not matter whether the cat is black or white as long as it catches mice.' The Chinese have turned the Yellow river, the 'Huang hue' once known as the 'sorrow of China' because of its 1,593 floods in the past four centuries, into its pride by using it as a metaphor to conquer China's travails. It is good, perhaps, for Bangladesh that the river of Chinese policy slowly meanders but does not suddenly change course. There is a method in the dragon's moods, reasons why it behaves as it does. The great challenge to the Bangladeshi policy makers would be to keep their country relevant to this emerging super-state entity, and not to allow it to become marginalised, as China rises in strength, power and influence.

✻

Notes

1. It was the French Emperor Napoleon Bonaparte who in the early 19th century described China as a 'sleeping dragon' preferring the world to leave it undisturbed.
2. See John J. Thacik, Jr, 'China's Rise at Stake in Power Struggle', *Asian Times*, September 2004. Singapore's minister mentor Lee Kuan Yew has suggested it be called a 'cultural renaissance'. *Straits Times*, 3 September 2009.
3. Wang Fei-Ling, 'Preservation, Prosperity, and Power: What motivates China's Foreign Policy', *Journal of Contemporary China*, vol. 14, no. 45, pp. 669–94.
4. Abanti Bhattacharya, 'China's Foreign Policy Challenges and Evolving Strategy', *Strategic Analysis*, vol. 30, no. 1, Jan.–Mar. 2006, pp. 182–86.
5. Jean-Pierre Cabestan, 'The China Factor: China between Multipolarity and Bipolarity', in Gilles Bouquerat and Frederic Grare (eds), *India, China and Russia; Intricacies of an Asian Triangle*, Singapore: Marshall Cavendish International Private Ltd., 2004, p. 86.
6. Chairman Mao Zedong's 'Theory on the Division of the Three Worlds and the Strategy of Forming an Alliance Against an Opponent', available at http://www.fmprc.gov.cn?Eng?Ziliao/3602/3604/t18008.htm (accessed 29 June 2009).
7. Ibid.
8. Cited in Henry Kissinger, *Diplomacy*, New York: Simon & Schuster, 1994, p. 725.
9. Kissinger had written: 'Beijing's diplomacy was so subtle and indirect that it largely went over our heads in Washington.' Ibid.

10. See Raja C. Mohan, 'Maritime Power: India and China Turn to Mahan', ISAS Working Paper No. 71, 7 July 2009.

11. 'Between Rising Naval Powers: Implications for Southeast Asia of the Rise of Chinese and Indian Naval Power', S. Rajaratnam School of International Studies, 18–19 November 2008.

12. Richard A. Bitzinger, 'China's Naval Ambitions: Aircraft Carriers will Make Waves', *Straits Times*, 10 April 2009.

13. See Frank W. Moore , 'China's Military Capabilities', Cambridge MA: Institute for Defense and Disarmament Studies, June 2000, available at http://www.comw.org/cmp/fulltext/iddschina.html (accessed 4 May 2009).

14. 'China's Strategic Nuclear Weapons', available at http://www.fas.org/nuke/guide/china/doctrine/huan.htm (accessed 4 May 2009).

15. Bitzinger, 'China's Naval Ambitions'.

16. Quoted in Fareed Zakaria, *The Post American World*, New York: W. W. Norton & Company, 2008, p. 89.

17. See http://tradinghelpdesk.wordpress.com/2009/07/15/Chinese-reserves-surpass-2-trillion/ (accessed 3 September 2009).

18. 'Crisis Focus: A Leg Up for China', *Beijing Review*, 15 April 2009.

19. Dominic Wilson and Roopa Purushothaman, 'Dreaming with BRICs: The Path to 2050', Goldman Sachs, Global Economic Paper No. 99, October 2003, available at http:// www2. Goldman. Sachs. com?insight?research/reports/99 pdf. Cited in Mohan, 'Maritime Power'.

20. 'Security and Opportunity for the Twenty-first Century', *Foreign Affairs*, Special Edition, Davos, 2008, p. 83.

21. 'Renewing American Leadership', ibid., p. 107.

22. The commissioner's office of China's Foreign Ministry in the Hong Kong SAR, available at http:// www/fmcoprc.gov.hk/eng/2gwjsw/t575979. htm (accessed 3 September 2009).

23. *Straits Times*, 15 September 2009.

24. For one such study, see Christopher J. Pehrson, *String of Pearls: Meeting the Challenge of China's Rising Power Across the Asian Littoral*, Strategic Studies Institute, United States Army War College, available at http://www.strategicstudiesinstitute.army.mil/pubs?display.cfm?Pubid=721 (accessed 5 July 2009).

25. See Yuan Jing-dong, 'The Dragon and the Elephant: Chinese-Indian Relations in the 21st Century', *Washington Quarterly*, Summer, 2007.

26. See Siddharta Srivastava, 'China Warms to Indo-US Nuclear Deal', *World Security Network*, 3 April 2006.

27. Jing-dong, 'The Dragon and the Elephant'.

28. Joseph E. Stiglitz, *Globalization and its Discontents*, New York: W. W. Norton and Company, 2002, p. 112.

29. Keith Bradsher, 'China is Taking Steps to Free its Currency', *International Herald Tribune*, 6 July 2009.

30. The author, then Bangladesh ambassador to the United Nations, was one of the two 'facilitators' of the president of the General Assembly charged with the task of negotiating the language of the draft principle, later to be adopted by the world leaders .The other 'facilitator' was Ambassador Roman Kirn of Slovenia.

31. For a study of a run-up to the crisis, see Iftekhar Ahmed Chowdhury, *The Roots of Bangladeshi National Identity*, ISAS Working Paper No. 63, 10 June 2009.

32. China and Pakistan enjoyed extremely close relations through the 1960s and beyond. The relationship was designed by both sides to offset India's preeminent role in South Asia. Pakistan, technically a US ally through its membership of the Central Treaty Organisation (CENTO) and Southeast Asia Treaty Organisation (SEATO) defence pacts, helped act as a bridge between the West and China, facilitating Kissinger's visit to Beijing in 1971 (see Henry Kissinger, *The White House Years*, Boston: Little Brown and Company, 1979, pp. 684–732). This relationship has sustained, though it has not precluded China over time from developing other connections in the region, including with Bangladesh, as also in due course, with India.

33. Even though President Field Marshal Mohammed Ayub Khan is generally seen as the architect of Pakistan's policy of friendship towards China, the process was initiated earlier by H. S. Suhrawardy, the Awami League prime minister of Pakistan, who visited China in the mid-1950s, as did his aide Sheikh Mujibur Rahman, who led the movement for Bangladesh.

34. The PPP projected itself as a pro-China socialist party, and Bhutto as a particular friend of China for having been instrumental in forging the 1963 China–Pakistan Boundary Agreement.

35. G. W. Choudhury, *The Last Days of Pakistan*, London: C. Hurst & Co., 1974, p. 211.

36. For a study of the attitudes of the radical Bengali parties towards the issue, see Talukdar Maniruzzaman, *Radical Politics and the Emergence of Bangladesh*, Dacca: Bangladesh Books International, 1978, pp. 51–52.

37. Tariq Ali, 'Pakistan and Bangladesh: Results and Prospects', in Robin Blackburn (ed.), *Explosion in a Subcontinent*, London: Penguin, 1975, p. 318.

38. *Mowlana Abdul Hamid Khan Bhashani's Appeal to World Leaders*, Dacca: Public Relations Department of the Government of the People's Republic of Bangladesh, pp. 2–3, undated. It is noteworthy that Bhashani himself took some time to bring his NAP entirely in line with the Awami League on the issue of the independence of Bangladesh.

39. For the text, see J. A. Naik, *India, Russia, China, and Bangladesh*, New Delhi: S. Chand and Co., 1972, Appendix 7, p. 138.

40. 'A Bengali's Grandstand View', *Far Eastern Economic Review*, 11 October 1974, p. 7.

41. Shirin Tahir-Kheli, 'The Foreign Policy of "New" Pakistan', *Orbis*, vol. 20, no. 3 Fall 1976, p. 735.

42. 'What are the Indian Expansionists Trying to Do?', *Peking Review*, vol. 14, no. 16, 16 April 1971, p. 7.

43. Choudhury, *The Last Days of Pakistan*, p. 212.

44. T. J. S. George, 'Peking's Pre-war Message to Bhutto', *Far Eastern Economic Review*, February 1978, p. 8.

45. For a full text of the speech, see *Peking Review*, vol. 14, no. 46, 12 November 1971, p. 5.

46. Kalim Siddiqui, *Conflict, Crisis, and War in Pakistan*, London: Macmillan, 1972, p. 14.

47. *Peking Review*, vol. 14, no. 49, 3 December 1971, p. 5.

48. Ibid.

49. Ibid., vol. 4, no. 10, 10 December 1971, pp. 8–10.

50. Kissinger, *The White House Years*, p. 906.

51. Ibid., p. 886.

52. *Peking Review*, vol. 14, no. 51, 17 December 1971, pp. 15–16.

53. Anwar Syed, *China and Pakistan: Diplomacy of an Entente Cordiale*, Amherst: University of Massachusetts Press, 1974, p. 152.

54. Interview with Moudud Ahmed, a key figure based in the headquarters of the Bangladesh government-in-exile in Mujibnagar, Dhaka, 19 July 1978.

55. *Crisis in Bangladesh Movement*, Bangladesh Foreign Ministry, Mujibnagar, 25 September 1971, pp. 5–6.

56. Ibid., p. 6. This shows that this fact was entered into the analysis of the government-in-exile's foreign office.

57. Motia Chowdhury eventually joined the Awami League and currently is a senior minister in the Awami League–led coalition of Sheikh Hasina. Menon is a member of parliament, elected in 2008, and his Workers' Party supports the present coalition.

58. Its editor, Enayetullah Khan, a brother of Menon, was to later become a cabinet minister and thereafter ambassador to Beijing.

59. Rounaq Jahan, 'Bangladesh in 1972: Nation Building in a New State', *Asian Survey*, February 1973, p. 207.

60. Anjali De, 'Soviet Strategy in Bangladesh', *Holiday*, 21 January 1973, p. 2.

61. *Far Eastern Economic Review*, 1 April 1972, p. 4.

62. *Bangladesh Documents*, vol. 7, no. 4, July–September 1972, p. 4.

63. At one stage Dhaka failed to follow up on a lead given by China. Kaiser obtained an offer by China to buy a quantum of Bangladeshi jute. Initially Bangladesh agreed to the trade in principle (*The Times of India*, 12 June 1972). Then, perhaps due to potential Indian unhappiness, Dhaka went back on it.

64. *Pakistan Times*, October 1973.

65. *Keesing's Contemporary Archives* (98-14 July 1974), p. 26610.

66. The delegation comprised Enam Ahmed Chowdhury, the director general of the Export Promotion Bureau, A. K. M. Moosa, a retired senior official, and M. L. Rahman, a businessman. Interview with Enam Ahmed Chowdhury, Dhaka, 28 February 2009.

67. *Pakistan Times*, June 1975.

68. *Bangladesh*, vol. 2, no. 4, Dacca, Ministry of Information and Broadcasting, 15 January 1977. Though Zia was at that time formally not the head of government but only the second ranking Bangladeshi, Chairman Hua Guo-feng, Mao's successor, broke protocol and personally received him at the airport.

69. For instance, see Dr Subash Kapila, 'Bangladesh–China Defence Cooperation Agreement's Strategic Implications: An Analysis', *South Asia Analysis Group*, Paper No. 582, 14 January 2003, available at http://www.southasiaanalysis.org?papers6/paper582.html (accessed 23 June 2009).

70. *The Hindu*, 9 April 2005. It may be worthwhile mentioning that Wen's eight-day visit to South Asia began with Pakistan and also included Sri Lanka.

71. Yang was hosted by the author who was the foreign advisor (foreign minister) of Bangladesh during the period of the caretaker government (2007–9).

72. The author was a member of the Bangladesh delegation, and participated in the talks.

73. *Asia Pulse News*, 17 September 2008, available at http://www.highbeam.com/doc/IGI-185205416.html (accessed 7 September 2009).

74. 'Maritime Security: The Case of Bangladesh', Bangladesh Institute of Peace and Security Studies, Dhaka, Issue Brief No. 4, January 2009.

75. *Daily Star*, 20 March 2010.

76. Vice President Xi Jinping, in course of this tour that covered Bangladesh, Laos, Australia and New Zealand was crisscrossing a region where 'China's growth is cause for both hope and anxiety', *Straits Times*, 26 June 2010. Abul Kalam Azad, the press secretary to Prime Minister Hasina of Bangladesh was quoted (same source) as saying that the Chinese vice president showed interest in helping build a US\$ 8.7 billion deep water port (Chittagong), intended to serve Nepal, Bhutan, southern China, Myanmar and northeastern India. This would demonstrate that India would also benefit from it and the project was not aimed at off-setting any Indian influence.

77. Embassy of the People's Republic of China, Dhaka, available at http://bd.china-embassy.org/eng/xwdt/t520614.htm (accessed 7 September 2009).

78. Rejaul Karim Byron, 'China Offers $1 billion for 5 Projects', available at http://www.thefinancialexpress-bd.com/2009/08/04/75246.html (accessed 6 September 2009).
79. Ibid. The nine-member Bangladesh side was led by Mosharraf Hossain Bhuiyan, secretary ERD. The Chinese team was headed by Vice Minister Chen Jian.
80. Nazmul Ahsan, 'China Interested to Finance Five Large Projects', *Financial Express*, 4 August 2009.
81. Byron, 'China Offers $1 billion for 5 Projects'.
82. For an interesting study of the opacity and 'hidden conditionalities' of Chinese aid, see Christopher Walker and Sarah Cook, 'The Dark Side of China Aid', *International Herald Tribune*, 25 March 2010.
83. For these data, see Iftekhar Ahmed Chowdhury, 'A Method in the Dragon's Moods: Why China Behaves as it Does', ISAS Working Paper No. 75, pp. 13–14.
84. Ahsan, 'China Interested to Finance Five Large Projects'.
85. BD News24.Com., 9 August 2009.
86. *Tibet's Waters Will Save China*, Chinese Ministry of Water Resources Report, Beijing 2005.
87. Brahma Chellaney, 'Sino-Indian Water Divide', *Lhasa Post*, 25 August 2009.
88. *Daily Star*, 20 March 2010.
89. Barrister Harun ur Rashid, 'India's Water Diversion Policy May Turn on Itself', *Daily Star*, 11 July 2009.
90. Richard A. Bitzinger, 'China's Reemergence as an Arms Dealer: The Return of the King?', *China Brief*, Jamestown Foundation, vol. 9, no. 14, 9 July 2009.
91. According to the Chinese, the UN Register is a register of 'legitimate transfers' and Taiwan being a province of China, any arms transfer to it by the US was 'illegitimate'. The US has now agreed not to make such mention, whereupon China decided to resume reporting.
92. Pranab Dhal Samantha, 'Breaking 10-year Silence, China Reveals its Now No. 1 Arms Supplier to Bangladesh', available at http://www.indianexpress.com/news/breaking-10year-silence-china-reveals-its/215320/ Posted online Sunday, September 2007 (accessed 8 September 2009).
93. See Iftekhar Ahmed Chowdhury, 'Bangladesh–China: An Emerging Equation in the Asian Diplomatic Calculations', ISAS Working Paper 105, March 31 2010.

3

Bhutan
Cautiously Cultivated Positive Perception

CAROLINE BRASSARD*

The main objective of this chapter is to critically assess the main factors that influence the Bhutanese view of the rise of China from various perspectives and for different stakeholders especially in the economic and political arenas. The key implications of China's growing geopolitical importance on Bhutan are multiple, including renewed emphasis on resolving the border dispute, pressure to develop the private sector and careful management of the relationship with India.

Up to now, there are no official diplomatic relations between China and Bhutan and there is a severe dearth of data on the depth and impacts of the economic and political exchanges between China and Bhutan. Consequently, the literature on China–Bhutan relations so far tends to focus on the historical linkages between the two countries. It seldom ventures into more recent issues such as Bhutanese perceptions of a rising China. This chapter is based on the most recent literature, available official data, recent media reports and more than twenty interviews, and focus group discussions from informants in Bhutan, China, India and Singapore.

This chapter comprises three sections. This first section begins with an overview of the historical origins of the cultural, economic and political relations between China and Bhutan, with a brief background on Bhutan's recent political and economic developments. Then, it discusses China's economic and defence growth in relation to Bhutan, and critically assesses the underlying geopolitical, cultural and historical factors influencing the Bhutanese perspective of a rising China, including the role of Tibet and India.

The second section looks at the specific factors that influence the positive and/or negative perceptions of the rise of China for different constituencies and stakeholders in Bhutan. First, from an economic and sectoral perspective, it begins with an analysis of the implications of China's international trade, foreign direct investment and foreign aid strategies. Second, from a political perspective, it delves into the political constituencies in light of the recent political developments in Bhutan. Third, from an international relations perspective, it discusses the influence of regional and international organisations such as the South Asian Association for Regional Cooperation (SAARC), Bay of Bengal Initiative for Multi-Sectoral Technical and Economic Cooperation (BIMSTEC) and Association of South East Asian Nations (ASEAN) as well as Bhutan's planned accession to the World Trade Organisation (WTO). Finally, from a security and defence perspective, it analyses the recent developments influencing the Bhutanese view of China.

The final section identifies the evolving nature of the Bhutanese views on China from various stakeholders and constituencies in the medium and longer term. In particular, it discusses the possible directions of Bhutan's engagement with China in relation to alternative economic and political scenarios in the future.

Historically, Bhutan's relations with its immediate neighbours, India and Tibet (dating from the 7th century A.D.) were linked to military and religious influences.[1] In the 18th century, Britain signed a peace treaty between the East India Company and Bhutan (in 1774) which formalised trade relationships between the British colonial powers in India and Bhutan. The Treaty of Sinchula (in 1865) established free trade between the British Empire and Bhutan, thereby ending possibilities for any levy or duties on British goods going into (or through) Bhutan.[2] This was a significant political and economic event given that, by the late 19th century, the export of Tibetan goods through Bhutan exceeded imports. Traditionally, Bhutan engaged in trade relations with Tibet, for example, by importing tea from China.

Although Bhutan is culturally, ethnically and linguistically related to Tibet, in Bhutan's perception of China's rise the role of Tibet is important for other reasons as well. The first, for political reasons, is the ongoing question of the Tibetan refugees. The second is for economic reasons because of potential border trade relations, and the impact of the new direct rail link between

Beijing and Lhasa. The third is for security reasons due to the unresolved border talks, and India's close ties with Bhutan. Each of these factors deserves to be examined carefully in this chapter, alongside the role of the power competition between India and China.

Tibetan refugees were welcome in Bhutan in the 1950s until the Bhutanese officially closed the border with Tibet following the uprising of Lhasa in the spring of 1959, the flight of the Dalai Lama into India and the infiltration of thousands of Tibetans into Bhutan.[3] Between 1974 and 1979, many Tibetan refugees that had settled in Bhutan but refused Bhutanese citizenship were deported. Kharat claims that this was done in order to maintain correct relations with China.[4] Many commentators argue that this is also in line with the formal invitation to China for the coronation of King Jigme Singye Wangchuck in June 1974.[5] Until now, the question of Tibetan refugees in Bhutan makes headline news.[6]

In the last twenty years, many cultural and political connections took place between the two countries, but Bhutan remains the only one of China's neighbours that does not have official bilateral relations. There are still relatively limited cultural, educational or other types of social relations between the two countries. Only a few Bhutanese students have been sent to China in recent years, for example, to study engineering. Nevertheless, the Bhutanese are increasingly and more confidently engaging with China at other levels. In 1990, a Bhutanese Sport Delegation participated in the Asian Games in Beijing. Bhutan also has an honorary consulate in Hong Kong, thanks to an agreement signed on 1 December 2000 to retain Bhutan's honorary consulate in the Special Administrative Regions of Hong Kong and Macau. Bhutan is an open supporter of the One China Policy and in 2002, Bhutan also supported China's stance on the Taiwan question by opposing Gaoxiong to host the 2002 Asian Games. In addition, as vice chairman of the 55th UN General Assembly, Bhutan supported China in rejecting Taiwan's participation motion in the UN.

Since 1999, a major technological development has begun shaping Bhutanese perceptions of China: the introduction of satellite television and the internet into many Bhutanese urban households. Some analysts argue that this has heightened the

Bhutanese knowledge of the changing geopolitical scene — and is also casting a negative influence on the Bhutanese cultural identity.[7] However, the impact of Chinese cyberspace is dwarfed by that of India. Nevertheless, thanks to the internet, recent diplomatic visits from China have received increasing public attention, contributing to a positive view of China's international outreach and demonstrating a more confident Bhutan on the international scene. For example, the national parliament of Bhutan newsletter of February 2009 includes a photo taken during the visit to the honourable speaker, Lyonpo Jigme Tshultim, by H.E. Mr Zhang Yan, the New Delhi–based ambassador of the People's Republic of China on 13 May 2008.[8]

Nevertheless, Bhutan's security and defence concerns have major implications on its sensitivity towards China's increasing international power. The unresolved border issue is still key to Bhutan's future political and economic relations with China.[9] Although relatively small, the 470 kilometres–long border between China and Bhutan remains peaceful. Kharat mentions that informal contacts with China via the Chinese embassy in the Indian capital took place in the early 1980s and Bhutan began to hold direct talks with China in 1984, to try to settle the boundary dispute.[10]

In 1998, Bhutan and China agreed to maintain peace and tranquillity on the Bhutan–China border during the 12th round of bilateral border talks.[11] This was the first bilateral agreement signed by the two countries, and showed how their relations had developed steadily over the years. The agreement states that 'the two sides agree to maintain peace and tranquillity in their border areas, pending a final settlement on the boundary question, and to maintain status quo on the boundary as before March 1959' and 'they will refrain from taking any unilateral action to change the status quo of the boundary'.[12] Although it appears that diplomatic relations between the two countries will not be possible before the border issue is solved, some media observers suggest that the opening of a Chinese embassy in Thimphu could be a tacit condition for a resolution of the border dispute.[13] During the 13th round of bilateral border talks in Thimphu in 1999, the Chinese added new dimensions by proposing the establishment of diplomatic relations and trade relations. There were signs of a 'package deal' that can be seen such as the Chinese shifting goal posts, by making boundary settlement as a condition to diplomatic and trade relations.

The 18th round of border talks occurred in Beijing in August 2006, and focused on the technicalities of the disputed claims. There are clear signs from the proceedings of the National Assembly of Bhutan that some stakeholders are putting pressure to resolve the border talks, for security and commercial reasons. For example, in the 84th and 85th parliamentary sessions (held respectively in June and December 2006) two types of concerns were expressed: First, from the population near the northern border areas over the building of roads by the Chinese; and second, mounting pressure to resolve the border issue on the part of the Bhutanese Chamber of Commerce.[14] The foreign minister of Bhutan, Lyonpo Ugyen Tshering, recently stated that the next round would be held 'as soon as possible', demonstrating the government's renewed commitment to resolving the issue.[15] In November 2007, the Chumbi Valley again attracted some media attention as Chinese forces dismantled several nearby unmanned posts. This tri-junction between Bhutan, India and China in the Siliguri corridor connects northeast India to the rest of India, and Nepal to Bhutan and shares borders with Tibet and Sikkim. Its strategic significance for the Indian military is obvious.

The most recent border talks, the first since democratisation in 2008, took place in Thimphu in January 2010 and dealt especially with the northwestern disputed sectors. For this 19th round, Assistant Foreign Minister Hu Zhengyue acted as the Chinese government representative and according to a press release from the foreign ministry, discussions were also held on 'bilateral, regional and international developments of mutual interest and concern'.[16] The talks concluded on an agreement to discuss the modalities for conducting a 'joint field survey' of the four disputed territories in the rich pastoral lands of northern Bhutan (Doklam, Charithang, Sinchulumpa and Dramana), amounting to 874 sq km.

But one cannot fully understand this dynamic without considering India's own border talks with China. According to Malik, since 2005, there has been a rapid deterioration in the Sino-Indian border talks due to 'China's increasing assertiveness, as evident in increased incursions in Arunachal Pradesh by the People's Liberation Army', which also borders East Bhutan.[17]

In addition, Wang Chongli, director of the Center for South Asian studies of the Institute of Asia-Pacific Studies at the Yunnan Academy of Social Sciences, stated that 'Bhutan's western border is close to Nathu La, the frontier port between China and India; the eastern border is connected to the disputed area of China and India; the narrow passage which connects the south west and north east areas, is not far from Bangladesh'. He further argues that 'the situation above tends to keep India vigilant and suspicious with regards to the development of Sino-Bhutan relations'.[18]

Up until the 1960s, Bhutan relied heavily on India for its foreign policy as well as its domestic policies and military aid. The economy of Bhutan is still tightly linked to that of India and its currency, Ngultrum, is pegged to the Indian rupee.[19] Bhutan's small military is still trained in India. Both countries have recently signed a free trade agreement which took effect in 2008 which also allows Bhutan's imports and exports from other markets to transit via India, thereby strengthening their ties further.

As per Ambassador Cheng Ruisheng, previously from the Chinese embassy in India, 'though without diplomatic relations, China has had friendly exchanges with Bhutan for many years which are very important for both countries to have a peaceful environment. However, China has very small volume of border trade with Bhutan and no economic aid to, or investment in Bhutan.'[20] The border trade volume between China and Bhutan is insignificant, especially when compared with Indian economic partnerships, and has limited potential for growth. As pointed out by Wang Chongli, 'China and Bhutan are bordered with high-altitude Himalayan Mountains which has no transportation facility. Thus, large-scale trade activities cannot be supported and Bhutan can hardly become a strategic path. The Zhangmu Port in border area of China and Nepal will remain the main station to connect the South Asian area through Tibet.'[21]

There may be other strategic interests at play which influence the Bhutanese perspective on China's increased international presence. In the words of Zhang Li, researcher at the Institute of South Asian Study of Sichuan University:

Economically, promoting economics and trade relations is helpful for China to expand its influence on Himalaya and Southern Asia subcontinent area. The strategic interests of China in engaging with Bhutan will be further deepened as the Qingzang railway extends to Southern Asia subcontinent and the opening of Tibet to South Asia. Strategically, Bhutan is a buffer area for China and India and thus it is geopolitically important. For example, the Dolan heights area in Bhutan under sovereignty debate has significant strategic interest since it is close to India's Siliguri Corridor in North West Bengal. This was shown in the recent controversy between China and Bhutan on the border patrol in the mentioned area.[22]

Indeed, in 2007, China's People's Liberation Army began building inroads near the Chumbi Valley which worried Bhutan and India given its closeness to the strategic Siliguri corridor.[23] This has been the subject of many parliamentary debates in the last two years in Bhutan.

Nevertheless, Ambassador Ong Keng Yong believes that, 'China's instinct is to stabilize relations with countries on its borders. During my time as ASEAN secretary general, I have seen a lot of statements about China wanting a peaceful neighborhood.' It now appears that sound conditions are there for the eventual resolution of the border issue in the foreseeable future. Perhaps the biggest obstacle is that the India–China boundary issue is also unresolved, and needs to be settled first, before the Bhutan–China border can be finally settled. In the words of Ambassador Ong again, 'if the Bhutan-China boundary dispute was settled first, that would antagonize the India-China border talks. Bhutan would not consent to do anything with China that would be constricting India's diplomatic space.'[24]

The border issue may appear to be a cat-and-mouse game. On the one hand, according to S. D. Muni, visiting senior researcher at the Institute of South Asian Studies of the National University of Singapore, 'China will not sign a border agreement with Bhutan until they have established official diplomatic relationship'. He adds, 'in the end, the Bhutan-China relations cannot be deferred forever . . .'[25] On the other hand, Thierry Mathou, associate researcher in the Himalayan Division of the French National Centre for Scientific Research (CNRS) in Paris, believes that:

> When the border [between China and Bhutan] will be settled, there will no longer be any constraints to the establishment of official relationship with China — which implies a lot. The Chinese are

ready to invest more in the terrestrial port of Haa, but Bhutan wants to go at its own rhythm. The day they sign an accord on the border, the speed of development with China will escape them as China will be too fast.[26]

Let us now turn to the factors influencing the view of various political constituencies in Bhutan on the rise of China. Given the recent political developments in Bhutan, a brief background on the political and institutional transformations of Bhutan in the last ten years is warranted first. On the institutional side, many of the structures in Bhutan are less than ten years old. Most of the key institutions and legislative reforms were implemented as the fourth King Jigme Singye Wangchuck began planning in 1998 to curb the power of the monarchy. He withdrew himself as the head of government in 2006 by abdicating in favour of his eldest son. This marked a major turning point in Bhutan's development.

The government's democratic reforms began in earnest in 1998–99 and the administrative decentralisation process came with the first local elections in 2002. The transition to a democratic system was preceded by the formation of an Anticorruption Commission in 2005, to ensure greater transparency and good governance. The first parliamentary elections were held on 24 March 2008, when about 80 per cent of the 320,000 registered voters cast their ballot. It was led by the Druk Phuensum Tshogpa (or the 'Bhutan Peace and Prosperity Party') which took forty-four of the forty-seven seats in the National Assembly. The remaining three seats went to the rival People's Democratic Party, whose leader, Sangay Ngedup, lost in his own constituency.[27] This election effectively meant the end of the century-old absolute monarchy.

The weak opposition of this new democracy is unlikely to challenge the cautious approach taken by the Bhutanese government or to put significant pressure to speed up a conclusion of the border talks. King Jigme Keshar Namgyal Wangchuck remains head of the state and Jigmi Y. Thinley, who already served twice as prime minister, was sworn in as the first democratically elected prime minister in Bhutan. All of his eleven ministers come from the civil service and most (but not all) of the elected people were already members of the National Assembly.

Another potentially significant political event occurred in February 2007, with the signing of a new India–Bhutan treaty, an update of a 1949 India–Bhutan treaty. According to Wen Fude, director of the Institute of South Asian Study at Sichuan University: 'Since the signing of the new India-Bhutan treaty in February 2007, Bhutan's government can formulate its own independent policy. Of course, by law Bhutan now can establish foreign relations with China without India's consent and India has no right to intervene. From this point of view, the new treaty can promote the development of China and Bhutan.'[28] But Thierry Mathou, from the CNRS in Paris, argues that 'the treaty of February 2007 in itself is not revolutionary, it merely states in writing a practice that was already taking place since the late 1980s and 1990s'.[29] According to Ambassador Ong Keng Yong, former secretary-general of ASEAN and currently director of the Institute of Policy Studies of Singapore, 'the update of the 1949 treaty is good, but does not imply any sudden opening-up of Bhutan. The experience of Tajikistan and Kyrgyzstan, when products from China flooded their domestic markets, was not unnoticed by the Bhutanese leadership.'[30]

Perspectives of China's Rise From Various Constituencies and Stakeholders in Bhutan

Given that Bhutan supports the One China Policy, this should strengthen the potential for deeper cooperation between the two countries. However, given that Bhutan's foreign relations are usually characterised as Indo-centric, the implications of the China–India relations on Bhutan's perception of China cannot be understated. Liu Jian, author of a book on Bhutan's international relations and chairman of the Department of South Asian Culture and Civilization Studies and vice director of the Center for South Asian Studies at the Chinese Academy of Social Sciences (CASS), believes that 'maintaining friendly relations and normal exchanges with Bhutan is also favorable for the China-India relations. Stable and friendly relations between the three countries are beneficial for the safety and development of each country.'[31]

There is no question whether Bhutan wants to use its relations with China to counter-balance its relations with India. Bhutan is a small state that can only afford a non-antagonistic strategy over its powerful neighbours India and China. Hence, due to the strength of the relationship between Bhutan and India, the relations between Bhutan and China, rather than being intimate, remain friendly. It has been argued that China's rapid economic growth underpins its increasing strength in South Asia.[32]

Bhutan's economic relations with its South Asian neighbours, in particular India, Bangladesh and Nepal, have an important role in shaping the Bhutanese view of China's increasing economic power. As an observer of SAARC, China sees great potential for cooperation, not only through trade, but also in sharing China's experience in poverty alleviation.[33] Through its position as an observer, China is able to gain a better understanding of the functioning of SAARC which in turn encourages multilateral cooperation and possibly bilateral relations with member countries such as Bhutan. In late April 2010, the 16th SAARC summit took place in Thimphu. A high-level senior Chinese delegation was sent, led by the executive vice minister of China, Mr Wang Guangya.[34] Discussions were held with Lyonpo Khandu Wangchujk, the minister in-charge of Foreign Affairs, reiterating the importance placed on bilateral relations and agreeing that an expert group would meet to discuss modalities for joint field assessment of the boundary issue.

Even if Bhutan sees China as a future major trade partner, the tensions between China and India will put significant pressure against further engagement between the two countries for many years to come. According to Table 3.1 and Table 3.2, official trade figures between Bhutan and South Asia since the 1980s demonstrate that Bhutanese exports have grown from 15 per cent of GDP in 1981 to more than 56 per cent of GDP in 2008. For the year 2006–7, the key export items from Bhutan were electricity and, as per media reports (representing respectively 26.5 and 16.8 per cent of total trade for 2006–7), also palm oil and copper wire. The principal imports for that year were diesel fuel, copper wires, crude palm oil and petrol.

Whether and what strategic interests are involved in the relations between China and Bhutan remain a matter of debate. According to Shen Dingli, vice dean of the School of International Relations at Fudan University, 'Bhutan will not play against China for other countries, nor will it play against other countries

TABLE 3.1: Exports in South Asia as a percentage of GDP (1981–2007)

Country	1981	1985	1990	1995	2000	2005	2006	2007
Bangladesh	5.3	5.6	6.1	10.9	14.0	16.6	19.0	22.0
Bhutan	15.2	14.7	26.5	37.3	28.4	35.4	31.6	58.2
India	6.0	5.3	7.1	11.0	13.2	19.9	22.1	21.3
Maldives	166.4	71.6	83.3	92.7	82.3	62.1	-	-
Nepal	12.9	11.5	10.5	25.0	23.3	14.6	13.6	12.5
Pakistan	12.3	10.4	15.5	16.7	13.4	15.7	15.3	13.9
Sri Lanka	30.5	26.0	30.2	35.6	39.0	32.3	30.1	29.2

Source: World Development Indicators online database, http://data.worldbank.org/
data-catalog/world-development-indicators (accessed 15 March 2009).

TABLE 3.2: Imports in South Asia as a percentage of GDP (1981–2007)

Country	1981	1985	1990	1995	2000	2005	2006	2007
Bangladesh	14.5	13.2	13.5	17.3	19.2	23	25.2	28.9
Bhutan	47.2	50.2	30.3	42.1	52.5	51.4	45.2	50.7
India	8.7	7.7	8.5	12.2	14.2	22.7	25.1	24.4
Maldives	209.0	66.8	74.0	77.2	65.9	62.1	-	-
Nepal	19.6	20.0	21.7	34.5	32.4	29.5	31.7	28.5
Pakistan	23.0	22.8	23.4	19.4	14.7	19.6	23.3	22.2
Sri Lanka	46.5	38.0	38.1	46.0	49.6	41.3	41.2	39.5

Source: World Development Indicators online database, http://data.worldbank.
org/data-catalog/world-development-indicators (accessed 15 March 2009).

for China. Therefore, there are no strategic interests involved.'[35]
But a different view is expressed by Liu Jian:

> The major strategic interest of engaging with Bhutan may not lie
> in economics, but in politics. China as a big country, being able to
> have good and equal relations with a small country, is able to show
> the world that China is peace-loving and can never be a dictator in
> international relations. This is helpful for China in engaging with
> the whole world.[36]

From an international relations perspective, one of the key
international events which will be influencing Bhutan's perception
of China in the coming years is its planned access to the World
Trade Organisation. In preparation of Bhutan's accession to the
WTO, a working party was formed in October 1999.[37] According
to India's *Financial Express*, Bhutan was likely to join the WTO
as early as 2009.[38] Bhutan in fact has not been able to join the
WTO even until mid-2011. Although Bhutan is a small market,
it offers some trade opportunities, as discussed in the following
paragraphs.

Bhutan's multilateral relation building has been more active in recent years, such as through the established organisation of the 'India–Bangladesh–Nepal–Bhutan' Bay of Bengal Initiative for MultiSectoral Technical and Economic Cooperation. In 2004, members of BIMSTEC signed a framework agreement to establish a free trade area by 2012, which should substantially facilitate trade relations between these neighbouring countries.[39] Meanwhile, the Kunming Initiative between China, India, Myanmar and Bangladesh, which began in 1999 and sought to improve communications between these countries, specifically through transportation developments via road, rail, waterways and air links, is also seen positively by the Bhutanese.

Unfortunately, efforts towards a comprehensive Trans-Asian Railway system have also been made by the United Nations Economic and Social Commission for Asia and the Pacific (UNESCAP) since the 1960s, but have met only with mixed results.[40] An improved sub-regional network between ASEAN and the India–China regions could eventually raise the impetus to broaden transportation linkages in the region, including improving links between China and Bhutan, although the presence of the highest mountain ranges in the world involves considerable infrastructural challenges and substantial financial support.

Moving to a sectoral perspective, several factors influencing Bhutan's view of China's international and economic stature can be identified. Among these are: China's foreign direct investment, prospects for foreign economic assistance and trade opportunities. Although China is currently the eighth largest exporter to Bhutan, total imports from China to Bhutan remain very low. However, in the last three years, there has been a clear upward trend, a sign of the increasingly positive opinion concerning Chinese products by the Bhutanese.

According to S. D. Muni: 'an important attraction for China is also in Bhutan's timber resources. Although Bhutan is renowned for its natural resources protection policies, at the same time, it has a massive program of reforestation which is one of the most successful in the world.' However, he adds that:

> The Chinese infrastructure is ready for trade, but on Bhutan's side, the trade infrastructure is weak. Trade in Bhutan is largely done in the southern belt of the country, including hydropower. In the North, there are physical constraints. There are immense gorges and

high mountains which make it difficult to trade, due to increased transportation costs which would be entailed.[41]

The Chinese government announced recently that official trade between China and Bhutan was minimal but that it had increased by 3,000 per cent from 2006 to 2007.[42] However, these figures are to be put into context. As shown in Table 3.3, based on data from the Chinese Ministry of Commerce, in the last eight years, official trade figures show no clear trend in Chinese exports to Bhutan, though there are signs of significant increase in the last two years.

TABLE 3.3: China–Bhutan trade, 2001–8 (US$ million)

Year	China exports	China imports
2001	160.0	2.0
2002	62.0	2.0
2003	197.0	0.5
2004	35.0	17.0
2005	46.6	0.2
2006	16.0	0.0
2007	539.0	0.0
2008 Jan-Jun	106.0	–

Source: Chinese Ministry of Commerce, 2008, http://english.mofcom.gov.cn/statistic/statistic.html (accessed 5 March 2009).

Based on Chinese official data sources, it is notable that Chinese imports from Bhutan are virtually negligible since 2005. However, the Bhutanese official trade statistics provide further details on Bhutanese exports specifically to Hong Kong. Accordingly, Bhutan's exports to Hong Kong for the years 2006 and 2007 represented respectively 15 per cent and 10 per cent of total exports. However, it subsequently dropped back to 0.5 per cent in 2008, which is comparable to earlier years. The main Bhutanese products exported to China in the last four years are various types of vegetables and fungus for consumption and medicinal purposes and coal (see Table 3.4).

Since 2007, there is some anecdotal evidence that there has been an increase in the imports of Chinese cars and pick-ups into Bhutan, as can be observed from the streets of the capital Thimphu. Also, more Chinese tractors for agricultural purposes can be seen in the rural areas than a few years earlier. In addition, many other Chinese goods may be coming into

TABLE 3.4: Main Bhutanese products exported to China (2004–7)

List of products exported to China

Micro Silicon
Vegetables (Fresh and Chilled)
Mushrooms of the genus agaricus
Dried vegetables (whole, cut, sliced, broken or in powder)
Cordyceps sinesis (fungus/herbal medicine)
Coal (briquettes, ovoid and similar solid fuels from coal)
Other coals

Source: Bhutan Chamber of Commerce and Industry and Bhutan Trade Statistics 2004, 2005, 2006 and 2007, National Statistics Bureau, Thimphu, http://www.nsb.gov.bt/ (accessed 5 March 2009).

Bhutan indirectly, either via India, Nepal or other countries, but official data remains unavailable. As of the end of 2008, the Royal Monetary Authority (RMA) (2009) reports that its total share of imports from China is 0.9 per cent, which places the country in fourth position after India, Japan and Singapore.[43] For the year 2008, Bhutan's imports from China show that trade centred on machinery, materials for communication and transportation, as shown in Table 3.5.

TABLE 3.5: Top 12 imports from China into Bhutan (2008)

Top 12 imports from China	Quantity	Value (Nu.)
Transmission apparatus	1,461.00	26,871,564.05
Machinery for liquefying air or other gases	13.00	20,208,642.23
Carbonaceous pastes for electrodes and similar pastes	702,000.00	19,196,361.81
Optical fiber cables	67,239.04	19,149,132.79
Machines for the reception, conversion and transmission	14.00	18,138,789.44
Machinery with 360 degree revolving (excavators)	5.00	15,287,973.10
Ready to assemble furniture	2,707.00	12,709,025.23
Electricity meters	18,250.00	11,518,638.49
Tires for motor cars	5,952.00	10,424,261.33
Air compressors mounted on a wheeled chassis	1.00	8,032,646.22
Reservoirs, tanks, vats and similar containers	4.00	7,761,493.91
Cars, diesel above 2500 cc	13.00	6,510,985.72

Source: Ministry of Finance, Department of Revenue and Customs, Thimphu (as of 1 October 2008), http://www.mof.gov.bt/ (accessed 15 March 2009).

Other recent trade-related activities occur on a smaller basis, for example, the iron ore and coke-oven plant project between Bhutan and Datong city in Shanxi Province, which began in 2008.[44] Zhang Li, researcher at the Institute of South Asian Study of Sichuan University, believes that 'in the long run, there will be great potential in trade of mechanical and electrical products, commodities, precious medicinal herbs and water power resources'.[45] Bhutan also attended the 18th border trade festival held in Tibet in 2008.[46] This could lead to resurgence in cross-border trade between the two regions.

From the perspective of the private sector, there is a strong sense of the great potential in developing tourism between China and Bhutan. The Bhutanese succeeded in attracting significant foreign direct investments in the tourism sector, especially since tourism was privatised in 1991. According to the Government of Bhutan, as of 1999, tourism was already the third most important source of foreign exchange, and a potentially larger source for the service sector and employment creation. Bhutan has a concept of 'high value low impact' guiding its tourism policy, making it attractive for eco-tourism and cultural tourism.[47]

In February 2003, Bhutan decided to join the World Tourism Organisation and was formally accepted as a member at the organisation's General Assembly held in Beijing in October of the same year. The RMA (2008) reports that tourist arrival increased by nearly 55 per cent between 2005 and 2006.[48] Today, about 200 private tour operators are currently in existence.[49] In 2007, the total number of tourists coming into Bhutan was over 21,000 and was expected to rise to 25,000 for 2008. However, partly due to the global financial crisis as well as an earthquake in September 2009, tourism declined by 31.5 per cent between 2008 and 2009.[50]

As part of its efforts to ensure sustainable economic growth, the Bhutanese government commissioned the consultancy firm McKinsey & Company in July 2009 for a period of two years, to provide advice on the project of 'Accelerating Bhutan's Economic Development'.[51] Their recommendations for the development of the tourism sector have been most debated (especially online) by the Bhutanese, as it constitutes a major source of employment. Based on the tenth Five Year Plan (FYP), annual tourist arrivals should increase to about 30,000 by 2012.[52] According to

McKinsey's projections, Bhutan can aspire to attract as much as 250,000 tourists per year.[53] Whether the recommendations from the McKinsey firm will impact Chinese tourists is an open but important question since the number of Chinese tourists coming to Bhutan has remained extremely low, as shown in Table 3.6.

Perhaps the highest potential for international trade between China and Bhutan comes from hydropower development. Indeed, hydropower is already Bhutan's major export and it is generally recognised as the engine of economic growth for Bhutan. However, as of 2009, it had been estimated that only 5 per cent of Bhutan's hydropower potential had been exploited so far.[54] There were positive signs of possible collaboration between Bhutan and China at the United Nations Symposium on Hydropower and Sustainable Development held in late October 2004 in Beijing, China.

TABLE 3.6: Chinese tourist arrivals in Bhutan (1999–2007)

Year	Number of arrivals
1999	11
2000	10
2001	27
2002	25
2003	23
2004	78
2005	234
2006	362
2007	504

Source: Tourism Council of Bhutan, Thimphu (2008), http://www.tourism.gov.bt/ (accessed 15 March 2009).

A recent McKinsey report indicates that between 1995 and 2007, the major mergers and acquisition deals with the Chinese in Asia have centred on natural resources from the oil and gas industry (more than US$ 9 billion) as well as transport industries (US$ 6 billion).[55] Should the Chinese be investing in Bhutan, these sectors would be attractive as they are in their infancy.[56] There are several areas where Bhutan's natural resources have been underexploited. For example, the southwest region of Bhutan is particularly rich in timber, which has yet to be exploited to its full potential. However, environmental policies in Bhutan dictate strict conservation rules which are unlikely to change in the foreseeable future.[57] The full extent of the mineral potential of Bhutan is still to be determined, since only about 30 per cent of the country's land has been assessed geologically. Very little is known as to its mineral wealth and its commercial value, which would attract heavy investment from countries such as China.[58]

Finally, the stance taken by Bhutan on supporting the 'One China Policy' largely could determine the extent of involvement from China in engaging in development assistance in the future. The latest poverty estimates from the ADB show that the percentage of the population living below the US\$ 1.35 per day Asian poverty line in consumption purchasing power parity (PPP) terms was nearly 36 per cent in 2003.[59] Bhutan receives foreign economic assistance, predominantly from India, followed by Japan and some additional technical assistance from Europe. However, the official aid received is still small, as shown in Table 3.7.

TABLE 3.7: Development assistance/official aid in Bhutan (in millions of US Dollars) (1981–2007)

Country	1981	1985	1990	1995	2000	2005	2006	2007
Bhutan	76.1	94.1	59.3	52.2	53	90	94	-

Source: World Development Indicators online database, http://data.worldbank.org/data-catalog/world-development-indicators (accessed 15 March 2009).

Bhutan's increasing pace of urbanisation also affects its perception of potential opportunities offered by international trade with China. It has been estimated that the number of people living in urban areas will quadruple between 1999 and 2020.[60] This poses a challenge to the Bhutanese government which must find ways to create productive employment for its citizens, especially the youth. At the same time, it creates further pressure on the country to open up to the opportunities offered by international trade and may prove to be a determining factor in China–Bhutan relations.

Medium- and Long-Term Prospects in Bhutan's Evolving Perceptions on China

This final section identifies the evolving nature of the Bhutanese views on China from various stakeholders and constituencies in the medium and longer term. In particular, it discusses the possible directions of Bhutan's engagement with China in relation to alternative economic and political scenarios up to the years 2020 and 2050, when China's projected economic size is expected to be the largest in the world.

The processes of decentralisation and administrative reforms, the recent democratisation process as well as the implementation of development policies in line with the Gross National Happiness (GNH) framework currently shape the Bhutanese view of the rise of China. Bhutan's vision for 2020 and its philosophy of development is summed up as: '[W]e have deliberately chosen to give preference to our understanding of happiness and peace, even at the expense of economic growth, which we have regarded not as an end in itself but as a means to achieve improvements in the well-being and welfare of the people.'[61] One of the key determinants of the development framework in Bhutan is based on GNH.[62] The GNH framework is based on four main components: the achievement of self-sufficiency in economic terms; the protection of the environment; good governance; and the promotion of local culture. The recent formation of the GNH commission demonstrates a new level of commitment on the part of the government.[63] This framework is being reinforced as a platform for policy making through the democratisation process, and also constitutes lenses through which it looks at the surrounding world.

The Government of Bhutan is currently in the midst of re-defining its role, to strengthen its capacity to face development challenges. As such, it is moving from a provider to an enabler of development, focusing on broadening the basis of development to achieve sustainable economic growth and raise standards of living and well-being. In the next decade, the importance of the Bhutanese private sector will inevitably receive greater precedence, as a way to provide employment for its growing population. Up to now, it has lagged behind expectations despite the recent emergence of small and micro enterprises, and family-owned enterprises such as restaurants, tea stalls and rice mills. But as part of Bhutan's need for economic diversification, priority will be increasingly given to the development of this sector, with an emphasis on producing well-trained entrepreneurs and improving the regulatory environment. This will simultaneously increase the international appeal of doing business with the Bhutanese,

and put enormous pressure and strain on its historical relationship with India, depending also on India's own relationship
with China.

Nevertheless, although equipped with many new institutions
that still need to gain experience, Bhutanese politicians are in
a better position to take a positive view concerning China's rise
and the potential benefits to opening up to its neighbour. Already,
there are signs that the new democratic government is pushing
forward for the settlement of the border dispute. This is also
evident from the increased pressure put by the private sector,
including from the Bhutan Chamber of Commerce and during
debates at the National Assembly. But for the coming few years,
the economic policy changes expected from the transition from a
monarchy to a two-party democratic system in Bhutan are likely
to be insignificant.

In the medium term, the single most important factor influencing the Bhutanese perception of China's rise is the status of
India–China relations. Clearly, the Chinese are ready and interested to do business with the Bhutanese, and would be moving
much faster were it not for the Bhutanese leadership's cautious
approach to ensure good relations with India. But in the next ten
years, the development and expansion of hydropower projects
and Bhutan's integration into regional and international economic
groupings such as the WTO are likely to force it to follow the
international current. At the same time, the increased importance
of China as a potential source of finance and as a development
actor in Bhutan is unlikely to materialise soon.

The recent international financial and economic downturn
also warrants important cautionary notes. Recently, the Chinese
media has been focusing on China's foreign policy to work with
the United States and the UK in redressing its economy after
the worse crisis it has faced in the last century.[64] Although this
has been noticed by the Bhutanese, they also recognise that
the economic and financial crisis will undoubtedly slow down
attempts at creating new partnerships with such a small country
as theirs.

There can be no doubt that the perceptions of China as the
world's largest economic power will create some factions, though
there is always some unpredictability in the public opinion in the
Bhutanese context. Ultimately, the young King Jigme Keshar

Namgyal Wangchuck and his newly elected parliament will undoubtedly demonstrate capability in dealing with positive and negative perceptions about the Chinese. But given the king's keen interest in politics and international relations and his outward outlook, these particular traits are also likely to influence a general positive view towards China.

In the longer term, economic changes are warranted in Bhutan but may take place very gradually. The Bhutanese have the reputation of being cautious in their foreign relations strategy and greatly concerned on any impact on their culture and values, a key aspect of the GNH framework. They have shown much astuteness in managing the different intrusions over the course of their history. Now more than ever before, Bhutan is faced with strong internal and external pressures, not least from technological advances speeding up the development of communication networks with the outside world.

From a strategic perspective, if the Bhutanese come to view, as claimed by some, that China is following a *hexiao, gongda* policy in South Asia, that is, uniting with the small (Pakistan, Bangladesh, Burma, Nepal and Sri Lanka) to counter the big (India), then it is likely to retain a negative view of China for many decades.[65] Should the Bhutanese choose to believe that China is not seeking to deny India its proper stakes in the game of international politics, their opening up to China will be extremely gradual and done with great care.

✻

Notes

* Excellent research assistance to conduct and translate interviews in China and Bhutan from Lin Hui, Liang Jing, Tashi Penjor and Sangay Thinley is greatly acknowledged. In addition to all the interviewees, the author would also like to thank the following persons for their help and guidance in writing this chapter: Pema Dechan Dorjee, Lam Dorji, Kencho Thinley, Sherab Chhojay, Choki Gyeltshen, Tandin Wangmo and comments from various anonymous reviewers. Any remaining mistake is my sole responsibility.

1. Gautam Kumar Basu, 'Bhutan's Foreign Economic Relations Integration with Global Capitalism or Dependency-Reversal', in G. K. Basu, *Bhutan: The Political Economy of Development*, New Delhi: South Asian Publishers, 1996, Chapter 5, pp. 61–85.

2. Ibid., p. 17.
3. In total, an estimated 80,000 Tibetans went into exile after the 1959 uprising. Martin Jacques, *When China Rules the World: The Rise of The Middle Kingdom and the End of the Western World*, London: Allen Lane, 2009, p. 253.
4. Rajesh S. Kharat, *Foreign Policy of Bhutan*, New Delhi: Manak Publications, 2005.
5. Also, according to the Ministry of Foreign Affairs of the People's Republic of China, in 1971, Bhutan voted for restoring China's seat in the UN. See http://www.mfa.gov.cn/eng/wjb/zzjg/yzs/gjlb/2686/t15851. htm (accessed 14 September 2009).
6. See, for example, http://www.reuters.com/article/worldNews/ idUSDEL25188520080401 (accessed 15 September 2009).
7. Dorji Penjore, 'Security of Bhutan: Walking Between the Giants', *Journal of Bhutan Studies*, vol. 10, Summer 2004, pp. 108–31, available at http://www.bhutanstudies.org.bt/pubFiles/v10-9.pdf (accessed 20 July 2011).
8. *Tshogdu News*, February 2009, available at http://www.nab.gov.bt/ publication/NewsletterEng2009.pdf (accessed 30 September 2009).
9. As of 2006, the ADB estimated a GDP per capita at purchasing power parity of US\$ 4,022, up from US\$ 2,385 in 2000. ADB, 'Key Indicators for Asia and the Pacific 2008', Manila: Asian Development Bank, 2008, p. 163, Table 2.2.
10. Kharat, *Foreign Policy of Bhutan*, p. 135.
11. See http://www.bhutannewsonline.com/bhutan_china.html (accessed 15 January 2009).
12. Kuensel Online, 'Joint Field Survey Next on Agenda', posted 14 January 2010, available at http://www.kuenselonline.com/modules. php?name=News&file=article&sid=14485 (accessed 18 June 2010).
13. Tibetan Review, '19th Bhutan-China Border Talk Held', available at http://www.tibetanreview.net/news.php?cat=2&&id=5333 (accessed 18 June 2010).
14. See http://www.nab.gov.bt/publication/4Agenda %20for%20the% 2084th%20Session.pdf (accessed 20 September 2009).
15. See http://www.nab.gov.bt/publication/5EngAgenda85.pdf (accessed 30 September 2009). See also Kuensel Online, 'Round 18 and Counting . . .', posted 31 December 2008 available at http://www.kuenselonline. com/modules.php?name=News&file=article&sid=11725 (accessed 9 March 2009).
16. Kuensel Online, 'Joint Field Survey Next on Agenda', posted 14 January 2010, available at http://www.kuenselonline.com/modules. php?name=News&file=article&sid=14485 (accessed 18 June 2010).
17. Mohan Malik, 'India-China Relations', Brief Analytical Report, Asia-Pacific Centre for Security Studies, (available at http://www.apcss.org/

core/BIOS/malik/India-China_Relations.pdf (accessed 20 September 2009).

18. Interview, 16 October 2008. In addition, the Mountain Kula Gangri in the northern part of Bhutan has been claimed by China, which results in a total area of around 38,000 square metres in Bhutan, compared to the earlier 45,000 square metres still shown in most international maps.
19. Exchange Rate Calendar Year average for 2009: 1 US dollar = 48.41 Ngultrums (Royal Monetary Authority Selected Economic Indicators) (December 2009, p. 70).
20. Interview, 27 September 2008.
21. Interview, 16 October 2008.
22. Interview, 7 October 2008.
23. See http://www.china-briefing.com/news/2008/09/08/a-changing-bhutan.html (accessed 19 March 2009).
24. Interview, 7 October 2008.
25. Interview, 17 September 2008.
26. Interview, 9 October 2008.
27. *International Herald Tribune*, 25 March 2008.
28. Interview, 27 September 2008.
29 Interview, 9 October 2008.
30. Interview, 7 October 2008.
31. Interview, 16 October 2008.
32. Jacques, *When China Rules the World*, p. 340.
33. See http://english.peopledaily.com.cn/200704/04/eng20070404_363592.html (accessed 14 September 2008).
34. Ministry of Foreign Affairs Press Release (27 April 2010), available at http://www.mfa.gov.bt/press-releases/press-release-10.html#more-376 (accessed 18 July 2010).
35. Interview, 13 October 2008.
36. Interview, 16 October 2008.
37. See http://www.wto.org/english/theWTO_e/acc_e/a1_bhoutan_e.htm (accessed 12 January 2009).
38. See http://www.bhutanobserver.bt/welcome-fdi-not-yet-wto-2/ (accessed 20 July 2011).
39. See www.wto.org/english/tratop_e/tpr_e/s182-02_e.doc (accessed 15 March 2009).
40. See http://www.unescap.org/ttdw/index.asp?MenuName=TheTrans-AsianRailway (accessed 18 March 2009).
41. Interview, 17 September 2008.
42. See http://www.state.gov/r/pa/ei/bgn/35839.htm (accessed 5 March 2009).
43. RMA, Selected Economic Indicators, Royal Monetary Authority, Thimphu, Bhutan, 2009, Table 23.

44. See http://www.dtsswxxzx.gov.cn/news.asp?id=1948 (accessed 14 January 2009).
45. Interview, 7 October 2008.
46. See http://tibet.mofcom.gov.cn/aarticle/sjixiansw/200809/2008090578 8015.html (accessed 14 January 2008).
47. Royal Government of Bhutan, 'Economic Development Policy of the Kingdom of Bhutan, 2010', available at http://www.mti.gov.bt/Tender/edp-2010.pdf (accessed 18 July 2010), p. 16.
48. RMA, 'Royal Monetary Authority Report 2006–2007', Thimphu: Royal Monetary Authority, 2008.
49. See http://www.tourism.gov.bt/about-tcb (accessed 15 March 2009).
50. Medha Bisht, 'Bhutan in 2009: A Retrospective View', New Delhi: Institute for Defence Studies and Analyses, 2010.
51. See http://www.bhutanobserver.bt/2010/bhutan-news/01/mckinsey-plans-vs-10th-plan.html (accessed 17 June 2010).
52. Bhutan's Tenth Five Year Plan (2008–13) is available at http://planipolis.iiep.unesco.org/upload/Bhutan/Bhutan_TenthPlan_Vol1_Web.pdf (accessed 20 July 2011).
53. Sonam Pelden, 'Will Bhutan Really Get 250,000 Tourists?' *Business Bhutan*, vol. 1, no. 6 (4 November 2009), available at http://www.businessbhutan.bt/?p=304 (accessed 17 June 2010).
54. World Bank estimates 2009, available at http://web.worldbank.org/WBSITE/EXTERNAL/COUNTRIES/SOUTHASIAEXT/BHUTANEXTN/0,contentMDK:22576906~PAGEpk:141137~piPK:141127~theSitePK:306149,00.HTML (accessed 17 June 2010).
55. *The McKinsey Quarterly*, 'China's Track Record in M&A', no. 3, June 2008, pp. 75-81 (see Exhibit 2), p. 77.
56. However, prospects are still bleak in the underdeveloped manufacturing sector in Bhutan, which is concentrated largely around food and wood processing.
57. For example, currently, forests cover about 74 per cent of the total territory and the long-term aim is for that proportion to be no less than 60 per cent.
58. Among some of the minerals known to be present are lead, zinc, copper, tungsten, graphite, iron, phosphate, pyrite and gold. Bhutan already mines dolomite, limestone, gypsum, coal, marble and quartzite but only a small portion is processed for export purposes. Royal Government of Bhutan, 'Bhutan 2020: A Vision for Peace, Prosperity and Happiness', Thimphu: Royal Government of Bhutan, 1999, p. 35.
59. ADB, 'Key Indicators for Asia and the Pacific 2008', Table 5.3a.
60. Royal Government of Bhutan, Bhutan 2020, p. 27.
61. Ibid.

62. The term Gross National Happiness was first coined by Bhutan's King Jigme Singye Wangchuk in 1972, and defines standards of living in more holistic terms, and is influenced by Buddhist and non-material values.

63. *The Kuensel*, 'GNH Takes Centre Stage', 19 January 2008.

64. See http://news.xinhuanet.com/english/2009-03/08/content_10971941. htm (accessed 9 March 2009). Malik, 'India-China Relations', pp. 1145–146. Malik also states that China is opposed to India's membership in the P-5 (UN Security Council), N-5 (Nuclear Club), ASEM (Asia-Europe Summit), APEC (Asia-Pacific Economic Cooperation) and EAS (East Asia Summit).

4

India
An Opportunity; and an Anxiety

SRIKANTH KONDAPALLI

China is our strategic partner. We have a multi-faceted relationship
with China. There is enough space — I have said so often — for both
China and India to develop and contribute to global peace, stability
and prosperity. We do not see our relations with China in antagonistic
terms. We have a large trading relationship, we consult each other
on global issues, whether in the G-20 process on climate change or
terrorism, and we share a common commitment to maintain peace
and tranquillity on our border.

There are, of course, issues which are complex such as the boundary
question. But we have agreed upon a mechanism to address this
matter. We wish to build a strong and stable relationship with
China. . . . But whether it is China or any country, we will ensure the
territorial integrity and unity of our country and protect the security
in every manner necessary. The House should have no misgiving on
that score.

—Prime Minister Manmohan Singh, 9 June 2009[1]

Recent events related to India–China relations have highlighted
the significance of security and strategic aspects. At the
'traditional security' level, in the last few years, the Chinese side
is firming up its position on the border dispute in the Arunachal
Pradesh and Sikkim sectors, with 270 border transgressions in
2008, infrastructure improvements in Tibet and China's military
modernisation efforts, rise in defence budget and successful
conduct of the anti-satellite test in 2007 and the interceptor
missile test in 2010. In response, India decided to despatch nearly
60,000 troops and deploy two squadrons (36) of Su-30 MKI
multirole fighter aircraft in Arunachal Pradesh, construct eleven
strategic roads connecting the trans-Himalayan border regions

and step up its military modernisation aspects. On the other hand, regarding the 'non-traditional security' aspects such as counter-terrorism, energy issues and hydrological data exchange of river waters, some recent cooperation between the two countries is visible. Economic interdependence is also increasing with bilateral trade exceeding $50 billion in 2008. Both are engaged in 'strategic dialogues' as well, with 'strategic and cooperative partnership' gaining currency in official discourse from April 2005. These nuances and complexities partly explain and influence the Indian perceptions today in the security and strategic arenas.

The structure of this chapter includes enlisting main factors influencing such perceptions, major issues and themes, disposition of important constituents and stakeholders in the Indian system with regard to China, and finally reflects on possible future directions of interactions between India and China at the regional and global levels. At the outset, a few caveats are necessary in these explorations. First, Indian institutional perceptions and assessments, much like the proverbial 'blind men of Hindustan', are multi-faceted. Second, these are changing due to the external and internal stimuli and hence altering perceptions as well as policy prescriptions. The Indian liberalisation programme from 1991, for instance, initiated a 'learn from China reforms' discourse in India.[2] Also, with the disintegration of the then Soviet Union and the spread of globalisation, India has to search afresh for its moorings and leverages once again, including in its relations with China. Third, the attempt here, given the wide canvas, is to treat the subject in a broad manner.

Factors Shaping Perceptions

Indian perceptions towards China are conditioned by several factors. First, the two largest states in Asia share a boundary which is not yet resolved. In 1960 border clashes erupted with the boundary issue as one of the triggers culminating in a full-scale border conflict in October 1962. Later, a number of talks between the two sides in 1960 and from 1981 till present, were conducted.[3] Complete normalisation of bilateral relations hinges on this crucial factor as the Indian side has pointed out time and again.[4]

A major theme underlying Indian perspectives is the socio-economic aspect. Indeed, the developmental imperatives of India stressed, to an extent, resolution of disputes through diplomatic negotiation processes rather than emphasising only on military-related initiatives that demand higher defence outlays.[5] It reflects a deeper understanding that such developing countries have a limit in pursuing a 'total war' national strategy. While this approach does not rule out military-related preparation of these countries, India has set its priorities on economic, technological and inclusive development as its overall national goals.

Third, while both India and China started at a similar nation-building and growth trajectory in the late 1940s, yet, in the last five decades of bilateral relations, national strengths indicate stark asymmetries. However, these are in the process of being bridged in the recent period as a result of growth in the Indian indicators. To some extent, Indian perceptions (as well as that of China towards India) are conditioned by this asymmetry in the power matrix.[6] Other related aspects are that China is the lone Asian country with veto power in the United Nations Security Council and in the current efforts to reorganise the UN system, its stance, as with that of the other members, would be crucial.[7] Additionally, China is also a recognised nuclear power with considerable clout in the global arms control and disarmament measures.[8]

Besides these issues, in general, the thrust of Indian foreign policy was on the goal to be autonomous in relation to other major powers and support for post-colonial and developing societies. As the then Soviet Union disintegrated in 1991, several important changes occurred in the direction of Indian foreign policy, even though there has been continuing emphasis on the independent nature of foreign policy. A corollary to this factor is the emphasis by India (and China) on aspects of multipolarity and multilateralism. Indeed, this aspect provides several opportunities for both India and China to come together such as on state sovereignty issues, emphasis on the United Nations Charter and non-interventionism in internal affairs of countries based on human rights violations, formation of strategic triangles, and the like.

A fifth factor is the current globalisation period in which several pan-regional and global issues need to be considered, specifically when both India and China are on the rise in economic, technological, military and other fields. This aspect has provided both opportunities to work together, and also challenges between these two countries such as cooperation in the World Trade Organisation (WTO) or competition in accessing markets or receiving investments and technologies from abroad. India cooperates with China on the energy exploration and distribution aspects (with an MoU signed in 2006) as well as on bringing forth a reasonable response from developed countries (such as at the Bali Summit meeting on climate change). For India, China's growth rates and market demands offer business opportunities — with investments of more than $1 billion (as compared to about $50 million in Chinese investments in India) and trade. India in 1995, 2004 and 2005 posted a favourable balance of payments position in the bilateral trade figures. India and China are also part of several multilateral institutions such as the East Asian Summit, Shanghai Cooperation Organisation (SCO), and South Asian Association for Regional Cooperation (SAARC). These new factors have brought about fresh demands on the bilateral relations and call for not purely bilateral and tactical manoeuvres, but strategic interactions between the two countries.

Constituents and Stakeholders

As with most large countries, the key policy makers and policy shapers in India towards China are too numerous to recount.[9] Yet, a generalised view indicates that as a democratic republic, in theory, the issue rests with the Parliament, specifically the Lower House (Lok Sabha), whose discussions and prescriptions are to influence the executive's decisions. Indeed, important policy perspectives are discussed and initiated for the executive to carry forward and implement such views. In 1993, seventeen standing committees (composed of members of parliament) were established by the Parliament with jurisdiction over all the departments and ministries (including home, defence and external affairs) of the government. These committees were tasked 'to concentrate on long-term plans, policies and the philosophies guiding the working of the Executive'.[10] A cursory look at these committees' recommendations reflects the checks and balances and guidelines on the executive's functioning. For instance, the standing committee on defence of the 10th Lok Sabha in its 6th report (1996) dealt extensively with defence policy, doctrine, strategy and the operational principles prescribed for the armed forces in waging war or sustaining and consolidating peace. Several officials, experts and think-tank personnel were summoned to explain why the country has not formulated a comprehensive defence policy despite the growing challenges. The then defence secretary's reply is worth citing, partly as it reflects on China as well. He stated:

> The primary approach of the nation or of the Government to ensure this [defence] doctrine is of two-fold. One is on the diplomatic and political front. Second is on the military front. Diplomatic and political efforts of the Government are centred around building bridges of peace in our neighbourhood. The Government is always on the forefront in this effort to have friendly relations with all our neighbours, even with our neighbours with whom we may have border disputes.[11]

With the nuclear and missile inventory of China increasing, the Lok Sabha is also a concerned party. In its recommendations to the government, the 12th Lok Sabha standing committee on defence, for instance, argued that

> the Government should go ahead full steam in a time-bound manner to develop full range of missiles in addition to the variants of 'AGNI' currently under development as a deterrent to potential enemies from using their ballistic missile capabilities against any of our assets.[12]

On other platforms as well, these committees were forthright in their observations. For instance, the 13th Lok Sabha committee was critical of the government and concerned defence agencies and suggested that there should be further strengthening of the conventional platforms of the country. It suggested that the government needs to acquire different cutting edge technologies and systems so that the country's security needs are well protected.[13] In the backdrop of the Kargil Committee Report, which went into the reasons for the intelligence failures in 1999, the 14th Lok Sabha committee in its report in 2007 recommended measures to developing 'a more efficient and cost effective national security system for the 21st century' and suggested revamping border units to form 'one border, one force'.[14]

Debates and discussions in Parliament between different political parties and personages on responses towards China — sometimes even acrimonious — are not unheard of. Indeed, on several occasions, the Indian Parliament echoed the sentiments of the people on China, as with other countries. Be it on the unresolved boundary dispute or the plight of nearly 5,000 Tibetan refugees who land in India every year, economic reforms in China or possible dumping of Chinese goods in the Indian market, Chinese support to Indian northeast rebels or Weapons of Mass Destruction (WMD) transfers to Pakistan — all these evoked sharp reactions in the Parliament and indicated the political barometer of the country.[15] Indeed, on the 1962 border clashes and the subsequent Parliament resolution in November of the same year on 'every inch of land to be recovered' all major political parties overtly abide by that resolution, although the mainstream parties such as Congress and Bhartiya Janata Party (BJP) have in the recent period toned down this position covertly.[16] The parliamentary left parties, mainly the Communist Party of India (CPI) and Communist Party of India (Marxist) (CPM) have a relatively more forthcoming position on China, although ideological rifts of the CPI with the Chinese Communist Party (CCP) are not unknown, specifically as an extension of the Sino-Soviet split of 1960.[17] The CPI and CPM delegations' visits to China and discussions with the CCP are frequent and cordial. These institutional interactions contributed to the close understanding between them.[18] Interestingly, the CCP, in its drive to form a 'united front', had opened up party-to-party contacts with the Congress, Bharatiya Janata Party (BJP), Janata Dal and others as well. While the ruling CCP has expanded contacts and influence with all major (including opposition) parties in India (as in other countries), the reverse has not happened so far.

As the highest political body to ratify any boundary settlement with China, the Indian Parliament's position is technically the most important.[19] More importantly, the process of political consensus and legitimacy is arrived at and accorded in this forum. Indeed, elite consensus on foreign policy issues had been the hallmark of India, although this was broken on several issues (including on China) and at several times.[20]

The next set of actors — the executive — in practice has become more influential on the China policy. Included in this are the different ministries — with the Ministry of External Affairs (MEA) as the most decisive but losing some influence to the Prime Minister's Office (PMO) from the 1980s. There are also ministries of defence (MoD), home affairs (MHA), petroleum, finance and commerce that vied for their say, albeit marginally. A 'China Study Group' (with expertise drawn from several secretaries, ministries, intelligence/security and think-tank circles) acts as a professional advisory group on China-related issues. The National Security Council Secretariat, formed by amalgamating several internal and external intelligence agencies, and National Security Council Advisory Board offer suggestions and recommendations to the prime minister on various issues, including on China.

From about the 1980s, the PMO has acquired considerable influence and in conjunction with the finance and petroleum ministries, has been able to exert pressure on MEA and MoD for a more forthcoming policy on China. The first prime minister, Nehru, dominated the making and pursuing of China policy, while for Shastri, the Gandhis and others, Pakistan loomed large over the Indian horizon. Many an Indian prime minister had their imprint on the China policy, advised as it was by several ministers, officials, politicians, journalists and others.[21] Prime Minister Rajiv Gandhi's visit to China in 1988 is considered to be 'path-breaking' due to the expansion in bilateral relations in different fields. Prime Minister Vajpayee, after citing China's clandestine transfers of nuclear and ballistic missiles to Pakistan as reason for the 1998 nuclear tests, proposed a 'forward looking' relationship with China in 2003. The current prime minister, Manmohan Singh, has repeatedly mentioned that India needs to learn from China in the economic field. More importantly, he said: 'There is enough space in the world for both countries to continue to grow and address the developmental aspirations of their peoples.'[22] Overall, in the last decade or so, Indian leaders adopted a policy of preserving strength and resolving issues through dialogue, maintaining economic growth rates and a multilateral approach.[23] The effect of all these, in some Chinese views, is to make India an 'attractive bride' for many.[24]

Most of the ministries listed here issue an annual report highlighting, apart from other events, the emerging policy postures towards China. The annexure provides for the last fifteen years of policy perspectives of the MEA and MoD, which are, as is evident, not necessarily on the same wave-length. Indeed, important differences between the two exist on how to deal with China.

However, at the cost of over-generalisation, we could sum-marise broadly that the MEA — as is obvious — looked at the China factor from the national interest angle. This explains partly the policies adopted vis-à-vis China — specifically on the border dispute, 'security concerns of each other should be respected', maintaining balance of power, etc.[25] In this context, last year's speech of the external affairs minister can be said to be a major departure in that for the first time perhaps, the MEA sought to explain the far-reaching impact that the rise of China could have on India. Speaking on 5 November 2008 at the National Defence College, Indian external affairs minister Pranab Mukherjee said:

> To my mind, the foremost among these [challenges to Indian security] would be (a) to cope with the rise of China; (b) maintenance of a peaceful periphery; and (c) managing our relations with the major powers. . . . We are today faced with a new China. Today's China seeks to further her interests more aggressively than in the past, thanks to the phenomenal increase of her capacities after 30 years of reforms. There are also new set of challenges which China poses such as the strategic challenge as China develops its capabilities in outer space; the geopolitical challenge as it reaches out to various parts of the globe in search of raw materials and resources.

The MoD, with command over the armed forces of the country, from 1962 to about 2001 almost uniformly viewed China with concern or even as a long-term challenge to Indian national security.[26] Currently, after an MoU was signed between the two defence ministers of China and India in May 2006 and the annual dialogue mechanisms began in November 2007, the tone of the MoD became relatively muted, although it 'continue[s] to realistically' monitor developments in China.[27] China's transfer of nuclear, ballistic missile parts/technologies to Pakistan, conventional weapons to other South Asian countries, its close relations with Myanmar from 1988, gradual entry into the Indian Ocean region, the anti-satellite test in January 2007 — all of these were highlighted as posing challenges to India.[28] To cope with this challenge, overtly or covertly, the policy prescription has been evolved through modernisation or even multilateral initiatives for cooperation with the US, Japan, Singapore and Australia.[29] These preparations were also highlighted by former army chief

Deepak Kapoor, who suggested in October 2009 that the forces are preparing for a two-theatre war (against Pakistan and China) under nuclear conditions. Next month, the defence minister A. K. Anthony suggested to the consultative committee of the Parliament on defence that India will strengthen the strategic assets in the northeast of India.

The Ministry of Home Affairs (MHA), likewise, with command over the paramilitary forces which actually control the bordering areas with China, had expressed concern over China's border consolidation and domination efforts and had repeatedly pointed to the border transgressions. The MHA has jurisdiction over the Indo-Tibetan Border Police (ITBP) deployed on the India–China border. This was raised after the 1962 war and currently has over twenty-six battalions of nearly 40,000 personnel. The ITBP controls nearly ninety-six Border Out Posts and patrols the border regions with China. It has also been engaged in overseeing mechanisms at border trade posts with China (established at Lipulekh, Shipki La and Nathu La) as well as conducting Indian pilgrimages to Man Sarovar Lake in Tibet. Another organisation under the MHA is the Sashastra Seema Bal established in 1963, mainly for counter-subversion and intelligence-gathering duties.[30]

Outside the government bodies are the track-II think-tanks, academic institutions or press corps that shape China policy. Being a relatively open society, the press corps — with its regular interactions in the 'power corridors' — disseminates policy perspectives on China (as with other countries/issues). On its own, the Indian press corps, as with its western counterparts, function as 'watchdogs' — unlike the Chinese media which acts as a 'mouth piece' (*houshe* 喉舌) of the establishment.[31] Besides, for several journalists, ideological differences (democracy vs authoritarianism) with China are pervasive. While very few Indian reporters are stationed in Beijing, China on the other hand has despatched several to cover events in India. Besides, the Chinese embassy in New Delhi invites Indian journalists to cover events positively in Tibet. With the exception of *The Hindu* and a few other newspapers, in general, the mainstream Indian press critically evaluates events in China.[32]

The academic community and the think-tanks — although limited in numbers and output — also reflect on the China policy and help shape Indian perceptions. While Robert Ash, David Shambaugh and Seiichiro Takagi had indicated in their recent work that the number of China watchers in US, Europe and Japan is increasing — as with their subjects of inquiry — India, with more than a billion people, is a relatively recent entrant in this field, even though Shanti Niketan near Kolkata has been a pioneer in Chinese language and religious studies from the 1930s.[33] The border clashes between the two countries and the subsequent cold war allowed only a few academic exchanges. The 1990s agreement on a cultural exchange programme between the two sides enhanced these interactions.[34] Besides Jawaharlal Nehru University, Delhi University and Shanti Niketan, several private and public institutions are coming up to impart Chinese language skills for prospective learners. Among the think-tanks, mainly focused in Delhi, notable are the Institute of Chinese Studies, Institute for Defence Studies & Analysis, Centre for Policy Research, Institute of Peace and Conflict Studies, United Services Institution, Indian Council for Research on International Economic Relations, Chennai Centre for China Studies and others. Some of these have bilateral tie-ups or academic/policy interactions with counterparts in China recently and have enhanced mutual interactions and networking.[35]

As bilateral trade between the two countries increased from a few million US dollars in the early 1990s to the 2008 figure of $50 billion, suitable business structures and interactions have cropped up to facilitate economic engagement. Confederation of Indian Industries (CII), Federation of Indian Chambers of Commerce and Industry and others have been active in the last decade to further this process. The CII opened a representative office in Shanghai in the 1990s for facilitating trade between the two countries.[36] It assisted several companies to establish themselves in China. The CII has today forged institutional contacts with several trade promotion bodies in China.[37]

Besides these, several thousands of Indian professionals are working in several cities of China from the last few years and may be considered as an important factor in India's China policy. However, their influence has been abysmally low in the past decades. Nevertheless, in the recent period, with reform and opening up and burgeoning trade and mutual visits, the space for expanding contacts and understanding has increased manifold between the two countries.

Indian perceptions as reflected through these constituencies and stakeholders are diverse and nuanced.[38] As such these issues are constantly changing due to internal and external stimuli. Socio-economic changes, political transformations, increase in the availability of research materials, global changes such as the end of bipolarity, globalisation, changes within Chinese political system, and the like have all contributed towards assessments and re-assessments on China as with other countries.[39]

To summarise, at different levels of the spectrum, Indian perceptions towards China over the last six decades have ranged from alliance formation, engagement (incremental, reluctant, controlled or full-blown), maintaining *status quo*, balance of power, counter-strategic encirclement, 'congagement' to even containment of China, although the engagement school has predominated in the actual policy towards China.[40]

Issues and Themes

India's security and strategic perceptions of China are shaped by historical images which are relatively few but overall amicable in disposition. These also reflect contemporary realities of nation-state and building process and future possibilities and considerations of growth, national power and stability. Overall, recent Indian perceptions were influenced by China's launch of reform and opening-up programmes from the 1970s and the lessons to be learnt from this experience, the protracted nature of talks for nearly three decades on the border dispute and the consequent uncertainty, if not instability on the border areas, ushering in stability in the region, the role of the United States, non-traditional security issues and the like. There is no doubt that recently such perceptions have become more diverse, complex, multi-pronged and sometimes even subtle.[41]

Part of the reason for the above complexity is due to the existence of a plethora of issues and themes, some resolved; yet others remained unresolved or have even become acute between the two countries. Some Indian policies also appeared contradictory in nature (viz., adoption of an engagement policy while at the same time giving a nod to military modernisation), while some have been shaped by different pressure groups and stakeholders as outlined earlier.

Foremost in the considerations of India is the security of the state, territory and sovereignty. These 'minimalist' foreign and security issues have been mentioned several times in the official and other reports over a period of time (see Annexure).[42] With regard to China, this issue is mainly reflected in the border dispute, China's position and support to insurgencies in Kashmir or the Indian northeast, providing alternative incentives or even pitching neighbours against India through their conventional/ strategic military capacity build-up, and possible build-up and operations in the Indian Ocean. Second, at the strategic level, the 'maximalist' foreign and security policy objectives and goals of India refer to the positive/negative stance of China on issues related to regional (Asian)/global aspects, multilateralism, nuclear issues and those pertaining to the long-term growth of India.[43]

To start with, Indian assessments note the positive direction in which China has been formulating its position on Kashmir. While in the 1950s, as a part of the bonhomie between the two sides, China desisted from making any explicitly negative comments on the Indian position on Kashmir. After relations soured in the 1960s, Beijing supported self-determination of Kashmiris or UN plebiscite as demanded by Pakistan. A pragmatic leadership in China in the 1980s took a relatively neutral position between India and Pakistan by supporting the sanctity of the line of control between these two states, peaceful resolution of the dispute and the like.[44] On another related issue — supply of small arms to Naga/other rebels in the Indian northeast — China appeared to have assured New Delhi from the late 1970s that this will be stopped.[45] However, during 2009–10 India criticised the revisions in the Chinese positions on Kashmir — reflected in China's investments in Pakistan Occupied Kashmir, issuing of stapled visas to Kashmiri students and invitation to the Hurriyat Leaders to visit China.[46]

On the border dispute, acrimony on both sides continues till this day.[47]Differing assessments on the border, border transgressions by patrols on either side, border domination through infrastructure developments and troop deployments, border migrations (of Tibetans) and border smuggling are all issues of security concern. An increasing number of transgressions by the patrols of Chinese frontier guards/Indo-Tibetan Border Police (ITBP) could pose security problems in the bilateral relations, although both governments have put in place some measures in 1993 and 1996 to address these issues. There has also been an attempt (first by China) at border domination in the last few decades. India expressed concern and attempted to respond to these challenges (see Annexure). Another Indian concern is the Chinese role in South Asia. Technically, as these are independent sovereign countries, China has the right to develop relations with any of these countries to mutual satisfaction. However, historical relations, strategic considerations, mutual suspicions, all provide for potential friction between the two countries. Here, China's 'all-weather' relations with Pakistan and its forays into Bangladesh, Nepal, Sri Lanka and Myanmar are cited as posing security concerns for India. Specifically, conventional, but most importantly, nuclear and ballistic missile technology/platforms/systems transfers from China to Pakistan were cited extensively by Indians.[48]

China's role in Nepal is also seen as a concern for India, as Kathmandu had concluded a treaty of friendship with India in 1950. China's arms transfers worth $200 million in 1987–88 led to frictions between New Delhi and Kathmandu.[49] China reportedly offered the then Nepal king small arms worth about $1 million to counter Maoists in 2005–6.[50] In September 2008, during the visit of Nepal's defence minister Badal to Beijing, China reportedly offered security assistance worth $1.55 million.[51] In May 2009 when Nepal's prime minister Pushpa Kamal Dahal wanted to sack the army chief, China reportedly backed Dahal, to the chagrin of India.[52]

China's agreement with Sri Lanka on arms transfers and infrastructure building is raising concerns in India. China transferred F-7 (MiG-21) aircraft to Colombo, in addition to rocket launchers, fast attack craft and others that were utilised to counter the Tamil rebels. More significantly, both countries signed an MoU for China's development of Hambantota port, which is a part of the so-called 'string of pearls'[53] Gwadar port in Pakistan, Chittagong in Bangladesh, Hyangyi, Sitwe, Kyepkau, etc. in Myanmar, Kra Isthmus project in Thailand, are all viewed as a part of this strategy, first to enhance China's energy security and second, in time of war, to be used as staging posts for China.

In addition to China's efforts of cooperating with the Indian neighbourhood, China's military modernisation is viewed in India either as a part of 'strategic encirclement' or 'marginalisation'. Specifically, any Chinese military activation or domination of the border areas opens the possibility of a two-theatre front for Indian forces. Indeed, in Indian wars with Pakistan in 1965 (border), 1971 (Bangladesh) and 1999 (Kargil), the Chinese side sent subtle, or even brazen, threats of mobilising troops near the border areas; though no major military move was made.

To elaborate further, from the overall Indian security point of view, China's military modernisation aspects have several dimensions. First, the British Indian government decided to carve a buffer zone in Tibet between itself, Qing dynasty of China and Czarist Russia, in the interests of the larger security of the empire.[54] After the Chinese military marched into Tibet in 1950, such a buffer zone effectively vanished and this brought pressures on India such as in 1962 and other periods. Further military modernisation of China and its occasional forays into Nepal reduced the comfort levels of Indian security further. Second, some in China (Colonels Wang Xiangsui and Qiao Liang) have advocated 'unrestricted warfare' as a mode of military engagement in the future. In 1999 China reportedly set up a special task force to engage in information warfare activities against several countries including India, the impact of which was visible in the reported increase in cyber attacks in India, as elsewhere.[55] Third, while China had denied any renewal of arms supplies to Indian northeast insurgents, recent reports indicated at least 'commercial' transactions from the ordnance factories in this regard.[56] Fourth, India and China have agreed to exchange hydrological data on the rivers flowing across the borders to forecast natural disasters. With reports about China's troops constructing artificial barrages for assured water supplies to troops at Zanda, Tololing and other places in Tibet, India has expressed concerns over the artificial dykes, such as Pareechu Lake that threatened to unleash floods in the lower reaches of Kinnaur and Spiti Valleys of Himachal Pradesh in the latter half of 2004. Large-scale construction activity is reported in Tibet leading to environmental degradation and damage to the lower riparian states such as India. The reported river diversion projects and construction activity at the 'Great Bend' of Yarlung Zangpo/ Brahmaputra further add to Indian concerns. While China has recently shown enthusiasm in engaging other countries at the multilateral fields, it still prefers a unilateral approach when it comes to river water issues with neighbours.

Although bilateral trade has contributed to increasing economic interdependence between the two countries, trade frictions, and more importantly security concerns on Chinese investments, are also increasing in India. In general, it is argued that there are no negative feelings in India about China on economic growth–related issues.[57] In April 2005, after the two premiers met, an annual financial dialogue mechanism evolved between the two countries, with three such dialogues conducted by January 2009.[58] During the ongoing global financial crisis, both sides had expressed the view that they should make efforts to overcome problems of western protectionism, greater role in international financial institutions, etc.[59] Nevertheless, neither the Chinese proposal for a free trade area was accepted by India (while Pakistan did in 2006), nor were Chinese investments in/or near security areas allowed. One of India's ministers, Jairam Ramesh, raised public objections on this issue in 2010, exposing divergent opinions within the Indian government. India is also reluctant to officially legitimise the Chinese-backed Bangladesh-China-India-Myanmar multilateral economic initiative (established in 1999).

To compound matters, with the worsening balance of payments position, India in the last few years has been resorting to anti-dumping procedures on Chinese goods. It was reported that from October 2008 to February 2009, India imposed seventeen trade remedy probes against Chinese products.[60] In January 2009, India imposed a ban on the import of Chinese toys.[61] This ban was for six months but was lifted under Chinese pressure. China also retaliated. On 29 December 2005, China announced anti-dumping investigations on the imported Nonyl Phenol originating from India.[62]

Another area where both countries signed a cooperative agreement, but in reality are competing, is the energy sector. As China became the second largest consumer and India notched up to the fourth position, in 2005–6, both countries conducted talks and concluded an MoU for cooperation in the energy drilling or distribution aspects so that mutual competition could be avoided.[63] However, competition between India and China is increasing abroad — India lost to China in Angola, Iran, Myanmar and Kazakhstan, although in other areas such as Sudan, cooperation is continuing.[64]

At the strategic level, Indian assessments realise that China has an advantage. While India was confined to the South Asia 'box' during the Cold War period, China's sights were set at the global level thanks to the Nixon visit and global shift in balance of power from Moscow to Beijing. While certain re-adjustments were made by Beijing in the post–Cold War period (such as the April 2005 'strategic and cooperative partnership'), Indian assessments on the whole assume some resistance from China. On the positive side, both have started strategic dialogues; the first such dialogue was conducted in Delhi on 24 January 2005, the second in Beijing on 12 January 2006, the third in New Delhi. These discussions included border issues, 'cooperation and coordination in regional and international affairs', etc.[65] Nuclear issues have also been discussed in other meetings, although there has been no perceptible change in the Chinese side away from the 1172 resolution at the UN Security Council (UNSC) of 1998. At the multilateral level, there had been some progress — nine trilateral meetings between Russia–India–China were held till 2008, India and China also interact at the Brazil–Russia–India–China (BRIC) meets (the last one in June 2009 at Yekaterinburg), also at the East Asian Summit, SAARC and SCO meetings. Besides, at the WTO and climate change proposals (such as at the Bali Summit and in the Copenhagen meeting in December 2009) as well, there has been some coordination between the two.

Yet, despite these, there has been some suspicion on both sides. While China is wary about the emerging US-India relations and India-Japan security cooperation, India is also concerned about the prospects for G2 (between US and China, in the wake of the financial crisis).[66]

Direction of Future Engagement

India–China relations have exhibited prospects for cooperation in multilateral fields although at bilateral levels progress has been tardy. While India has been keen on resolving the bilateral issues, China has been reluctant to expeditiously resolve the issues 'left over by history'. In this context, the future direction of engagement between the two countries is hard to predict.[67] Nevertheless, it can be argued that as developing and nuclear countries, with rational leaderships, since the cost-benefit balance could be adverse in case of a conflictual relationship, both are likely to pursue engagement policies, even if limited. The recent decisions at Yekaterinburg (June 2009) to renew border talks, and more importantly, to set up a hot line is an indication. Also the realisation that both countries have enough space to thrive in Asia and beyond appears to be a tactical arrangement for some time to come.[68]

Nevertheless, from the Indian foreign policy point of view, increase in Chinese diplomatic and military activity and interactions with the Indian neighbourhood constrains Indian activity in these regions. Specifically, alternative incentive structures provided and nurtured by China in this region exert pressure on India in terms of intense diplomatic attention and activity. This is detrimental to attention that ought to be paid to other regions, thus effectively keeping Indian attention engaged to the South Asia 'box' at the cost of its strategic rise in other regions and sectors. Bilateral security cooperation between the two countries is reflected in two aspects: growing understanding on the necessity to counter terrorism and further strengthen confidence building measures (CBMs). As a part of this counter-terrorism effort, both India and China have instituted a joint working group and share intelligence regarding counter-terrorism efforts. Second, to stabilise borders and expand cooperation, both countries have initiated several CBMs including flag and border personnel meetings, joint exercises (between navies in November 2003 and December 2005; between armies in mountaineering expeditions and as observers in each other's military exercises) and an MoU was signed in May 2006 between the two defence ministers on expanding military exchanges and dialogues.[69] In October 2007, both armies held joint exercises for the first time in Chengdu Military Region (Kunming) and later this was followed by a similar 'hand-in-hand' exercise in India (Belgaum) in 2008. However, all these CBMs are conflict preventive in nature and have not yet shown concrete signs of trust building between the two countries.[70]

At the military level, India for long had adopted a strategy of 'deterring Pakistan and dissuading China'. Nevertheless, with the Chinese missile threat (from Qinghai and Yunnan) and missile transfers to Pakistan increasing by 2001, India appeared to be on the course of graduating from the above strategy to that of 'deterring Pakistan and deterring China'.[71] This implies not only enhancing its nuclear stockpile and developing and deploying

Agni III missiles of 3,000 km and above range but also configuring long-range aircraft for nuclear missions and efforts to build second strike nuclear capability.[72] As a result, Indian defence spending has to be raised to meet the Chinese challenges. This may lead to an arms race between the two countries in the years to come.

Conclusions

A few generalisations and conclusions can be drawn from the above analyses of Indian security and strategic concerns on China. First, and most importantly, Indian official perceptions need to factor China at three levels, viz., national strategy of sustaining economic development for a long period of time, foreign policy objectives of protecting national interests through an engagement policy and the military strategy of protecting sovereignty and territorial integrity through modernisation, mobilisation of military assets and alertness. To arrive at a fine balance between these three levels, Indian policy makers have to walk on the razor's edge. Second, while India accords high priority to China in the overall security and strategic aspects, the same is not the case with China, which considers the US as its primary focus. While Pakistan used to occupy major space in the Indian security debates, currently China is looming large on the horizon, partly with the realisation that Pakistan has been propped up by Beijing in an 'all-weather' relationship since 1962. This is viewed as constraining Indian options in Asia and beyond. Indian rise in economic, military and soft power domains during the last decade provides the canvas for a shift from Pakistan towards China. The US reassessment in the recent period on improving relations with India acknowledges this process. Third, in recent years, Indian perceptions on China have expanded from traditional security issues (sovereignty, territorial integrity, military, balance of power) to also include non-traditional security issues (energy, environment, migration, pandemics, terrorism, etc.). Fourth, while most of these indicate the predominance of elite and state-centric perceptions, in the last few years due to people-to-people contacts and expanding trade and tourism, perceptions are becoming more broad-based.

✸

ANNEXURE

Key statements/events of India on China, 1993–2008

Year	Key statements in Ministry of External Affairs Annual Reports	Key statements in Ministry of Defence Annual Reports
1993–94	The peace and tranquillity agreement was termed as an 'important step forward towards normalising bilateral relations and developing them on positive lines . . . [and] creating a tension-free atmosphere'.	There has been a perceptible improvement in India–China relations (due to the 1993 agreement). China has embarked on an ambitious programme of modernisation of its armed forces . . .
1994–95	The peace and tranquillity agreement 'will make progress . . . to clarify the line of actual control and remove potential confrontation in areas where forces are in close proximity'.	(positive contributions of the 1993 agreement on peace and tranquillity noted)
1995–96	1993 agreement implemented by pulling back four India and Chinese posts, two on each side, in 'close proximity'.	There has been a steady and substantial improvement in India–China relations . . .
1996–97	CBMs signed during Jiang Zemin's visit. Both agreed to work for 'Cooperative and constructive relationship into the 21st century'.	(PLA modernisation is a concern for India.) Upgradation of China's logistic capabilities all along the India–China border, for strengthened air operations has to be noted.
1997–98	Bilateral relations exhibited 'steady progress'. Expression of concern on China's assistance to Pakistan in the nuclear and missile fields.	(China's military modernisation and transfer of weapons to Pakistan and Myanmar) . . . directly affect India's security.
1998–99	'Cooperation to be maximised and tensions minimised, mutual concerns addressed and thus, issues solved.'	. . . the nuclear tests conducted by India . . . have helped forge a relatively stable national security environment for India . . . (China's WMD transfers to Pakistan is a concern). India does not regard China as an adversary . . .

1999–2000	India reiterated its policy of seeking a 'long-term and stable relationship with China'.	The PLA is being restructured with a view to enhancing its trans-border military capability by improving mobility, firepower and ensuring better coordination in joint service operations.
2000–1	We seek a long-term, stable relationship in which both sides are responsive to each other's concerns.	. . . China is working towards the goal of achieving Superpower status in the new millennium. . . . It is rapidly modernising its Armed Forces and is building political and military bridges with a large number of countries in our neighbourhood. Every major Indian city is within reach of Chinese missiles. . . . The asymmetry is strongly in favour of China . . .
2001–2	India's policy is to develop 'mutual trust and confidence'.	. . . there are continuing reports of transfer of missile parts and components technology to Pakistan (from China). . . . China continued to provide military assistance to Pakistan and Myanmar . . .
2002–3	'Efforts continued to build on the growing convergence of interests.'	China . . . is passing through a period of rapid economic growth and modernisation with the aim of achieving great power status in the shortest time possible . . . every major Indian city is within reach of Chinese missiles and this capability is being further augmented to include Submarine Launched Ballistic Missiles (SLBMs). The asymmetry in terms of nuclear forces is pronouncedly in favour of China and is likely to get further accentuated as China responds to counter the US missile defence programme. China's close defence relationship with Pakistan takes a particular edge in view of the latter's known belligerence and hostility to India and its acquisition of nuclear assets.

(Continued....)

(Annexure Continued....)

Year	Key statements in Ministry of External Affairs Annual Reports	Key statements in Ministry of Defence Annual Reports
2003–4	The first-ever Joint Declaration issued during PM's visit in June and stressed 'qualitatively new relationship' and multipolarity.	China is modernising rapidly, building up its 'Comprehensive National Power'. . . . China's close defence relationship with and regular military assistance to Pakistan, including assistance in the latter's nuclear and missile programmes at critical stages, its build up in the Tibet Autonomous Region, its military modernisation, its nuclear and missile arsenals, and its continental and maritime aspirations, require observation.
2004–5	India continued to view bilateral relations with China in a positive spirit, seeking friendly, cooperative, good neighbourly and mutually beneficial relations on the basis of the Five Principles of Peaceful Coexistence and mutual sensitivity to each other's concerns and aspirations.	The US retained its position as the pre-eminent world power though the nascent challenge posed by a fast growing and modernising China was too strong to be ignored. . . . China's rapid modernisation elicited both awe and nervousness in some quarters. China's close defence relationship with and military assistance to Pakistan continued. We will also continue to monitor development of military infrastructure by China in India–China border areas and its military modernisation, including in the maritime sector.
2005–6	. . . India–China relations transcended bilateral issues and have acquired a global and strategic perspective.	China's military modernisation, with sustained double digit growth in its defence budget for over a decade as also the development of infrastructure in the India–China border areas, continues to be monitored.
2006–7	The trend of development and diversification of India–China relations further intensified during the year.	The Chinese assistance to Pakistan's nuclear and missile programme has been a matter of concern as it has adversely impacted on India's national security environment. We have also taken note of the recent destruction by China of one of its own satellites in polar orbit through direct ascent anti-satellite test.

2007–8	India–China relations remain a high priority of India's foreign policy. . . . India–China relations today are of regional and international significance. . . . It was recognised that the Strategic and Cooperative Partnership should be based on strong, diversified and mutually beneficial economic ties.	'We continue to realistically analyse the growing economic and military capacities of China and the infrastructural developments in Tibet. Accordingly, we are constantly reviewing and upgrading our strategic and conventional postures so that our national security is not compromised.'
2008–9	Defence cooperation has contributed to enhancement of mutual trust and cooperation. . . . Both countries have also interacted constructively on regional and international issues.	'India has a strategic and cooperative partnership with the Peoples Republic of China which has further progressed. . . . The two countries are seeking to build a relationship of friendship and trust based on equality, in which each is sensitive to the concerns and aspirations of the other. . . . China's defence modernisation needs to be monitored carefully in the foreseeable future for the implications that it can have on the security and defence of India.'
2009–10	'China is now India's largest trading partner . . . temporary restrictions imposed (on border trade) by the Chinese authorities in connection with the Beijing Olympics and Paralympics in 2008 . . . (were lifted) . . . defence cooperation between India and China maintained a healthy momentum.	

Source: Government of India, Ministry of External Affairs, *Annual Report* (New Delhi: Policy Planning and Research Division, Ministry of External Affairs, various years) and Government of India, Ministry of Defence, *Annual Reports* (New Delhi, Ministry of Defence, various years).

Notes

1. See 'PM's Reply to the Debate in the Lok Sabha on the President's Address', available at http://pmindia.nic.in/speech/content.asp?id=787 (accessed 22 July 2009).

2. This is reflected in Indian prime minister Manmohan Singh's several statements on the necessity for Mumbai to learn from Shanghai, setting up Special Economic Zones, joint ventures, timely completion of projects, etc.

3. These include three talks at Beijing, Rangoon and New Delhi in 1960, eight talks in 1981–87, fifteen Joint Working Group meetings from 1989 to 2005 and thirteen Special Representative meetings till 2009.

4. See John Lall, 'The Sino-Indian Border Problem as a Leftover of History', in Surjit Mansingh, *Indian and Chinese Foreign Policies in Comparative Perspective*, New Delhi: Radiant Publishers, 1998, pp. 442–56.

5. Indeed, during Nehru's times, the Indian defence budget was relatively low, although from Indira Gandhi onwards this was hiked, partly to cope with challenges from China. Nevertheless, on the whole, Indian defence allocations are relatively less as compared to that of the Chinese since the 1950s. See Jasjit Singh, *India's Defence Spending: Assessing Future Needs*, New Delhi: Knowledge World, 2000, pp. 14–15. In 2009, China's official defence allocation was about $70 billion, while that of India was less than half at $32.7 billion.

6. See John W. Garver, 'Asymmetrical Indian and Chinese Threat Perceptions', in Sumit Ganguly (ed.), *India as an Emerging Power*, London: Frank Cass, 2003, pp. 109–34. A latest Chinese rendition is reflected in 'India's Unwise Military Moves', *Global Times*, 11 June 2009, available at http://english.people.com.cn/90001/90777/90851/6676088.html (accessed 22 July 2009).

7. While former US secretary of state Rice had mentioned certain features (rising power, geopolitical location, democracy, etc.) as contributing factors in the US decision to support a country for the UNSC seat, no specific statement or move was made by the US to support India. However, in the case of China, as reflected in the joint statements and trilateral declarations (at Dalian and Yekaterinburg), there has been an increasingly favourable, if not decisive and explicit, disposition towards Indian candidature in this regard. See Muchkund Dubey, 'The United Nations as a Foreign Policy Arena for India and China', in Mansingh, *Indian and Chinese Foreign Policies*, pp. 187–96.

8. Here the 1998 United Nations Security Council Resolution No. 1172 (in which China actively participated in passing the resolution) and the negotiations leading up to the 2008 International Atomic Energy Agency and Nuclear Suppliers Group deliberation on waiver for India in the civilian nuclear trade (in which the Indian national security advisor

mentioned his 'disappointment' at the Chinese role) are of considerable importance to India. See 'NSG Waiver: India Issues Demarche to China', *The Times of India*, 7 September 2008. See also, K. Subrahmanyam, 'Don't Get Fooled by China', *The Times of India*, 28 August 2007.

9. A comprehensive work in this direction is J. N. Dixit, *Makers of India's Foreign Policy: Raja Ram Mohan Roy to Yashwant Sinha*, New Delhi: HarperCollins, 2004.

10. See 'Parliamentary Committees', available at http://www. parliamentofindia.nic.in/ls/intro/p21.htm (accessed 22 July 2009).

11. See Standing Committee on Defence (1995–96) Tenth Lok Sabha Sixth Report, March 1996, *Defence Policy, Planning and Management*, New Delhi: Lok Sabha Secretariat, p. 4.

12. Standing Committee on Defence (1998–99) Twelfth Lok Sabha First Report, New Delhi: Lok Sabha Secretariat, July 1998, p. 3. See also V. K. Nair, 'Armed Forces, Nuclear Weapons and China's Foreign Policy', in Mansingh, *Indian and Chinese Foreign Policies*, pp. 176–86.

13. Standing Committee on Defence (1999–2000) Thirteenth Lok Sabha Seventh Report, 'Modernisation of the Indian Air Force', New Delhi: Lok Sabha Secretariat, December 2000, p. 3, on strengthening the Indian Air Force for 'protecting the country from the aggressor'.

14. Standing Committee on Defence (2006–7) Fourteenth Lok Sabha Twenty Second Report, *Review of Implementation Status of Group of Ministers* New Delhi: Lok Sabha Secretariat, July 2007, pp. 4 and 63.

15. See Nancy Jetley, *India–China Relations, 1947–1977: A Study of Parliament's Role in the Making of Foreign Policy*, New Delhi: Radiant Publishers, 1979. For extensive coverage of different political parties' views on China, see also http: //parliamentofindia.nic.in/ (accessed 26 June 2010). For an eloquent view on the need to guard 'strategic frontiers' of India see former foreign minister and till recently BJP leader Jaswant Singh, *Defending India*, New Delhi: Macmillan Publishers, 1999. Jaswant Singh suggests here that '. . . in the absence of any social, cultural, political or economic commonality or interdependence, a band policy of "improving relations" with China could, over time, convert into an opiate, consequentially persuading us to mortgage the future yet again for illusions about the present'. See p. 270. For another (of the Congress Party till recently) foreign minister's views, see K. Natwar Singh, *My China Diary, 1956–88*, New Delhi: Rupa & Co, 2009.

16. The Congress Party suggested that it will improve relations with (in that order) 'United States, the European Union, the Russian Federation, China, Japan and the ASEAN countries. . . . The Congress will continue the process of normalizing, strengthening and expanding India's relations with China, which is the most important factor affecting Asian security and stability.' See 'Security, Defence and Foreign Policy', available at http://aicc.org.in/new/security-agenda.php (accessed 26

June 2010).On the other hand, a search of the BJP's website indicated sixty-two hits for China referring to speeches or remarks made by the BJP leaders. The content mainly included criticism of China in terms of the unresolved border dispute, strategic challenges from China in the Indian neighbourhood, learning from the Chinese economic reforms, etc. See http://www.bjp.org/index.php?searchword=china&option=com_search&Itemid=&x=3&y=8 (accessed 2 June 2009).

17. See Taufiq Ahmad Nizami, *The Communist Party and India's Foreign Policy*, New York: Barnes & Noble, Inc., 1971, pp. 222–56.

18. For instance, recently, during a visit by CPM delegation members in December 2008, CCP politburo member Li Changchun said that CCP would 'step up exchange and cooperation' with CPM. See 'Communist Parties of China, India Eye Stronger Ties', *Xinhua*, 2 December 2009, available at http://english.people.com.cn/90001/90776/90883/6544776.html (accessed 8 January 2010).

19. On the contrary, it was argued that the 1967 Unlawful Activities Act enacted by the Parliament, besides overriding previous laws, permits cessation of territory by treaty and allows the state (through officials of the state) to ratify the boundary. For this view, see A. G. Noorani cited in Mohan Guruswamy and Zorawar Daulet Singh, *India China Relations: The Border Issue and Beyond*, New Delhi: Viva Books Private Limited, 2009, pp. 123–24.

20. Yet, on the border dispute with China, specifically on the Arunachal Pradesh issue, the Congress, BJP, left parties and others were at the same wave length, although each differed on the approaches to resolve the dispute. However, on defence cooperation with the US and multilateral exercises, Indian left parties were apprehensive that these may pitch India against China. On the US–India civilian nuclear agreement as well the left parties' position indicated to lack of consensus resulting in a vote on this issue in the Indian Parliament on 22 July 2008.

21. Significant nuances remained in all their perspectives on China, Tibet, the border dispute and other issues, though. To outline a few, while Nehru–Krishna Menon took a relatively benign view of relations with China, Sardar Vallabhbhai Patel cautioned Nehru on India's China policy. Patel said on 7 November 1950: 'The Chinese Government has tried to delude us by professions of peaceful intentions. . . . The tragedy . . . is that the Tibetans [had] put faith in us; they chose to be guided by us; and we have been unable to get them out of the meshes of Chinese diplomacy or Chinese malevolence. [With the Chinese entry into Tibet], India's defence has to concentrate on two fronts simultaneously.' Indira Gandhi, moving away from idealism, initiated measures to become self-reliant in nuclear and missile programmes in the light of the Chinese progress in these fields. Morarji Desai was also critical of China's position on Tibet, even though he normalised

relations with China by sending his foreign minister Vajpayee in 1979. Rajiv Gandhi, unencumbered by rigid ideological positions, further expanded relations with China. I. K. Gujral's initiatives on CBMs in 1996 with China and furthering of the Look East Policy also have implications on the Indian policy. Patel, Indira Gandhi, Desai, Rajiv Gandhi, Gujral quoted in Dixit, *Makers of India's Foreign Policy*, pp. 67, 70, 128, 177 and 183, 202–3 and 222 respectively. For another useful source, see Harish Kapur, *Foreign Policies of India's Prime Ministers*, New Delhi: Lancer International, 2009.

22. 'PM Calls for Increased Economic Engagement between India and China', 13 January 2008, available at http://pmindia.nic.in/pressrel. htm (accessed 28 January 2008).

23. For instance, see Manmohan Singh, 'PM's Address to IFS Probationary Officers', 11 June 2008, available at http://pmindia.nic.in/lspeech. asp?id=689 (accessed 2 June 2009).

24. Interviews in China during May–June 2007 and November–December 2008.

25. This is based on Srikanth Kondapalli, 'Policy Perspectives on India–China Interaction', *Indian Foreign Affairs Journal*, New Delhi, vol. 2, no. 1, January–March 2007, pp. 75–87. Within the MEA some major changes have taken place in the last decade in terms of its perspectives on China. A more realist perspective is visible in Jagat Mehta, 'India–China Relations: Review and Prognosis', in Mansingh, *Indian and Chinese Foreign Policies*, pp. 457–83; J. N. Dixit, *Indian Foreign Policy and Its Neighbours*, New Delhi: Gyan Publishing House, 2001, pp. 219–70; S. K. Singh et al., *External Affairs: Cross Border Relations*, New Delhi: Roli Books, 2003 and Rajiv Sikri, *Challenge and Strategy: Rethinking India's Foreign Policy*, New Delhi: Sage Publications, 2009, pp. 92–111. Others had suggested that continuing the engagement policy would best serve India's interests vis-à-vis China. See C. V. Ranganathan and Vinod C. Khanna, *India and China: The Way Ahead After 'Mao's India War'*, New Delhi: Har Anand Publications, 2003. This school had a dominant influence on the MEA till recently. However, some in the 'younger' generation call for 'soft balancing'. See Venu Rajamony, 'India-China-U.S. Triangle: A "Soft" Balance of Power System in the Making', *Center for Strategic and International Studies*, available at http://www.csis.org/saprog/venu.pdf (accessed 15 March 2002). This is an upcoming school in the MEA, strengthened, as it were, with the growing relations with the US, specifically in the back drop of the civilian nuclear technology cooperation agreement.

26. In 1998, the then defence minister George Fernandez reportedly said that China is India's potential enemy number one. However, he visited China during the SARS crisis in 2003 and mended fences. In June 2008, the defence minister A. K. Antony, speaking at the

commanders' conference, said: 'To a maximum extent, we will try to avoid confrontation' with China. See 'India Wants No Confrontation with China: Antony', *The Indian Express*, 10 June 2008.

27. Government of India, *The Ministry of Defence Annual Report*, 2007–8, p. 23.

28. See Srikanth Kondapalli, 'Chinese Military Eyes Southern Asia', in Andrew Scobell and Larry Wortzel (eds), *The PLA Shapes the Future Security Environment*, Carlisle Barracks, PA: US Army War College & The Heritage Foundation, 2006, pp. 197–282, available at http://www. strategicstudiesinstitute.army.mil/pdffiles/PUB709.pdf (accessed 8 April 2008).

   Soon after this test, the Indian air force announced its interest in setting up an aerospace organisation to meet such challenges, while the Indian army as well made preparations in this direction by formulating its Space Vision 2020. See 'Indian Army Looks to "Catch Up with China" in Space Warfare', PTI News Agency, 22 October 2007. See also 'Now, Space Cell to Keep an Eye on China's Plans', *The Times of India*, 11 June 2008, available at http://timesofindia.indiatimes.com/India/File_Now_space_cell_to_keep_an_eye_on_Chinas_plans/articleshow/3118491.cms (accessed 22 June 2008).

29. Government of India, *The Ministry of Defence Annual Report 2006–07*, p. 6. For an overall view of these developments, see V. R. Raghavan, *India–China Relations: A Military Perspective*, New Delhi: Gyan Publishing House, 1998.

30. Government of India, The Ministry of Home Affairs Annual Report (various years).

31. See Pallavi Aiyer, *Smoke and Mirrors: An Experience in China*, New Delhi: The Fourth Estate, 2008.

32. For instance, according to a *Times of India* editorial, on the eve of the post-poll scenario in India and its future course: 'A larger role on the global stage and a more assertive geopolitical positioning are not indicative of aspirational overreaching but prerequisites for safeguarding India's national interests.' See 'Chinese Checkers', *The Times of India*, 22 May 2009.

33. See Robert Ash, David Shambaugh and Seiichiro Takagi (eds), *China Watching: Perspectives from Europe, Japan and United States*, London: Routledge, 2007.

34. As a part of the normalisation of relations between the two countries, in the early 1990s both initiated not only exchanging scholars but also conducted performances by cultural troupes in various cities in India and China. The latter included mostly traditional classical theme performances such as on 'Journey to the West', Ramayana, etc.

35. The Institute of Chinese Studies (ICS) and Centre for Policy Research have been the institutional partners for the Bangladesh-China-India-Myanmar sub-regional grouping that was established in 1999 and has conducted annual meetings in these four countries. The ICS is also an institutional partner in promoting India-Russia-China trilateral as well as economic multilateralism through the Bo Ao Forum for Asia.

36. It was reported that when the Dalai Lama participated in one of the conferences of the CII at New Delhi, the Chinese ire led to the closure of the CII office in Shanghai, only to be reopened after 'assurances' from the CII.

37. See CII, 'Country Briefing: China', 2003. It stated: 'China has come to be an ideal manufacturing base for Indian companies, a joint-venture partner, a growing market and an excellent trade partner', p. 120. See http://www.ciionline.org/ (accessed 8 April 2007).

38. One set of Indian intellectuals suggested that poverty and economic development are main security issues facing India. Hence, the national strategic and security perspectives should focus on building the economy for the foreseeable future. See Kanti Bajpai and Amitabh Mattoo, *The Peacock and the Dragon*, New Delhi: Har Anand Publications, 2001, p. 248. Jasjit Singh, 'India's Strategic and Security Perspectives', *Strategic Analysis*, vol. 13, no. 5, August 1990, pp. 479–81. Another set clearly had power status in sight. Overwhelming intellectuals that Baljit Singh interviewed in India in the early 1960s expressed their distrust towards China, specifically in its relations with Pakistan. See Baljit Singh, 'Pundits and Panchsheela: Indian Intellectuals and Their Foreign Policy', *Background*, vol. 9, no. 2, August 1965, pp. 127–36. Today, the situation may not be completely different, although 'China market as an opportunity' is a new mantra these days, specifically among the commercial lobby. According to Karsten Frey, in a brief survey of the Indian strategic community's perceptions about China vis-à-vis the nuclear option, a majority of them are 'preoccup[ied] with status considerations'. See Karsten Frey, *India's Nuclear Bomb and National Security*, London: Routledge, 2006, chapter 6, pp. 111–21, see p. 114. An overwhelming Indians that the Chicago Council on Global Affairs interviewed in mid-2006 considered the rise in China's military prowess with concern. See Chicago Council on Global Affairs, 'The United States and the Rise of China and India: Results of a 2006 Multination Survey of Public Opinion', Chicago: The Chicago Council on Global Affairs, 2006, pp. 37–38, available at http://www.thechicagocouncil.org (accessed 2 June 2008).

39. It was argued that Gorbachev's Vladivostok speech in 1986 improved Sino-Soviet relations and impacted on India-Soviet-China relations. See Mira Sinha Bhattacharjea, 'New Equations, Hard Decisions',

in Verinder Grover (ed.), *China, Japan and India's Foreign Policy*, New Delhi: Deep and Deep Publications, 1992, pp. 171–72. Maryam Daftari, 'Sino-Indian Relations and "Encounters": Challenges and Opportunities in the Nineties', *China Report*, vol. 30, no. 3, 1994, pp. 283–93, here p. 283 for the argument that the 1990s were times of international strategic flux and realignment and that multipolarity provided opportunities for China and India to come together. Faisal O Al-Rfouh, 'Sino-Indian Relations: From Confrontation to Accommodation (1998–2001)', *China Report*, vol. 39, no. 1, January– March 2003, pp. 25–28.

See for an Indian view on the Tiananmen Square incident in 1989, Giri Deshingkar, 'The PRC at Forty: The Security Dimension', *China Report*, vol. 26, no. 4, 1990, pp. 351–64, here p. 351. The Government of India, on the other hand, viewed this incident as an 'internal' matter of China and refused to be part of the western sanctions on China.

40. See Subhash Kapila, 'China-India Strategic Alliance — Should Not be Unthinkable: An Analysis', *South Asia Analysis Group*, May 2005, available at http://www.saag.org (accessed 8 June 2005).

41. A conference held at Chennai with the participation of retired officials, scholars and professionals in October 2006 exhibited this diverse nature of the bilateral relations. See 'India-China Relations in the New Era', *ORF Discourse*, vol. 1, no. 4, December 2006, available at http://www. orfonline.org (accessed 8 June 2005).

42 These underline that India has no territorial ambitions. However, one Lok Sabha Standing Committee on Defence, as cited earlier, suggested building up 'out-of-area' contingency strength, ostensibly to preserve the Indian system from attacks from outside.

43. The word 'strategic' appeared in the India–China official lexicon in the April 2005 joint statement during the visit of premier Wen Jiabao. It could be surmised that part of the reason for this entry is related to the Indian GDP reaching nearly $1 trillion, growing Indian reach, improving relations between India and US, etc.

44. See Sheldon W. Simon, 'The Kashmir Dispute in Sino-Soviet Perspective', *Asian Survey*, vol. 7, no. 3, March 1967, pp. 176–87; Swaran Singh, *China–South Asia: Issues, Equations, Policies*, New Delhi: Lancer's Books, 2003; Bal Raj Madhok, *Kashmir: The Storm Centre of the World*, Houston, Texas: A. Ghosh Publishers, 2002, pp. 74–81; C. Raja Mohan, 'Kashmir: Remaking the Bridge Linking India, Pakistan and China', IDSS Commentaries, 22 August 2005, available at http:// www.idss.edu.sg (accessed 18 September 2005).

45. Srikant Dutt, 'China and the Hill Peoples of South-east Asia and North-east India', *China Report*, vol. 17, no. 3, 1981, pp. 3–16.

46. See 'Mirwaiz Seeks China's Help to Resolve Kashmir Dispute', 24 March 2010, available at http://soskashmir.wordpress.com/2010/03/

(accessed 18 April 2010) and 'Hands Off Projects in PoK, India Tells China', 14 October 2009, available at http://news.rediff.com/report/2009/oct/14/hands-off-projects-in-pok-india-tells-china.htm (accessed 18 April 2010).

47. On border dispute as a security problem between the two countries, see John W. Garver, *Protracted Contest: Sino-Indian Rivalry in the Twentieth Century*, New Delhi: Oxford University Press, 2001, chapter 3 and Srikanth Kondapalli, 'India–China Border Perspectives', in *A Presentation Collection for Conference on India in 21ˢᵗ Century: External Relations*, Shanghai: Shanghai Institute of International Studies, 2002, pp. 129–49.

48. See C. V. Ranganathan, 'The China Threat: A View from India', in Herbert Yee and Ian Storey (eds), *The China Threat: Perceptions, Myths, and Reality*, London: Routledge Curzon, 2002, p. 294; Brahma Chellaney, *Securing India's Future in the New Millennium*, New Delhi: Orient Longman Limited, 1999, pp. 406–7 and p. 382; Nimmi Kurian, *Emerging China and India's Policy Options*, New Delhi: Lancer Publications, 2001, p. 68; see also, Sumit Ganguly, 'India's Pathway to Pokhran II: The Prospects and Sources of India's Nuclear Weapons Program', *International Security*, vol. 23, no. 4, Spring 1998, pp. 148–77.

49. See Garver, *Protracted Contest*.

50. See D. S. Rajan, 'China Adjusts Fast to the Situation in Nepal — Implications', C3S Paper No. 202, 14 August 2008, available at http://www.c3sindia.org/india/309 (accessed 18 August 2008).

51. See Sudeshna Sarkar, 'China Steps Up Military Ties with Nepal', *The Hindustan Times*, 6 December 2008.

52. This was denied by China. See 'China Disputes Indian Media Report of Political Interference in Nepal', *Xinhua*, 12 May 2009, available at http://english.people.com.cn/90001/90776/90883/6656326.html (accessed 4 July 2009).

53. Gurpreet S. Khurana, 'China's "String of Pearls" in the Indian Ocean and Its Security Implications', *Strategic Analysis*, vol. 32, no. 1, 2008, pp. 1–39.

54. In the light of China's entry into Tibet and as a part of the overall dynamics in bilateral relations, India articulated its Tibet policy in 1954 (when in a border trade aspect Tibet was obliquely referred to as a part of China), 1988 (when Tibet was considered to be an *autonomous* part of China), and 2003 (when Tibet Autonomous Region was considered as a part of the People's Republic of China). To ameliorate China's sensitivities, India further imposed restrictions on the Dalai Lama by barring any 'political activities' from the Indian soil. India also mobilised about 16,000 police forces to protect the Olympics torch march in 2008. For an overview of the subject see Amar Jasbir Singh, 'The Tibetan

Problem and China's Foreign Relations' in Mansingh, *Indian and Chinese Foreign Policies*, pp. 243–79 and Ajay B. Agarwal, *India, Tibet and China: The Role Nehru Played*, Mumbai: NA Books International, 2003.

55. See M. Shamsur Rabb Khan, 'China's Cyber Warfare', Article No. 2597, 18 June 2008, available at http://www.ipcs.org/whatsNewArticle1. jsp?action=showView&kValue=2613&status=article&mod=b (accessed 4 July 2008) and 'China Mounts Cyber Attacks on Indian Sites', *The Times of India*, 5 May 2008, available at http://timesofindia.indiatimes. com/India/File_China_mounts_cyber_attacks_on_Indian_sites/ articleshow/3010288.cms (accessed 4 July 2008).

56. This was denied by China. See 'China Refutes Reports of Helping Anti-govt Groups in India', *Xinhua*, 3 November 2008, available at http://english.people.com.cn/90001/90776/90883/6525740.html (accessed 2 December 2008).

57. Pieter Bottelier, 'India's Growth from China's Perspective', *Margin: The Journal of Applied Economic Research*, vol. 1, no. 1, 2007 pp. 119–38, see p. 120. There is also a growing literature on comparative advantages, niche area, etc. in the simultaneous rise of these two countries. See Rita Dulci Rahman and Jose Miguel Andreu, *China and India: Towards Global Economic Supremacy?* New Delhi: Academic Foundation, 2006; P. Jagdish Gandhi, *India and China in the Asian Century: Global Economic Power Dynamics*, New Delhi: Deep and Deep Publications, 2007; Chen Kuan-I and Joginder S Uppal, *India and China: Studies in Comparative Development*, New York: The Free Press, 1971 and Subramanian Swamy, *Financial Architecture and Economic Development in China and India: A Comparative Perspective*, New Delhi: Konark Publishers, 2006.

58. 'China–India Financial Dialogue Discusses Co-op on Fight against Crisis', *People's Daily*, 23 January 2009, available at http://english.people. com.cn/90001/90776/90883/6580338.html (accessed 4 February 2009).

59. See 'Address by Secretary (ER) at CII Conference on "India–China: Drivers of the Asian Century in a Post-Crisis World', 4 March 2009, available at http://meaindia.nic.in/speech/2009/03/04ss01.htm (accessed 8 July 2009).

60. This led to a loss of about $1.5 billion for China. See 'China, India Discuss Trade Disputes, Call for Regular Communication and Coordination', *Xinhua*, 20 March 2009, available at http://english. people.com.cn/90001/90776/90883/6618131.html (accessed 4 April 2009).

61. 'China's Industrial Association Strongly Dissatisfied by Indian Toy Ban', *Xinhua*, 11 February 2009, available at http://english.people. com.cn/90001/90776/90883/6590610.html (accessed 4 April 2009).

62. See 'Public Announcement of the Ministry of Commerce on Preliminary Adjudication of Anti-dumping Case Concerning Imported Nonyl Phenol Originating from India and Taiwan Region', China's Ministry of Commerce, 10 July 2006, available at http://www.isinolaw.com/isinolaw/english/detail.jsp (accessed 24 July 2006).

63. See B. K. Sikdar and A. Sikdar, *India and China: Strategic Energy Management and Security*, New Delhi: Manas Publications, 2004, pp. 311–31.

64. Indrani Bagchi, 'India, China at Loggerheads', *The Times of India*, 27 August 2005, available at http://timesofindia.indiatimes.com/articleshow/1211953.cms (accessed 2 September 2005).

65. 'China–India Strategic Dialogue Manifests Partnership', *People's Daily*, 12 January 2006, World News Connection File Number 985, Accession Number 219700118.

66. 'Washington Draws India in Against China', *People's Daily*, 8 July 2005, World News Connection File Number 985, Accession Number 210300049; Lin Chuan, 'South Asia Becomes a Target That China and the US Compete to Woo', Zhongguo Tongxun She, 10 April 2005, World News Connection File Number 985, Accession Number 205850293.

Brahma Chellaney, *Asian Juggernaut: The Rise of China, India and Japan*, New Delhi, HarperCollins Publishers, 2006 and Bill Emmott, *Rivals: How the Power Struggle Between China, India and Japan will Shape Our Next Decade*, London: Allen Lane, 2008.

67. See Francine R. Frankel and Harry Harding (eds), *The India–China Relationship: Rivalry and Engagement*, New Delhi: Oxford University Press, 2004.

68. See the then Indian defence minister George Fernandez's speech in K. Santhanam and Srikanth Kondapalli (eds), *Asian Security and China 2000–2010*, New Delhi: Shipra Publications, 2003.

69. W. P. S. Sidhu and Yuan Jingdong, *China and India: Cooperation or Conflict?* Boulder: Lynne Rienner Publishers, 2003.

70. For instance, in April 2009 it was reported that the Indian Military Operations directorate conducted a simulated exercise 'Divine Matrix' with a 2017 scenario of an India–China war. See Rahul Singh, 'Indian Army Fears China Attack by 2017', *The Hindustan Times*, 26 March 2009. This was denied by the Chinese foreign ministry spokesman. See 'India's Drill Report "Surprises" Chinese Govt', *China Daily*, 1 April 2009, available at http://english.people.com.cn/90001/90776/90883/6626802.html (accessed 4 July 2009). Again, the Indian air force chief said in May 2009 that China is a 'greater threat' to India than Pakistan. See 'China Bigger Threat than Pakistan, Says IAF Chief', *The Times of India*, 24 May 2009.

71. Ninan Koshy had argued that India's nuclear doctrine shifted from 'regional limited deterrent' to that of 'regional overall deterrent'. See 'Looking from India at the Spy Plane', May 2001, available at http://www.fpif.org (accessed 2 July 2001).

72. In October 2007, India succeeded in testing Agni III while in December 2007 it had tested an interceptor missile as a part of its ballistic missile defence system. There are also plans by the Indian navy to acquire strategic nuclear submarine from Russia on lease or through its indigenous programme.

5

China and India
Growth Outcomes and Economic Exchanges

BIBEK DEBROY AND AMITENDU PALIT

In a long-term and secular sense, economic growth in emerging Asia (including China and India) appears de-linked from growth in developed countries. This, of course, doesn't imply that cyclical growth fluctuations in the developed world don't impact economic activity in emerging Asia. Nevertheless, the growth trajectories in China and India — the two largest economies of emerging Asia — do appear to be traversing fairly distinct courses. The International Monetary Fund's (IMF) forecasts for 2009 and 2010 indicate real gross domestic product (GDP) growth in China and India at 6.7 per cent and 8.0 per cent and 5.1 per cent and 6.5 per cent respectively. The actual growth rates might turn out to be more robust than the predicted ones and more impressive than those witnessed in the rest of the world. The explanations behind the better growth performances primarily pertain to stronger economic frameworks coupled with endogenous sources of growth based on domestic consumption and investments as well as limited exposure to toxic assets of failed global banks and financial institutions and ample foreign exchange reserves.

Given the growth expectations within China and India and their implications for employment generation, the performances in 2009 and 2010 will be distinctly moderate. Confronted with the economic deceleration following the onset of the global financial crisis, both China and India eased monetary policies and imparted additional fiscal stimuli. The size of the fiscal stimulus was larger for China, which is understandable given the greater fiscal space available in China. The IMF estimates the additional fiscal stimulus for China at 0.4 per cent in 2008 and 3.2 per cent in 2009. The corresponding estimates for India are 0.6 per cent in both years. There are, however, concerns about what the fiscal stimuli will be used for and the capacities of the national administrative systems to deliver the outputs from these stimuli.

The near-term economic outlooks in both countries need to be tempered in the light of the relatively slower growth in trade, foreign investment and development assistance flows following the global slowdown. Economic deceleration is also expected to at least marginally affect poverty-reduction and employment-generation effects of growth due to diversion of resources to fiscal expansion programmes and limited fiscal space available to governments due to falling revenues. The World Bank's revised configuration of income poverty line at US$ 1.25 per day indicates head-count ratios for the poor at 20 per cent–plus range in rural China and almost double in rural India. Growth and poverty-reduction efforts for China and India depend not only on the financial crisis, but also the food and fuel crises preceding it, since food accounts for a disproportionately large share in the consumption baskets of the poor. The food, fuel and financial crises can be interpreted as a movement away from what were the earlier growth trajectories in China and India. The growth trajectories will resume sooner or later though the global environment might be different.

This chapter examines the economic policies and resultant quality of economic growth achieved by both countries with particular emphasis on the progress of economic reforms. In the light of the qualitative growth trajectories and the global outlook in a post-crisis economic order, the chapter examines bilateral economic relations and the future outlook for such relations from an Indian perspective.

India's Economic Policies and Growth Outcomes

India's market-oriented reforms adopted from the early 1990s can be divided into two broad categories. The first of these are reforms pertaining to the external sector and include removal of quantitative restrictions (QRs) on exports, elimination of export subsidies and introduction of export incentives, phased reduction in import duties, introduction of a broadly market-determined exchange rate with a convertible rupee, a liberal policy on foreign institutional investments, opening up different production segments to foreign direct investments (FDIs) and introduction of a modern and enabling foreign exchange management legislation. The second category essentially comprises reforms concerning the domestic economy. These include reforms in both product markets (agriculture, industry and services) as well as factor markets (land, labour and capital). Compared to the first category of reforms, the pace and progress has been more patchy and uneven across segments in the second category. This is, however, understandable given the prevalence of political economy considerations in domestic economic reforms compared to the external ones. Much of India's possibilities regarding sustaining an 8 per cent–plus growth trajectory in the medium term will depend upon its success in pursuing and implementing some key reforms in the domestic economy. A few of these are discussed here.

Rural Reforms

More than 70 per cent of India lives in rural areas.[1] It is important to distinguish between rural and agricultural reforms because the former extend beyond agriculture. Agriculture reforms include tackling pending measures such as allowing corporate sector involvement in agriculture, removing state controls on production, marketing and distribution of agricultural produce, refocusing public investment in agriculture from input subsidies to development of infrastructure and extension services, creating efficient distribution chains, promoting contract farming, revamping credit and insurance and freeing land markets. The most important component of rural reforms pertains to creation of physical and social infrastructure, which, along with agriculture reforms, can create significant non-farm employment opportunities in rural India.

Taxation Reforms

India's import tariffs continue to remain much higher than the rest of the BRIC (Brazil–Russia–India–China) in both agriculture and industrial products. Bringing down these tariffs in a phased manner is an important pre-requisite for India's closer integration with world trade.[2] The thrust of the other indirect tax reforms has been set out. A composite goods and service tax (GST) to be accompanied by withdrawal of other diverse taxes such as central excise, central sales tax, state-level sales tax, entry tax, stamp duties, transportation taxes and so on. The GST is not only expected to create a common market for goods and services in the country but is also required for making the export incentive system WTO-compatible, introduce appropriate countervailing duties and allow better defence against anti-subsidy and anti-dumping investigations. There is a parallel exemption issue for direct taxes, both for personal income taxes and corporate taxation.

Public Expenditure and Civil Service Reforms

Reforming public expenditure for improving its quality is arguably one of the more difficult set of reforms since it involves coordinated actions by the central government, state governments as well as local bodies. A substantial chunk of public expenditure is on non-asset-creating avenues such as interest payments, wages and salaries and pensions. These expenditures are inflexible in the short run, though in the long run they can be significantly reduced by limiting government borrowings and liabilities. Reforming the bureaucracy is a key issue in this regard as such reforms are not only expected to improve delivery of public goods but are also expected to reduce public expenses.

Law Reforms

The salient aspects of legal reforms include statutory law reform, expediting dispute resolution and reforming administrative law for reducing procedural costs. Statutory law reform includes rationalisation and harmonisation across statutes enacted at various points in time, eliminating archaic laws, removing the scope of state intervention in several statutes and introducing new, contemporary and enabling legislations in several segments of the economy. Despite a new Arbitration Act since 1996, conciliation/ mediation is still not credible. An estimated backlog of around 28 million pending cases reflects poorly upon the ability of the legal system to deliver speedy justice.

Administrative law reform pertains to relationships between the citizen and the government and transactions between an enterprise and the government. The latter can be divided into three phases of an enterprise's existence — entry, functioning and exit. The former involves birth certificates, death certificates, land titles, requirements for establishing individual identities and accessing public services. Sustained protests against rent-seeking and ineffective delivery of public services have led to passage of the Right to Information (RTI) Act of 2005. There has, however, been little progress on facilitating exit in the formal sector of the Indian industry, a factor that continues to constrain industrial expansion in several cases.

Why have the required reforms not been implemented? The political economy, unfortunately, has not permitted the emergence of durable consensus on most of these aspects. A closer look into 'lack' of consensus indicates such lack to be most conspicuous about the role of the government and core governance areas. The latter for any state ought to be ensuring law and order, an efficient dispute resolution mechanism and intervention in certain segments of physical and social infrastructure, occasionally through financing rather than actual provisioning. Unfortunately, the outcomes have been rather unsatisfactory in these core areas primarily on account of the Indian state concentrating on multiple objectives that are often probably less significant than these core functions.

Notwithstanding the lackadaisical movement on several domestic reforms with the exception of the financial sector, analytical research and medium-term predictive outlooks are considerably optimistic about India's growth prospects. Some of these are not concerned with overall economic prospects, but concentrate instead on segments like out-sourcing and software exports. The latest period of robust growth for the economy — 2003–4 to 2007–8 — has led to the growth of the opinion that the Indian economy experienced a structural break in the year 2003–4, by picking up a base-line trend growth of 8.5 per cent or thereabouts from an earlier level of 6–6.5 per cent in the 1990s.

There are several reasons for such a belief. First, the domestic savings rate has increased along with the investment rate, leading to convergence between East Asian (and Chinese) investment rates and those in India. Indeed, in this regard, the popular notion that growths in India and China are primarily consumption-led and investment-led respectively is no longer correct. Second, India's incremental capital/output ratio (ICOR) is now around 4, which indicates that achieving an annual real growth of 9 per cent is distinctly feasible.[3] In this regard, it is important to note that the share of agriculture and allied activities in India's GDP is declining, while that of services is increasing. The service sector tends to have a lower ICOR. If services are growing relatively fast, then the sectoral shift from agriculture to services itself increases GDP growth as a statistical inevitability. Third, the effect of export growth on India's GDP growth is perhaps not always explicitly recognised. Fourth, while the demographic dividend and India's demographic transition is recognised, its impact on GDP growth is not always factored in. Growth projections are usually based on capital inputs, ignoring labour, and the Indian labour force is expected to grow at just below 2.5 per cent a year between now and 2020. This should itself add a clear percentage point to GDP growth, problems of education, skills and morbidity notwithstanding. Fifth, India has a young population with a median age of 24. This has significant positive implications for entrepreneurship in a country like India where new-generation private sector entrepreneurship has been a key driver of growth and economic change. Thus GDP growth can very well be at around 9 per cent between 2010 and 2015 with the possibility of accelerating upward to 10 per cent between 2015 and 2020.

Chinese Economic Reforms and Growth Outcomes

A comparison of different indicators across economic, social and human development categories (Table 5.1) indicates that notwithstanding a sharp improvement in India's trend rate of growth since 1991, it falls behind in comparison to China. With the exception of a few qualitative indicators (freedom and governance-type) China is ahead of India in virtually every economic indicator. Such a lead on the part of China remains impressive even if Chinese statistics are viewed with some degree of circumspection.

Chinese reforms date back to 1978 — more than a decade before India took decisive steps to move towards a market-based economy. The salient features of these reforms were decentralising control over state-owned enterprises (SOEs) by increasing the authority of local bodies and plant managers, subsequent privatisation of SOEs, dismantling the rural commune system and replacing the same with a household responsibility system,

TABLE 5.1: The China–India comparison

	China	India
GDP (PPP), US$ billion[i]	7,035	2,997
GDP per capita (PPP) US$[ii]	5,943	2,787
Human Development Index (HDI)[iii]	0.781	0.609
Life expectancy at birth (no. of years)[iv]	72.7	64.1
Adult literacy rate (per cent)[v]	93.0	65.2
Combined enrolment ratio (per cent)[vi]	68.7	61.0
Poor population (per cent)[vii]	13.4	41.6
Global Hunger Index[viii]	7.1	23.7
Under-5 mortality rate[ix]	2.4	7.6
Under-nourished population (per cent)[x]	12	20
Doing Business Rank[xi]	83rd	122nd
Global Competitiveness Index Rank[xii]	30th	50th
Index of Economic Freedom[xiii]	53.2	54.4
Corruption Perception Index[xiv]	3.6	3.4

Source: The data in the table has been compiled from statistics obtained from following sources: 1. International Monetary Fund (IMF); 2. United Nations Development Programme (UNDP); 3. International Food Policy Research Institute (IFPRI); 4. World Bank; 5. World Economic Forum; 6. Heritage Foundation; 7. Transparency International.

Notes: i. PPP implies purchasing power parity. The figures are as reported by the IMF statistics for the year 2007. See http://imf.org (accessed 4 August 2011).

ii. The figures are for the year 2008 and as reported by the IMF. See http://imf.org (accessed 4 August 2011).

iii. The index is prepared by the UNDP and is reported for the year 2008. See Human Development Report 2008, http://www.undp.org/publications/annualreport2008/downloads.shtml (accessed 4 August 2011).

iv. For the year 2008 as reported by the UNDP. See http://www.undp.org/publications/annualreport2008/downloads.shtml (accessed 4 August 2011).

v. Same as in 7.

vi. Ibid.

vii. Estimated in terms of population living below $1.25 a day; UNDP, 2008, http://www.undp.org/publications/annualreport2008/downloads.shtml (accessed 4 August 2011).

viii. As estimated by the International Food Policy Research Institute (IFPRI) for 2008, see http://www.ifpri.org/publication/2008-global-hunger-index-key-findings-facts (accessed 4 August 2011).

ix. Ibid.

x. Ibid.

xi. Estimated by the World Bank for the year 2009. See http://www.doingbusiness.org (accessed 4 August 2011).

(*Table 5.1 continued*)

(Table 5.1 continued)

    xii. Prepared by the World Economic Forum, 2008, http://members.
        weforum.org/pdf/GCR08/GCR08.pdf (accessed 4 August 2011).

    xiii. Scores for the year 2009 as reported by the Heritage Foundation. See
        http://www.heritage.org/index (accessed 4 August 2011).

    xiv. Scores for the year 2008 as reported by the Transparency International.
        See http://www.transparency.org/policy_research/surveys_indices/
        cpi/2008 (accessed 4 August 2011).

greater use of market-based incentives for augmenting agricultural production, opening up the economy to foreign trade and investment and improving economic infrastructure. The labour market reforms implied an end to the 'iron rice bowl' (*tie fan wan*) system.[4] The system, while guaranteeing job security and steady income and benefit flows, led to overstaffing of SOEs in urban areas. The benefits of the system, however, were only selectively available in rural areas with migration controlled through the household registration system (*hukou*). As a result, the rural labour force was not only surplus but also prevented from participating in industrialisation. Labour market reforms — one of the most critical structural changes introduced in the Chinese economy that provided industries access to large chunks of cheap workers — were actually done in parts in both urban and rural segments rather than as an unified whole.

The Indian official perspective often highlights labour market reforms as a key driver of China's economic success.[5] It also attributes the same to the incentives offered to manufacturers through lower indirect taxes, better infrastructure, particularly availability of electricity as well as social infrastructure and large FDI inflows.[6] There is recognition that China has handled its factor markets — particularly labour and land — much better, including contentious issues of land acquisition, compensation, rehabilitation and resettlement, which have had important implications for infrastructure development, enterprise growth and urbanisation.

Both for infrastructure and urbanisation, as well as economic reforms in general, comparisons between the political economy of resistance in China and India become inevitable. Chinese decision-making is found to be much more decentralised compared to India's, notwithstanding devolutions to states and the constitutional sanctity given to *panchayat*s and urban local bodies in India. There are also inevitable references to the absence and presence of democratic institutions in the two countries and their respective effects on economic performances. In this regard, there are arguments suggesting a 'democracy tax' in India that essentially underscores the greater cost (in terms of delays and resources) of pushing through reforms in a democracy.[7] It is, however, doubtful whether this trade-off exists at all.[8]

Bilateral Economic Relations

China and India granted each other 'most favoured nation' (MFN) status in 1984. At the time, China was experimenting with the initial policies guiding its transition to a 'socialist market economy', while India was still very much an inward-looking economy. Despite periodic frictions over outstanding political issues such as border disputes and contentions over Arunachal Pradesh and Tibet, neither side has ever discouraged the growth of economic engagement. Trade through land borders resumed after a long hiatus in 1992 with an additional trading post coming up in 1993.

The growth in bilateral trade between the two countries has been nothing short of spectacular with China emerging as India's second largest trade partner and India also developing into one of China's largest trade partners. Bilateral trade has grown most rapidly in the current decade following China's entry in the World Trade Organisation in December 2001 and the onset of robust economic growth cycles in both countries since 2003. During the period 2003–4 to 2008–9, bilateral trade has increased from US$ 6.9 billion to US$ 41.8 billion (Table 5.2) by growing at an average annual rate of 44.8 per cent. The annual rate of growth in trade during the period was actually averaging a remarkable 53.4 per cent till it contracted in 2008–9 due to the outbreak of the global financial crisis.

A much-discussed feature of the bilateral trade has been its accentuating imbalance. The balance of trade (merchandise trade since data on services exchange is not available) has been in China's favour with the Chinese trade surplus increasing over time. India's trade deficit with China accounts for nearly a fifth of its entire merchandise trade deficit with the trade gap with China enlarging from US$ 1.1 billion in 2003–4 to US$ 23.2 billion by 2008–9 (Table 5.1). Alarmist impressions about the growing imbalance arising from spectres of cheap Chinese imports

TABLE 5.2: India–China bilateral trade (2003–4 to 2008–9)

Year	Export	Import	Trade	Export Growth (per cent) (Y-o-Y)	Import Growth (per cent) (Y-o-Y)	Trade Growth (per cent) (Y-o-Y)
2003–4	2.9	4	6.9	...		
2004–5	5.6	7.1	12.7	90.0	75.1	81.4
2005–6	6.8	10.9	17.7	20.4	53.1	38.6
2006–7	8.3	17.5	25.8	22.6	60.5	46.0
2007–8	10.8	27.1	37.9	30.7	55.4	47.5
2008–9	9.3	32.5	41.8	−14.4	19.9	10.3

Source: Department of Commerce, Ministry of Commerce & Industry, Government of India. The Export Import Data Bank is available at http://commerce.nic. in/eidb/default.asp and Foreign Trade Performance Analysis is available at http://commerce.nic.in/ftpa/default.asp (accessed 3 August 2011).

Note: Y-o-Y: Year-on-Year

flooding India usually overlook the fact that the deficit expanded primarily on account of high demand for raw materials and intermediates from a robustly expanding Indian manufacturing. Chinese imports of coking and steam coal, inorganic and organic chemicals, fertilizers, iron and steel, pearls and precious stones, machinery and equipment and project goods imports have met significant resource demands of Indian producers during their latest phase of expansion.[9]

Excessive concerns over the trade imbalance also tend to overlook the fact that China has emerged as a key export market for India. China is now India's third largest export market following the United Arab Emirates (UAE) and the US.[10] Indian exports to China are dominated by minerals with ores, slag and ash comprising more than half of Indian exports wherein iron ore exports are frontrunners followed by chromium and lead ores.[11] China is the largest consumer of India's iron ore and accounts for 92 per cent of such exports by India. Granite and refined petroleum oil exports to China are also increasing along with plastic polymer, cotton, ferro-alloys, refined copper, electrical transformers and telephone apparatus equipment exports. Empirical analysis of the competitiveness of Indian exports in the Chinese market, however, indicates that such exports are relatively less competitive than similar exports from Southeast Asian countries in several product categories. This is a serious constraint impeding growth of Indian exports in China.[12]

Contemporary economic engagement has not been restricted to movement of goods alone; cross-border capital flows have also started picking up fast. Chinese firms are showing keen interest in specific segments of India's infrastructure. These particularly include electricity generation, construction, telecommunications and iron and steel. Firms such as Huawei Technologies and Sinosteel have been active in India for several years. On the other hand, Chinese consumer durable producing firms such as Haier and Lenovo have become household names in India. At the same time, the presence of Indian firms in China is also on the rise. Unlike Chinese firms in India, Indian firms operating out of China are much less noticeable in infrastructure or construction; they are mostly visible in IT and IT-enabled services (ITES) and in certain select segments of manufacturing. Leading Indian IT firms such as Tata Consultancy Services (TCS), Wipro, Infosys, as well as pharmaceutical and component manufacturing firms such as Ranbaxy, Dr Reddy's Laboratories and Bharat Forge are present in China.[13] The investment pattern of Chinese and Indian firms, in India and China, respectively, clearly reflects alignment in line with their respective comparative advantages with Chinese firms concentrating on building infrastructure assets and Indian firms on IT and knowledge-intensive activities.

The Way Forward

The pace and quality of economic reforms has been distinctly different between China and India. China began reforming its economy much earlier than India; it also followed a different approach to reforms. This involved correcting distortions in its factor (viz., land, labour) markets prior to reforms in the product markets. At the same time, China also reformed its agricultural and rural economy far more effectively. In contrast, Indian reforms have hardly improved productivity and efficiency in agriculture. Indian manufacturing has also failed to take off in a meaningful manner with the result that industry does not contribute even a third of the country's national output. However, economic reforms have strengthened the services sector of the economy, which has enabled India to integrate more closely with the world economy. India's recent economic progress owes a lot to the outstanding enterprise and aggressive business initiative displayed by a new generation of visionary entrepreneurs.

In the aftermath of the global financial crisis, China and India stand poised to resume their journeys as the world's two fastest growing economies. The global economic outlook, particularly the sluggish (in certain cases almost negligible) pace of recoveries in advanced country markets, conveys to both the importance of looking at each other closely for new economic opportunities. Rapid growth in both countries will undoubtedly inspire greater transactions with each other. Formalisation of trade relations through a bilateral trade pact can be of considerable help in gainful exploitation of the existing synergies.

A bilateral trade agreement between the two countries will also partly reflect the disappointment of both with the lack of progress in multilateral trade negotiations that has encouraged China and India to focus on regional trade agreements (RTAs). A significant part of the negotiating efforts towards creation of RTAs has been directed at trade partners in the Asian region. The China–ASEAN Free Trade Area (CAFTA) has become functional from 1 January 2010.[14] One of the largest trade areas in the world covering a population of almost 2 billion and trade volume of US$ 4.3 trillion, the CAFTA not only extends preferential tariffs to goods from either side, but also includes services and investment.[15] China, Japan and Korea are examining the feasibility of a trilateral FTA, while talks between China and Australia on a mutual trade pact are also at an advanced stage.[16] These regional trade initiatives on the part of China entailing widening the domain of its existing markets requires India to impart additional attention on driving RTAs, with specific focus on its east. A trade pact with China should be an important component of this agenda. India's relatively backward eastern and northeastern regions can benefit significantly through economic integration with Southeast Asia and China.

There are several reasons why formalisation of bilateral trade relations between China and India has not proceeded despite a report prepared on the subject by a Joint Study Group (JSG). One of the key reasons, as mentioned earlier, is the overarching fear that Indian manufacturing is not cost competitive and will be deluged by Chinese imports, once the latter get easier access in the Indian market. Indian manufacturing is certainly not as cost competitive as China's. However, that should not be taken as a ground for apprehending 'dumping' of Chinese imports. The bulk of India's anti-dumping investigations have been directed against China.[17] It is difficult to say how many of such moves have been precipitated by anxiety as opposed to genuine 'anti-market' and WTO-incompatible moves. At the end of the day, panic responses through the WTO grievance redressal route or shying away from a formal bilateral trade pact, are not the options for gaining competitiveness. The latter can be acquired only through expeditious domestic policy reforms that correct existing distortions in land and labour markets and reduce transactions and operating costs for Indian manufacturing.

The similarity of concerns between the two economies also provides them the common ground for collaborations. One of the most apt concerns in this regard is the cooperation over climate change. The Copenhagen Summit in December 2009 found both countries preparing in collaboration for pushing an action agenda that was more consistent with their development concerns and burden-sharing aspects. The climate change agenda is expected to draw both countries closer in the foreseeable future. There could be other similar concerns produced by the shifting dynamics of a globalised world order that may encourage both countries to explore greater collaboration.

It is important to note that on the economic plane, bilateral relations have not become inordinately strained. On the contrary, economics probably provides the best ground for pragmatic and positive exchanges between the two countries. This is notwithstanding the odd friction over contentious issues such as permits for Chinese workers in electricity and construction projects in India. In international forums such as the IMF, World Bank, WTO, G20 and the East Asian Summit (EAS), China and India have not yet adopted conflicting positions, unlike in non-economic domains like the UN, specifically the Security Council, or nuclear issues.

Both countries, obviously, have to accept the reality that in a globalised world, competition between the two fastest growing economies is inevitable since both are trying to secure additional strategic space. Such competition will create tensions over access to greater natural resources, commodities and energy. A case in point is the continent of Africa. There are concerns on the Indian side over Chinese FDI and aid beyond that deployed in Africa for obtaining larger strategic gains. Beyond Africa, perceptions of some potential strategic conflicts are also visible in South Asia and Southeast Asia.

Stated in simple terms, however, both countries are learning to adjust to each other's economic rise and the impact that their respective rises will have on the global economy. In this regard, it appears that there is quite a bit of mutual respect between two countries. At the same time, there is also a carefully crafted pragmatism guiding bilateral engagement on both sides. The pragmatism is based on the assumption that while certain outstanding political differences will take time to resolve, such differences should not affect economic interaction and mutually beneficial cooperation. Prevalence of such pragmatism in the medium term should see much stronger bilateral ties with economics providing the fundamentals of the bonding.

❋

Notes

1. According to the latest available Census of India (2001), 72.2 per cent of the country's population lives in rural areas.
2. India's simple average bound tariff rate is 50.2 per cent, while Brazil's, China's and Russia's are 31.4 per cent, 10.2 per cent and 11.4 per cent respectively. Russia is not a member of the WTO. Information on tariffs of the other countries is available from World Tariff Profiles (2010) of the World Trade Organisation (WTO), available at http://www.wto.org/english/thewto_e/whatis_e/tif_e/org6_e.htm (accessed 3 August 2011).
3. The ICOR measures the additional units of capital required for achieving an additional unit of output. A lower value of ICOR indicating lesser units of capital required for obtaining an additional unit of output suggests greater efficiency in use of capital and also implies that relatively lesser infusion of capital can generate more growth.
4. A porcelain or clay rice bowl breaks upon being dropped, whereas an iron bowl does not, thereby allowing its repeated use. The metaphorical implication is that employees went unpunished despite repeated mistakes.
5. 'Various studies indicate that Indian labour laws are highly protective of labour, and labour markets are relatively inflexible. . . . Perhaps there

are lessons to be learnt from China in the area of labour reforms. China, with a history of extreme employment security, has drastically reformed its labour relations and created a new labour market, in which workers are highly mobile.' *Economic Survey,* Ministry of Finance, Government of India, available at http://indiabudget.nic.in (accessed 4 August 2011).

6. See (a) *National Strategy for Manufacturing,* National Manufacturing Competitiveness Council, Government of India, 2006, http://nmcc. nic.in/pdf/strategy_paper_0306.pdf (accessed 3 August 2011), (b) The Indian prime minister's address delivered to a conference of chief ministers on Panchayati Raj, June 2004 and (c) *Eleventh Five Year Plan (2007–2012), Inclusive Growth,* vol. 1, Planning Commission, Government of India, New Delhi: Oxford University Press, 2008 for various references in official documents to lessons to be learnt from China's economic success.

7. In cross-country correlations, it is impossible to establish a link between GDP growth and democracy. The relationship is simply not robust enough, especially if one excludes natural resource-based economies.

9. The assertions are on the basis of bilateral trade in goods. Data on bilateral trade in services is not available in public domain. The actual volume of trade would be much larger including services.

10. Amitendu Palit, 'Why Fear Cheap Chinese Imports?', *Financial Express,* 13 November 2009, available at http://www.financialexpress.com/news/whyfearcheapchineseimports/544836/ (accessed 4 April 2010).

11. See http://commerce.nic.in/ftpa/cnt.asp (accessed 26 December 2009).

12. See http://commerce.nic.in/eidb/ecntcomnext.asp (accessed 18 December 2009).

13. See Amitendu Palit and Shounkie Nawani, 'India–China Trade: Explaining the Imbalance', Institute of South Asian Studies (ISAS), National University of Singapore (NUS), Working Paper no. 95, October 2009, available at http://www.isasnus.org/events/workingpapers/94.pdf (accessed 26 December 2009).

14. See http://www.indianembassy.org.cn/DynamicContent.aspx?MenuId =3&SubMenuId=0 (accessed 26 December 2009).

15. See http://www.isas.nus.edu.sg/Attachments/PublisherAttachment/ISAS_Insights_96_-_Email_-_India's_Look_East_Policy_(Revised)_06042010133656.pdf (accessed 9 April 2010).

16. Ibid.

17. See http://www.mofat.go.kr/english/econtrade/fta/consideration/KCJ/index.jsp (accessed 27 December 2009).
See http://www.reuters.com/article/idUSPEK18244120090331 (Accessed 27 December 2009).

18. See *Annual Report, 2005–06*, Directorate General of Anti-dumping and Allied Duties, available at http://commerce.nic.in/traderemedies/ ANNUAL_REPORT_2005_2006.pdf?id=1 (accessed 4 August 2011). China accounts for almost 50 per cent of India's anti-dumping investigations. There is a problem with matching Indian data on anti-dumping investigations with WTO data, since the classifications are different. There is greater leeway with anti-dumping procedures against China, since China's accession agreement to WTO doesn't allow it to have 'market economy' status until 2016.

6

Nepal
A Benign Neighbourhood Power

Shambhu Ram Simkhada

The genesis of the term 'Rising China' may invoke debates, but the qualifier 'rising' is used so often that it seems part of the name.[1] Impressive economic growth, steady defence modernisation, political and diplomatic confidence and the spectacular Olympics in Beijing have secured China's place on the global 'high table'.[2]

Nepal's relations with China are age-old and it is a close witness to China's phenomenal rise in modern times. Asymmetric in size and power and with different political systems, Nepalese see China as a friendly neighbour ready to help whenever it can and a benign power maintaining a 'hands off' policy in its internal affairs.[3] In such a context, the mainstream Nepali perception of Rising China is friendly and favourable.

Perceptions are formed by one's understanding of history, cultural and religious affinities, and crucial external relations and roles affecting internal developments. Perceptions change with political predispositions, world views and interests of changing political elites, their socio-economic, cultural and religious priorities. To quote Henry Kissinger, 'Personality and policy could never be fully divorced'.[4] In 'Hypotheses on Misperception', Robert Jervis says perceptions, when they deteriorate into misperceptions, can create havoc.[5] While China is rising, Nepal is changing the entire spectrum of its politics, history, culture, religion, values, institutions and actors. An understanding of such changes is essential in empathising with Nepal's perceptions of a rising China.

What strikes one about China is not just its physical size and mammoth economic momentum, but also the surprise it has often sprung on outside observers. Although coloured largely by the stereotypes nurtured over time, with unprecedented access to information and knowledge, national perceptions are also influenced by regional and global developments. There are, of course, questions of space and time; or, is it politics or economics, war or peace that determine the rise and fall of great powers? Tibet, the central cord linking China–Nepal relations, has many strings and knots that demand a much deeper and wider understanding to keep it intact.

Beyond conceptual complexities, external dynamics and internal changes, a common concern of most Nepalese when talking of a rising China is the historical experience of conflict and violence associated with the rise and fall of great powers. Most prosperous democracies of today are built on the foundation of the 'happiness of the people' leveraged with social safety and economic prosperity but subordinated to the demands of national security. With this knowledge and experience, the central questions in the minds of most Nepalese as we observe and admire the rise of China today are: Will it remain a peaceful process as it has been so far? And how skillfully will the drivers of the 'Four Modernisations' speed-craft navigate towards the democracy lane, with Chinese characteristics, based on some basic universal values?[6]

In trying to explore this complex subject, for thematic clarity and methodological simplification, this chapter is divided into three sections. In the first we will analyse China's impressive economic growth and defence modernisation and discuss how Nepalese look at those developments as well as China's political and diplomatic role. In the second section, major constituencies that help create, cultivate, and sustain Nepal's perceptions of a rising China are identified and explained with a discussion of how the equations among them could change and how such changes may in turn influence perceptions. In the third section, an attempt is made to draw a picture of China–South Asia relations and how this relationship is likely to evolve over time economically, strategically as well as politically and diplomatically. The chapter ends with a three-scenario analysis and some concluding thoughts.

China's Economic Growth and Defence Modernisation:

On the correlation between a nation's economic growth and military capability, historian Paul Kennedy writes in his *Rise and Fall of Great Powers*, 'wealth is usually needed to underpin military power, and military power is usually needed to acquire and protect wealth'.[7] China's defence modernisation is the outcome of its growing economic strength and as the economy grows, China will further strengthen its military capability and modernise its defence forces.

To delve a little deeper into China's economic growth, defence build-up, its political and diplomatic roles, let us first turn to Table 6.1 which presents a comparative profile of China on four separate dimensions, namely background and social infrastructure, state of economy, security, and politics vis-à-vis nine other states, on a total of twenty-four variables. In physical size, China is third after Russia and USA, but in population, it overtakes every other country. In ethnic homogeneity, China enjoys an obvious advantage, although the riots in Tibet in 2008, and persistent violence in Xinjiang show China is not immune from the complexities of identity politics. In literacy, it has already overtaken Brazil and India but what is even more striking is its share of the tertiary level students in science, mathematics, and engineering enrolled as a percentage of the total in universities, which happens to be the highest (53 per cent). Although the R&D human power is significantly behind Japan, USA, Russia, and Germany, it is far ahead of Brazil, Indonesia and India. The shift in Human Development Index (HDI) in the forty-five years between 1960 and 2005 was, moreover, a significant one.

In the economic sector, whereas the Gross National Income (GNI) per capita is way down compared to the top economies of the world, China is surging ahead faster than a number of developing economies with a total GNP that ranks favourably with the highest ranking states. The figure for trade shows a high dependence outside (72 per cent) and in FDI, China ranks next only to the USA. Whereas the figures for poverty and inequality appear to give it a medium status, column B9 in the table shows it as the most opaque system. The figures in the security sector

TABLE 6.1: A comparative profile of China

Countries	A1 Surface area sq. km² (000)	A2 Population million	A3 Ethnic Homogeneity Index (EHI) %	A4 Internet Users (mn)	A5 Adult Literacy %	A6 Tertiary Students in Sc., Maths & Eng (% of Total)	A7 Researcher in R&D per mn Pop	A8 HDI 1960	A9 HDI 2005	B1 Arable Land %	B2 Urbanisation %	B3 GNI US $ bn	B4 GNI per capita PPP US $	B5 Trade as % of GDP	B6 FDI US $ bn	B7 Pop below income poverty $1 a day %	B8 Inequality	B9 Opacity Index	C1 Defense Budget US $ bn	C2 Total Armed Forces (000)	C3 Pop/Soldier Ratio	D1 Governance	D2 Gross Human Rights Violation (GHRV)	D3 Press Freedom
1. Brazil	8,515	192	–	25.9	89	22	344	.394	.800	7	84	1,133	9,370	26	18.8	7.5	65.8	61	13.1	287	641	0.09	4	31
2. China	9,598	1,320	88	111.0	91	53	708	.248	.777	11	40	3,121	5,370	72	78	9.9	12.7	87	29	2,255	580	-0.21	3	80
3. Germany	357	82	–	48.7	100	31	3,261	.841	.935	34	75	3,197	33,820	85	43.4	–	7.1	64	30.2	285	290	1.45	1	13
4. India	3,287	1,123	11	50.6	61	25	119	.206	.619	54	29	1,069	2,740	49	17.4	34.3	9.5	64	22	1,325	848	0.06	4	42
5. Indonesia	1,904	226	24	18.0	90	28	207	.223	.728	13	48	373	3,580	57	5.5	18.2	6.6	75	2.5	302	729	-0.87	4	47
6. Japan	378	128	100	86.3	100	23	5,287	.686	.953	12	66	4,813	34,600	68	-6.7	–	4.5	60	44.7	260	492	1.19	1	23
7. Nepal	147	28	30	.17	49	14	59	.128	.534	16	16	10	1,040	45	-7mn	24.1	9.3		.1	69	385	-0.46	2	57
8. Russia	17,098	142	12	23.7	99	18	3,319		.802	12	73	1,071	14,400	68	30.8		23.3	84	18.8	1,027	140	-0.64	4	60
9. S. Africa	1,219	48	12	3.6	–	18	307	.464	.674	12	69	274	9,560	45	-0.1	10.7	42.5	60	3.4	56	843	0.36	4	23
10. USA	9,632	302	50	203.8	100	–	4,605	.865	.951	19	81	13,887	45,850	76	180.6	–	16.6	36	460.5	1,546	191	1.41	–	15

Note: Figures are rounded to the nearest percentage point where appropriate.

Abbreviations: HDI = Human Development Report; WDR = World Development Report; WABF = World Almanac and Book of Facts (WABF), New York: Pharos Books, 2007, pp. 745-845.

Col. A: 1-WDR 2009, TAI; Ibid, T1, T5; 3_Kurian, T 32; 4_WABF 2007, Nations of the World, pp. 745-845; 5-WDR 2009, T1; 6-HDR 2002, T10; 7-HDR 2007, T13; 9-Ibid, T2;

Col. B: 1-WDR 2009, TAI; 2-HDR 2007/08, T5; 3-WDR 209, T1; 4-Ibid.; 5-WDR 2009, T1; TB4; 6-Ibid., T4; 7HDR 2007/08, T3; 8 HDR 2002, T13; 9-Global Corruption Report 2001 (Berlin: Transparency International, 2001), p. 278.

Col. C: 1-WABF 2007, pp. 745-845, 2-HDR 2006, T22; 3-Calculated from cols. A2 and C2 show China with the largest army in the world but a defence budget that is a small fraction of what the US spends with a pop-soldier ratio significantly below those of Germany, Japan, Russia and US. The negative figure for governance (-0.21) vis-à-vis many others suggests considerable work remains to be done in political modernisation; India faring better in that regard. But even here, China is ahead of Indonesia and Russia, even if in Gross Human Rights Violations (GHRV), it stands midway, faring worst in press freedom.

On the whole, China stands favourably in the economic sector, but in the political sphere, it may have a long way to go. On this overall canvass, an attempt will now be made to paint a picture of China's economic development, security policy, politics and diplomatic role.

Chinese Economic Miracle — Growth, Development and Progress (GDP)

To reclaim the status as a global power the People's Republic of China (PRC) embarked on economic growth above all else.

- **Impressive Economic Growth**: Between 1978 and 2007, China's GDP rose from 364.5 billion Yuan to 24.95 trillion.[8] Political stability for economic growth and economic growth absorbing the abundant supply of labour in turn nurtured political stability.

- **Successful Poverty Reduction**: Between 1981 and 2004, China's population consuming less than a dollar a day fell from 65 per cent to 10 per cent and the absolute number of the poor dropped from 652 million to 135 million.[9] The average income of the urban population increased from 343 Yuan in 1978 to 13,786 in 2007 and of farmers from 134 to 4,140. Today's China claims that the economy of shortage that plagued China for a long time has ended.[10] China remains a developing country but it has set a goal of becoming a moderately prosperous nation within the next twenty years.

- **Challenges**: Rapid economic growth has brought new challenges. Food safety, industrial security, structural-institutional problems as well as the depletion of natural resources are serious issues. China has become one of the most unequal societies. Chinese leaders have marked corruption control as one of their top agendas, confirming its growing menace. Population policy faces a serious dilemma. Unless the one child policy is changed, China could lose its advantage of abundant and cheap labour for the 'factory of the world'. If the policy is relaxed, population growth and pressure on demand for jobs and resources could become unmanageable.[11] At the same time, China is the largest producer of CO_2 emissions; it has the largest number of polluted cities and rivers and has one of the worst population/arable land ratios making food security and fresh water critical. Transition from a centrally planned to a consumer society can further aggravate social problems.

- **Development**: To address the challenges, China diversified its economic development. Massive increases in investments on Research and Development (R&D), Intellectual Property (IP) protection, legislation and enforcement, and growth in registration of patents, trademarks and domain names indicate how fast it is diversifying and integrating itself into the global economy. This year China has allocated US$ 9.2 billion for key technology R&D.[12] It is now the world's largest user of mobile phones (670 million) and the internet (298 million) with 91 per cent of these users having broadband connection. China now creates its own brand names, is entering the auto sector and has started making airplanes.

- **Progress**: From growth and development, China moved towards enhancing efficiency with equity, social welfare and environmental protection in order that all people can share in the fruits of development and step up their efforts to build an environmentally sustainable, economically progressive and socio-politically harmonious society.[13] It also stresses the importance of giving a better role to the market forces in allocating resources, promoting the establishment of a modern system of property rights and corporate management but also improving the state's macroeconomic regulations, overcoming the faults in the market itself, and ensuring dynamic, efficient and sound economic operation.[14]

- Given its high external dependence how would the current global financial crisis affect China? Foreign direct investments and exports are important, but some people see domestic shifts in investments and consumption as the main factors responsible for China's growth.[15] The government's stimulus package equivalent to US$ 586 billion aims to boost domestic demand and consumption. By placing orders of over US$ 12.2 billion of imports from Europe and continuing to invest in US financial instruments, China wants to keep the global economy open and avoid the global financial crisis leading to 'beggar thy neighbour' policies of trying to cure domestic economic problem by restricting imports.[16]

Security Policy: Defend, Deter and Deny (3Ds)

China's defence modernisation is motivated by the need to maintain stability at home, peace in the neighbourhood and to contribute to a peaceful global order. Through its military strength China seeks to defend its interests, deter any threats and deny victory to any outside involvement in the event of flare-ups in the Taiwan straits, Tibet and Xinjiang.

- China seems keen to dispel the fear of its rise as a threat to others. It is strengthening the PLA, reducing the number of defence personnel but focusing on better training, equipment and technology with particular emphasis on strategic capability, space research, and naval build-up to deal with new sources of threat and non-traditional security responses.[17]
- Competing demands of defence modernisation and social necessities and the need to channel available resources to non-military use is nowhere more pressing than in the PRC. While a general mark of opacity characterises China's overall decision-making (see Table 6.1), it may be the mode of managing its relative weakness. The publication of the White Paper on Defence, participation in joint military exercises and friendly missions, the 60th anniversary celebrations of the PLA navy with fourteen foreign navies taking part may be attempts to open up, dispel doubts and anxieties abroad, and build confidence. It may also reflect increasing

confidence and display of growing power to deter and deny. China's economic rise and military buildup make some of its neighbours nervous and give others discomfort but China wants to dispel the fear of its rise as a threat to others by invoking the old Maoist doctrine: 'If others do not make aggression toward us, we will not do it to others. If others do infringe upon us, we must retaliate.'

Politics: Reform, Replace and Reclaim (3Rs)

Reform of its politics, retaining aspects of Marxism, Leninism and Mao Zedong's thoughts that work, and replacing what does not, using ideology only in so far as it serves the national cause, emerged as the central mottos in China's post-Mao political agenda. What works and what does not is decided by the Communist Party of China (CPC).

If the vision of reclaiming past glory seemed somewhat uncertain earlier, Deng's reforms have started to make it a reality. The party and the state have delivered; people's livelihoods have improved and 'the Chinese nation . . . is now standing firm in the East'. Political power in the grip of the CPC made all this possible; so, trust the party leadership to decide on the substance, style and speed of political reforms. This in a nutshell is China's politics today.

- As reforms started to bear fruit, retaining the ideological foundation and organisational base of the CPC under a carefully groomed leadership totally committed to the core principles of the '3Rs' became the principal plank of China's politics. But they also stress on reforms to building a new generation of ideas: 'Socialism with Chinese Characteristics' under Deng, the Three 'Rs' under Jiang Zemin, and the 'Scientific Outlook of Development' under Hu Jintao.[18]
- In China, the challenge to the monopoly of power of the CPC is dealt in line with the policy of 'nip-in-the-bud'. Ruthless ousters of leaders 'deviating' from the party line and suppression of unauthorised protests with an iron fist are examples even as within the system reforms and opening up accelerate. 'Idealised expectation' of economic reforms bringing immediate and automatic transformation of China's politics into a western-style liberal democracy

creates problems of perception. The gradualist nature of political reform causes frustration. Some critics think the present generation of Chinese leaders is trying to undo the reforms started earlier but Chinese leaders claim, 'Political reforms are deepening and the people's right to run the country is better protected through the promotion of socialist democracy'.[19]

Diplomacy: Cooperate, Contain and Counteract (3Cs)

China's leaders made a dispassionate assessment that to reclaim their place in history, they needed a long period of stability at home, peace in the neighbourhood and beyond. To achieve these goals, China adopts a multi-directional diplomacy of cooperation as far as possible, containment if necessary and counteraction when absolutely essential. China decided, 'In foreign policy, national interests overrode ideological differences'.[20] This realpolitique comes from its national humiliation (*gauchi*) as well as resolve to reclaim its greatness. Henry Kissinger recounts how during his secret visit to China, Premier Zhou Enlai shared his fear 'that Europe, the Soviet Union, Japan, and the US might decide to carve China up again'.[21] Now China displays greater confidence that 'China cannot develop in isolation from the rest of the world, nor can the world enjoy prosperity and stability without China'.[22] By the phrase *tao guang yang hui*, translated as 'hide our brightness . . .', and the satire, 'the day before yesterday, I was an old friend of China; today I'm a new enemy', Deng Xiaoping and Lee Kuan Yew were cautioning that national self-confidence does not mutate into great power arrogance and ultra-nationalist chauvinism, confusing right from wrong, friends from foes.

- **China–US Relations**: The ambivalence in China–US relations reflects the admiration for US power and determination to match it, but also the realisation that their paths are different and China has a long way to go. Present Sino-US interests converge on economics. The United States' investment, technology and market played an important role in China's economic transformation. China, in turn, has invested a large part of what it has gained from its exports in buying US financial instruments and assets partly financing the massive US appetite for consumption, housing and international commitments. Eighty-two per cent of China's $2 trillion in foreign exchange reserves is in US dollars.[23] This compels both to work together. But, it is also causing unease on both sides, the American president saying, 'We can't keep borrowing from China' and the Chinese Premier admitting, 'We are concerned about the safety of our assets. To be honest, I am definitely a little worried.'[24]

- US dependence on China is growing in dealing with North Korea, Iran and Sudan as well as security concerns, resources use and climate change. But 'lack of U.S.-China cooperation does not stem from failure to recognize how much China matters. . . . It derives from mismatched interests, values and capabilities.'[25] With growing competition for markets, influence over Europe, natural resources and massive Chinese investments in Africa and the western hemisphere, the 'sole superpower' in duress may face increasing pressure to reassert the 'superiority of its values' and strategic power. The US's insistence on the 'universal' application of democracy and China's retaliation with the assertiveness of its growing national power and international clout could escalate into containment of each other at bilateral, regional and multilateral levels.

- Economic strain and political stress interfaced with security concerns such as the 'US trying to encircle China' and 'Chinese conquests of the "pivot" area which would make China the dominant geopolitical power', create a recipe for one trying to counteract the other.[26] While China may be unable to match US power far beyond its borders, it seems prepared to counter any outside pressure on its 'Five Nos': Tibet, Taiwan, Xinjiang, economic interests and human rights.

- Good Sino-US relations are vital for global peace, stability and prosperity. Characterising this relationship, the former US secretary of state, Madeline Albright, in her memo to the president writes 'you will welcome China's economic integration while worrying about the eventual impact of its ascendency on peace, democracy, and our own leadership'.[27] The best way to resolve the dilemma is through dialogue and diplomacy.

Relations with EU and Russia

Paul Kennedy thinks China sees the 'world of the future very much like the world of the past . . . (where) the powerful have the real say'.[28] But now it may be starting to appreciate the 'soft power' of the EU. The bilateral China–EU trade in 2008 reached a massive US$ 425.5 billion, though a crisis in the Euro zone and pressure on the Chinese Yuan have changed this linkage. The Euro is in the basket of currencies on which the Chinese RMB has been pegged. Brussels and Moscow could be important centres between Beijing and Washington in a multipolar world order.

Relations with Developing Countries

China continues to nurture ties with the developing world, retaining its distinctiveness but also remaining a part of them reflected by the nomenclature Group of 77 and China in the UN. China joins a 'likeminded' group in the UN's Human Rights mechanisms and supports the non-aligned movement from outside.

Sino-Japanese Relations

These relations are underscored by growing economic ties but continuing political and diplomatic unease. China's relation with North Korea, particularly on the issue of making East Asia a nuclear weapons–free zone will be testing its diplomatic skill. The grouping of the Association of South East Asian Nations (ASEAN) plus Three and the Joint Fund to stabilise Asian currencies are signs of China strengthening links with East and South East Asia. The Boao Forum and the Asia Pacific Economic Cooperation (APEC) further enhance China's diplomatic role.

International Organisations (IOs)

Economic growth, military strength and political clout will give China an increasingly important voice in international financial institutions (IFIs), the World Trade Organisation (WTO) and regional organisations such as the Asian Development Bank (ADB), and further strengthen its already vital role as a permanent member of the UN Security Council (UNSC). As China rises, its role in IOs will also come under greater scrutiny; its role for a coordinated Asian position in the UN, the restructuring of the UNSC to reflect current global realities and a voice for the developing world will be parameters on which the diplomatic role of a rising China will be perceived.

Constituencies Creating, Cultivating and Sustaining Nepal's Perceptions of a Rising China

Legend says a saint named Manjushree came from the north and with his powers, drained the water, making Kathmandu a fertile valley suitable for human settlement. Nepali princess Bhrikuti, married to a Tibetan emperor in 620 A.D., is believed to have brought Buddhism into Tibet and China by Nepali Buddhist scholars.[29] Bhrikuti's temple is a major tourist site in Lhasa and the White Pagoda constructed by Nepali sculptor Arniko stands prominently on the outskirts of Beijing. There are accounts of Chinese travelers visiting Nepal as early as the 4th century A.D. These historic, religious and cultural exchanges have created enduring perceptions of China. Against such a perspective, how do the people of Nepal view China today? To respond to such a query we first turn to the results of some recent surveys.

Empirical data on image and issue surveys are rare. One study which tried to identify the level of cognition of neighbours among the mass public brought out a curious fact: even non-neighbours were selected as neighbours, explained by high level of illiteracy (still over 50 per cent), although nearly three-fourths could clearly name China, which came second in the cognitive scale of neighbourhood ranking.[30]

In another survey, China figured as the first choice for the two front-runner left parties, Communist Party of Nepal–United Marxist Leninist (CPN–UML) and United Peoples Front of Nepal (UPFN) (who rank India as second) and second for NC but third for Nepal Sadbhawana Party (NSP) which ranks Japan as second after putting up India as its first choice. The perceived significance of a country is apparently determined by the party ideology.[31]

Another query by Himal Media in 2005 to identify country preference for peace mediation in Nepal brings out 15 per cent choosing China as a possible mediator, as the fourth choice, after India (36 per cent), UN (24 per cent), and USA (20 per cent) in a sample of 3,000 respondents.

Still another more recent survey in 2008 took up the importance the Nepalese people gave to the role of countries about what is going on in Nepal at present. China stood fourth in the category of the 'very important' in the response given by both the citizens and the MPs, superseded by India, the UN and the USA, respectively. However, MPs tended to view China as far more important in their responses compared to the citizens. Inference could thus be drawn that the level of importance attributed to a country is determined by the status and political awareness of the respondent. The rankings by both groups of respondents are similar for all the countries except for Japan and the UK for which the position is reversed. Table 6.2 indicates these preferences.

TABLE 6.2: Role of international community in Nepal's internal affairs

Q: How important is the role of the countries (or international community) (China, India, Japan, UK, USA, European Union [EU], UN) in what is going on in Nepal today?

(Total Respondents) = 4,089 (Figure in Denomination of N is the total number of respondents for each country)

Country or Int. Community	Citizens (N-4,089)			MPs (N-300)		
	N	Valid %	Rank	N	Valid %	Rank
China	635/2288	27.8	4	131/395	44.4	4
India	1,338/2646	50.6	1	227/297	76.4	1
Japan	398/2128	18.7	6	26/292	8.9	7
UK	324/2002	16.2	7	47/294	16.0	6
USA	883/2309	38.2	3	160/298	54.7	3
EU	419/1751	23.9	5	93/295	31.5	5
UN	957/1966	48.7	2	206/297	69.4	2

Source: Krishna Hachhethu with Sanjay Kumar and Jiwan Subedi, *Nepal in Transition: A Study on the State of Democracy*, Stockholm: International IDEA, 2008, pp. 120–21.

• Historically, Nepal enjoyed monopoly over lucrative trade with Tibet. With the road linking Kathmandu with Lhasa, many small traders thrive in the new market of consumer products that include clothes and shoes and electronics. One can presume that the consumer goods at affordable rates create a favourable impression of China. China now makes mobile phones, computers and cars, attracting a large body of businessmen and high-end consumers. The quality, reliability and terms of trade of these products can influence perceptions of this category of Nepali consumers.
• The Federation of Nepalese Chambers of Commerce and Industries (FNCCI) and the Chamber of Commerce (CC)

bring together the government and the private sector to deal with policies related to China. Nepal receives a large number of Chinese tourists and many western tourists visiting the Tibet Autonomous Region (TAR) of China go through Nepal. Growing road and airline links make tourism a vital mode of interaction between the two sides.[32] The Nepal–China Investment Promotion Centre monitors Chinese investments in Nepal.

Intellectuals play a crucial role in creating perceptions. But in Nepal, even the Central Department of Political Science at the Tribhuvan University (TU), for long the only institution of higher learning in the country, has started a course on China, along with one on Japan, only recently. The Center for Nepal and Asian Studies (CNAS) started analysing major developments in politics, economics, foreign and security policies of China along with many others publishing the annual *CNAS Year Review* during the late 1980s. But, in the absence of support and encouragement from the state, the effort has fizzled out. Certain non-governmental institutions like the China Study Center, China Information Centre, Arniko Samaj, media houses and individuals do some valuable work. But a comprehensive academic platform for a dispassionate discourse on Nepal's perception of Rising China on the scale that the agenda deserves does not yet exist.

A diplomat-strategist once wrote 'foreign policy is made not in reaction to the world but rather in reaction to an image of the world in the minds of the people making decisions'.[33] With the ongoing upheaval in politics, the principal actors in Nepal are changing. China itself is changing so much that it looks different to different people.

Nepal's reward or 'revenge of geography' means the Nepali landscape cannot be painted without knowing the brushes and colours of competing demands of the major external actors. As an epicentre of the political, economic and strategic cooperation and competition among the major powers, 'prescriptive' donors and intrusive International Non-government Organisations (INGOs), Nepali society is 'exposed', elites are divided and politics is polarised to the extent that not just the public but the nation-state itself, as the central institution responsible for domestic politics, economic/security policies and foreign relations, is lost. The confusion is apparent and everywhere, in the street, and among scholars, political parties, media and official policy. An analysis of the manifestos of the three main political parties during the Constituent Assembly (CA) election of 2008 shows some nuances. The Nepali Congress states 'the relationship between the two friendly neighbors India and China will be further strengthened on the basis of the principles and norms of international relations'. The UML only stresses 'Nepal will not allow its territory to be used for any activities against the interests of friendly countries'. The Communist Party of Nepal-Maoists (CPNM), now United Communist Party of Nepal (UCPN) says 'Special effort will be made to strengthen the relations with two big neighbors India and China'. The CPNM further claims to discard the traditional buffer state notion by a policy of 'acting as a dynamic bridge in the interrelationship between the two countries'. Declarations and pronouncements of leaders of all three major parties confirm the perception of China as a friendly neighbour although they have very divergent world views within them.[34]

The rise of the United Communist Party of Nepal-Maoists as a major political force has created a new 'complex'. Other political actors have been forced to react to the Maoists' agenda in Nepal today when Mao's own homeland has moved so far beyond in the path of reform (*gaige kaifang*). China maintained longstanding close relations with the now abolished monarchy. Even as the Maoists' movement strengthened and Nepal's internal conflict spread China continued to distance itself from the Nepali Maoists who were waging their so-called People's War (PW) from 1996 to 2005. After the abolition of monarchy, China realises it cannot ignore the Maoists. So, it may be testing them.

Soon after taking office in August 2008 the Maoist prime minister Pushpa Kamal Dahal attended the closing ceremony of the Beijing Olympics, ignoring the tradition of past Nepali PMs visiting India first, as some saw it, although the PM himself tried to explain the China visit as a special one and called his India visit a little later as his first official visit. Other senior Maoist leaders, including Defence Minister Ram Bahadur Thapa and Communications Minister Krishna Bahadur Mahara visited Tibet besides their official trips to Beijing in 2009. In various ways, Maoists were trying to convince China of their 'equi-proximity' policy between the two neighbours and allay the suspicion of their external support base when fighting the PW.

After the Maoists came to power, China sent a number of academic, political, economic and security delegations including one led by Foreign Minister Yang Jiechi and another by the deputy head of the People's Liberation Army, Lieutenant General Ma Xiaotian. The political and academic visits demonstrated China's wish to strengthen relations at the political level and upgrade its limited exchanges at the non-state level. The high-level PLA visits reflected China's security concerns. The new draft Treaty of Peace and Friendship to replace the one signed in 1960 presented by Assistant Foreign Minister Liu Jieye in 2009 was particularly significant.

The Chinese Communist Party maintains friendly relations with the NC and CPN-UML. During the visit of the NC delegation led by party vice president Prakash Man Singh and co-chaired by the head of the International Relations Department, Sujata Koirala, foreign minister since 2009, at the invitation of the CPC, China's leaders emphasised that changes in Nepal's politics do not affect the traditional friendly party-to-party relations. A ministerial-level CPC delegation attended the national convention of the CPN-UML and a high-level delegation led by newly elected president Jhala Nath Khanal visited China soon after that in 2009.

China sent a high-level delegation to the convention of the Madheshi Janadhikar Forum (MJF) in 2008. Its president, then foreign minister in the Maoist-led government, which many speculate had to resign in May 2009 for its overt overtures towards China, visited China. The leader of the splinter wing of the CPNM led by Matrika Yadav, also from the Madhesh region, was also invited to China. Interestingly, the CPC apparently has not yet extended an official invitation to the UCPN.

Regardless of their original platform, is it normal for Nepal's Maoists not to entertain ideological affinity with the successors of the great 'helmsman' to whose name, after all they owe their rise to power? On its part, does China too have any choice or reason but to recognise them as a force to reckon with now? How this relationship develops will profoundly affect Nepal's politics and consequently Nepal's perceptions of China. Equally significant will be the roles of the MJF, the splinter of the UCPN and other political parties as well as developments within the NC and the UML. The increased levels of exchanges not only indicate China's growing interest in Nepal but also a search for 'reliable friends' after the abolition of monarchy. The death of G. P. Koirala, leader of the NC and former prime minister, is likely to widen and intensify this search.

Which way will the traditionalist political base shift now that monarchy has been abolished? How will the democratic-progressive political mainstream fair within the new national, regional and global co-relation of forces? How will China position itself in case of a monarchist-republican, Hindu-secular or Maoist-other political parties/NA showdown if the CA fails to promulgate the new constitution again and Nepal enters into yet another phase of conflict?

How political events will play out and influence Nepal's perception of a rising China is difficult to predict. But some trends are emerging. China considers developments in Nepal too important from its own political, economic, diplomatic and security perspective. So, unlike its traditional 'hands off' policy it will try to position itself to actively exercise all three dimensions of its foreign policy in Nepal.[35]

As China's 'Go West' policy accelerates, extending major infrastructure works into the bordering areas, China–Nepal economic relations, trade, tourism, investments and financial assistance could swell to a new level, consolidating the already formidable economic and business constituency that is an important stakeholder in reinforcing Nepal's positive perception of a rising China. Chinese investments in Nepal have increased significantly and these will grow in the years to come.[36] How this constituency interacts with the formidable India and western political, economic and security lobbies would need in-depth analysis. But the proximity of geography and the role of the large international community in Nepal cannot be ignored.

Large numbers of students now go to China for higher studies. China also sends teachers for Chinese language courses in several institutes in Nepal. The Kathmandu University has established the Confucius Institute to promote the study of Chinese language and culture. A number of Nepali publishers are also supplying textbooks to China. A large number of official, business, political parties' and civil society/academic delegations are invited to

China. Meanwhile the number of such delegations from China is also increasing. Such exchanges will certainly help create new impressions of its achievements and cultivate new perceptions of China.

The Nepal Army (previously the Royal Nepal Army) was known to be under the direct control of Nepal's monarchy which was reasonably friendly towards China. Now that Nepal is a republic, China's interest in Nepal's army is growing as reflected by the visits of high-profile Chinese military delegations, their meetings with senior army and other security officials as well as interest in the integration of the Maoist combatants.[37]

Media plays a vital role in shaping perceptions and influencing policies. According to the Media Directory of the Department of Information, Government of Nepal, currently there are 4,871 newspapers of which 365 are dailies and 1,778 weeklies. Ten televisions channels and some 100 radio stations play a critical role as a source of information and viewpoints. But all of them depend on the major global networks as their source for international news. Many media outlets, mostly the vernacular weeklies, are also under the influence of some political parties or groups making them highly biased in their coverage.

Growing global interest in the Himalayan ecosystems, research on melting glaciers and high altitude health conditions and medicines to Tibetan culture, society and tourism are bound to create a spill-over on both sides of the Himalayas. Hollywood actors use local TV channels in Kathmandu to promote the Tibetan cause. Press reports of the Tibetan Youth Congress activities, pressure to reopen the Office of the Dalai Lama and demonstrations by Tibetans in front of the Chinese embassy or the UN office and China's reaction are bound to give headaches to officials in Kathmandu. The Khampa movement, till the closing of its Mustang camp in 1974 after operations by the Nepal army, was believed to have been linked to the sudden departure of some foreigners supposed to have been engaged in academic work but apparently involved in something else. Even trekking and mountaineering can draw political attention as some trekkers tried to unfurl a Tibetan flag just before the Beijing Olympics in 2008. Media highlights on the visits of Kathmandu-based ambassadors to Nepal's tourist destinations such as Mustang (which was the centre of the Khampa movement) show that tourism too has political and security interests. Table 6.3 tries to broadly classify some of these constituencies to illustrate their nature, components, interests and roles.

Gunnar Myrdal once said every theory contains the seed of an *a priori* thought. Any China watcher is aware of the intensity of pro-Tibet demonstrations and the interest they attract from certain civil society organisations, NGOs and INGOs, human rights groups and activists and even some sections of the international community and the media. The increase in the number of monasteries and monks is visible around Kathmandu. The visit of some members of Nepal's Constituent Assembly to meet the Dalai Lama on the initiative of some NGOs, in 2009, the reaction of the Chinese embassy and the explanation of the foreign ministry became public recently. One can assume that what comes to the public domain is a small fraction of the larger contention over Tibet playing out in Nepal.

Given the paucity of data and information in the open academic discourse, it is not only difficult to identify particular organisations broadly classified in the table but impossible to either suggest how they will change or affect Nepal's perception of a rising China right now. Despite these difficulties, two general observations, however, may be in order. First, compared to the state to state interactions at the para- and non-state levels (political party to parties, enterprises to enterprises and people to people levels as well as international organisations — intergovernmental and non-governmental) interactions are likely to increase. Second, as such interactions grow, both the proximity and sensitivity marking Nepal–China relations are likely to emerge as delicate but crucially significant elements in sustaining and changing perceptions. How both sides respond to such interactions could impinge on the traditional Nepali perceptions of a rising China.

China and South Asia

The eight members of the South Asian Association for Regional Cooperation (SAARC) are situated at the southern edge of the Eurasian landmass having vital links with the heartlands of Central Asia and the sea lanes of the Indian Ocean. All SAARC members are developing countries and China shares common borders with five of them. China and South Asia combined

TABLE 6.3: Constituencies and their prospective roles in Nepal–China relations

Constituency	Components	Nature of Interest and Role Area	Track Level and Continuity I = Formal State II = Elite Middle Class III = Public (Mass)	Level of Functioning at Present (1–5 pt very low to very high scale)
1. Political	Government, Pol. Parties, Bureaucracy, Diplomatic Sector	Historical, Power Relations, Policy Making and Planning Regular	I	Medium
2. Military	Army, Police Force	Security	II	Low Intermittent
3. Commercial	Traders, Industrialists	Part Historical, Economic (Business, entrepreneurship)	II, III Fragmented	Low
4. Professional/ Academic (Socio-cultural)	Teachers, Professors, Area Experts, Observers, Students, Tourists, Artists, Non-resident Citizens	Historical, S&T, R&D, Education, Socialisation, Mobilisation	II, III	Low Sporadic
5. Media	Journalists (Press, Electronic Media)	Communication, Image Formation	II	Low Occasional
6. Civil Society	NGOs, Friendship Organisations	Bridge-building, Solidarity	II, III	Very Low Rare
7. Regional	SAARC and Agencies	Interaction, Collaboration	I, II	Very Low Rare
8. Transnational	INGOs, MNCS	Mediation, Cooperation, Trade	II	Very Low Sparse
9. Global	UNO, World Bank	Mediation, Reconciliation, Resource Flow, Technology Input	I, II	Low Rare
10. Non-statutory	Insurgents, Spoilers	Image Attrition, Balance of Stakes and Interests	II, III	Medium to Low Occasional

Source: Compiled by the author and his research team.

represent almost 12 per cent of the world's area, 43 per cent of the world's population, 26 per cent of the armed forces and considerable arms expenditure, three of the world's recognised nuclear powers, are home to most of the world's major religions and civilisations, and have a variety of political systems. Together, China–South Asia relations are economically and diplomatically significant, strategically vital and politically crucial.

China–South Asia Economic Cooperation

China and South Asia together represent one of the most important areas of economic growth and cross-border trade. The level of development and structure of their economies, some dependent on agriculture and export of mainly primary products, others already moving up in the value chain, high-tech and IT, make the two sides of the Himalayas highly complementary to each other.

For improving China–South Asia cooperation both sides will have to improve their infrastructure internally as well as across their borders. They can join hands in the development of transport, communication and transit as well as energy (hydro, wind and solar power). South Asia needs infrastructure for economic development and China and India have the interest and resources to build that. Japan also, as an observer in SAARC, adds to the potential of such cooperative development. The increasing focus of China to its southwest along with massive build-up of infrastructure and investment and the recent decision of SAARC to start a train service from Pakistan to Bangladesh via India and Nepal create great potential of enhanced China–South Asia economic cooperation.

By creating better connectivity, tourism can be one of the most important avenues of further cooperation between the two sides. Labour mobility too can improve productivity and strengthen cooperation. Situated between the world's two countries with the largest populations, fastest growing economies and because of its friendship with both, Nepal enjoys tremendous potential as a transit point for trade, tourism, investment, transport and communication.

Rich history, culture, traditional wisdom and modern knowledge create great potential for strengthening the understanding of different political experiences and development thinking.

Exchange programmes between Chinese and South Asian academic institutions can enhance 'partnership in ideas' crucial for cooperation in policies and programmes.

China's huge trade surplus with the US–EU but deficit with South East Asia is an indication of its role as an engine of growth for that region. Vivek Bharati suggests, 'Very soon China will most probably integrate South Asian countries into its manufacturing economy'.[38] India's economy could also do the same for South Asia.

Poverty is the main problem of South Asia, its eradication one of the main goals of SAARC. Chinese experience in poverty reduction could be useful for SAARC.

China–South Asia Security Relations

The South Asian security environment is complicated by its historic 'outward look' and extraregional interests. This has brought Rising China increasingly closer to the South Asian security scene.

India–China relations will profoundly influence South Asia–China cooperation. The ground breaking visit of the late prime minister Rajiv Gandhi in 1988 opened the door for a new era in India–China relations. One of India's most senior leaders and present finance minister, Pranab Kumar Mukherjee, quotes Chinese Premier Wen Jiabao as saying, 'The time when China and India enjoyed friendly relations lasted 2000 years or 99.9 percent of total time of our interactions. . . . The conflict between our two countries only lasted two years or less than 0.01 percent of the total time of our interactions.' Highlighting the difference between the rise of great powers in Europe and Asia, Mukherjee himself writes: 'It is imperative that we create such collaborative spaces that feed each other's strength and do not exploit the differences.'[39]

Strategic partnership between two emerging global superpowers is a positive development. Their relations with other SAARC members will impinge on their bilateral ties. China is one of Pakistan's key strategic allies. Pakistan is also a strategically of the United States.[40] This relationship has been strengthened by Pakistan's frontline position in the US war on terror. China's concerns could only increase with increasing US troops in Afghanistan. This will lead China to further consolidate the security side of the Shanghai Cooperation Organisation (SCO) as well as strengthen relations with Iran in the West and Myanmar in the east. As China does not see South Asia as a real threat, relations between them can strengthen regional peace and security.

South Asia has already been identified as 'the most dangerous place on earth'. South Asia remains a 'hot spot' in China's security thinking whereas others see China's ascendency leading to an eventual situation of confrontation. Some observers have gone to the extent of warning that a confrontation first between India and China and then China and America is inevitable making Nepal a *Kuruchhetra* (battlefield).[41] Bharat Verma, a recognised defence expert and editor of the *India Defence Review* goes so far as to predict a Chinese attack on India by 2012.[42]

China, India and Pakistan's nuclear weapons capability makes the central Himalayas the most nuclear-locked region of the world. Afghanistan, the latest addition to SAARC, and Pakistan, one of its founding members, are the focal points of the world's superpower's *war on terror*. Sri Lanka is just emerging from a devastating ethnic war; Bangladesh and parts of India are under strain. With internal turmoil, intra-regional discord and extra-regional demands, all that is needed to push the region over the threshold is a trigger. Such a scenario naturally makes Nepal vulnerable and Nepalis extremely sensitive and worried.

China–South Asia Political/Diplomatic Relations

China and South Asia have different political systems and experiences but share many common problems. Poverty and political violence are the main problems of South Asia and China has tackled these problems differently.

While China enjoys a greater degree of ethnic homogeneity and internal stability, the violence in Tibet last year and Xinjiang recently demonstrates that it is not immune from problems of ethnic conflict besides other challenges of change. On internal conflicts in its neighbourhood, to the extent that it thinks they are not serious, China will 'watch the fire from the other side of the river'. It will get involved only if it must and will do so in support of the government. This explains China's role in Nepal during the Maoist insurgency or its support to Sri Lanka in its fight against the LTTE.

Nepali Maoists successfully challenged the traditional Nepali state and increasing tactics of violence of the Indian Maoists is creating problems in India. The undercurrent between China and India, but also involving neighbours, is reflected in the serious reports coming from non-official channels so far on both sides. These cases make greater China–South Asia consultation and cooperation extremely important to prevent the politics of conflict and chaos taking a greater toll on both sides of the Himalayas.

China and India can act as twin engines to lift the region out of poverty and political violence by strengthening SAARC and SCO. China and South Asia together represent an over-whelmingly large majority of troop contributions to UN's peace-keeping work. Would it not make sense for them to start thinking of cooperation to extinguish the fire engulfing their own house and neighbourhood as they go around the globe doing that so splendidly?

Proximity adds vitality but also complexity and sensitivity in inter-state relations demanding high priority and careful hand-ling.[43] Tibet looms large in China–South Asia relations. The presence of the Dalai Lama and a large number of Tibetan refugees in India and Nepal cannot be wished away. The advocates of the traditional Tibetan cause may see the present Dalai Lama as their last best hope whose departure from the scene would greatly weaken their cause. Thus Dalai Lama's age and health could exert pressure on the supporters of the Tibetan cause to intensify their campaign, perhaps around some of the anniversaries and the Shanghai Expo as they did before the Beijing Olympics. China may succeed in getting Nepal and India to clamp down harder on the Tibetan refugees on the South Asian side but China will have do its part to prevent unrest within or the outflow from Tibet. As a large power, India can exercise its options. But, given the centrality of Tibet in China–Nepal relations, how they respond to the diverse demands of the various national and international actors, remaining steadfast to the One China Policy is going to test the diplomatic skill of Nepal's republican rulers.

The Himalayas represent both the connection and separation of China and South Asia creating the ambivalence of closeness and distance at the same time. But if the British, French, Germans, Swiss, Italians and Austrians can connect and interconnect through networks of tunnels underneath the ocean and across the Alps, aircrafts in the sky and remodel their statecrafts through vertical and horizontal evolutions of their institutions, why can't the great trans-Himalayan civilisations that dominated the early world start thinking about combining their traditional wisdom and modern knowledge for a new stage of China–South Asia relations?[44]

China's efforts to impress everyone that its rise is not at the cost of others have historical underpinnings. To quote a respected western scholar, 'the Chinese apparently never plundered and murdered — unlike the Portuguese, Dutch, and other European invaders of the Indian Ocean' later.[45] Such assurances notwithstanding, lessons of history that 'the rise of a new power has often led to war, whether caused by the desire of that power to spread its wings or the attempt by rivals to smother it in the nest' cannot be ignored.[46] Wise consul does suggest 'China's rise need not lead to war' but hastens to warn 'but this doesn't mean war or other violent clashes won't happen.'[47]

A trans-Himalayan institute of higher learning bringing thinkers from both sides to create new convergence of ideas and ideologies for a peaceful and tolerant, democratic-progressive political centre, promoting economic prosperity and eradicating violence emanating from political extremism and religious fundamentalism could go a long way in building trust, confidence and credibility for a new future of China and South Asia rising together in peace and cooperation. This could develop the foundation for a new Asian partnership for peace.

Great Power Syndrome and Scenario Analysis

Nepal is located between India and China. That is a fact of geography. China and India are changing. That is also a reality. It may yet be too early to hypothesise that Rising China and Shining India will take on the garb of Great Powers soon, despite hangovers of history and memories on either side (*Middle Kingdom* and *Greater India*). But the relevance such a curiosity induces is hard to deny outright. The question that comes to mind then is: Will China and India go the way of the other great powers as and when they do attain the status anticipated for them in the future? If they do, how are the relations between them likely to affect Nepal?

All the five dimensions of great power status — physical size (area, population and strategic location), economic growth, military strength (power), cultural base, and political will are likely to favour China and India towards such status sooner or later. But what form such a development takes is going to be determined by five elements, consequences of the overall rise, but which in the long term can also profoundly influence the ultimate outcome, even the sustenance and the destiny of each state. These are: hegemonic and non-hegemonic roles played by each actor, the use and avoidance of coercion in demands projected, the competition vs cooperation modes evolved in sharing resources, the success of the future international regime in observing global ethics and enforcing a humanitarian rule of law and mediating conflicts, and finally, the level of alienation and acceptance from the global community. What happens to China and India as great powers in the future is thus going to be the product of interplay of these five elements.

It is also against this same background that a threefold scenario may be envisaged at this point. Scenario one posits an authoritarian polity with robust economy, secure military strength, aggressive nationalism, and assertive power projection in the neighbourhood and beyond. In Scenario two, contradictions of the politics of identity and livelihood, socio-economic disparities and dislocations and massive environmental disasters, products of an increasing gap between the rulers and the ruled in the absence of adequate political spaces to address them could bring implosion spawning conflict and instability at home and massive trans-border flows of populations causing instability also in the surrounding areas. A more likely and desirable scenario, however, is the third, an arduous if relatively painless transformation into a democratic-accommodative order, just and tolerant society at home and sober foreign policy sustaining the peaceful rise (*heping jueqi*) of China.

Neither Mao's nor Deng's departure brought the chaos that many feared. If the world community cooperates, the erstwhile power rivals condescend and compromise and the new leaders manage the challenges of change with wisdom and foresight, China's future transformation can yet prove to be more painless and freer from the risks and insecurities for itself, its neighbourhood and beyond. Nepalese remain hopeful of this last scenario for tomorrow even as they watch and admire the spectacular rise of China today.

Conclusions

The last year of the first decade of the 21st century, 2009, dubbed as the Asian Century, is an important year for China. It was the sixtieth year of the founding of the PRC and the first year after the successful Beijing Olympics. In-between these sixty years China has gone through many ups and downs but on the whole it has achieved significant successes in economic development, defence modernisation, political reforms and integration into the global system through its diplomatic role. Despite its impressive transformation China remains a developing country but it has set a clear goal of becoming a moderately advanced nation within the first half of this century.

China's early emphasis on economic growth is being diversified to a broad-based development to ensure progress for a prosperous, sustainable and harmonious society. Its security policy of defend, deter and deny seeks to maintain stability at home, peace in the neighbourhood and to contribute to a peaceful global order. China's politics is focused on reforms retaining the ideology of Marxism-Leninism and Mao Zedong thoughts only so far as they serve the national cause, replace what does not work to ultimately reclaim its rightful place as a great power. China's foreign policy is an extension of its clearly defined national interest (goal), diplomacy as a tool to cooperate with the developed world, neighbours and developing countries as far as possible, contain if necessary and counteract when absolutely essential. With these policies China is marching resolutely towards its goal. Although passing through some traumatic times, particularly since the introduction of Deng Xiaoping's reforms and opening up, China has made great achievements. The 2008 Beijing Olympics is the most spectacular show-case of this success.

While China is rising, Nepal has been undergoing radical changes. Despite internal upheavals Nepalese perceptions of a rising China continue to be favourable and friendly. If there is a trace of concern it has to do with the stereotypes of history or the dilemmas societies have encountered in their course of history making. The anxiety is exacerbated by Nepal's own recent traumas reinforced by the surrounding environment in South Asia.

But these experiences may also help in creating, cultivating and sustaining a more favourable perception of China and what it has been able to achieve so far; maintaining stability at home, eradicating poverty and improving the living standards of its people and contribute to prosperity in the neighbourhood and peace in the world. Such a perception could provide impetus for an enhanced level of interaction not just between China and Nepal but with the whole of South Asia, further strengthening trans-Himalayan cooperation. This surely will depend on what happens in Nepal, South Asia and elsewhere. But the main role, as the prime mover and shaker in this show will, no doubt, be that of China itself.

❋

Notes

1. Although many of the ideas behind the concept of the peaceful rise of China are said to have come from the New Security Concept formulated by China's think tanks in the mid-1990s, the term itself was first used in a speech by the former vice principal of the Central Party School in late 2003 during the Boao Forum for Asia. However, the term proved controversial among the Chinese leadership, in part because some officials thought the use of the word 'rise' could connote the fall of someone else and fuel perceptions that China is a threat to the established order. So, at the 2004 Boao Forum President Hu Jintao used the phrase 'China's peaceful development'. See 'Lee Kuan Yew Reflects', *Time Asia*, 5 December 2005 on the rise of China. Also see Madeline Albright, *Memo to the President: How We Can Restore America's Reputation and Leadership*, New York: Harper Perennial, 2001, p. 201 and Kishore Mahbubani, *The New Asian Hemisphere: The Irresistible Shift of Global Power to the East*, New York: Public Affairs, 2008.

2. In addition to the sporting side, the successful hosting of the Olympics represents national status in terms of individual caliber, political stability, economic prosperity and national prestige, power and security. The author was in China soon after the Beijing Olympics and could observe the confidence, almost a sense of having come of age, in Chinese political and government leaders and people for having hosted such a successful Olympics. See also discussion paper by Shambhu Ram Simkhada, 10 January, 2009 Kathmandu Nepali Congress, International Relations Department Discussion with Prof. Zhang Yuyan, director, Institute of Asia Pacific Studies and the delegation of the Chinese Academy of

Social Science, Nepal Research Visit programme with Nepali scholars and professionals.

3. Before being declared a republic in 2008 Nepal was a Hindu kingdom. In 1995 Nepal was ruled by a Marxist-Leninist minority government for nine months and in 2008-9 a coalition government under Prime Minister Pushpa Kamal Dahal, president of the Communist Party of Nepal-Maoist (CPNM) came to power. Both the communist governments were popularly elected.

4. Walter Issacson, *Kissinger: A Biography*, New York: Simon and Schuster, 2005, p. 344.

5. Klaus Knoor (ed.), *Power, Strategy and Security*, New Delhi: Asian, Books, 2nd Reprint, 1987, pp. 152-77.

6. The Four Modernisations are Economy, Agriculture, Science and Technology and Defence.

7. Paul Kennedy, *The Rise and Fall of the Great Powers: Economic Change and Military Conflict from 1500 to 2000*, London: Fontana Press, Collins Publishing Group, 1989, p. xvi.

8. Speech at the meeting marking the thirtieth anniversary of reform and opening up by Hu Jintao, general secretary of the CPC Central Committee, 18 December 2008.

9. 'From Poor Areas to Poor People: China's Evolving Poverty Reduction Agenda', An assessment of poverty and inequality in China, report of the Poverty Reduction and Economic Management Department, East Asia and Pacific Region, The World Bank, Washington DC, March 2009.

10. See speech at the meeting marking the thirtieth anniversary of reform and opening up, p. 3.

11. See *Global Times*, 14 May 2009.

12. *China Daily* via Xinhua, 13 May 2009.

13. See speech at the meeting marking the thirtieth anniversary of reform and opening up.

14. Ibid.

15. Albert Keidel, 'China's Economic Rise — Fact and Fiction', Policy Brief 61, July 2008, Carnegie Endowment for International Peace, p. 4.

16. See *Beijing Review*, 7 March 2009.

17. White Paper on National Defence, 2008, available at http://english. gov.cn/official/2009-01/20/content_1210227.htm (accessed 14 August 2011).

18. Ibid.

19. See Derek Scissors, 'Deng Undone The Costs of Halting Market Reforms in China', *Foreign Affairs*, vol. 88, no. 3, May/June 2009, pp. 24-39.

See speech at the meeting marking the thirtieth anniversary of reform and opening up.

20. Henry Kissinger, *Years of Upheaval*, Canada: Little Brown and Co., 1982, p. 67.
21. Ibid., p. 49.
22. See speech at the meeting marking the thirtieth anniversary of reform and opening up.
23. *The International Herald Tribune*, 20 May 2009.
24. See http://www.bloomberg.com/apps/news?pid=newsarchive&sid=aJsS b4qtILhg&refer=worldwide (accessed 14 August 2011). Also see http://www.guardian.co.uk/world/2009/mar/14/china-us-economy (accessed 14 August 2011).
25. Elizabeth C. Economy and Adam Segal, 'The G-2 Mirage, Why the United States and China Are Not Ready to Upgrade Ties', *Foreign Affairs*, vol. 88, no. 3, May/June 2009, pp. 14–23.
26. See Robert D. Kaplan, 'The Revenge of Geography', *Foreign Policy*, no. 172, May/June 2009, p. 96.
27. Madeleine Albright, *Memo to the President*, p. 203
28. Kennedy, *The Rise and Fall of the Great Powers*, p. 178; Also see Kissinger, *Years of Upheaval*, pp. 44–71.
29. See V. K. Manandhar, *Cultural and Political Aspects of Nepal-China Relations*, New Delhi: Adroit Publishers, 1999.
30. Krishna Hachhethhu, 'State of Democracy in Nepal: Survey Report', Kathmandu: SDSA/N and International IDEA, 2004, p. 94.
31. Dev Raj Dahal, 'Legislators' Attitude on Foreign Policy', in *Political Parties and the Parliamentary Process in Nepal: A Study of the Transitional Phase*. Kathmandu: POLSAN, 1992, Table 3, p. 282.
32. The official announcement of Nepal as the ninth country of China's tourism destination was made in 2000.
33. See Joshua Cooper Ramo, *The Age of the Unthinkable*, New York: Little Brown and Company, 2009, p. 13.
34. When Nepal faced shortages of petroleum products due to some payment problems with India foreign policy advisers of the Interim prime minister and president of the NC, G. P. Koirala were saying they had received assurances from China that it would supply petroleum and even construct a pipeline across the Himalayas, even as the Chinese ambassador in Kathmandu was cautioning that it was not so easy. During the CPNM-led coalition with MJF president as foreign minister, the Chinese foreign minister assured Nepal of assistance to protect its sovereignty and territorial integrity; a senior Maoist leader says 'Unlike . . . China keeps its words' reflecting their perceptions of China although others see limits up to which China would be willing or able to go and hence caution about over-using the 'China card'.

35. See 'Chin ko Nepal Najar' (China's Nepal View), *Nepal National Weekly*, Kantipur Publications, Sunday, 10 Jestha, 2066 (16 May 2009).

36. See 'Chiniya Paisako Ohiro (Flood of Chinese Money)', *Nepal National Weekly*, Kantipur Publications, Sunday, 32 Saun, 2066 (16 August 2009).

37. Ibid.

38. S. D. Muni and Suranjan Das (eds), *India and China: The Next Decade*, New Delhi: Observer Research Foundation & Rupa, 2009, p. 30.

39. Ibid., p. 18.

40. See Waheguru Pal Singh Sidhu and Jing-dong Yuan, *China and India: Cooperation or Conflict?*, Boulder: Lynne Reinner, 2003.

41. See Guihong Zhang, 'India's Perceptions of a Rising China; An Assessment', *South Asian Survey*, vol. 13, no. 1, 2006, pp. 93–102. Late Samuel Huntington's *Clash of Civilizations*, somewhat mistakenly, is seen as representing the school of thought of the inevitability of America's confrontation with a rising China. But his hypothesis as well as conclusions warn of the dangers of the universalist notions of one's cultural values and hence desist them from using it to impose on other cultures and civilisations. See Samuel Huntington, *The Clash of Civilizations and the Remaking of World Order*, London: The Free Press, Simon & Schuster UK Ltd, 2002 p. 316. On Nepal's nervousness, see Ramesh Nath Pandey, 'Ke Dakshin Asia Ko Manchitra Pherindaichha' (Is the Map of South Asia Changing?), *The Kantipur daily*, Kathmandu, Monday, 16 February 2009.

42. See *The Times of India*, 12 July 2009.

43. See Shambhu Ram Simkhada, 'Complexities of Nepal's Foreign Policy', paper presented at the seminar organised by the Institute of Foreign Affairs, Ministry of Foreign Affairs, Kathmandu, December 2008.

44. The State evolution idea can be found in Shambhu Ram Simkhada, 'Global Human Rights Agenda: Emerging Issues' in Ajit M. Banerjee and Murari Raj Sharma (eds), *Reinventing the United Nations*, India: Prentice Hall, 2007.

45. Kennedy, *The Rise and Fall of the Great Powers*, p. 7.

46. Albright, *Memo to the President*, p. 209.

47. Ibid.

7

Pakistan
Perceptions and Responses of an All-weather Friend

IFTIKHAR A. LODHI

The rise of China as a major economic, political and military power on the world stage could not be anything but a welcome development for Pakistan. Both countries enjoy a unique relationship affirmed by the rhetoric of 'indispensable' friendship that is 'deeper than the Arabian Sea and higher than the Himalayas'.[1] However, the rise of China when viewed in the context of post–Cold War post-9/11 geopolitical developments in the region puts some constraints on Pakistan's strategic environment as well as on the Sino-Pak *entente* cordial.

The post–Cold War geopolitical environment in the region is profoundly different from the one in which Sino-Pak relations were founded, deepened and strengthened. The collapse of the Soviet Union and the end of the 'communist threat' in all of its manifestations, militarily as well as ideologically, has profoundly changed US policies globally as well as in the region. The regional actors like China and India too have tailored their policies according to the new geopolitical environment. Consequently, the 1990s witnessed increasing US efforts for promotion of democracy and free market ideology; China and India liberalising their economies and improving their erstwhile bitter relations; India jettisoning its pro–Soviet Union non-aligned approach and the United States reaching out to India as part of its global strategy to sustain the US primacy; America continuing its engagement with China albeit with increasing criticism of the latter for not accelerating economic and political reforms.

Whereas China and India emerged as winners, Pakistan, on the other hand, 'lost out seriously' at the end of the Cold War.[2] Once Pakistan's utility as a front line ally against the Soviet Union ceased, the US slapped sanctions against Pakistan because of the latter's secret nuclear weapons programme. Pakistan was left 'high and dry' to deal with the spillovers from the US-backed 'jihad' in Afghanistan against the Soviet intervention, that is, the civil war in Afghanistan (1990–96), nearly four million refugees, a growing arms and drug trade and Islamist militancy.[3] When the hardcore Islamist Taliban rose to power (1996–2001) in Afghanistan, Pakistan supported them. This strained Pakistan's relations with other neighbours including its all-weather friend China, which were apprehensive of Taliban's extremist policies.[4] Furthermore, Pakistan's support for the militant independence movement in Indian-held Kashmir came under criticism from India and the US — both earlier 'estranged democracies' now eyeing a strategic partnership. Islamabad was increasingly branded as 'supporter of terrorism' in contrast to its erstwhile much appreciated policy of support for the US-backed 'jihad' in Afghanistan. India, envisioning a greater role for itself in the emerging world order, launched a massive diplomatic campaign which increasingly isolated Pakistan in the international community. Consequently, Pakistan's strategic environment deteriorated vis-à-vis India, which it perceived as the primary security threat.[5]

It is in this backdrop that the rise of China needs to be considered for evaluating Pakistani perceptions. China's rise, precipitated by its economic liberalisation and integration into the world system, is a result of three decades of gradual transformation of China's domestic and foreign policies enunciated in the concepts of 'peace and development', 'socialism with Chinese characteristics', 'peaceful development' and the 'new security concept'.[6] The 'grand strategy' adopted by the Chinese for their conduct in the 21st century subordinates national defence to economic development.[7] This translates into non-confrontation, constructive engagement, cooperative and responsible behaviour in regional and international organisations with ever greater emphasis on economic development, interdependence and unity of their country. From this Chinese perspective follows the greater Sino-US engagement, the Sino-Indian *rapprochement*, and the fight against 'three evils' (terrorism, separatism and extremism) contributing, in one way or the other, towards a rethinking of China's South Asian policy beginning from the mid-1990s.[8]

As a result, China increasingly adopted a more cautious approach towards Pakistan reflected in China's relatively neutral position on the Kashmir issue and Chinese apprehensions on Pakistan's support for the Taliban government in Afghanistan.[9] Beijing is also concerned about the spread of Islamic extremism in the adjacent Muslim-majority Xinjiang region of China. Therefore, Beijing has welcomed the US-led war on terror and Pakistan's efforts to combat Islamic extremists. Sino-Pak cordial relations continue unabated, albeit with growing restraint because of China's policy to improve its relations with India and to allay Indian and American suspicions on alleged Sino-Pakistan nuclear and missile cooperation. Furthermore, keeping peace and stability in its peripheries and building its image as a 'responsible stakeholder' of the international community are the two top priorities for China today.

Therefore, how China's policy of 'peaceful development' evolves under domestic and international compulsions would have a direct bearing on China's South Asia policy and consequently on Pakistan's perceptions. A second factor influencing the mutual perceptions of China and Pakistan would be the likely direction of the US–India strategic partnership, apparently to contain China but also a matter of grave concern for Pakistan. Finally, how Pakistan's internal and external strategic environment (the war on terror, socio-politico-economic crisis and Indo-Pak relations) evolve under the current discourse would be another critical factor in forming perceptions and responses of the two countries towards each other.

This chapter aims to look at Pakistani perceptions of China's rise and its responses. It does so by looking at the sources of Pakistan's strategic perceptions and historical evolution of the perceptions of the two countries in the first and second parts. The third section traces the Pakistani perceptions of China's peaceful rise and its regional implications. The fourth section looks into Pakistan's response and the trends in its relations with China. The fifth section identifies stakeholders in Sino-Pak relations and their perceptions. Finally the chapter extrapolates the future scenarios where the respective perceptions of national interests in Pakistan and China can diverge or further converge.

Pakistan's Strategic Environment and China

Three factors largely shape Pakistan's strategic environment and consequently perceptions of its policy makers. First, the creation of Pakistan on the slogan of 'a homeland for the Muslims of the Indian subcontinent' in 1947 through the partition of the Indian subcontinent resulted in hostile relations between a weak Pakistani state and a much stronger India. Consequently, a regional power imbalance persisted. Pakistan perceives India as an 'existential threat' having 'problems in coming to terms with Pakistan's existence'.[10] While the Kashmir dispute between the two countries, an unfinished agenda of the partition, remains the core conflict, there are socio-historical factors which run much deeper. One such factor is Pakistan's persistent refusal to accept Indian hegemony. Both have fought three wars and many border battles. Near-war tensions have been a persistent feature of Indo-Pak relations with many short-lived peace talks. In 1998, both countries became overt nuclear powers. Even if the Kashmir dispute is resolved, hostilities between the two countries are unlikely to recede in the foreseeable future.[11]

Second, Afghanistan is the second most intractable and complex security problem faced by Pakistan and this has both internal and external dimensions. Afghanistan has persistently been of some concern in Pakistan's strategic thinking for some reason or other at different times; the unrecognised border between the two countries, Afghanistan's irredentist claims on a large Pakistani territory (apparently larger than Afghanistan's own Pushtun population and territory), Afghanistan's close links with pan-Pushtunistan separatism, the Soviet and Indian support for the Afghan governments' hostilities towards Pakistan and the Soviet military intervention in the 1980s followed by a Civil War in the 1990s.[12] Pakistan supported the Taliban government with a view to have a friendly regime in Kabul, until the latter was attacked and overthrown by the United States in reaction to the 9/11 terrorist attacks.

Overnight, Pakistan reversed its policy of supporting the Taliban and decided to support the US war in Afghanistan. However, this has led to further instability, both in Pakistan and Afghanistan. Militancy and violence has spread into Pakistan with enormous social and economic costs estimated at US$ 35 billion.[13] The Karzai government in Kabul is perceived unfriendly in Islamabad and closer to New Delhi. Islamabad views Indian involvement in Afghanistan detrimental to Pakistani interests. This only exacerbates Pakistan's sense of insecurity.[14] When seen in the context of China's rise and the growing US–India strategic partnership, these developments have divided the strategic community in Pakistan as well as in China on the question of American intentions in the region.[15] Afghanistan's strategic importance for Pakistan's security and economic development can not be over-emphasised.

Finally, for Islamabad, the challenge of economic development of the country remains as arduous as ever. Pakistan's deteriorating economy has reached a persistent crisis level. For Pakistan, China is an attractive source of much needed investments. Similarly, Pakistan's large consumer market presents huge opportunities for China. Pakistan provides China a strategic link to critical West Asian energy resources, making it the potential 'trade and energy corridor'.

Traditionally, to meet its economic needs and to correct regional power imbalance, Pakistan has sought assistance from major powers.[16] Immediately after Pakistan's creation, the Pakistani westernised elite, cognisant of Cold War geopolitics and Pakistan's geostrategic importance, approached the United States for economic and military assistance. The United States did not oblige.[17] It was only after the Eisenhower-Dulles' containment policy against the Sino-Soviet bloc that US and Pakistan signed a Mutual Defence Assistance Agreement in 1954 followed by Pakistan's membership in the US-led alliances South East Asian Treaty Organisation (SEATO) and the Central Treaty Organisation (CENTO). For the US, Pakistan fitted as an ideological as well as geographical bulwark against the expanding 'communist threat'.[18] However, 'none of these arrangements addressed Pakistan's main concern that was India'.[19] Pakistan also tried to nurture good relations with other regional powers including China and the Soviet Union.

Reaching out to China

Pakistan was one of the first countries to recognise communist China and established diplomatic relations in 1951. Pakistan supported communist China's claim for the UN seat. It abstained from a western attempt to label China as an aggressor in the United Nations during the Korean War.[20] During the Afro-Asian conference in 1955, Pakistan was able to assuage Chinese apprehensions on the former's joining of the US-led alliances and China showed, unlike the Soviet Union, a greater understanding of the Pakistani sense of insecurity and compulsions.[21] High-level official visits followed and in 1961, both countries initiated a border settlement dialogue which was concluded in 1963 delineating their boundary by the give and take of a few hundred square miles of territory on both sides.[22] New Delhi objected to this agreement having a claim on the territory that Pakistan had acceded to China. A number of agreements were also signed between China and Pakistan which marked the beginning of close cooperation through trade, technological and cultural exchanges, civil aviation links and the Karakoram Highway.[23]

Shared Geography, History and Perceptions

The ancient Silk Road connected modern day China and Pakistan for thousands of years and served as a vital trade and cultural link at the crossroads of the Indian subcontinent, the Arab world, the east and the West.[24] Buddhism spread to China in the 1st and 2nd centuries from the Gandhara region in the northwest of today's Pakistan.[25] Islam and Christianity also spread to China from this region in the succeeding centuries during the reigns of various northwest Chinese, Turk and Persian dynasties in the region. However, the Russian incursions in central Asia and the European colonisation of South and Southeast Asia during the 18th and 19th centuries disconnected the two regions. Furthermore, maritime trade replaced the land links. By the end of the 19th century, a declining Qing dynasty (1644–1911) was conceding the British and Russian encroachments in southwest China and their rivalry completely severed the links between the two regions.[26]

These links were to be revived only in the 1960s, through the Karakoram Highway. The Karakoram Highway, like the ancient Silk Road, was a rare link between China and the world. Similarly, Pakistan offered an isolated China aviation and diplomatic links to the outer world during the heydays of the Cold War despite being a member of SEATO directed against China. Pakistan's courtship with China was called 'an unfortunate breach of free world solidarity' by Washington, which in retaliation threatened to suspend economic and military aid.[27] Why would Pakistan, an impoverished Islamic country with 40 per cent of its budget and all of its defence requirements dependent on the United States, risk its relations with its powerful patron for friendship with a poor isolated communist China? The answer to this question is the key to understanding Pakistani perceptions of China and the evolving strategic environment.

Shared Perceptions of the United States and India

A conventional answer often advanced in respect to this question points to the Sino-Indian 'War' of 1962 and 'Sino-Pak shared hostilities towards India'.[28] However, this largely Indian and western point of view is a gross simplification of the events leading up to the Sino-Pakistan *entente,* the turbulent history of the partition (1947) and Cold War politics. This point of view fails to explain Pakistani overtures to China throughout the 1950s when Sino-Indian relations were termed '*Hindi Chini Bhai Bhai*' (Chinese and Indians are brothers) and more importantly, Pakistan was part of the US-led military alliance aimed against China. For all intents and purposes, such a line of argument seems to overlook the facts about Indian aggressive hegemonic ambitions against its neighbours; the overt and covert role of the United States in destabilising the region, pitting one Asian power against the other and using its military pacts with Pakistan for its own interests while compromising the vital interests of Pakistan.[29]

In fact, the primary factor pushing Pakistan towards China was the US economic and military aid to India, a pro-Soviet leader of the Non-alignment Movement, at the cost of Pakistan, the 'most allied ally'. For China, embracing Pakistan provided many benefits including (a) breaking away from the US encirclement (b) a valuable link to the Muslim and the western world and a gateway to the Indian Ocean, (c) a credible counterweight to Indian hegemonic designs which was at that time being assisted by the Soviet Union and the United States perceived by China as hostile powers.

In the late 1950s, there was a tilt in the US policies in favour of India.[30] The latter received US$ 6 billion of economic aid between 1951 and 1964 excluding the pledges from other western countries through the Aid India Club in contrast to Pakistan which received only US$ 3 billion during the same period.[31] This US tilt towards India was felt, resented and complained about in Pakistan as early as in 1956 and the civil society questioned the very rationale of joining the US alliances. Pakistani newspapers cited the Indian example as to how non-alignment could pay from both sides of the fence.[32] In 1958, Prime Minister F. K. Noon, widely considered pro-western and weak on India, declared in the parliament, 'our people, if they find their freedom threatened by Bharat [India], will break all pacts [CENTO and SEATO] and shake hands with people [Soviet Union and China] whom we have made enemies because of others [US]. Let there be no mistake about it.'[33]

In 1959, China found an 'Indian hand' in the Tibetan uprising and Sino-Indian cordial relations started to deteriorate. The Dalai Lama and his followers fled to India and were given asylum. The American Central Intelligence Agency (CIA) was running a major covert operation against China from Indian territory in close cooperation with the Indian government.[34] In this deteriorating environment, Indian incursions into Chinese territory under the Forward Policy drove a final nail into the coffin of Sino-Indian cordial relations. China retaliated with force in June 1962, regained its territory, and announced a unilateral ceasefire in November without capturing even the areas over which it had a claim or the Indian territories that lay at its mercy.[35]

While the 1962 'war' remained a border conflict for China and Pakistan, it would become a mainstay of India's security and foreign policy. A closely interlinked development was the growing Sino-Soviet rift. The Soviet Union sided with India during this conflict. For China, the collusion of these three hostile powers (US, USSR, India) posed a security predicament. It might have reminded China of the past when imperial powers preyed on it in the 19th century. China concluded from the events between 1959 and 1963 that India was a hegemonic power, a continuation of British imperialism and that China is still surrounded by hostile powers.[36]

In Pakistan's strategic thinking, the US decision to rush military supplies to India during the 1962 Sino-India border conflict was a watershed event. During the conflict, the US tried to press upon Pakistan the danger of 'Chinese expansion' and urged Pakistan not to take advantage of the situation. Nevertheless, Pakistani perceptions and military calculations were completely different. From the Pakistani point of view India was the aggressor, China was not driven by any expansionist agenda, and the conflict was a 'direct outcome of distorted and fallacious thinking on the part of Mr. Nehru'.[37]

Pakistan complained bitterly about the no-strings-attached US military and economic assistance to India during this time, which it feared would be used to its disadvantage. The United States had earlier declined a blanket security cover to Pakistan if a non-communist state attacked Pakistan.[38] Pakistan also resented the fact that the West had failed to convince India, despite all military and economic assistance, for the settlement of the Kashmir dispute.[39] The policy makers and people in Pakistan started to believe that Anglo-American powers were not interested in resolving its Kashmir dispute with India.

In 1965 Pakistan and India went to war. The US not only declined to extend any help but also terminated economic and military assistance to Pakistan. Starved of armaments, Pakistan turned to China. This marked the beginning of close defence cooperation between China and Pakistan. Although US–Pakistan relations gradually normalised, it left a deeper mistrust of the US in the Pakistani mindset.[40]

China showed its steadfast support for Pakistan in the coming years. While China did not fulfill Pakistani expectations to get militarily involved in case of confrontations between India and Pakistan, it rendered maximum diplomatic assistance. Despite criticism from some quarters, the Chinese role was well appreciated in Pakistan.[41] As Pakistan's influential newspaper *Dawn* wrote in an editorial, 'China has been a great friend of Pakistan. Let us honour this friendship by being rational and realistic and not by imposing unnecessary burden and strain on this friendship.'[42]

Role of the Soviet Union

The Soviet Union supported India during the 1965 and 1971 wars. Therefore, Pakistan harboured, along with the US and China, great suspicions of the Indo-Soviet cooperation. The Sino-Soviet split brought a radical change in both US and China's policies resulting in the Sino-US *détente* for which Pakistan played the role of a facilitator. The shared enmity towards the Soviet Union of these three strange bedfellows brought a tripartite marriage of convenience. In the late 1970s, the Soviet Union militarily intervened in Afghanistan, ostensibly to save the 'socialist revolution' from conservatives supported by the US and Pakistan. India's muted response to the Soviet intervention in Afghanistan further estranged these two blocks.[43] Pakistan felt threatened from the Soviet-Indian nexus. Islamabad found the US and China eager to support Pakistan, both of which had a vested interest in containing the Soviet Union. For the next decade, these three countries would work in tandem to run the largest covert operation in the history of CIA, training and arming the Afghan 'mujahidin' to fight the Soviets. If the US pro-Indian policies in the late 1950s and early 1960s were vital in bringing China and Pakistan together, the Indo-Soviet nexus in later years played a critical role in cementing Sino-Pak ties.

Shared Insecurities and Identity of Interests

Both China and Pakistan share a deep sense of insecurity. Territorial integrity from external and internal threats, economic development, and maintenance of order coupled with building a national identity remain primary preoccupations of the two states. The horrors of the partition and mistreatment by the Indians and British have left deep and long-lasting scars on the Pakistani psyche. The Pakistanis were to develop paranoia that was expressed by Pakistan's founder Mohammad Ali Jinnah when he lamented that a 'mutilated, truncated, moth-eaten Pakistan' was given to him.[44] The failure of the international community to resolve the Kashmir dispute and the humiliating dismemberment of Pakistan by the Indian military intervention during the 1971 East Pakistan crisis only reinforced this paranoia. Pakistan at times also faced grave internal threats in terms of ethnic strife and separatism with external links to the Soviet Union and India.

China's humiliating experiences from the Opium Wars, imperial Unequal Treaties, the US nuclear threats, the Japanese and Russian occupations, the US encirclement during the Cold War, and most recently the US attempts to contain China generate a similar kind of paranoia in the Chinese psyche.

It also faced internal threats and civil wars. A seasoned scholar on China, Wang Gungwu puts it succinctly:

> Since the second half of the 19th century, there has been the threat of the breakup of Qing dynastic China. That threat was to reduce China to the lands occupied only by the Han Chinese. It had begun with the idea of something that western maps called China Proper, as distinct from a China including at least Manchuria, Mongolia, Xinjiang, and Tibet. The Russians succeeded in detaching Mongolia from Republican China in 1924, and this tempted Japanese to do the same to Manchuria seven years later. There are some groups who would like to repeat this process for Xinjiang on behalf of the Uighurs, and for Tibet on behalf of the Tibetans. Yet others would be prepared to risk war to see that Taiwan be removed as well.[45]

According to a former Pakistani ambassador, both China and Pakistan are interested in correcting [enduring] injustices through peaceful negotiations.[46] China has demonstrated this by its words and actions, particularly in the case of Taiwan. It has relentlessly pursued a policy of patience and dialogue. China has time and again advised Pakistan against military options in Kashmir and urged it to 'settle the dispute with dialogue'. Nevertheless, both countries remain committed to each other's territorial integrity.[47]

Both China and Pakistan are developing countries. Both seek a level playing field in the global economic system and coordinate to promote interests of developing countries. Both have extended their diplomatic support to each other whenever the question of territorial integrity has arisen. Both adhere to the five principles of peaceful coexistence and promote regional cooperation and multilateralism within the UN system. The latter becomes more important in the post-9/11 international system which has been threatened by preemption, interventionism, coercive diplomacy and unilateralism.[48]

China's Peaceful Rise

China is a transition state emerging from its poor past through commendable statecraft and has its own unique features. The perceptions on the rise of China among the Pakistani scholars and strategic community can be broadly summarised as follows:[49]

(a) The rise of China is a stabilising factor in the international system;

(b) 'China certainly shows no signs of becoming a challenger to the US';[50]

(c) Neither does China pose a threat to any country nor does it seek hegemony;

(d) Many do hope that China would be able to dilute US hyper-power by promoting multilateralism through the United Nations and regional forums of cooperation;

(e) China will uphold its tradition of 'five principles of peaceful coexistence';

(f) Chinese South Asia policy seeks stability and cooperation in the region;

(g) China's rise is an opportunity for the developing countries in the region;

(h) 'A long-standing consensus persists among Pakistanis that the alliance with China is not only indispensable but also more than likely to endure';[51]

Pakistani scholars and policy makers alike believe that China has developed a fairly consistent and coherent grand strategy in the past decade.[52] At the core of this strategy remain the goals of peace and development spelt out in China's White Paper on Peaceful Development.[53] From an isolated socialist past, China has come a long way since the policy of reforms and openness was launched in 1978. China has realised that the objectives of modernisation and development can only be followed with increasing integration in the world economy. From this Chinese objective follows a policy of achieving a conducive and enabling international environment, particularly in the neighbourhood.

China's tremendous developmental agenda also requires increasing natural resources and markets for trade and invest-ments. Beijing has been pursuing a very proactive engagement with the world. China became a member of the World Trade Organisation (WTO) in 2001. It has been playing a construc-tive role in regional and international organisations. Playing by the rules and becoming a 'responsible stakeholder' in the existing international structures while marginally pushing for reforms consistent with its ambitions and interests seem to be the mainstay of the evolving Chinese foreign policy.[54] It has been engaged in ASEAN+3, Asia-Pacific Economic Cooperation (APEC), ASEAN Regional Forum (ARF) and has been spearheading the Shanghai Cooperation Organisation (SCO). China has resolved its border disputes with all its neighbours (India being the only exception) with generous concessions; has played a vital role in six party talks over the North Korean nuclear issue; has coordinated with the major economic powers in managing the global financial crisis; has joined the US war against terrorism; has resisted unqualified support of one or the other on the US-Iran standoff.[55] Even in China some have called it a policy of appeasement. Nevertheless, this seems to be the course of action of the Chinese foreign policy in the coming years, which has been dubbed by a Chinese scholar as 'learning to live with hegemony'.[56] Pakistani scholars' and policy makers' assessments endorse this view. Their views also seem to endorse the following observation made by a China hand, David Shambaugh, that in Asia, China is seen 'as a good neighbor, a constructive partner, a careful listener, and a non-threatening regional power'.[57]

China continues to enjoy enormous goodwill in Pakistan across the board. There is no power group in the Pakistani civil and military establishment which feels uncomfortable with the growing power of China, nor does any political party from right or left express any apprehension. Despite the fact that China has lately toned down its support for the 'Kashmir cause', a central piece of Pakistani foreign policy, yet there is no public criticism from any lobby.

The US and India Factors

Islamabad has, or so it seems, a greater understanding of China's rise and its concomitant geopolitical developments in the region. Pakistan has been treading carefully in its relations with China. That is why Pakistan has not gone in 'panic mode' over restrained Chinese policy towards Pakistan, particularly with regard to Kashmir, and China's 'intricate endeavor to sell friendship to India'.[58] China has taken greater interest in SAARC and expects to play a constructive role as an observer. Beijing has been encouraging both Pakistan and India for regional cooperation and to continue dialogue, besides calling for restraint during Indo-Pak tensions.[59] As a Pakistani scholar wrote after the Kargil crisis:

They have been telling us to divert resources from guns to development . . . there is some merit in the Chinese prescription for peace and stability in South Asia. . . . Whether or not we can follow the Chinese example, their advice to Pakistan has been in line with what they have themselves been practicing since the launching of the modernization campaign.[60]

Pakistan seems to heed Chinese advice. Pakistan has even welcomed the Chinese 'constructive role' after the Mumbai attacks in diffusing tensions between India and Pakistan.[61] During President Obama's visit to China in November 2009, the US and China agreed to cooperate in 'bringing about more stable, peaceful relations in all of South Asia'.[62] However, New Delhi objected to any Chinese role in South Asian affairs.[63] India has persistently rejected calls for any third party mediation in its confrontations with Pakistan.

Notwithstanding, Beijing has been reassuring Pakistan that its friendship with India need not be at the cost of a good friend like Pakistan. Both the countries share 'enduring strategic interests' which include (a) apprehensive yet close relations of the two with the United States, (b) mutual recognition of the economic and strategic importance of each other, (c) keeping Indian hegemonic designs in check. While Islamabad has generally welcomed Sino-Indian improved ties, it appears that strategists in Pakistan as well as in China remain ambivalent about the success of Sino-Indian rapprochement at best.[64] On the other hand politicians and scholars have been generally more optimistic.[65]

The United States remains a critical factor in both Chinese and Pakistani thinking. For Pakistan, the US remains a self-interested ally often at odds with perceived Pakistani interests, particularly vis-à-vis India. However, both China and Pakistan are neither willing nor capable of challenging American supremacy. On the contrary, both have a vested interest in engaging the US. Nevertheless, because of their troubled history of relations with the US and perceived clash of interests, both China and Pakistan remain wary of the United States and its strategic partnership with India.[66]

China sees the post-9/11 developments in Afghanistan and the region with some concern, presenting challenges as well as opportunities. On the one hand the US invasion of Afghanistan helped China to allay its concerns (and a source of tension with

Pakistan) about spreading Islamic militancy through the Taliban in its Muslim-majority Xinjiang province and beyond. The 9/11 events also brought the US back as a major stakeholder in the economic wellbeing of Pakistan and managing the South Asian crisis, a difficult challenge for China. On the other hand, this also brought the US and NATO military forces to the Chinese doorstep and halted growing Chinese influence in central Asia.[67]

Both Pakistan and India have been in a mutually zero-sum relation with respect to their relations with the United States and China. Improvements in relations of one with either of these powers tend to negatively impact the other's relations with that country. A frequent allegation made by India is that the military and economic support that Pakistan receives from the US or China undermines India's security interests in the region. This criticism becomes sharper in case of Sino-Pak defence and strategic cooperation, which India perceives as Chinese attempts to 'bog India down in regional affairs' and to thwart Indian global ambitions vis-à-vis China. In case of US–Indian defence cooperation, Pakistan complains about its security predicament. Pakistan's anxieties grow further also when there is close Sino-Indian cooperation. Nevertheless, all four actors remain engaged in a delicate balancing act with ever increasing mutual cooperation. Both India and Pakistan continue to expect from major powers, namely the United States (and lately China), to influence others' course of action. Pakistan even goes further to invite these powers for mediation while India insists on bilateralism.[68]

The prevailing sense in Pakistan is that in the long run Sino-Pak relations will continue to grow irrespective of the Sino-Indian ties.[69] There are virtually no quarters in Pakistan that feel uncomfortable with the rise of China, rather policy makers in Islamabad believe that a strong China will keep playing a constructive role in the stability of South Asia and will also keep a check on the growing US–India strategic partnership. Islamabad, hard pressed from all sides, particularly by the Indo-US strategic partnership and deteriorating economic situation, has attuned its policies accordingly, particularly with regard to the Kashmir issue. Islamabad seems to be heeding the Chinese advice to focus on economic development of the country putting thorny issues aside. For that China has extended full economic cooperation.

Economic Cooperation

The rise of China has brought enormous opportunities for Pakistan. The economic relations of the two countries have been growing steadily in the recent years in the fields of energy security, trade, investment, and people-to-people contacts, pointing towards a more self-containing relationship. This is a completely new dimension in the Sino-Pak bilateral relations which historically have been dominated by government-to-government political, strategic, and defence cooperation. There is a growing need and desire on both sides to tap the comparative advantages of each other. As Tanvir Ahmed Khan, a former foreign secretary and ambassador of Pakistan said, 'a new bilateral alliance has emerged and at its heart lays the promise of Pakistan as a conduit of energy and strategic commodities'.[70] It is the strategic location of Pakistan which Islamabad wants to use for accessing the Chinese economic growth.

From the Chinese perspective, Pakistan offers great opportunities for exports and investments. Pakistan is a growing consumption-led economy; a population of 160 million makes it the sixth largest market in the world. Chinese business interest in Pakistan has been increasing steadily. Bilateral trade between the two countries has grown by almost 50 per cent annually, from a few hundred millions in the early 1990s to US$ 1.5 billion in 2001 and to US$ 7 billion in 2008 (see Figure 7.1). Both countries have set targets to increase trade to US$ 15 billion by 2011.[71]

The China–Pakistan Free Trade Agreement (FTA) came into effect in 2008. The FTA, not surprisingly, resulted in Pakistan's trade deficit with China rising sharply, as most of the increase in the trade volume was in terms of Chinese exports to Pakistan, with Pakistani exports recording only modest growth (see Figure 7.1).[72] The government is of the opinion that the FTA will help in raising competitiveness, bring down production cost and will benefit consumers.[73] Policy makers in Islamabad realise that it is important to engage China in a long-term win-win relationship even if there are some short-term costs involved. Outweighing the costs are the benefits of this engagement, which are manifold for both countries ranging from increased investment flows to Pakistan to long-term geopolitical gains.

Part of the long-term benefits for Pakistan are greater Chinese investment, particularly in infrastructure and developmental

FIGURE 7.1: Pakistan's trade with China (1994–2008)*

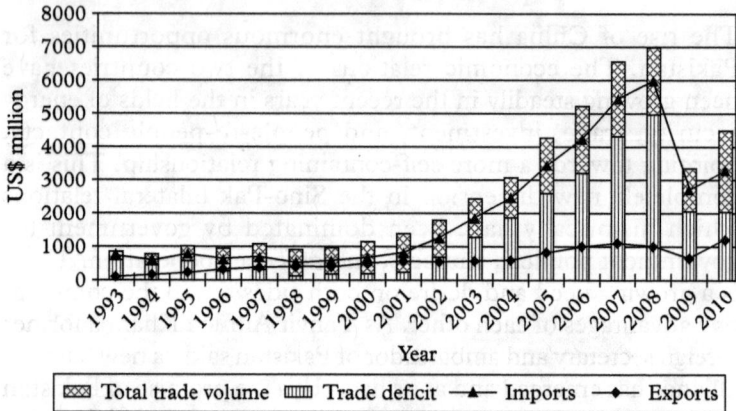

Source: Calculated from the State Bank of Pakistan's annual publications.

projects, which are crucial to Pakistan. The extent of Chinese economic engagement is reflected in the growing number of public and private projects and joint ventures. Chinese investment in Pakistan has been growing steadily and reached US$ 6 billion in 2007.[74] More than sixty Chinese firms with 10,000 Chinese personnel are operating in Pakistan, undertaking over 120 projects in different sectors including oil and gas, information technology, telecommunications, power generation, engineering, automobile manufacturing, infrastructure and mining sectors. Both governments are encouraging their business leaders to take part in the consumer and financial sectors in Pakistan, which have been growing rapidly.

Both governments are also encouraging hitherto overlooked people-to-people contacts. Many initiatives have been taken in recent years to increase cultural exchanges involving universities, the business community and political parties. Tourism has been growing steadily. In 2008, some 100,000 Pakistanis visited China and vice versa. Similarly, there has been a sudden growth in the number of students from each country studying in the other. Many universities in Pakistan have been offering Chinese language courses. Latest in a row of such initiatives is the Pak-China Friendship Cultural Complex inaugurated by Prime Minister Yousaf Raza Gillani in Beijing on 24 October 2009.

Besides, China is heavily investing in Pakistan. Many of the projects undertaken or assisted by China are major infrastructure projects with long-term strategic and economic implications. These include the Chashma Nuclear Power Plant, Saindak Copper Mining, Thar Coal Power Plant, upgradation of the Karakoram Highway, Coastal Highway, and the Gwadar Port. A number of hydropower plants, refineries, railways, exploration and mining projects are also expected in the near future. These projects not only help Pakistan in its overall development efforts but also reduce its dependency on international financial institutions, whose financial assistance comes attached with many conditions. These projects also have the effect of indirectly increasing the Chinese stake in Pakistan's economy, stability and ultimately politics. Of these, the most significant are the Gwadar Port, Karakoram Highway and the rail link between China and Pakistan. These interconnected projects termed as the 'trade and energy corridor' have geopolitical implications as well.

The Trade and Energy Corridor

Pakistan is located at the crossroads of three important Asian regions and offers connectivity through what has been termed as the 'trade and energy corridor'. The corridor vision includes oil and gas pipelines, railways and road links with Iran, Afghanistan, China, and the central Asian states. China is not the only country buying into this corridor concept by providing financial and technical assistance to Pakistan. For example, the Asian Development Bank (ADB) is providing US$ 500 million for Pakistan's highway infrastructure and is actively supporting the Turkmenistan-Afghanistan-Pakistan-India (TAPI) gas pipeline. The World Bank, Russia and China, all have shown interest in the Iran-Pakistan-India (IPI) gas pipeline, large dams, and electricity imports from Tajikistan and Kirghizstan.[75] All these endeavours will not only effectively meet Pakistan's development plans and growing energy needs but will certainly accelerate regional interdependence and economic development.

For China, the acquisition of oil and gas assets abroad and securing their transportation to China is a top priority to ensure its economic growth stays on track. The strong US military presence controlling the sea lanes of communication (SLOCs), through which Chinese oil and gas are imported, is a matter of concern for China, especially given the fact that it already feels encircled by the United States and its strategic partnership with India.[76] Two such choke points, from where 60 per cent and 80 per cent of the total Chinese oil imports pass through, are the Straits of Hormuz and Malacca, respectively.

Having no blue water navy of its own, China has been pursuing a multipronged strategy. It has searched for alternative routes such as the Kra Canal in Thailand; an oil pipeline across Malaysia; onshore oil and gas pipelines from Myanmar, Central Asia, and Russia; strategic oil reserves; modernisation of its navy; and building/assisting commercial and naval ports in friendly countries along the shipping routes. The Gwadar Port of Pakistan in the long run can serve as an alternative energy supply route from the Middle East to western China. There have also been discussions to build an oil and/or gas pipeline (Trans-Karakoram pipeline) from Gwadar to China.[77] China has been involved in the Iranian and Saudi energy sectors in the recent years. Both countries have shown interest in supplying oil/gas through a pipeline via Pakistan. China and Iran are also likely to join a consortium proposed by the UAE to build an oil refinery in Gwadar.[78]

Defence Cooperation

China has been Pakistan's largest arms supplier for more than four decades, followed by the United States and France (see Table 7.1). From 1950 to 2008, 36 per cent of Pakistan's total defence imports were from China and 23 per cent from the US. Pakistan started off with virtually zero indigenous defence industry which led it to ally with the US. However, faced with the perils of reliance on foreign suppliers during its war with India in 1965 and 1971 (see Figure 7.2), Pakistan was determined to diversify the range of its arms suppliers and in the long run to develop and improve its domestic defence industries ultimately achieving 'self-reliance' in arms, ammunition and weapons systems.[79]

Besides approaching France and China among others, Pakistan embarked on an ambitious plan of defence production by establishing the Defence Production Division. Within a few years the Pakistan Ordinance Factory was revamped and various defence production facilities were built including Heavy Industries Taxila (HIT), Heavy Mechanical Complex (HMC)

TABLE 7.1: Top five arms suppliers to Pakistan

Pakistan: Top Five Arms Suppliers (US$ million at 1990 constant prices)						
	1950–60	1961–70	1971–80	1981–90	1991–2000	2001–8	Total
China	0	700	2,347	2,497	2,314	1,390	9,248
USA	1,087	459	593	2,383	449	1,091	6,062
France	0	473	1,463	356	672	747	3,711
Ukraine	0	0	0	0	1,280	92	1,372
Italy	0	0	17	178	421	194	810
Others	1,196	566	347	851	897	687	4,544
Total	2,283	2,198	4,767	6,265	6,033	4,201	25,747

Source: Stockholm International Peace Research Institute Arms Transfer Database, 6 November 2009.

FIGURE 7.2: Pakistan's defence imports, US vs China

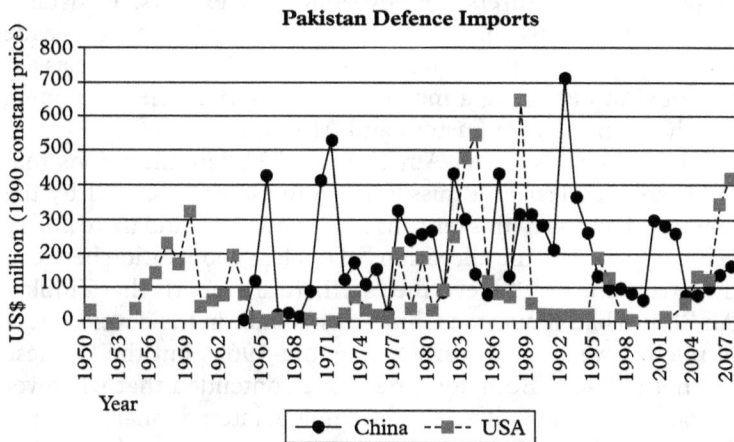

Pakistan Defence Imports

Source: Stockholm International Peace Research Institute Arms Transfer Database, 6 November 2009.

and Pakistan Aeronautical Complexes (PAC). China has been instrumental in providing military supplies as well as technical assistance and technology transfer.[80]

During the 1990s, arms embargo on Pakistan by the US (including twenty-eight F-16 aircrafts for which Pakistan had already paid) led to a further resolve for self-reliance and diversification.[81] Today Pakistan is manufacturing arms for use by all the three wings of its armed forces, many of them under Chinese license.[82]

The events of 9/11 brought the US back as an important arms supplier mainly because of the resumed sales of F-16 fighter aircrafts and specialised counter-terrorism equipment like Cobra gunship helicopters. Nevertheless, there has been a major shift away from US dependence.[83] If this trend continues and the US does not approve some high-tech weapons systems (such as theatre missile defence system) for Pakistan, by 2015 the US may not be any significant source of defence supplies to Pakistan.

Currently, Pakistan is manufacturing in collaboration with China the JF-17 Thunder aircrafts, F-22P frigates, and T-59 Al-Khalid/Al-Zarrar main battle tanks. The two countries also have plans for the joint production of Airborne Warning and Control System (AWCS).[84] The JF-17 and battle tanks with various other defence manufacturers are envisioned for exports. Pakistan's defence exports also have grown exponentially in the last decade reaching the US$ 300 million mark in 2008. The country has the potential of becoming a major arms supplier to the developing South Asian, Middle Eastern and African markets.[85]

There have also been American and Indian allegations that Pakistan's nuclear and missile programme was assisted by the Chinese. However, 'this remains a nebulous area, and there is little evidence to verify the allegations of nuclear cooperation between the two countries'.[86] Nevertheless, there are reports that Zulfikar Ali Bhutto had requested Chinese assistance in the development of nuclear weapons as early as the mid-1960s but the Chinese did not oblige.[87] Both countries have contended that whatever cooperation there is, is within the ambit of international treaties.[88] China has offered Pakistan sustained cooperation in the nuclear field, so much so that it has even moved in February 2010 to give Pakistan support in the civil-nuclear field on the line of similar Indo-US cooperation.

Constituencies influencing Sino-Pak ties

The cabinet headed by the prime minister is the supreme security and foreign policy making authority in Pakistan.[89] The parliament can also make laws related to Pakistan's external affairs.[90] However, such were the internal and external circumstances in which Pakistan was born that the army and the bureaucracy ascended to carry out state- and nation-building projects instead of the parliament and political parties.[91] As a result, the security and foreign policy of the country has remained largely a civil-military bureaucratic enterprise. Consequently these institutions have 'lent their worldview to other institutions and groups'.[92] However, this does not imply that their worldview was necessarily clashing with the overall strategic culture of the country, including the mainstream political forces.

In Pakistan's sixty-two years of chequered polity, the first eleven years (1947–58) marked the rule of non-parliamentary forces followed by frequent army rule for thirty-three (1958–71, 1979–89, 1999–2008) years. Although democratic governments were in office from 1989 to 1999, the years were characterised by an intense power struggle between the army and civil governments and between the two largest political parties, the Pakistan Peoples Party (PPP) and the Muslim League (ML). Only the six years (1971–77) of Zulfiqar Ali Bhutto of PPP are considered the era of genuine civilian supremacy.[93]

Despite the overarching role of the military, Pakistan primarily remains a constitutional state.[94] Even the military rulers are compelled to keep a façade of civilian rule, manipulate the domestic political environment from behind the curtain, and accommodate popular demands. Recently, there have been suggestions to assign a constitutional role to the Pakistan National Security Council, a consultative body comprising the armed forces chiefs and senior members of the executive and the legislature to coordinate national security policy.

Since Pakistan's relations with the United States, China and India have security underpinnings of great consequences, the Pakistan military remains the single most important stakeholder in its relations with China. As discussed earlier, the nature of defence cooperation between the two countries is a telling evidence of the armed forces' dispensation towards China. The military-to-military ties between the two countries are strong with frequent exchange visits and joint military exercises.[95]

However, it is interesting to note that, institutionally, Pakistan's armed forces have been oriented in the western tradition, its doctrines, strategies, warfare techniques, and ethos — a legacy of the British colonial rule and alliances with the United States. The Pakistan military still has close military personnel contacts with the US military. Its officer corps are trained in Britain and America.[96] More importantly, the US has helped the Pakistan army in consolidating its political power against democratic forces, which are considered in Washington weak and at times hostile toward the United States.

The Pakistan military would like to have close relations with both the United States and China and keep its options open. However, Pakistan's present alliance with the United States is increasingly becoming difficult to manage. Both countries harbour a deep mistrust of each other. Since 9/11 there has been an increasing polarisation. While the Islamist sympathisers have been marginalised, not all moderates favour all American policies.[97]

It is also interesting to note that it was the *Qaid-e-Awam* (leader of the people) Z. A. Bhutto of the Pakistan Peoples Party who played a key role in cementing ties with China under President Ayub and later when he himself became prime minister.[98] During the only period of complete civilian supremacy (1972–77) in Pakistan, Sino-Pak relations were deepened and strengthened. Nevertheless, the PPP of today is altogether a different party from that of the 1970s. It has distanced itself from the policies that Bhutto was advocating. Though the three PPP governments between 1990 to 2009 have continued with the standard line that relations with China are the corner stone of Pakistan's foreign policy, they have been more inclined towards the US.[99] The only mention of China in its 2008 election manifesto was in these words:

> The PPP believes in good neighbourly relations with Afghanistan, India, Iran and the Peoples Republic of China. The Party also believes in further strengthening relations with the USA, Canada, European Union, Japan and the Commonwealth.[100]

The current PPP regime owes its existence to Washington in large part. The former allegedly played a critical part in negotiating a deal between President Musharraf and the PPP. Nevertheless, President Zardari has shown a lot of enthusiasm towards China by visiting the country every three months.

The two Pakistan Muslim Leagues (PML-Nawaz and PML-Qaid-e-Azam group), both right of the centre parties, have shown more praise and enthusiasm for China. While the PML-Q could be dismissed as a hotchpotch of politicians who gathered around President Musharraf, the PML-N is known for its less favourable dispensation towards the United States, particularly with regard to the US war on terror and perhaps the US support for Musharraf who came to power by disposing the PML-N government.[101] During his last government, the leader of the PML-N, Nawaz Sharif, said at the eve of Pakistan's nuclear tests:

> China is against expansionism in spite of being several times more powerful than India in respect of its strength and defence capabilities, while India is an expansionist country. We constantly pointed towards this fact but the major powers did not pay any attention to this and continued to believe in false pronouncements made by Indian rulers. Under these circumstances, it was but natural for us to get worried. We expressed this worry in every way. I even proposed that the United States, Russia, and China use their good offices to protect Asia from the nuclear arms race.[102]

While the PPP 2008 election manifesto made only one indirect passing reference to China, the PML-N 2008 election manifesto mentions the United States only once accusing it for the support of President Musharraf because he is fighting 'America's proxy war'. On the other hand on China it states:

> China has been a time tested friend of Pakistan. Every effort would be made to strengthen and enhance this relationship, so as to make it truly strategic, by imparting greater substance and depth to it.[103]

The Islamic parties, despite their weak electoral support, like Jamaat-e-Islami and Jamiat-e-Ulamai Islam (JUI) have a relatively larger clout in the civil-military establishment as well as in inspiring the public opinion, particularly on foreign policy issues.[104] If not in their love for China, at least these parties favour China in their antagonism towards the US and India. There have been suggestions in the Pakistani Urdu media from these parties that to offset American pressure on Af-Pak and war on terror, Pakistan should work with China to form AfPIChS — Afghanistan, Pakistan, Iran, China, and Saudi Arabia. Irrespective of their merits, such sentiments inform the public opinion in Pakistan. These kinds of suggestions might have soothing effects on Chinese ears, only if they were not having problems with their own jihadis in Xinjiang province.

While some countries from OIC condemned the Chinese heavy-handed response to the July 2009 riots in Xingjian,

Pakistan, with its transnational Islamic parties, played a critical role in toning down the OIC statements concerning the riots.[105] Pakistan unequivocally condemned the rioters and agreed with the Chinese assessment that western powers have been fanning the flames in Xinjiang like the previous year's Tibet riots during the Olympics. The group accused of the riots, the World Uyghur Council, is supported by America.[106]

The public debate in Pakistan over its relations with China is relatively mute when compared to the heated debates and street protests when it comes to the United States and India. The primary reason for this is China's strict adherence to the five principles of coexistence and non-interference in the domestic affairs of Pakistan. It also eschews megaphone diplomacy leaving marginal room for civil society to discuss issues of bilateral concern. The civil society in Pakistan, traditionally oppressed, particularly the media, have come a long way to play a larger role in the country and may very well succeed in influencing foreign policy even if at the margins. A case in point is the 2008 elections which brought about the democratic change after nine years of President Musharraf's military rule. The civil society generally favours good relations with all the countries while China enjoys a special respect for its impressive economic growth and support for Pakistan.

According to the 2009 Pew Global Attitudes Survey, 80 per cent of Pakistanis view China as a partner as opposed to only 9 per cent who view the US as a partner. It is interesting though that the unfavourable opinion of China amounts to 3 per cent less than the 6 per cent in China itself. A Pakistani scholar writes:

> China's clout stems from its historic support for Pakistan vis-à-vis India and the perception that it is a non-intrusive and non-exploitative ally. The latter is linked not just to China's softer diplomatic rhetoric but also its aid strategy. Although Chinese assistance to Pakistan over the years has paled in comparison to U.S. aid, it has made more of an impact, with few strings attached, it has focused on long-term financing and large infrastructure projects instead of direct economic aid that is often squandered by the leadership or on the ground.[107]

The business community is another important stakeholder in Pakistan's relations with China. The Pakistani bourgeoisie has traditionally been very weak and in constant clash with the overwhelmingly powerful feudal elite.[108] They have been oriented towards the lucrative western markets for decades. But it has been changing gradually for various reasons. The forces of globalisation have compelled the government to patronise the business community if Pakistan were to achieve economic viability. Whereas the Sino-Pak FTA may have adversely affected some quarters, others have benefited too. There are enormous opportunities for joint projects with Chinese companies, with capital readily available from the two governments.

Future Scenarios

From this discussion it becomes obvious that both Pakistan and China interact in a very complex strategic environment and form nodes of multiple strategic triangles namely US–China–India, US–China–Pakistan, China–India–Pakistan, US–India–Pakistan. To extrapolate on the future direction of relations, these discussions of perceptions provide sufficient grounds. More often than not, Sino-Pak decisions would be in reaction to the decisions made in Washington and New Delhi.

Strain in Relations

Despite all the rhetoric of friendship, the possibility of some strains in Pakistan's relations with China can not be ruled out. One such development, from the Pakistani perspective, could be a complete and persistent policy of China to 'appease the US' and 'sell friendship to India' even at the cost of Pakistan, under some internal or external compulsions. From the Chinese perspective an Islamist take over in Pakistan with hostile designs towards Chinese interests in Xinjiang and central Asia could push China to join the US and India in reining in such a regime. However, chances of such developments remain very remote.

Alliance

An aggressive US policy to contain China, particularly in the Indian Ocean and the greater Middle East in which India becomes a full US partner could possibly force China to seek an alliance with Pakistan. This will be a very difficult situation for Pakistan, as Pakistan may not like to choose sides given the influence of the pro-US lobby which definitely would be countered in a similar attempt by a pro-Chinese lobby to side with the US in this situation. For Pakistan, it may like to seek alliance with China when faced with an attack from India or the US. However, given the Chinese compulsions, its peaceful development policy, and experience during the 1965 and 1971 wars reflect that it would be hesitant to come to rescue Pakistan militarily. Therefore this scenario too remains unlikely.

Status Quo (with improved interdependence)

What is the likely course of relations between the two countries is status quo. For the Chinese status quo is in the best interests of all the parties involved. In this situation China would like to work with both the US and India to eliminate the threat of terrorism and improve Indo-Pak relations gradually. For Pakistan, as discussed earlier, there are not many options left to choose. Given the urgency of its domestic crises and in absence of any favourable option becoming available to it in the near future, Pakistan is also likely to continue on the path of status quo with greater engagements with all three actors. However, it would like to maximise benefits from all the actors having an interest in the stability of South Asia. India in this case could play a greater role by allaying Pakistan's fears.

Concluding Remarks

This chapter has argued that despite the tectonic shifts in the geopolitical landscape of the region after the end of the Cold War, the underlying strategic interests of China and Pakistan have not changed much. Pakistan's strategic culture continues to be shaped by the security predicament posed by its much stronger adversary India. The war on terror, continued instability in Afghanistan (and its adverse domestic impact) and deteriorating economic situation has further intensified Pakistan's sense of insecurity; consequently there is an ever growing need for diplomatic, security and economic assistance from abroad.

Although the United States has been a source of military and economic assistance since 2001 and has shown interest in forging a long-term relationship, the deep mistrust of that country and the current US-India strategic partnership keeps Pakistan on its toes. As a result, Pakistan continues to see the United States as a self-interested unreliable ally and relations between the two remain uncertain at best. China, on the other hand, enjoys enormous goodwill across the board in Pakistan and is perceived as an 'all-weather friend'. There is a conviction among the Pakistani strategists that China and Pakistan share enduring strategic interests imposed on them by geography and history; keeping a check on Indian hegemony not the least of all.

However, there is definitely more to Sino-Pak entente cordial than the India factor. For Pakistan, the rise of China presents enormous economic opportunities in the shape of investments in its critical infrastructure and manufacturing sectors. This also presents an opportunity for Pakistan to become a 'trade and energy corridor' in the long run for China and central Asia. For China, Pakistan offers a large market for its exports and expanding enterprises. Pakistan's strategic location is critical for both Chinese commercial as well as strategic objectives like securing a smooth flow of energy resources. Therefore there is a growing cooperation between the two countries pointing towards a self-sustained relationship.

China has been following a policy of 'peaceful development', from which follows the Sino-US engagement, the Sino-Indian *rapprochement* and the fight against three evils (terrorism, separatism, extremism). As a result, China has adopted a more cautious approach towards Pakistan, particularly in the latter's interaction with India, be it the Kashmir issue, Islamist militancy, or alleged nuclear and missile cooperation between the two countries. Pakistan seems to have fully comprehended Chinese compulsions in this respect. Therefore, Pakistan has been treading carefully in its relations with China and has made an effort not to overreact against a restrained Chinese policy towards Pakistan. On the other hand, there is also an understanding that Pakistan is too important for China to be abandoned. Therefore Islamabad has been reorienting its relations with China giving top priority to economic relations.

❋

Notes

1. Speech by Mr Luo Zhaohui, ambassador of China to Pakistan, 6 June 2006, available at http://pk.china-embassy.org/eng/zbgx/t327077.htm (accessed 2 May 2010).

2. Sandy Gordon, 'South Asia After the Cold War: Winners and Losers', *Asian Survey*, vol. 35, no. 10, October 1995, pp. 879–95.

3. President Pervaiz Musharraf interview with Charlie Rose, 25 September 2006, available at http://www.charlierose.com/view/interview/208 (accessed 2 May 2010).

4. See, for example, Fazal-ur-Rahman, 'Pakistan's Relations with China', *Strategic Studies*, (Winter 1998), pp. 55–87.

5. For a detailed discussion on Pakistan's threat perceptions, see Sahar Shafqat and Kanishkan Sathasivam, 'In India's Shadow: The Evolution of Pakistan's Security Policy', in Uk Heo and Shale Asher Horowitz (ed.), *Conflict in Asia: Korea, China-Taiwan, and India-Pakistan*, London: Praeger, 2003, pp. 119–38.

6. See, for example, Zheng Bijian, 'China's "Peaceful Rise" to Great-Power Status', *Foreign Affairs*, vol. 84, no. 5, Sep./Oct. 2005, pp. 18–24; Xu Genchu, 'China's Peaceful Development and Rising Military Strength', *Chinese Foreign Affairs Journal*, vol. 83, Spring 2007; 'China's Peaceful Development Road', Information Office of the State Council of the People's Republic of China, December 2005, available at http://www.china.org.cn/english/features/book/152684.htm (accessed 2 May 2010); 'China's Position Paper on the New Security Concept', Ministry of Foreign Affairs, Peoples Republic of China, July 2002, available at http://www.mfa.gov.cn/eng/wjb/zzjg/gjs/gjzzyhy/2612/2614/t15319.htm (accessed 2 May 2010).

7. 'White Paper on China's National Defence', December 2000, available at http://www.china.org.cn/e-white/2000/index.htm (accessed 2 May 2010); Ahmed Faruqui, 'The Complex Dynamics of Pakistan's Relationship with China', *IPRI Journal*, vol. 1, no. 1, Sep.–Nov. 2001, pp. 1–17; On China's grand strategy for the 21st century, see, for example, Yunling Zhang and Shiping Tang, 'China's Regional Strategy', in David Shambaugh (ed.), *Power Shift: China and Asia's New Dynamics*, California: University of California, 2006, pp. 48–70; Pervaiz Iqbal Cheema, 'The China Threat: A View from Pakistan', in Herbert Yee and Ian Storey (ed.), *The China Threat: Perceptions, Myths and Reality*, New York: Routledge Curzon, 2002, pp. 306–9; Maqbool Ahmad Bhatty, 'China's Peaceful Rise and South Asia', IPRI Paper 13, Islamabad: Asia Printers, August 2008, pp. 26–27; Michael Pillsbury, *China Debates the Future Security Environment*, Washington DC: National Defense University Press, January 2000; Michael D. Swaine and Ashley J. Tellis, *Interpreting China's Grand Strategy: Past, Present, and Future*, Washington: RAND Corporation, 2000.

8. This change in China's South Asia policy is noted by many scholars, see, for example, Cheema, 'The China Threat', Faruqi, 'The Complex Dynamics of Pakistan's Relationship with China' and Bhatty, 'China's Peaceful Rise and South Asia'; see also Ghulam Ali, 'China's Kashmir

Policy: Back to Neutrality, *IPRI Journal*, vol. 5, no. 2, Summer 2005, pp. 48–61; Robert G. Sutter, *China's Rise in Asia: Promises and Perils*, Maryland: Rowman & Littlefield Publishers, 2005, pp. 231–48; John W. Garver, 'Sino-Indian Rapprochement and the Sino-Pakistan Entente', *Political Science Quarterly*, vol. 111, no. 2, Summer 1996, pp. 323–47; Zhang Guihong, 'U.S. Security Policy toward South Asia after September 11th and Its Implications for China: A Chinese Perspective', January 2003, Washington: Henry L. Stimson Centre, Briefings, available at http://www.stimson.org/regions/south-asia/essays (accessed 2 May 2010); Mira Sinha Bhattacharjea, 'India-China-Pakistan: Beyond Kargil-Changing Equations', *China Report*, vol. 35, no. 4, Oct.–Dec. 1999, pp. 493–99.

9. Ibid.

10. Marvi Memon, 'Reorientation of Pakistan's Foreign Policy after the Cold War', in Mehrunnisa Ali (ed.), *Readings in Pakistan Foreign Policy 1971–98*, Karachi: Oxford University Press, p. 404; Shafqat and Sathasivam, 'In India's Shadow'. Kindly note that there is a growing constituency in Pakistan and India that has worked for peace between the two countries.

11. Hopes have been raised in the post-9/11 strategic environment from unprecedented progress in the peace dialogue and the goodwill gestures from both sides, ostensibly under US pressure. If peace means anything substantial than merely no-war then it may take decades to establish peace between the two countries. Scholars from the two countries and abroad generally agree that there is more to the hostilities than Kashmir. See, for example, Husain Haqqani, 'Pakistan's Endgame in Kashmir', *India Review*, vol. 2, no. 3, July 2003, pp. 34–54; Rajesh Basrur, 'South Asia's Persistent Cold War', ACDIS Occasional Paper, November 1996, pp. 2–3, available at https://www.ideals.illinois.edu/bitstream/handle/2142/15/Basrur%2520OP.pdf?sequence=1 (accessed 2 May 2010); Kripa Sridharan, *Indo-US Strategic Engagement* New Delhi: MacMillan, 2009, pp. 67–73; Robert Wirsing, 'Pakistan's Strategic Options: From the Cold War to the War on Terrorism', in Saeed Shafqat (ed.), *New Perspectives on Pakistan*, Karachi: Oxford University Press, 2007, pp. 370–73; Hu Shesheng, 'Role of SAARC Observers: China's Perspective', in S. D. Muni (ed.), *The Emerging Dimensions of SAARC*, New Delhi: Cambridge University Press, 2010.

12. The 2,640 km long Durand Line that divides the two countries, and the Pushtun and Baluch tribes on both sides of the border, is not recognised by Afghanistan even today.

13. Pakistan Budget FY 2009–10, available at http://www.mofa.gov.pk/Pages/Budget-Speech-09-10_Eng.pdf (accessed 2 May 2010).

14. See, for example, Barnett R. Rubin and Ahmed Rashid, 'From Great Game to Grand Bargain: Ending Chaos in Afghanistan and Pakistan',

Foreign Affairs, vol. 87, no. 6, November/December 2008, pp. 30–45; Fahmida Ashraff, 'India-Afghanistan Relations: Post 9/11', *Strategic Studies*, vol. 27, no. 2, 2007.

15. See, for example, Wang Jisi, 'China's Changing Role in Asia', in Kokubun Ryosei and Wang Jisi (eds), *The Rise of China and a Changing East Asian Order*, Tokyo: Japan Center for International Exchange, 2004, p. 16; Sutter, *China's Rise in Asia*, p. 245.
16. Cheema, 'The China Threat', p. 305.
17. Shuja Nawaz, *Crossed Swords: Pakistan, Its Army and the Wars Within*, Karachi: Oxford University Press, 2008, pp. 93–103.
18. Following on Mackinder's geographical line of argument, among others, Sir Olaf Caroe, the last governor of the NWFP, argued that (West) Pakistan and Iran are not only important geographically but Islam presents an ideological bulwark against the expanding communist threat. This idea later formed the basis of President Eisenhower and Secretary Dulles' containment policy in South West Asia. For a detailed discussion on the topic see Lloyd Rudolph and Susanne H. Rudolph, 'The Making of US Foreign Policy for South Asia', *Economic and Political Weekly*, vol. 41, no. 8, 25 February 25–3 March 2006, pp. 703–9; Peter Brobst, *The Future of the Great Game*, Ohio: The University of Akron Press, 2005; Olaf Caroe, *Wells of Power: The Oilfields of South-Western Asia: A Regional and Global Study*, London: Macmillan, 1951.
19. 'Pakistan', Country Studies Series by Federal Research Division, Library of Congress, United States, available at http://www.country-data.com/cgi-bin/query/r-9896.html (accessed 2 May 2010).
20. K. Arif, *Pakistan's Foreign Policy*, Lahore: Vanguard Publishers, 1984, p. 274, quoted by Shahzad Akhtar, 'Sino-Pakistan Relations: An Assessment', *Strategic Studies*, vol. 29, no. 2 and 3, 2009, pp. 65–89, here p. 65.
21. Cheema, 'The China Threat', p. 303.
22. W. M. Dobell, 'Ramifications of the China-Pakistan Border Treaty', *Pacific Affairs*, vol. 37, no. 3, Autumn 1964, pp. 283–95.
23. Mohammad Ahsen Chaudhri, 'Strategic and Military Dimensions in Pakistan China Relations', in Mehrunnisa Ali (ed.), *Readings in Pakistan Foreign Policy 1971–98*, Karachi: Oxford University Press, 2001, pp. 317–29.
24. 'Silk Road', in *Encyclopædia Britannica*, from Encyclopædia Britannica Online, available at http://www.britannica.com/EBchecked/topic/544491/Silk-Road (accessed 2 May 2010).
25. John E. Hill, *Through the Jade Gate to Rome: A Study of the Silk Routes during the Later Han Dynasty, First to Second Centuries CE*, South

Carolina: BookSurge, 2009, p. 29; John M. Rosenfield, *The Dynastic Art of the Kushans*, New Delhi: Munshiram Manoharlal, 1993, p. 41.

26. Inasmuch as the 1907 Anglo-Russian Convention declared Tibet, Afghanistan and parts of Iran as buffer zones between the two empires.

27. 'Pakistan: Courtship in the Air', *Time Magazine*, 6 September 1963; Arif Hussain, *Pakistan: Its Ideology and Foreign Policy*, London: Frank Cass & Co., 1966, p. 109.

28. B. R. Deepak, 'Sino-Pak Entente Cordiale and India', *China Report*, vol. 42, no. 2, 2006, pp. 129–51; Garver, 'Sino-Indian Rapprochement and the Sino-Pakistan Entente'.

29. See, for example, Mansoor A. Kundi, 'Politics of American Aid: The Case of Pakistan', *Asian Affairs*, vol. 29, no. 2, April–June 2007, pp. 22–39; Mohammed Ayoob, 'Pakistan's Alliance with the United States, 1954–1965', Ph.D. thesis, University of Hawaii, 1966, available at http://scholarspace.manoa.hawaii.edu/handle/10125/11839 (accessed 2 May 2010).

30. See, for example, Nawaz, *Crossed Swords*, pp. 193–200; Abdul Sattar, *Pakistan Foreign Policy: 1947–2005*, Karachi: Oxford University Press, 2007, pp. 60–64; Hussain, *Pakistan*, p. 109–26.

31. Ayoob, 'Pakistan's Alliance with the United States', p. 179.

32. Ibid., p. 180; also see Sattar, *Pakistan Foreign Policy*, p. 62.

33. *The Chronicles of Pakistan*, 8 March 1958, available at http://www.therepublicofrumi.com/chronicle/1956.htm (accessed 2 May 2010).

34. For a detailed discussion of the role of CIA in the Tibetan uprising and the Indian Forward Policy leading to the 1962 Indo-China conflict see Kenneth Conboy and James Morrison, *The CIA's Secret War in Tibet*, Lawrence: University Press of Kansas, 2002; Neville Maxwell, 'Henderson Brooks Report: An Introduction', *Economic and Political Weekly*, vol. 36, no. 14/15, Apr. 14–20, 2001, pp. 1189–1193; Neville Maxwell, *India's China War*, New York: Anchor Books, 1972.

35. Ibid. Also see Dobell, 'Ramifications of the China-Pakistan Border Treaty'; Hussain, *Pakistan*. Bhatty, 'China's Peaceful Rise and South Asia', pp. 54–55.

36. John W. Garver, 'China's Decision for War with India in 1962', 2004, available at http://www.people.fas.harvard.edu/~johnston/garver.pdf (accessed 2 May 2010); Dobell, 'Ramifications of the China-Pakistan Border Treaty'; Bhatty, 'China's Peaceful Rise and South Asia', pp. 54–55.

37. Mohammad Ayub Khan, *Friends Not Masters*, Karachi: Oxford University Press, 1967, reprint by Islamabad: Mr Books, 2006, pp. 160–66; 'In Anguish, Not Anger', *Times Magazine*, 30 November 1962.

38. Ibid.
39. Ibid. Hussain, *Pakistan*, p. 109; Sattar, *Pakistan Foreign Policy*, pp. 60–64.
40. See, for example, Hussain, *Pakistan*, pp.110–26.
41. Ibid.
42. Ibid.
43. Mohammed Ayoob, 'India Matters', *The Washington Quarterly*, vol. 23, no.1, 2000, pp. 27–39.
44. 'East Pakistan: Poor Relations', *Times Magazine*, 14 July 1958.
45. Wang Gungwu, *Ideas Won't Keep: the Struggle for China's Future*, Singapore: Eastern University Press, 2003, p. 5.
46. Bhatty, 'China's Peaceful Rise and South Asia', p. 77. The author here seems to talk more about enduring injustices rather than historical injustices.
47. Mahmud, 'Sino-Pak Ties'; Zaid Haider, 'The China Factor in Pakistan', *Far Eastern Economic Review* October 2009, full version available at http://64.151.79.128/?p=131 (accessed 2 May 2010).
48. Humayoun Khan, 'A Historical View of China's Foreign Policy towards Great Powers', *Strategic Studies*, vol. 26, no. 2, 2006, available at http://www.issi.org.pk/old-site/ss_Detail.php?dataId=391 (accessed 2 May 2010).
49. For detailed discussions see the various studies cited in this chapter.
50. Bhatty, 'China's Peaceful Rise and South Asia', p. 79.
51. Ibid. See also Wirsing, 'Pakistan's Strategic Options' and Garver, 'Sino-Indian Rapprochement and the Sino-Pakistan Entente'.
52. See, for example, Cheema, 'The China Threat', Bhatty, 'China's Peaceful Rise and South Asia', Faruqui, 'The Complex Dynamics of Pakistan's Relationship with China'; Khan, 'A Historical View of China's Foreign Policy towards Great Powers'; Khalid Mahmud, 'Sino-Pak Ties: India Factor', *Dawn*, 14 April 2001; Shehzad H. Qazi, 'United States' Attempts to Balance the Rise of China in Asia', *IPRI Journal*, vol. 9, no. 2, Summer 2009, pp. 32–48.
53. White Paper on Peaceful Development Road, The State Council of China, December 2005, available at http://www.china.org.cn/english/2005/Dec/152669.htm (accessed 2 May 2010).
54. Ibid., also see Bhatty, 'China's Peaceful Rise and South Asia'.
55. Ibid.
56. Jia Qingguo, 'Learning to Live with the Hegemon: Evolution of China's Policy Toward the United States since the End of the Cold War', *Journal of Contemporary China*, vol. 14, no. 44, 2005, pp. 395–410.
57. David Shambaugh, 'China Engages Asia: Reshaping the Regional Order', *International Security*, vol. 29, no. 3, 2004/2005, pp. 64–99, here p. 95.

58. Mahmud, 'Sino-Pak Ties';
Ali, 'China's Kashmir Policy'.

59. Starting from the 1996 visit of President Jiang Zemin, China has consistently played a constructive role and urged both India and Pakistan to solve their issues through dialogue. For further discussion, see Iftikhar Lodhi and Rajshree Jetly, 'Sino-Pak Relations: Retrospect and Prospect', in Tan Tai Yong (ed.), *South Asian Perspectives: Societies in Transition*, Delhi: Macmillan Publications, 2010, pp. 153–86.

60. Mahmud, 'Sino-Pak Ties'.

61. Statement by Pakistan's ambassador to China, available at http://www.pakembassy.cn/statement_7.html (accessed 2 May 2010).

62. Joint Statement by President Obama and Chinese President Hu in China, 17 November 2009, available at http://www.america.gov/st/texttrans-english/2009/November/20091117155448eaifas0.846615.html&distid=ucs (accessed 2 May 2010).

63. 'US–China Seek Role in South Asia, Irked India Says No', 19 November 2009, Zee News, available at http://www.zeenews.com/news580042.html (accessed 2 May 2010).

64. See, for example, Bhatty, 'China's Peaceful Rise and South Asia', p. 71, Cheema, 'The China Threat', and Jisi, 'China's Changing Role in Asia'.

65. See, for example, Mahmud, 'Sino-Pak Ties' and Jisi, 'China's Changing Role in Asia'.

66. When asked, the Chinese officials have resorted to the line that they are not affected by the Indo-US nuclear deal or partnership. See, for example, Lodhi and Jetly, 'Sino-Pak Relations'.

67. See, for example, John W. Garver, 'China's Influence in Central and South Asia', in David Shambaugh (ed.), *Power Shift: China and Asia's New Dynamics*, California: University of California, 2006.

68. Sattar, *Pakistan Foreign Policy*, p. 248; Kripa Sridharan, *Indo-US Strategic Partnership*, New Delhi: Palgrave, 2009, p. 73.

69. 'Ahmed Ejaz, an expert on Asian security at the University of Punjab, believes that for China, the stakes are far too great for it to turn its back on Pakistan', quoted in 'Pakistan and China: A Fraying Friendship?', *Time Magazine*, 19 February 2009; Lodhi and Jetly, 'Sino-Pak Relations'.

70. Tanvir A. Khan, 'New Developments in Pakistan–China Relations', *Arab News*, 20 April 2007, available at http://www.arabnews.com/?page=7&section=0&article=95216&d=20&m=4&y=2007.

71. Lodhi and Jetly, 'Sino-Pak Relations'.

72. There have also been fears that the cheap Chinese goods may hurt Pakistan's domestic industry. However, these fears appear baseless as Chinese high end value-added exports to Pakistan mainly compete with imports from other countries.

73. Prime Minister Shoukat Aziz speaking at a conference organised by the ISSI, Islamabad. Proceedings available at http://www.issi.org.pk (accessed 2 May 2010).

74. Lodhi and Jetly, 'Sino-Pak Relations'.

75. Iftikhar Lodhi, 'IPI or TAPI?', in Marie Lall (ed.), *The Geopolitics of Energy Security in South Asia*, Singapore: ISEAS Publications, 2008.

76. International Institute of Strategic Studies, June 2002, available at http://www.iiss.org/conferences/the-shangri-la-dialogue/press-coverage/press-coverage-2002/the-economist---china-feels-encircled (accessed 2 May 2010).

77. Lodhi, 'IPI or TAPI?'.

78. Ibid.

79. Malik Qasim Mustafa, 'Pakistan Defence Production: Prospects for Defence Export', *Strategic Studies*, vol. 24, no. 4, 2004, available at http://www.issi.org.pk/journal/2004_...article/5a.htm (accessed 2 May 2010.

80. Ibid.

81. Ibid.

82. A survey of *Millitary Balance 2009*, IISS (available at http://www.iiss.org/publications/military-balance/the-military-balance-2009 [accessed 2 May 2010]) confirms this author's personal communications with various high level officials and experts that the Pakistan military is predominantly using Chinese technology.

83. See, for example, Pakistan section in *Military Balance 2009*, International Institute of Strategic Studies; Pakistan's Military Inventory, Global Security website, available at http://www.globalsecurity.org/military/world/pakistan/air-force-equipment.htm (accessed 2 May 2010).

84. 'Central and South Asia Caribbean and Latin America', *The Military Balance 2009*, vol. 109, no. 1, pp. 329–62.

85. 'Official Claims Big Rise in Arms Exports', *Dawn*, 18 July 2008.

86. Lodhi and Jetly, 'Sino-Pak Relations'.

87. George Perkovich, 'The Nuclear and Security Balance' in Francine R. Frankel and Harry Harding (ed.), *The India-China Relationship: Rivalry and Engagement*, New Delhi: Oxford University Press, 2004, pp. 178–218, here p. 200, quoted in Lodhi and Jetly, 'Sino-Pak Relations'.

88. W. John Garver, 'The Future of the Sino-Pakistani Entente Cordiale' in Michael Chambers (ed.), *South Asia in 2020: Future Strategic Balances and Alliances*, Strategic Studies Institute, USA, 2002, pp. 385–448, here p. 405, quoted in Lodhi and Jetly, 'Sino-Pak Relations'.

89. See, for example, Javid Husain, 'The Process of Foreign Policy Formulation in Pakistan', Briefing Paper No. 12, PILDAT (April 2004), available at http://www.pildat.org/Publications/publication/FP/

The%20Process%20of%20Foreign%20Policy%20Formulation%20i n%20Pakistan.pdf (accessed 2 May 2010).
90. Ibid.
91. For a detailed discussion see Hamza Alvi, 'The Army and the Bureaucracy in Pakistan Politics', in A. Abdel Malek (ed.), *Armee et Nations dans les Trios Continints*, Alger 1975 (Original paper in English, mimeographed), quoted in Mohammed Waseem, 'Civil-Military Relations in Pakistan', in Rajshree Jetly (ed.), *Pakistan in Regional and Global Politics*, New Delhi: Routledge, 2009, p. 186.
92. Waseem, 'Civil-Military Relations in Pakistan', p. 186.
93. Ibid.
94. Ibid.
95. Lodhi and Jetly, 'Sino-Pak Relations'.
96. For a discussion on the Pakistan army and its strategic culture, see, for example, Brian Cloughley, *A History of the Pakistan Army*, Karachi: Oxford University Press, 2000; Brian Cloughley, *War, Coups and Terror: Pakistan's Army in Years of Turmoil*, New York: Skyhorse Publishing, 2009. Nawaz, *Crossed Swords*.
97. See, for example, how there was a difference of opinion on the decision whether Pakistan should join the American war on terror. Pervez Musharraf, *In the Line of Fire*, New York: Free Press, 2006. Similarly, many Pakistani retired generals have come out in public to express their opinions against the war on terror.
98. Pakistan's foreign policy available at http://www.bhutto.org/relations. htm (accessed 2 May 2010).
99. Rajshree Jetly, 'Forthcoming Pakistan Elections: A profile on Benazir Bhutto', ISAS Brief No. 36, 13 December 2007, available at http://www. isasnus.org/events/backgroundbriefs/37.pdf (accessed 2 May 2010).
100. The PPP manifesto, available at http://www.ppp.org.pk/manifestos/2008. pdf (accessed 2 May 2010).
101. See, for example, Ishtiaq Ahmed, 'Forthcoming Pakistan Elections: A Profile on Benazir Bhutto', ISAS Brief No. 37, 19 December 2007, available at http://www.isasnus.org/events/backgroundbriefs/38.pdf (accessed 2 May 2010).
102. BBC, 28 May 1998, available at http://news.bbc.co.uk/2/hi/world/ monitoring/102445.stm (accessed 2 May 2010).
103. PML-N Manifesto, available at http://www.pmln.110mb.com (accessed 2 May 2010).
104. Iftikhar A. Lodhi, 'Forthcoming Pakistan Elections: A Profile on the Islamic Parties', ISAS Brief No. 39, 26 December 2007, available at http://www.isasnus.org/events/backgroundbriefs/40.pdf (accessed 2 May 2010).

105. 'Pakistan Saved China from Embarrassment on Xinjiang Violence: Chinese Ambassador', *Daily Times*, 5 September 2009.
106. Ibid.
107. Zaid Haider, 'The China Factor in Pakistan'.
108. Imran Ali, 'Political Economy of Pakistan', in Rajshree Jetly (ed.), *Pakistan in Regional and Global Politics*, New Delhi: Routledge, 2009, p. 186.

8

Pakistan
Challenge of China's 'Second Rise'

SHAHID JAVED BURKI

China is rising again. This time, the change is taking place in response to Beijing's policy responses to an external eco-nomic crisis. Beijing has handled domestic economic crises earlier but this time around, the structural impact on the country's economy and its relationship with the outside world will be very different and considerably more profound. How China will change and how that change will influence the world — not just the global economy but also the international political order — are the subjects that have begun to receive some attention in academic and policy circles. This chapter attempts to bring out some of the issues that should inform the debate. It also discusses the impact China is likely to have on Pakistan, one of its neighbours in South Asia. China and Pakistan have enjoyed what is often referred to as an 'all-weather relationship' to distinguish it from the off and on relationship it has had with the United States.[1] As China's status in the community of nations improves and as it develops the institutional means to conduct its business with the United States, would it continue to pay the kind of attention it has given in the past to Pakistan? We will provide some tentative answers to this question.

This chapter has seven parts. The second part, following this introduction, looks at China's 'second rise' — a phrase used to underscore the point that the policies adopted this time by Beijing to pull the country out of what economists now call the 'Great Recession of 2008–9' will not only deeply affect the structure of the Chinese economy but also the global economic system. The third part examines China's rise in the context of a theoretical framework economic historians have developed to understand how and why relatively backward economies sometimes catch up with the leaders. In China's case it is in the process of catching up with the United States in terms of the size of its national product after it overtook Japan in 2010. It is the latter development— that China rather than Japan is now the largest Asian economy — that is of great consequence for the smaller economies of Asia such as Pakistan. The fourth part is a discussion of China's rise on the global economic system, as there will be a profound change in the structure of the global economic system in order to accommodate China's rise. The fifth part of the chapter looks at the impact China's economic prominence will have on Pakistan. The sixth part discusses President Asif Ali Zardari's state visit to China in mid-July 2010. The chapter concludes with a brief summary of the argument presented about China and the impact it is likely to have on its smaller neighbours such as Pakistan.

China's 'Second Rise'

There is now consensus among policy analysts the world over that China is well on the way to becoming a power house in the global economy. Even if it does not become the world's largest economy in one and a half to two decades — as some believe that it might — it will certainly be the second largest, behind the United States. The fact that the country's economy has begun to recover at a faster pace than was expected in the spring of 2009 is a testimony to its strength. At that time the global economy was in a deep recession — economists have begun to refer to it as the 'Great Recession of 2008–9' — and the Chinese dependence on the markets in developed countries was expected to hurt it badly. That did not happen. In the summer of 2009, the World Bank issued a new forecast on China's growth rate which was put at 7.2 per cent. This was a long way down from the 11.9 per cent in 2007 but was still remarkable, given the sluggishness in other parts of the world. China is likely to achieve this impressive rate of growth in spite of a fall in the rate of real export growth from 20 per cent in 2007, to 8 per cent in 2008 and to a forecast of minus 10 per cent in 2009. In 2009, the Chinese GDP increased by 9.6 per cent and in 2010 by another 10.3 per cent. According to one assessment, 'China may have accounted for as much as 2 percentage points of annualized growth in inflation-adjusted world output in the second quarter of 2009'.[2] This was possible since the country was no longer that dependent on exports for growth as was believed before the present crisis hit the globe. It may lead the emerging economies towards 'decoupling', a concept according to which these economies are no longer linked with the world's rich nations, moving in tandem with them.

China's rapid recovery from the setback caused to its economy by the deep recession in the West — in particular in the United States, its largest trading partner — was on to two counts: the aggressive response by the state to the decline in the rate of economic growth and the rapid, but still not fully understood, restructuring of its economy. In 2008 Beijing moved decisively to prevent a sharp decline in GDP by injecting large sums of public funds into the economy. A stimulus package of Rmb4,000 billion (US$ 585 billion) was launched largely to further develop physical infrastructure — roads, railways, airports, ports, bridges and tunnels. The money flowed from the federal budget to the state-owned agencies responsible for building and maintaining infrastructure. It was spent quickly by bringing forward the projects that were already included in the current five year plan or were at the planning stage. The United States also provided a large dose of public money to stimulate its economy; $200 billion more than the Chinese amount. But the American programme mostly went into encouraging consumption such as 'cash for clunkers' according to which the consumers could trade in their old cars for new ones. The Chinese put money into developing physical infrastructure.

Beijing's main concern was with rising unemployment. Some 20 million workers — mostly migrants from the countryside — were laid off by the industries in the private sector that depended almost entirely on exports to the West. Under the Chinese system of human resource management, the unemployed workers were required to return to their villages. Beijing was fearful that this return would make the countryside restive. Given the country's history, Beijing is always alert to the possibility of 'peasant rebellions'. The rising by the Uighur minority in the summer of 2009 can be partly attributed to the economic slowdown which took a heavier economic toll on the western provinces such as Xinjiang, the home-province of the community, than in the country's more developed eastern parts. This happened in spite of the fact Beijing had initiated a ten-year economic development plan to narrow the gap between the western and eastern provinces.

One consequence of this large stimulus to the economy was a significant increase in the share of the public sector in the Chinese economic system. This reversed the trend of the last two decades when the authorities encouraged the state sector to shrink in size in the expectation that people who lost jobs in the state-owned enterprises (SOEs) would find employment in the rapidly expanding private sector. This approach differed markedly from the one adopted by the countries that once made up the Soviet Union and those in Eastern Europe as they switched their ideologies. Communist Europe adopted capitalism by following the 'big bang' approach. The Chinese, ever pragmatic, opted for the gradualist approach. One consequence of the way the Chinese handled the economic downturn in 2008–9 was to interrupt this process of transferring workers from the public to the private sectors of the economy by creating space for them in the state sector. One unintended consequence of this was the strengthening of the role of the state in the economy which will be used to handle the opportunities created and the problems posed by its unique urbanisation experience.

China: In the "Catch-up Game"

Studying catch-up economies became a popular pursuit as economists began to understand the process of economic growth.[3] The first insightful study in this area was done by the Harvard economic historian Alexander Gercshenkron.[4] He first studied the industrial revolution in England and concluded that it came about because of a fortuitous combination of a number of circumstances; in particular, technological revolution and entrepreneurship. He then turned his attention to Western Europe. Once England had shown the way, the countries that had been left behind were anxious to catch up. Those who aspired to catch up with England were the countries in the immediate neighbourhood. France was the first one to work on that process with the French state playing an active role. Germany was the second country to play the catch-up game. In its case, it was a close relationship between finance and industry that helped the country to get even with the front runner.

The United States joined the game in the last few decades of the 19th century. In the US case, natural endowments and a government structure that allowed a great deal of space to private entrepreneurship helped. America not only caught up with Europe, it overtook it in terms of the size of its national product and the average per capita income of its citizens. This happened in the period leading up to the First World War. Europe, weakened by the war, was left behind by the United States, and for about three decades it was the sole economic Superpower.

After the Second World War it was Japan's turn to successfully play the catch-up game. By the end of the 1970s, in terms of average per capita income, it was equal to that of the advanced countries of Western Europe and also with the United States. It was not able to overtake the US in terms of the size of its economy simply because it had a much smaller population. Japan's extraordinary story of economic success was studied by scholars from several disciplines. Ezra Vogel, a Harvard University socio-logist, was one of them whose 1979 book, *Japan as Number One*, became a best seller.[5] He argued that Japan, by combining a style of governance with a culture that supported entrepreneurship, had found a unique way to promote economic growth. It would not be long before Japan would have the largest economy in the world and income per capita much larger than the United States.

The Japanese model of growth involving an active role by the state, large investments in the development of the human resource and focus on exports, was adopted by a number of countries of East Asia. They were able to accelerate their rates of growth to the point where, by the first decade of the 21st century, Singapore's per capita income approached the levels of America and Western Europe while South Korea joined the Organisa-tion for Economic Cooperation and Development (OECD). The Paris based OECD is considered to be the rich countries' club. Both Singapore and South Korea were included among the countries that came to be called East Asia's 'miracle economies'.[6] In Japan as well as in the miracle economies of East Asia, the state created the economic environment in which the private sector could freely operate, flourish and compete in the domestic eco-nomy. By maintaining an undervalued exchange rate the gov-ernments of these countries also made it possible for domestic producers to export their products.

While China was not initially counted among the miracle economies, its growth picked up in the early 1980s and has been maintained for more than a quarter century. China's economy, in achieving high rates of growth, has gone through two phases. In the first, the country followed the model of growth pursued by the miracle economies of East Asia by relying on exports. The second phase started with the Great Recession of 2008–9 in the global economy. In dealing with the sudden deterioration in the state of the global economy, the Chinese began to reorient their economy towards domestic consumption. They put in place structural changes that will have profound implications for its future and for the rest of Asia.[7]

China's second rise 'could accelerate Japan's economic decline as it captures Japanese export markets, its crushing national debt increases, and its ageing population grows less and less productive — producing a downward spiral', wrote Hiroko Tabuchi in *The New York Times*. 'At stake are more than regional bragging rights: the reversal of fortunes will bring an end to a global economic order that has prevailed for more than 40 years, with ramifications across arenas from trade and diplomacy to, potentially, military power', he continued.[8] Though recent wild swings could delay the reckoning, many economists expect Japan to cede its rank as the world's second largest economy sometime next year, as much as five years earlier than previously forecast. Some Japanese observers were disconcerted at these developments:

> Now many here ask whether it is destined to be the next Switzerland: rich and comfortable, but of little global import, largely ignored by the rest of the world . . . the per-capita gross domestic product of Japan which, surged past that of the United States in the late 1980s, stalled at $34,300 in 2007; it is now a quarter below American levels and 19th in the world.[9]

However, unlike the countries of Western Europe in which the rate of economic growth also stalled, both income inequality and poverty rose in Japan. In 2009 unemployment stood at 5.7 per cent, while prices and wages were falling fast. Japan's economy shrank at an annualised rate of 11.7 per cent in the first three months of the year before recovering to a modest 2.3 per cent annual rate of growth in the second quarter. China also surpassed

Japan in having the biggest trade surplus and foreign currency reserves, as well as the highest steel production. And in 2011 China could overtake Japan as the largest automobile producer. China became Japan's largest trading partner in 2006 and China-bound exports were among the first signs of recovery in the 2008–9 slump. Based on current growth and currency trends, C. H. Kwan (the author of the forthcoming *China as No. 1*, a kind of update of Ezra. F. Vogel's 1979 best seller) forecast that the Chinese economy could surpass that of the United States in 2039. And the date could move up to 2026 if China lets its currency appreciate by a mere 2 per cent a year.[10]

The Chinese economy, on the other hand expanded by 9.6 per cent in 2009, while the Japanese economy shrank by 3 per cent for the year before returning to an anemic growth of about 1 per cent in 2010. The Chinese economy grew about 10 per cent a year for most of the last two decades. According to Hiroko Tabuchi, 'over that period the Japanese economy stagnated as huge public works projects aimed at reviving the economy went toward protecting moribund industries instead of fostering new ones. . . . In 1988, Nomura Securities issued a ranking of companies by market capitalization, and 8 of the top 10 were in Japan, topped by Nippon Telegraph and Telephone. As of July this year, not a single Japanese company made to the global 10. The list was dominated by companies based in China and the United States; Toyota Motor, now the largest Japanese firm, ranked No. 22, at $144.5 billion, and only five other Japanese companies made the top 100. The richest man in Japan, the retailing entrepreneur Tadashi Yanai, was 76th in the most recent global Forbes list, behind moguls from countries like Mexico, India and the Czech Republic — a far cry from the late 1980s when Japanese industrialists like the railroad tycoon Yoshiaki Tsutsumi were among those at the top.'[11]

As countries develop, growth tends to slow down. Annual growth in the Japanese gross domestic product averaged 10.4 per cent in the 1960s and 5 per cent in the 1970s, but only 4 per cent in the 1980s and 1.4 per cent in the 1990s, according to a study by Goldman Sachs. In the first decade of this century, growth has been even slower. Would China follow the same pattern? A slowdown in the Chinese economy has been predicted ever since the country began to register double digit increases in its GDP.

That did not happen for a number of reasons, among them, most importantly, was the pragmatism shown by the leadership groups in Beijing. Since the Chinese economy began to take off — a process that began in 1979 with the ascent to power of Deng Xiaoping, Beijing has seen two changes in leadership — from Deng to Zhiang Xemin and from Zhiang to Hu Jintao. But one thing remained constant: the focus of the leadership on economic development. In addition, unlike Japan, China still has a very large reserve of labour that can — and will be — moved from less to more productive jobs in the economy. This will result in increases in worker productivity which, in turn, will contribute to a high rate of economic growth.

The passing of economic leadership from Japan to China will have enormous consequences for other countries of Asia. While our concern is with economics, it is useful to say a word about politics. Japan was less assertive in international affairs, leaving that role to the United States. The US was thus able to dominate the Pacific region. In China, the US is bound to face some competition. The American administration headed by President Barack Obama put forth the argument that the era of great-power competition is over. The American president declared during a speech in July 2009, delivered before an audience made up mostly of Chinese officials, that relations with China 'must no longer be seen as a zero-sum game'. According to the more conservative elements in the American foreign policy establishment such as Robert Kagan and Dan Blumenthal:

> Unfortunately, that is not a reality in Asia. Contrary to optimistic predictions just a decade ago, China is behaving exactly as one would expect a great power to behave. As it has grown richer, China has used its wealth to build a stronger and more capable military. As its military power has grown, so have its ambitions. This is especially true of its naval ambitions. Not so long ago, China experts believed that it was absurd for China to aspire to a 'blue water' navy capable of operating far from its seas, and yet the country is investing large sums of money in acquiring a modern navy.[12]

China's growing military strength will have consequences for India that has ambitions of its own as an emerging quasi-superpower and also for Pakistan as it seeks to balance India's growing presence in the South Asian region by getting even closer to China. However, economics is the main subject of analysis in this chapter. Here as well, China's eclipse of Japan as the most important Asian economy will have profound implications for the rest of Asia.

When Japan was the rising economic power and the most important economic player in Asia, it conducted its relations with the other Asian countries on purely economic and humanitarian terms. In the case of its trade with other Asian countries, it bought what was needed by its rapidly growing industries and sold the surpluses its industry produced. In developing its aid programme, it focused more on poverty and on the development of infrastructure than was the case with other large donors. It did not use aid either to promote its own economy in pursuit of its geopolitical interests. And, since it was considerably more developed than other countries of Asia, it did not compete with them.

China, of course is different. It differs in at least three ways. Its industry competes with those in the rest of Asia. This is particularly the case with the industries in such low-wage economies as in South Asia. Second, it is searching for the resources it needs and is using its aid programme to gain access to the resource-rich countries in Africa and Central Asia. At the African summit held in the Egyptian resort of Sharm-al-Sheikh in November 2009, it announced that it will double its aid programme to sub-Saharan Africa from $5 to $10 billion. And, third, it uses its economic contacts for geopolitical purposes. Its close economic relations with Pakistan have always been motivated by that consideration.

Impact of China's Second Rise on the Global System

How will this new China affect the global economy and its political system? As Britain's prime minister Gordon Brown wrote in an op-ed piece for the *New York Times* on the eve of the opening session of the 2009 UN General Assembly:

> After 1945, the world — fresh from a devastating conflict — summoned its energies to build a new international order. Now we are being tested again. In the days and months ahead, our collective resolve must hold across all the challenges [the world faces]. If it can, something

bigger and even more lasting than the great reconstruction of the post-war era is possible: the creation of the first truly global society.[13]

Although Prime Minister Brown did not say that China will be an important component of this 'global society', it was clear that this will indeed be the case. A day before the Brown article appeared in the newspaper, President Hu Jintao of China surprised the international community by presenting his government's plans to address the problem of climate change. He thus put China in the lead of the effort rather than be cast in the role of a country interested in its own economic future rather than in the long-term health of the globe. How will the world accommodate a richer and more assertive China?

It is possible to contemplate four possible futures for the global economy and how these might shape the international economic and political systems. All three will have considerable consequences for South Asia. We can argue that the world is moving away from unipolarism when the United States was the undisputed leader. That this may happen has led to some talk about G7 or G8 being replaced by G20, a larger grouping of states than the more restrictive G7. This would mean slowing the move towards the creation of a multilateral system that receives direction from a much broader grouping than G7 or G8. In this context, the role played by G20 was seen to expand. This group includes, in addition to G8, the twelve largest emerging economies from all parts of the world. It has met three times since November 2008 when it was reconstituted at the heads of state level. It met in Washington in November under the chairman-ship of lame-duck US president George W. Bush; in London in April 2009 presided over by Prime Minister Gordon Brown; in Pittsburgh in July 2009 chaired by Barack Obama, the new US president, and at Toronto chaired by Canada's prime minister Stanley Harper. It was supposed to come up with a new structure for managing the global economy. This would have led to the development of a new form of multilateralism. This did not occur and may not happen for the simple reason that G20 was being built on top of a system that had creaky foundations. The focus remained on the United States and Western Europe. The latter, in particular — and for reasons that we will mention briefly later — is no longer the most vibrant part of the global economy.

There may not, after all, be such a widening of influence and reshaping of the global economy as was believed would be the case when the Great Recession of 2008–9 began. Instead, America and China may institutionalise their cooperation on issues that concern them as well as those that matter for the global economy. The slow move towards multipolarism may be preempted by the continuing strength of the economy of the United States and what is called the 'second rise of China'. That this may be happening was demonstrated by the inaugural session of the Strategic and Economic Dialogue between Washington and Beijing held in Washington in the closing days of July 2009. Both sides fielded large delegations and the discussions covered a large number of issues of mutual interests. In his opening address, President Barrack Obama said that the United States–China relationship will 'shape the 21st century'. With that he virtually launched the 'G2' without giving it that name.

It can also be argued that what we are seeing is the emergence of a multi-centric world. Such global configuration will reshape not only the global economy but also the international political system. We could see a global system with as many as seven centres of economic activity — the United States, Japan, China, India, Brazil, South Africa and the European Union. The first six of these will try and create their own spheres of influence. The European Union is still in a formative phase with a considerable dispersal of power among the nation states that are its members. For as long as it does not find a way of working as one entity able to pull its weight in unison, it will not be able to create much of an impression on other parts of the world. Europe and Japan are also two parts of the post-industrial world that have as yet to find a way out of the demographic cul-de-sac in which they find themselves with declining rates of fertility. A declining population and aversion to compensate it through immigration will inevitably produce less economic dynamism. India may not be able to match China's economic success any time soon.[14]

The remaining six economic centres could, if circumstances permit, create their own spheres with a greater prospect of clashes than is likely in a bipolar world. These clashes will occur in the areas where the different spheres come into contact. The most likely places where this may occur are in Central and South Asia, and the Middle East. Not only will this result from competition for geographic space — which was the reason in the past for clashes between centres of power. There will, in addition, be economic reasons for conflict. In a global system increasingly short of scarce resources vital for sustaining development, there will be immense competition for energy and water and possibly also some minerals vital for development. However, systems with many poles are inherently less stable compared to those dominated by one or two powers as was the case in the post–Second World War period.

A fourth likely scenario is also possible. If the United States and China become the two dominant powers, the global system will have three and not two tiers — the two global powers, four or five regional powers and the rest. In the former case each major power will seek to circumscribe the other by creating economic and political alliances close to the other power. This will create some tension of the type that characterised the 'Cold War' period in which the United States and the Soviet Union challenged each other. The United States then built a chain of alliances around the Soviet Union and China — this was when it regarded China as an extension of the Soviet Union — while Moscow tried to recruit Cuba and a number of small Central American states as partners. Moscow also encouraged a number of developing countries to remain unaligned. The Non-aligned Movement in which India played the role of a leader had the consequence of limiting the reach of the United States.

However, America and China may not confront each other the way the United States and the Soviet Union did during the Cold War. This is for two reasons. They are economically much more dependent on each other than the Soviet Union and the United States ever were. China needs the US markets and technology, Washington requires Chinese surplus capital. Also, neither China nor the United States has expansionary territorial ambitions. That was not the case with the Soviet Union which was constantly trying to expand its sphere of influence, if need be by the use of military force. This was evident in its intervention in Afghanistan in 1979. A G2 system, therefore, may be more stable. The current thinking in the United States emanating from a number of policy institutions on both coasts of the country sees the coming global arrangement from the bipolar perspective, in part because such a system is familiar to the policy makers as well as policy analysts. This is one reason why the administration of

President George W. Bush paid so much attention to cultivating a new relationship with India. There is a simple idea behind this. Developing India as a counter-weight to China will further America's interests, particularly in Asia.

It is difficult at such a fluid period in the world's history to predict with some confidence as to which of these four ways the globe will go. That said, a somewhat higher probability can be attached to the fourth of these four scenarios. Nonetheless, it would be useful to study all three with greater analytical depth.

There is a virtual consensus among those who watch global economic trends that one consequence of the Great Recession of 2008–9 will be to raise China's position in the global economic and political systems. As an expert on globalisation has observed, the Great Depression accelerated the decline of Britain and the rise of America. The world that emerges from the Great Recession will be shaped largely by China and America, the one rising and the other declining, both in relative terms, as global powers.[15] Elsewhere, the author has described China's remarkable recovery from the global recession as its 'second rise' — second since its basis is very different from the one which produced the previous rise.[16]

We have also suggested in another study that one inevitable consequence of China's second rise will be the eventual replacement of such policy making forums as the G7, G8, G20 with the G2. The G2 will involve the United States and China. The well-attended America–China dialogue in Washington in the summer of 2009 set the stage for the founding of the G2. It will probably move towards a formal arrangement. This development will structure the global economy and the associated political system into three tiers: the G2 at the top, the second tier powers such as Brazil, Germany, India, Japan, Russia and possibly South Africa in the middle, and the rest of the world at the bottom. The G2 will effectively oversee the globe, the second tier powers will create their spheres of influence in their neighbourhood and the rest of the world will seek association with one or both of the supra-systems.[17]

China: Relations with Pakistan

Analysts and policy makers in Pakistan have examined their country's relations with China from the perspective of what is usually termed as an 'all-weather friendship'. It was initially based on the security interests of the two countries. The relationship has survived several changes in the two countries. In the 1950s and most of the 1960s China had been isolated, with little contact with the outside world. This was in part because of the ideological preference of the first generation of the Chinese leadership. They believed that contacts with the outside world would contaminate the citizenry and bring in ideas and attitudes that would harm the vision of Mao Zedong and his associates. But China was staying away from the world not only because its leaders wished it that way. To a certain extent, isolation was also forced upon communist China. There was concern in the United States about the spread of communism in Asia. Washington believed that Beijing was actively engaged in spreading the communist ideology. Pakistan provided an outlet to help China break out of its isolation when it suited the Chinese leadership to have some contacts with the outside world. Its national carrier, Pakistan International Airlines (PIA), was the only link that China had with the world.

Beijing's choice of Pakistan as a partner was somewhat surprising. India was ideologically much more compatible with China than Pakistan was at the time it was governed by President Muhammad Ayub Khan, Pakistan's first military leader. The Pakistani president was far closer to the West than to China; he had willingly enrolled his country as a member of two US-sponsored alliances aimed at the containment of communism — the Central Treaty Organisation (CENTO) and the Southeast Asia Treaty Organisation (SEATO). India, on the other hand, had eschewed alliances with the We/st. Jawaharlal Nehru, the country's first prime minister along with Indonesia's Soekarno, Ghana's Kwame Nkrumah and Egypt's Gamal Nasser had advocated the middle way. Unlike Pakistan's Ayub Khan all of them had fought or opposed western domination of their countries. They were not inclined to align themselves with the former colonial powers. Accordingly, they founded the Non-aligned Movement. Pakistan stayed out of the NAM, joining it only after the collapse of the Soviet Union.

Pakistan had its own reasons for befriending China. It felt insecure because of the perceived Indian threat. The historic animosity between India and Pakistan since 1947, the broader international context of the Cold War, and India's defeat in the Sino-Indian war of 1962, created an atmosphere of hostility and entrenched suspicions in the subcontinent. Among other reasons, the underlying calculus that cemented the partnership between the two countries was India: For China, Pakistan was a low-cost secondary deterrent to India, and for Pakistan, China was a high value guarantor of security against India.

The most tangible benefit to Beijing for having developed good relations with Islamabad came in 1971 when President Richard Nixon decided to visit China in order to find a solution to the war in Vietnam. It was with Pakistan's assistance that initial contacts were made between Washington and Beijing. It was from Islamabad and in a plane operated by PIA that Henry Kissinger went to Beijing to prepare the ground for President Nixon's visit. Pakistan's involvement with the American president's dramatic visit to the People's Republic went beyond providing cover to Kissinger for his visit and transport for taking him there. There was an active involvement on the part of a number of senior officials. This is how Nixon recalled Pakistan's role in his autobiography:

> On December 9 [1970] Chou En Lai sent word through [Pakistani] President Yahya that my representative would be welcome in Peking for a discussion of the question of Taiwan. Chou stressed that the message did not come from him alone but had been approved by Chairman Mao and by Lin Piao, still a powerful figure at that time. With characteristic subtlety, Chou concluded with a play on words. 'We have had messages from a Head through a Head to a Head.' Through Pakistani Ambassador Agha Hilaly we replied that any meeting should not be limited to a discussion of Taiwan, and we proposed that Chinese and American representatives meet in Pakistan to discuss the possibility of a high level meeting in Peking in the future.[18]

China rewarded Pakistan for its help. For four decades since then, it stood by Pakistan's side during many crises. It helped Islamabad in difficult economic times. It aided Pakistan's efforts to develop a defence industry when Islamabad's access to modern weaponry was severely restricted. And it served to provide some comfort to Pakistan by giving it mostly verbal support in its long-standing quarrel with India. Most of the time the last item in this list was Pakistan's real agenda in developing a close relationship with China. It is also an area of Pakistani concern where China was least helpful.

Half a century later, China is well integrated with the outside world while Pakistan, because of the rise of Islamic extremism, is isolated. The only foreign airlines that go to the country are either from East Asia, including China Air, or from the Middle East. When in the late 1950s, Pakistan and China reached out to each other, the two countries had about the same level of income per capita. Both economies were dependent on agriculture and both traded very little with the world outside. Since then China has seen its economy grow at an average rate of 9 per cent a year. That of Pakistan has increased by less than 4 per cent. The Chinese economy is now seventy-four times its size in the late 1950s. Pakistan's has increased a bit more than sixfold. The structure of the Chinese economy has changed significantly over the last fifty years. It has developed its industry to the point where it has become a major supplier of increasingly sophisticated products to the world market place. In early 2010, it surpassed Germany as the world's second largest trading nation after the United States. Pakistan remains a relatively backward economy still relying on agriculture and low value added manufactures for a significant proportion of its total output and for the bulk of its exports.

Pakistan in the late 1950s did not look to China for economic help. Now China is usually the first port of call for the Pakistani leaders whenever they find themselves in economic difficulties, which is often the case. In 1996–97, I was personally involved as Pakistan's finance minister in getting financial help from China because of my close relations with its senior leaders. I was able to secure a low-priced loan of US$ 500 million from Beijing to pay the bills that were due from such 'preferred creditors' as the IMF and the World Bank. The default on them would have plunged Pakistan into a deep financial crisis. Beijing was approached again in 2008 by Pakistan to provide it with financial relief as it struggled once more with a serious balance of payments crisis. But this time China indicated that its assistance should be sought within the context of a multi-year strategic framework and not for solving one particular crisis.[19] Nonetheless China is participating in the 'Friends of Democratic Pakistan' initiative by providing some balance of payments support. But longer-term assistance will depend on the clear articulation of an economic strategy that Pakistan should formulate and pursue keeping in mind the changes that are occurring in the global economy. China would want such a strategy to be of benefit to both countries.

There were other occasions when Beijing came to Islamabad's help not only to provide financial assistance but also to assist Pakistan in the area of defence technology. From Pakistan's perspective but not from that of the rest of the world, the most important area of involvement for China was the help it gave for the development of Pakistan's nuclear weapons programme. The extent of China's help to Pakistan was recently revealed by *The Washington Post* on a front page story as President Barack Obama headed to Beijing to hold wide ranging talks with the Chinese leaders including the need for controlling nuclear proliferation. It appears that in 1976 Prime Minister Zulfikar Ali Bhutto negotiated a deal with China's Mao Zedong to help Pakistan develop a nuclear bomb to balance India's efforts in the field. India had exploded a nuclear device in 1974 and Bhutto had promised that his countrymen will be 'prepared to eat grass' to develop a nuclear capability of its own. In 1980, four years after Mao's death, China secretly shipped uranium hexafluoride to Pakistan, allowing a laboratory near Islamabad to begin producing enriched uranium. Pakistan's progress was slow but it was in a hurry to develop a bomb before the West imposed sanctions on it. Therefore, China in 1982 shipped 50 kg of enriched uranium to Pakistan to fuel two bombs. In return, engineers from Pakistan helped the Chinese to establish a modern uranium enrichment plant.[20] Pakistan also supplied China some of the short-range missiles it had received from the United States during the first war in Afghanistan. These were 'reverse engineered' and became part of the Chinese arsenal.

However, Beijing resisted Pakistan's efforts to involve it directly in its long-enduring conflict with India. In Pakistan's wars with India in 1965 and 1971, while Islamabad attempted to enlist Beijing on its side, the latter kept itself at a safe distance, confining its assistance to the supply of weapons and some words of encouragement.

In spite of the fundamental changes in the situation of the two countries, the close relationship they had forged half a century earlier has been maintained. But the reasons why they continue to depend on each other have changed. When the Chinese analyse their relations with Pakistan, they view them in two different contexts: Pakistan's help in providing China access to the sea on its side and the balance Pakistan could provide to the rapid rise of India. Even now China is looking to Pakistan to find access to the Indian Ocean and to the countries in the Middle East. In some of the conversations I had with the senior leaders of China, when I was in charge of the World Bank's programme in that country, they indicated to me that their efforts to break out of the constraint imposed by geography with Pakistan's help were not fully successful. On a separate occasion, a Chinese prime minister, in a conversation with me, pointed at the map of his country that hung on the wall of his office to explain to me his predicament. He emphasised that China was the only large country that had access to the sea only on one side. It was landlocked on the remaining three sides. Pakistan could help it to gain access to the sea from its western side through a system of roads and ports. Some of this was done with the construction of the all-weather Karakoram Highway, and China's participation in the construction of the port at Gwadar. However, the Chinese, always impatient for results, seemed not to be fully satisfied with the progress that was made on the Pakistani side. But this is history. What about the future?

President Zardari in China

President Asif Ali Zardari spent five days in the country between 6 and 11 July 2010, visiting Beijing and Shanghai. This was his fifth visit to the country but the first state visit as Pakistan's president. The visit came at a time when Pakistan faced a difficult economic situation and while China was engaged in the process of redefining its economic objectives. China was catching up with the more advanced countries in the global economy. In 2010 China overtook Japan as the second largest economy in the world after the United States. For Asia, China's rise would be different from the earlier rise of Japan. While Japan had anchored its economy in the West, China was focusing to a much greater extent on leading the rest of Asia towards development and modernisation. This raises the question whether the discussions the Pakistani team had with China's senior leaders during the Zardari visit recognised the importance for their country of the massive structural change that was occurring in China. This change will be of great consequence for the future of the Chinese economy, its position in the global economic system and its relations with the countries in its immediate neighbourhood. How Pakistan should respond to China's evolving situation in the global system given the long relationship between the two countries is a question of some importance for all of Asia.

President Zardari was escorted to the Great Hall of the People in Beijing by his two daughters. *China Daily* covered the Pakistani president's visit extensively. It carried his picture alongside President Hu Jintao on the first page of the newspaper and quoted the Pakistani president telling the Chinese leader that his daughters wanted 'very much to see you in person' hoping the meeting would inspire the younger Pakistani generation to continue its 'all-weather and time-tested friendship with its Asian neighbor'.[21] By bringing his children along for the visit, Zardari was giving a clear signal to the Chinese leadership. He was carrying on the work initiated by his father-in-law, Prime Minister Zulfikar Ali Bhutto, in the late 1950s and early 1960s. Bhutto was then foreign minister in the cabinet headed by General Muhammad Ayub Khan, Pakistan's first military leader. Under Bhutto's stewardship Pakistan established a close working relationship with the Chinese. China then was isolated partly because of its ideological preferences but partly also because of a *cordon sanitare* thrown around the country by the United States.

Warm relations between China and Pakistan have survived many leadership changes in the two countries. By bringing his children along to the meeting Zardari was telling the Chinese leaders and people that he was preparing the next generation to carry on the work initiated by the earlier generations. 'The only way I could do justice to the memory of my late wife and my late father-in-law was to make sure that my first state visit as president was to China,' he told President Hu Jintao as he began his meeting with the Chinese leader. 'I'm hoping to take the China–Pakistan friendship further along. It is a duty that history has bestowed upon me.' In his response President Hu acknowledged the legacy of the Bhutto family in developing the China–Pakistan friendship. 'Ali Bhutto and Benazir Bhutto made prominent contributions to the initiation and development of China-Pakistan friendship which the Chinese people will never forget,' he said. 'China attaches great importance to the China-Pakistan relationship and has always made the development of the relationship China's diplomatic priority.'[22]

It was reported that since the Pakistani president assumed his present office the two countries had concluded sixty agreements, opening up a number of new avenues for Chinese investment in Pakistan. The Hu–Zardari meeting on 7 July lasted for 100 minutes and witnessed the signing of six deals in the fields of law, housing, agriculture and media cooperation. These were all new areas of collaboration between the two countries. The visit and the associated meetings also covered some of the traditional areas in which the two countries have been involved. The most important of these was the development of Pakistan's energy resources.

The Pakistani president told Chinese business heads in Beijing that 'Pakistan was facing an acute power shortage and intended to add tens of thousands of megawatts of power to its national grid in the next 25 years through combined hydro, coal, gas, nuclear and renewable energy resources'. The Chinese response was encouraging. According to *China Daily* 'an executive of China's Three Gorges Corporation which runs the huge hydro power dam in central China indicated that it was agreed to invest more than $100 billion in two hydro-power projects in Pakistan'.[23]

The question of China's support for developing nuclear power in Pakistan also came up. This issue had acquired some significance following questions raised by the American administration about the understanding China and Pakistan had reached earlier in the area of nuclear power development. China National Nuclear Corporation had signed an agreement with the Government of Pakistan in February 2010 to finance the construction of two new reactors. Washington was concerned whether the promised assistance by China to add to the nuclear capacity already built at Chasma in the Punjab met with Beijing's international obligations. Beijing gave repeated assurances to the international community that its current and future nuclear commerce would be in total compliance with its commitment to the Nuclear Non-proliferation Treaty. This assurance was repeated to the Indian national security adviser Shiv Shankar Menon who left Beijing the day the Pakistani president arrived in the Chinese capital. Menon spent four days in China during which he met with Prime Minister Wen Jiabao. He said before leaving China that he had discussed China's assistance to Pakistan in the nuclear area. 'They told us that what they are doing will be in accordance with their international obligations. We will wait and see where this is going,' he said while talking to the press before leaving for India.[24]

Ye Hailin of the Chinese Academy of Social Sciences spoke about the controversy and said that the decades-long Chasma project was legal and also had nothing to do with other countries. He said that China has always been supervised by the International Atomic Energy Agency and future nuclear cooperation with Pakistan will depend on the demand of that country for using nuclear power to meet its large energy shortfall. 'Our cooperation is not a show, not a demonstration. It is decided by our need.'

The expression of concern by New Delhi and Washington about the cooperation between Beijing and Islamabad was surprising since they themselves had concluded a deal which was clearly outside the NPT framework. The Americans had used considerable political muscle for the international community to accept their agreement with India.

Conclusion

In looking at the future we should ask the following question: will there be a change in the basis of the Sino-Pakistan relationship, particularly when China's position in the world alters in many fundamental and remarkable ways, while Pakistan continues to weaken economically, politically and socially? As discussed in an earlier section, the world is passing through a period of deep financial crisis which is likely to profoundly influence China's position in the world. There will be a restructuring of the global economic system. This puts Pakistan in an interesting position. It will be a relatively large country — at least in terms of the size of its population — that borders a member of the G2 (China) and one of the second tier powers (India). What would be the implications of this economic geography for Pakistan? How should Pakistan manage its external economic and political affairs in light of this reshaping of the global system? These will be two of the several questions that Pakistan's policy makers need to reflect on.

Separate from the global economic malaise, there is also a series of crises affecting Pakistan. From 2008 on Pakistan was buffeted by a perfect storm: its economy was under great stress, its political system remained unsettled, and it had to deal with the rise of Islamic extremism that many analysts and policy makers in the West as well as in Pakistan believed to pose an 'existential threat' to the country. The third storm — the rise of Islamic extremism — brought the United States army right to Pakistan's borders. The United States is once again taking a look at its Afghan strategy. There was a point of view, advanced in particular by Vice President Joe Biden, that the focus should be on Pakistan rather than on Afghanistan. According to him, Pakistan received only $1 of American assistance per citizen compared to $30 for Afghanistan. He believed that this imbalance needs to be corrected. Therefore, Pakistan has to deal not with two but three large countries although the third — the United States — is not on its immediate borders. What are the choices available to it?

These choices will involve a balancing act for Pakistan. It will entail working with the United States, China and India to stabilise Afghanistan; working with the United States to overcome insurgencies in the tribal areas; working with India to find a solution for the problem of Kashmir that does not involve changes in the state's boundaries; working with China to develop some of the sectors of the economy in which the Chinese have interest; granting India and China transit rights through its territory. The best way of developing an overall strategy that addresses these issues is to find a new basis for Sino-Pakistan relations, since that will be central to Pakistan's efforts to break out of the crises that have overwhelmed the policy makers in Islamabad.

✳

Notes

1. The phrase, 'an all-weather relationship' was used once again by President Asif Ali Zardari when he went to China on a state visit in mid-July. The Zardari visit is discussed in greater detail later in the chapter.
2. Stephen Roach, 'I've Been an Optimist on China. But I'm Starting to Worry', *Financial Times*, 29 July 2009, p. 20.
3. For a detailed study of this phenomenon, see Shahid Javed Burki, 'Asia in the "Catch-up" Game' I, ISAS Working paper 106, 9 April 2010 and 'Asia in the "Catch-up" Game' II, ISAS Working Paper, 107, 10 May 2010.
4. Alexander Gerschenkron, *Economic Backwardness in Historical Perspective: A Book of Essays*, Cambridge, Mass.: Belknap Press of Harvard University Press, 1962.
5. Ezra F. Vogel, *Japan as Number One: Lessons for America*, New York: Universe, 1999.
6. The miracle economies were studied by the World Bank in an influential study that, for the first time, identified the state as an important player in economic development. The World Bank, *The East Asian Miracle: Economic Growth and Public Policy*, New York: Oxford University Press, 1973.
7. Shahid Javed Burki, *The Rise of China: How It Will Impact The World*, Institute of South Asian Studies, Insight No. 80, 6 August 2009.
8. Hiroko Tabuchi, 'China's Day Arriving Sooner than Japan Expected', *The New York Times*, 2 October 2009, pp. B1 and B2.
9. Ibid.
10. Ibid.
11. Ibid.
12. Robert Kagan and Dan Blumenthal, '"Strategic Reassurance" that Isn't', *The Washington Post*, 10 November 2010, p. A15.
13. Gordon Brown, 'All Together Now', *The New York Times*, 23 September 2009, p. A35.
14. This point is well developed in a recent article by an Indian economist. See Shankar Acharya, 'Rising India Labors in the Shadow of Asia's Real Giant', *Financial Times*, 29 July 2009, p. 7.
15. Harold James, *The Creation and Destruction of Values: The Globalization Cycle*, Cambridge, MA: Harvard University Press, 2009.
16. Shahid Javed Burki, 'China's Second Rise', *The Business Times*, Singapore, 11 August 2009.
17. Burki, *The Rise of China*.
18. Richard Nixon, *The Memoirs of Richard Nixon*, New York: Grosset and Dunlap, 1978, p. 547.
19. This was indicated to the author by President Asif Ali Zardari in a meeting in Islamabad in November 2008.

20. Jeffrey Smith and Joby Warrick, 'A Nuclear Power's Act of Proliferation', *The Washington Post*, 13 November 2009, pp. A1 and A13.

21. Xiao Yang, 'Children Lead the Way into the Meeting', *China Daily*, 7 July 2010, p. 1.

22. Xuiao Yang, 'Zardari Visit Cements All-weather Friendship', *China Daily*, 9 July 2010, p. 4.

23. Ibid.

24. Ibid.

9

Sri Lanka: China as a Model of Growth and Modernisation

JAYANTHA DHANAPALA AND JOHN GOONERATNE

Sri Lanka's geopolitical location in South Asia undoubtedly dominated its international relations during its ancient and medieval history. Thereafter, during the period of four-and-a-half centuries of western colonial rule from the 16th century A.D. to 1948, it was Europe that was perforce the main international partner, although social, cultural and some trade relations with India continued. It was only with the regaining of independence in 1948 that Sri Lanka was able to adopt a global approach. National interest drove the island-nation into closer alliances with the Non-aligned Movement (NAM), the Group of 77 and the South Asian Association of Regional Co-operation (SAARC) while remaining a member of the United Nations and the Commonwealth.

Throughout the centuries, based on its strategic location at the centre of the Indian Ocean, political, cultural and economic contacts with China existed but the perception of China remained that of a huge, powerful and distant Asian power. Buddhism was an important link that led to contacts as early as in the 3rd century B.C. with the Chinese monk Fa Hsien being among the most important pilgrims in 411 A.D.[1] Attempts by China to take the Tooth Relic of the Buddha from Sri Lanka failed but did not cause rancour. Not being on the Silk Route, Sri Lanka was, however, involved in trade with China through what is now described as 'the silk road of the sea'.[2] Neither the 1411 abduction of the Sri Lankan King Vira Alakesvara by the famous Chinese Admiral Zheng He nor the stoning of Sri Lankan (then Ceylon) Embassy in Beijing by the Red Guards in the 1967 Cultural Revolution, over the seizure of a consignment of Mao badges by Colombo, upset the even tenor of Sino-Sri Lanka relations.[3] The adoption of western stereotypes of the Chinese, encouraged by the presence of a small Chinese minority, was mixed with an admiration of China's cultural riches and her resistance of Japanese and western imperialism.

This even keel of relations enabled the perception of the emergence in 1949 of the People's Republic of China (PRC) as a welcome transition of an ancient civilisation, which, like Sri Lanka, had been subjected to exploitation by colonial powers, into a united and independent country. Independent Sri Lanka was pursuing a middle path in foreign policy even before articulating its non-aligned stance and stayed clear of blocs like the South East Asian Treaty Organisation (SEATO).[4] There was no threat perception from 'Red' China. The ideological content of the revolution that caused this transition was not an obstacle and so three months after the establishment of the PRC Sri Lanka recognised new China in January 1950.[5] It supported the restoration of China's representation in the UN and its membership in all international bodies.[6] It has since followed a 'One China Policy' consistently and resisted all efforts of Taiwan to enter the UN and to have relations with Sri Lanka. Recognition of China in 1950 was followed in 1952 by the mutually beneficial Rubber-Rice Barter Agreement in defiance of US legislation with Sri Lanka losing US aid as a result. A brief lurch into anti-China rhetoric by the pro-western Sir John Kotelawela at the 1955 Bandung Conference was an aberration never repeated just as Mrs Sirimavo Bandaranaike's 'rapacious West' speech in Beijing came to be regretted.[7] In 1957 the more liberal S. W. R. D. Bandaranaike government established diplomatic relations with China and the USSR.[8] Successive Sri Lanka governments had good relations with China as a staple element in their foreign policy with little disagreement among the parties even when a pro-Beijing communist party existed. The Sino-India war of 1962 saw Sri Lanka attempting to mediate while maintaining a stance of neutrality.[9]

A similar neutrality was maintained in the Sino-Soviet dispute while the Sino-US rapprochement under Nixon was welcomed. An opportunity to join the Association of South East Asian Nation States (ASEAN) in 1967 was declined mainly on the basis that it was perceived as an alliance to contain China. Chinese aid was made available to Sri Lanka irrespective of whether the SLFP or the UNP was in power and trade continued to expand although the old Rubber-Rice agreement had expired. As a developing country, China's development model was viewed with interest as an alternative especially for agricultural development where intermediate technology and the commune system without its coercive elements provided some attraction. With the watershed economic reforms in 1977 towards a market economy in Sri Lanka and China's own reforms under Deng Xiao-ping, a close parallelism in economic development policy continued, especially in poverty alleviation and rural development areas. Increasingly China also became a source of investment. In sum, Sino-Sri Lanka relations were regularly cited as a model of relations between a big and small country with different political systems. Sri Lanka's perception of itself was that of a proud ancient civilisation vested with the historic task of protecting the Buddha Dhamma symbolised by the custodianship of the Sacred Tooth Relic and it pledged to maintain its sovereignty, unity and territorial integrity. Thus the rejection of any sphere of influence or bloc let alone the notion of subjecting herself to hegemonism was a fundamental part of her foreign policy. China was perceived to respect this position unvaryingly. The elaborate extent to which China treated Sri Lanka as an equal, at times even seeking its expert advice on legal and other issues, was deeply appreciated.

The pressure of the internal conflict within Sri Lanka caused by the separatist-terrorist group, the LTTE, resulted in a strain on Indo-Sri Lanka relations. India was not a reliable supplier of arms and the perception of China (and Pakistan) as a more reliable friend pledged to a policy of non-interference in the island's internal affairs grew. This source of arms was also a pillar of diplomatic support in international gatherings on human rights and later in the Security Council. China thus emerged as a means of balancing Sri Lanka's inescapable proximity to India. The reduction of Sino-Indian tensions and the emergence of both Asian giants as power houses in the global economy made the task of balancing relations between them easier. Possible future scenarios will be examined in our penultimate section but it seems unlikely that the positive perceptions of the past will change unless China goes through a Cultural Revolution–like violent upheaval and/or becomes an aggressor nation.

Sri Lanka's Perspective on China's Economic and Defence Growth

In a way, it were the sheer market conditions and sources of commodities badly needed by the two countries that forged the nature of modern Sri Lanka–China relations. Depending largely on the export of three products — tea, rubber and coconut — and with a steep drop in world rubber prices, and a sharp increase in the largely imported staple food of rice, Sri Lanka found in China a country that had difficulty in obtaining the strategic product of rubber, because of US sanctions, and plentiful rice that could be exported. It was in this background of mutual trade and economic need that the China–Sri Lanka Rubber-Rice Agreement of April 1952 was signed. This agreement is seen as the first step in a long journey of Sri Lanka–China relations to date.

Similar to a 'Rising China' at the present time, then it was a 'Red' China that the US and western countries were worried about. Times have changed, and so have the ways in which any country on the rise is handled. But, at that time, the provisions of the Battle Act precluded the continuing of US assistance to Sri Lanka because of the Rubber-Rice Agreement of April 1952.[10]

Sri Lanka's relations with the US have come a long way since. And so have Sri Lanka–China relations. There is a tendency at formal occasions such as state visits between Sri Lanka and China, to paint the state of relations as a marriage made in heaven. However, that is to miss out a lot of the details of the texture of Sri Lanka–China relations that lend it an enduring quality.

During the early post-independence years, the governments in Sri Lanka were seen as right wing and although Sri Lanka recognised the People's Republic of China in January 1950, it did not formally exchange ambassadors with Beijing until 7 February 1957. Colombo not only discouraged diplomatic contacts with China but, indeed, went to the extent of banning any import of communist books, magazines, films, etc. 'This clearly reflected the strength of anti-China sentiment that was predominant in Sri Lanka during those initial years.'[11] Nevertheless, economic self-interest led to the Sri Lanka–China Rubber-Rice Agreement of April 1952, and laid the foundation for building future Sri Lanka–China relations.

Even after that, the domestic politics of the two countries occasionally impinged on the bilateral relationship, but without affecting the trade relationship between the two countries.[12] The March 1965 elections brought UNP back in power, reasserting its pro-western perspective. And it was also the period of the Cultural Revolution in China, the seizure of Mao badges by Colombo, and the stoning of the Sri Lanka Embassy in Beijing by the Red Guards.

With the return of the SLFP to power in 1970, leading a left coalition, Sri Lanka–China relations were in higher profile. However, that bilateral relations were not conditioned purely by political events was made clear with the next change of government in Sri Lanka in 1977, when the UNP under President Jayewardene returned to office, and both countries revived their economic initiatives. 'To recall, both China and Sri Lanka had begun their economic opening up and reform about the same time, and these were to make them perfect candidates for economic partnership.'[13]

Meanwhile, the Sri Lanka–China relationship was gathering other dimensions, in addition to the trade and economic base. China gifted five high-speed naval boats to the Sri Lankan navy in 1972; it completed the Rs 35 million Bandaranaike Memorial International Conference Hall (BMICH) in May 1973. That her munificence was politically even-handed was indicated by building Sri Lanka's Supreme Court complex in the 1980s and more recently, in 2007, the building of the National Performing Arts Theatre costing US$ 23 million — the entire cost of which was borne by China.

There were, in addition, several loans that were granted to Sri Lanka.

The trading relationship itself was put on a firmer foundation through several institutional arrangements:

- 1952 April — The China–Sri Lanka Rubber-Rice Agreement.
- 1982 — A Trade and Payments Agreement of a general nature between the two countries was signed in September 1982, which provided Most Favoured Nation (MFN) treatment for products of exports and imports of the two countries. And a Joint Trade Committee between China and Sri Lanka was established.

- 1984 — In pursuance of article VI of the trade agreement between the governments of China and Sri Lanka signed on 21 September 1982 in Colombo, the first meeting of the Sri Lanka–China Joint Trade Committee was held in Beijing from 13 to 21 November 1984. The two delegations agreed to arrange for business visits by delegations of both countries, hold trade fair exhibitions, etc., improve the exchange of information by the commercial organisations of both countries and exchange indicative lists of products that were available for export according to the laws of the two countries. The agreement was signed on 16 November 1984 forming the Sri Lanka–China Joint Trade Committee into which the 1982 agreement was amalgamated.
- 1994 — The Sri Lanka–China Business Cooperation Council, which is a private sector initiative, was established on 6 June 1994. Its primary objective is to promote and enhance mutual interaction between the private sectors of the two countries, with a view to further enhancing bilateral trade and investments between them.
- 2005 April — An Agreement on Further Development of Bilateral Economic and Trade Relationship between Sri Lanka and China was signed during the visit to Sri Lanka of Mr Wen Jiabao, prime minister of China.
- 2009 — on 25 July 2009, an Investment Facilitation Agreement was signed between China Development Bank and the Central Bank of Sri Lanka. Under this agreement, China Development Bank will initially place a US dollar deposit with the Central Bank of Sri Lanka, while also progressing towards long-term economic ties between the two institutions.
- 2010 — In June 2010, six agreements were signed in the areas of information technology, maritime ports, economic and technological cooperation and southern transportation development. The two governments also signed an agreement for the maintenance and development of the Bandaranaike Memorial International Conference Hall (BMICH) which is a donation from China. The signing of agreements took place in the presence of Prime Minister D. M. Jayaratne and Chinese vice premier Zhang Dejiang.

At present China has provided assistance to Sri Lanka on several major projects:[14] The Colombo–Katunayake expressway, the Southern expressway (Pinnaduwa to Matara), the Sri Lanka Railways and Sri Lanka's second international airport in Hambantota.

China has agreed to provide a loan of US$ 252 million, that is, 85 per cent of the estimated cost for the Colombo-Katunayake expressway which is US$ 292 million. The project which was started in 2000 is being constructed by the Metallurgical Group Corporation of China. The completion of this project will enable commuters to reach Sri Lanka's international airport in Katunayake in a matter of 15–20 minutes.

The Southern expressway is largely funded by the Asian Development Bank and Japan International Cooperation Agency; however, China's Exim Bank has agreed to give US$ 162 million for the project. The China Harbour Engineering Corporation Ltd. (CHEC) has been awarded the construction of a section of a 34.5 km long stretch of this highway. In June 2010, the Road Development Authority (RDA) signed an agreement with a Chinese company for the construction of the last stage of the Southern Expressway from Pinnaduwa to Godagama. In addition, it is expected that the Exim Bank will provide assistance in the construction of roadways in the north and east of the island which includes the reconstruction of the A9 road.

The extension plans for Matara-Katargama railway line were finalised by June 2010. The whole project however is expected to be completed by 2014 in three phases with an estimated cost of $350 million.[15] In addition, China has already provided assistance through an agreement signed with China National Machinery Import and Export Corporation to provide 100 railway carriages to the Sri Lanka Railway Department. Fifteen power sets were provided by China South Locomotive and Rolling Stock Corporation Ltd. US$ 100 million has also been provided by Exim Bank to acquire further infrastructure for the Sri Lanka railways. China, through the Exim Bank, has also offered a concessional loan to Sri Lank of US$ 200 million to build an international airport in Mattala, Hambantota. The project is to be commissioned in December 2011.

The nature of trading and economic relationship between the two countries has also begun to change qualitatively, from one of primarily state-to-state trading, to where it is now, with more of the private and business sectors involved on both sides.

Sri Lanka also viewed the other developing areas of the bilateral relationship as not having strings attached, and not based on ideological compulsions. One area that began in the late 1970s was in defence purchases. With several Tamil groups advocating secession starting to form in the late 1970s, and receiving Indian sponsorship and training after 1983, sources for defence purchases became a priority concern of Sri Lanka. And China became one of the more dependable sources for a variety of arms acquisitions which continues to date.

The nature of the bilateral relationship was, naturally, not impervious to the changes taking place in the geopolitical environment in South Asia and beyond. Of greater relevance were China's engagements with India and Pakistan, in particular. Overtly cooperating or having friendly relations, but covertly competing, the smaller countries in South Asia, like Sri Lanka, get drawn into this cooperative/competitive syndrome. As a result, any transaction Sri Lanka has with China or Pakistan draws India's hypercritical attention and in turn, the smaller countries see Pakistan and China as a counterweight to India's sometimes overbearing postures in South Asia.

China and India fought a war in 1962 but since then the two countries have not allowed the boundary dispute to be a stumbling block to improving bilateral relations. In the current phase of globalisation and market economies, the two countries are considered economic giants in Asia. Nevertheless, they are also in competition with each other, fed by the need in the West to balance a rising China.

The very complicated state of relations between India and Pakistan has been described as the result of being 'separated at birth'.[16] Pakistan holds India responsible for the bifurcation of its country, and the creation of Bangladesh in 1971. The relations between the countries fluctuate between high and low tension and in this context, Pakistan has developed relations with China as a counterweight to India.

Sri Lanka has its own problems with India, mainly as part of a small country-next-to-a-very-big-country syndrome. However, on balance, the plus factors outweigh the problem areas. There are also times when Sri Lankan issues get aggravated as India's domestic issues (Tamil Nadu politics) are worked out at the expense of Sri Lanka. Nevertheless, maybe as a result of its size and location, Sri Lanka does not deliberately manipulate its relations with China as a counterweight in the bilateral relationship with India.

Sri Lanka views China more from the angle of its economic strength and as a strong and beneficial trading partner. Sri Lanka does look to China for military hardware to meet its domestic requirements. But these requirements do not need the source to be a major military power, as this military hardware is meant purely for a domestic conflict. Basically Sri Lanka does not see China's modernisation of its military as a threat to either the global or regional balance of power or one that could adversely affect Sri Lanka's national interest.

The late minister of foreign affairs, Lakshman Kadirgamar in a lecture titled 'The Peaceful Ascendancy of China: A South Asian Perspective' delivered on 28 December 2004 at the China Institute of International Studies in Beijing made the following statement:

> The question the world, particularly other Asian countries, asks themselves is no longer whether China will rise but in what way it will rise, and what level its rise will reach.

> The core issue seems to be whether China will rise peacefully or whether it will go the way that historically other world or regional powers have gone, namely, expanding their influence and interests by military means.

> China's relations with its neighbouring countries have markedly improved in recent times and the peripheral environment is relatively stable.

> The general situation is conducive to China's realisation of the strategic goal of building an affluent society through concentration on sustainable economic growth and all-round development of the social sector, thus blazing a trail for a peaceful rise which is diametrically different from the ways other major powers rose in history.[17]

In the same speech, the late minister aptly outlined Sri Lanka's relations with China as follows:

> I believe that the relationship between the two countries whch began, as I have said, many, many centuries ago, is based on a secure foundation, the principles of panchasila. . . . China has never sought to influence the domestic politics of Sri Lanka. Over the years China has proved to be benign and sincere with no ulterior motives for

befriending Sri Lanka. She has never tried to dominate, undermine or destabilize Sri Lanka. She has come to our rescue with timely assistance on several occasions when there were threats to Sri Lanka's national security and territorial integrity. And even on those occasions China never tried to strike a quick bargain in a crisis. There have been no strings attached to Chinese aid.[18]

Sri Lanka–China relations, strongly anchored in mutually beneficial interests, are not without the occasional buffeting from both domestic and regional squalls. An interesting case of then and now is provided by the case of the Sri Lanka–China Maritime Agreement (1963) and the Sri Lanka–China Agreement on the Hambantota Project (2007).

Sri Lanka entered into a Maritime Agreement with China on 25 July 1963 to promote Sri Lankan and Chinese vessels, operating from ports in their respective countries, to engage in foreign trade, cargo and passenger services.[19] The agreement was tabled in parliament thereafter. This agreement was signed during the period of an SLFP government.

The deputy minister of defence and external affairs speaking in parliament on 30 August 1963 referred to criticisms being made about the *bona fides* of the Maritime Agreement. That the criticisms were being made from within the left parties was obvious when the deputy minister said that no objections were raised when a similar agreement was signed with the USSR on 22 February 1962. 'I do not know whether it is the ideological conflicts which are creating these problems between the two Governments and whether there are sections of their counterparts in this House,' the deputy minister observed.[20]

On 11 March 1965, with a general election in the offing, and the opposition UNP trying to make election propaganda with allegations about the 'real' objective of the Maritime Agreement, Prime Minister Mrs Bandaranaike made the following observations in parliament:

> The Maritime Agreement with the People's Republic of China is no secret Agreement, and it would need either a fertile imagination or a prejudiced mind to read into that Agreement the idea that Ceylon had, through this Agreement, handed over Trincomalee harbour to the Chinese. The maritime Agreement with China was not merely made public, but it was actually tabled in Parliament in August 1963, and discussed during the budget debate of that year.[21]

A point to note is the fact that when the General Election of 1965 resulted in the election of a UNP-led government no attempt was made to abrogate the Maritime Agreement with China.[22]

The suspicions about the Maritime Agreement were not confined to the domestic politics of Sri Lanka. As to who entertained such suspicions is clear from the Press Communiqué issued (8 February 1963) by the Ministry of Defence and External Affairs, Government of Ceylon, on 'Alleged Offer of Naval Base to China'.[23] A report originating from London dated 6 February, under the caption 'Naval Base in Return for Long-term Gains — Peking's Deal with Ceylon'.[24] The report states that 'Soviet bloc diplomats here have a report that China wants to acquire a naval base in Ceylon in return for substantial long-term economic assistance. Discreet inquiries being made by them led to their belief that the subject was discussed during Mrs Bandaranaike's recent visit to Peking.' The report goes on to say that:

> These sources agree that there is no reason at all why Ceylon should consider a proposal which will have the greatest implications for the security not only of India but for the whole of South East Asia. Still they are unable to dismiss it. They argue that China has stepped up its activities in Africa and need some staging posts in the Indian Ocean. The Soviet bloc as a whole appears concerned over the Chinese activities in Africa.

The reactions to the Sri Lanka–China Agreement on the Hambantota Project (2007) to be discussed later in this chapter, are reminiscent of the reactions to the Sri Lanka–China Maritime Agreement of 1963. There is no Soviet bloc now. It is not Trincomalee (after the Indo-Lanka Agreement of 1987), but Hambantota now. Then there is the 'string of pearls' strategy to contain India. These are some of the pressures — domestic, regional and beyond — that bilateral relations and agreements are heir to, and Sri Lanka–China relations are no exception.

Sri Lankan Stakeholders In Sri Lanka–China

Since the days of the Rubber-Rice Agreement of 1952, Sri Lanka and China relations have developed a multi-dimensional relationship, involving facets such as trade, tourism, investments, defence, energy and education. As such, there are now more stakeholders that benefit from Sri Lanka–China relations, and, also, work towards further strengthening it. Rising China is seen from Sri Lanka for its trade, economics and related areas, rather than for any benefits from its military potential. The various stakeholders act complementarily since their interests do not contradict each other.

Addressing a seminar in Colombo, Dr Saman Kelegama, executive director of the Institute of Policy Studies pointed out that:[25]

> (Sri Lanka's) exports to China are not very significant. Last year, it was about US$ 25.5 million, compared to what we import from China, which amounted last year to about US$ 780 million. Consequently, we had a trade deficit of about US$ 754 million.

But, he said,

> As an economist I would not give much importance to this trade imbalance, because we are now living in a globalised world, when a particular country engages in international trade, with some countries, we will have a trade deficit.

and the way out is 'the important point is that we can reduce this deficit by increasing Sri Lanka's exports to China'.[26]

Speaking specifically on China's emergence in the world economy, he asked 'What are the implications of China's emergence in the world economy? Sri Lanka exporters should focus on increasing the exports of value-added products to China.' A suggestion he made was:

At present most of the major exports occur in raw form. Now if you look at Zirconium Ores and Raw Coconut oil, they all go in raw form, not in value added form. Even Tea and Natural Rubber, they are going in raw form. We can earn far more foreign exchange earnings if they go as value-added products. China's growing middle class, expected to reach 400 Million in 2010, provides a major market for Sri Lankan exporters. One country cannot have comparative advantage in producing each and every good and service. So always there is a niche market. So Sri Lanka can capture niche markets in China with the rapid growth of the middle class population and their purchasing power increasing.[27]

Speaking of the oft voiced fear of Chinese Imports, Dr Kelegama said: 'Then, there is also the fear of Chinese imports flooding domestic market. But we have to see the import of Chinese goods positively in the context of the items that are not produced domestically.'[28]

Investment was a growing area of Chinese activity in Sri Lanka. Kelegama pointed out that 'China has become a major investor in Sri Lanka. . . . Major sectors, in which foreign investment was received, included the apparel sector, textiles, services, transport equipment, and food products. These sectors all have significant importance in Sri Lankan economy, as export items and as having a role in economic performance. As China continues to grow, it is likely to increase the FDI in Sri Lanka.'[29]

The statistics in Table 9.1 provided by the Chinese official sources show the inflow of FDI from China between 2006 and 2009 and that they have indeed grown in the last four years.

TABLE 9.1: Status of FDI inflow from China over the past four years

Year	China's FDI Stock (In US Dollars, Million)
2003	6.543
2004	6.790
2005	15.430
2006	8.460
2007	7.740
2008	16.780

Source: Adapted from Nilanthi Samarnayake, 'Are Sri Lanka's Relations With China Deepening? An Analysis of Economic, Military and Diplomatic Data', *Asian Security*, vol. 7, no. 2, pp. 119–46, Table 4, p. 129.

In 2009, China's assistance to Sri Lanka in the form of grants, loans and credit totalled US$ 1.2 billion amounting to 54 per cent of the US$ 2.2 billion which Sri Lanka received from foreign countries and multilateral agencies in that year.[30] China now ranks number 1 among Sri Lanka's foreign direct investors moving up from its position of number 18 in 2006.

Trade

China is the fourth largest trading partner of Sri Lanka, and third and twenty-seventh in the list of major import and export partners for Sri Lanka according to the 2008 statistics of the Sri Lanka Customs/Export Development Board. The total trade turnover between Sri Lanka and China which stood at 25,774 million

Sri Lankan Rupees in 2002, increased to 125,250 million Rupees in 2008, which is an increase of just short of 500%.[31] Sri Lanka's exports to China comprise tea, spices, coconut fibre products, natural rubber, precious and semi-precious stones and readymade garments, while products such as fabrics, machinery, chemicals, tractors, vehicle spare parts and vehicles are imported from China creating a negative trade balance for Sri Lanka.

Nevertheless, as Mr T. K. Premadasa, head of Corporate Affairs and Communication of the Sri Lanka Export Development Board observes:

There has been a significant increase of Sri Lanka exports to China since 2000, mainly due to the bulky export of mineral sands as zirconium ores and rutiles, coir fiber and electrical components etc. (Table 9.2). The exports of mineral sands from Rs 10 million in 2001 inspiringly propelled up top Rs 226 million in 2008. Coir products worth of Rs 6 million in 2000 ascended to Rs 1,142 million in 2008. Apart from the above increase in exports, an intrinsic ascendancy in tea and natural rubber sector was recognised.

China accounted 0.45% of total exports from Sri Lanka to the world. But on the current trend it is optimistic that China will increase the potential items of exports from Sri Lanka exports such as rubber products, tea, spices, confectioneries and seafood etc.[32]

In the area of government-to-government cooperation in the promotion of trade, there has been close contact since the early

TABLE 9.2: Trade between Sri Lanka and China, last twenty years (rupees in million)

Year	Imports	Exports	Balance of trade	Total trade turnover
1985	1,921.0	464.0	−1,456.7	2,384.3
1988	3,336.2	762.6	−2,573.6	4,098.8
1989	3,695.9	128.5	−3,567.4	3,824.4
1992	5,302.3	65.0	−5,237.3	5,367.3
1993	7,224.6	142.5	−7,102.1	7,387.1
1994	7,731.6	91.3	−7,640.3	7,822.9
2000	19,027.0	258.0	−18,769.0	19,258.0
2004	45,945.0	1,742.0	−44,203.0	47,687.0
2005	63,370.0	2,864.0	−60,506.0	66,234.0
2008	120,069.0	5,181.0	−119, 888.0	125,250.0

Source: The data from the year 1985 to 2005 have been adapted from T. K. Premadasa, 'Sri Lanka–China Trade Relationship', *Asian Tribune*, 20 October 2007, http://www.asiantribune.com/node/7893 (accessed 26 August 2011). The data for the year 2008 was collected by the authors.

days of the Rubber-Rice Agreement. China being an upcoming market, both at the Ministry of Trade in Colombo, and the Sri Lanka Embassy in China, there have been a number of trade and investment promotional activities carried out between Sri Lanka and China.

Cooperation in matters of trade has been also carried out in forums like the United Nations Conference on Trade and Development (UNCTAD), where China and Sri Lanka have played active roles since its inception. This cooperation is seen in the World Trade Organisation also, where China is now a member, and where issues affecting developing countries come up.

Three institutions very active in the area of promoting business with China are:

(a) the Board of Investment of Sri Lanka (BOI),
(b) Sri Lanka–China Business Council, and
(c) the Federation of Chambers of Commerce and Industry of Sri Lanka (FCCISL).

BOI

Started as the Greater Colombo Economic Commission, which was established in 1978 to generate development in the outskirts of Colombo, it was re-constituted as the Board of Investment of Sri Lanka (BOI) in 1992, with its mandate encompassing the entire island. The Board of Directors drawn from the private and public sector and its several departments are geared to facilitating the investment process.

China with its 'Going Global' overseas investment policies and diversified investment interests has been identified as a focus country in the BOI's promotional plans. The BOI has also participated in a number of trade fairs in China. There is a strong belief within the organisation that China will play a pivotal role in the global economy, and in the Asian continent in particular.

A significant number of small- and medium-scale Chinese companies have already invested in various sectors such as fisheries, textiles/apparel, housing, manufacturing, agriculture, etc. There are already thirty-five Chinese companies that operate under the special incentives the BOI offers investors. There are in addition forty-six other Chinese enterprises that operate under the normal laws of the country. They are in areas such as embroidery services, deep sea fishing, bicycles, apparel and textile products, sewing thread for export, shoes, garments, fabric and related products, cellular mobile telephone service, and cashew nut shell oil. The small-scale enterprises operating under the normal laws of the country are engaged in restaurants, medical centres, trading houses and manufacturing of soya and other products.

The BOI signed an MOU with the Chinese company Huichen Investment on 30 June 2009, to develop and manage the BOI Special Economic Zone dedicated to Chinese enterprises at Mirigama. The BOI conducted two seminars on 27 and 31 March 2009, titled 'Investment Opportunities for Chinese Entrepreneurs at the Sri Lanka Embassy'.

With the economic boom in China and expanding capital reserves, the BOI is targeting investments in different areas especially in large-scale infrastructure projects. Some projects which have been entered into are as follows:

(1) Hambantota Port Development
The Government of Sri Lanka and Exim Bank of China entered into an agreement pertaining to the construction of the Hambantota port in October 2007. China has agreed to fund 85 per cent of the USD 360 million mega port development project. The Exim Bank of China would extend a Buyer's Facility amounting to US$ 307 million with an interest rate of 0.90 per cent. For all record purposes, the offered interest rate by the Exim Bank of China was very competitive and advantageous to Sri Lanka.

The primary objective of the Hambantota Port Development was to synchronise the different aspects of development such as shipping, trans-shipment, shipbuilding, bunkering, the handling of large-scale fuel products and facilitating and addressing the rapid increase of exports and imports among others. The port of Colombo does not have sufficient space and capacity to meet the demand.

This project, however, has generated a lot of comment on the Indian side as having defence implications for India. This is how *The Times of London* reported on these defence concerns of India in an article dated 2 May 2009.[33] Jeremy Page, the South Asia correspondent of the weekly writing on the location of the project, Hambantota, states:

This is where China is building a $1 billion port that it plans to use as a refueling and docking station for its navy, as it patrols the Indian Ocean and protects China's supplies of Saudi oil. Ever since Sri Lanka agreed to the plan, in March 2007, China has given it all the aid, arms and diplomatic support it needs to defeat the Tigers, without worrying about the West.

Even India, Sri Lanka's long-time ally and the traditionally dominant power in South Asia, has found itself sidelined in the past two years — to its obvious irritation. 'China is fishing in troubled waters,' Palaniappan Chidambaram, India's Home Minister, warned last week.

The Chinese say that Hambantota is a purely commercial venture, but many US and Indian military planners regard it as part of a 'string of pearls' strategy under which China is also building or upgrading ports at Gwadar in Pakistan, Chittagong in Bangladesh and Sittwe in Burma.[34]

However, H. E. President Mahinda Rajapakse in an interview with Jyoti Thottam of *The Time* dated 13 July 2009 has refuted such conspiracy theories by stating that the request for China to fund the Hambantota port development project came from Sri Lanka and not China:

(Question) What do you think China's strategic interest is in this port?

(President): I asked for it. China didn't propose it. It was not a Chinese proposal. The proposal was from us; they gave money. If India said, yes, we'll give you a port, I will gladly accept. If America says, we will give a fully equipped airport — yes, why not? Unfortunately, they are not offering to us.[35]

(2) Power plant

A Technical and Commercial Agreement was signed on 17 March 2006, to establish a 3×300 MW coal fired power plant at Norochcholai, Puttalam district, with an estimated investment of US$ 455 million. The contract was signed by the Ceylon Electricity Board (CEB) and the National Machinery Export Cooperation of China. The initial ground work, that is, development of land and the road network have already been started by the CEB and Road Development Authority.

Electricity supply to the power plant site has been completed with the construction of a 1.73 km 32 KV line and a 160 KVA transformer. The extension of the low voltage lines near the power plant site and the new resettlement housing projects have also been completed.

The Government of Sri Lanka is considering the possibility of accelerating the Norochcholai Coal-Power Project, which is expected to add another 300 Mega Watts to the national grid. This is a move to meet the emerging power crisis. The project is due to be completed in 2012 (Table 9.3).

TABLE 9.3: Top Chinese projects in operation (as at the end of 2008)

Name of the Enterprise	Activity	Investment (In Rupees Million)	Employees (Numbers)
Tigo (Pvt) Ltd	Cellular mobile telephone service	23168.9	463
Textured Jersey Lanka (Pvt) Ltd	Fabrics & related products	5019.4	1751
Creative Cycles (Pvt) Ltd	Export bicycle wheels	394.1	232
Collins Fashion (Pvt) Ltd*	Apparel & textile products	212.6	636

*China and Taiwan

Source: Sri Lanka, Bank of Investment. As tabulated in Dr Saman Kelegama, 'China–Sri Lanka Economic Relations: An Over View', Presentation to the Sri Lanka–China Business Forum Organised by the Ceylon Chamber of Commerce, 25 September 2009. http://www.ips.lk/news/newsarchive/2009/20-9-9-china-business-china-presentation.pdf (accessed 27 August 2011).

(b) Sri Lanka–China business council

With a very large number of Sri Lankan business establishments active in China, the Sri Lanka–China Business Council was established on 26 April 2001, under the aegis of the Ceylon Chamber of Commerce. The Council was formed at the request of the Ministry of Foreign Affairs with the main objective of promoting trade, investment, services and tourism between Sri Lanka and China.

Among the objectives of the Business Council are:

- To promote trade, tourism and services between Sri Lanka and China, and, in particular, to promote exports from Sri Lanka to China.
- To encourage Chinese investment and the establishment of joint ventures in Sri Lanka between Chinese and Sri Lanka investors.
- To exchange information on trade and investment with the appropriate bodies in China.
- To promote Sri Lankan participation in international fairs in China.
- To cooperate with the Government of Sri Lanka in the pursuit of the above objectives.

The council consisted of 129 members as of 31 March 2007. They were very active in organising a variety of events such as a thirteen-member delegation visit from the China Council for the Promotion of International Trade (CCPIT Beijing) to Sri Lanka which took place from 13 to 15 May 2006, in order to offer an opportunity for the Sri Lankan members of the Council to establish contacts with the visiting delegation.

With a view to enhance trade and investment opportunities between Sri Lanka and China, a catalogue exhibition pertaining to Chinese products and services was organised for the second successive year by the Council in association with the Embassy of the People's Republic of China on 26 May 2006. A selection of over 150 catalogues from several categories was displayed at the exhibition. The exhibition was also successfully held in June 2008 following a seminar which covered the areas of: doing business in China, the Asia-Pacific Trade Agreement, exporting to China — exploring emerging opportunities and sharing experience through trading with China.

Federation of chambers of commerce and industry of Sri Lanka (FCCISL)

The other major organisation of business establishments in Sri Lanka is the FCCISL. Some of the main activities recently organised by them are the following:

- FCCISL led a Sri Lankan business delegation to Kunming Fair/China South Asia Business Forum and was awarded the first prize for best participation in 2007.
- FCCISL led a strong Sri Lankan trade delegation to South Asian countries and organised a commodity fair in Beijing in 2007–8.
- FCCISL led a Sri Lankan delegation in April 2009 to the Chinese Mechanical and Electrical Hardware Exposition in the city of Jiang Yan.

Military

An area of very great importance, and involving the country's national security, was the need for the security forces of the country to be properly equipped to meet the separatist challenge posed, at first, by several Tamil militant groups from the early 1970s, and later, since the 1980s, from the Liberation Tigers of Tamil Eelam (LTTE). The sources of obtaining the needed hardware were not plentiful. India as a source for such imports was compromised by the fact that in the early stages, India was arming and training these Tamil militant groups. Several suppliers in the West often had their own restrictions as to which countries they could export to, based on human rights conditions. The limited suppliers of military equipment for Sri Lanka therefore included China, Pakistan, Israel, Russia, Ukraine and the Czech Republic. The US and UK, also, did supply some military equipment.

There is a natural confidentiality in the case of military items imported/exported. The following information is gathered from available public sources: Sri Lanka used to import its military equipment through Norinco and the regularity and quantity of imports was such that Norinco maintained a bonded warehouse in the southern port city of Galle since 1993.[36] China reportedly exported ammunition, anti-tank guided missiles, rocket launchers and shoulder-fired surface-to-air missiles, deep penetration bombs and rockets, mortar ammunition, night vision devices, security equipment, tanks, F7G jets, naval vessels, radars, communication equipment and other assistance to Sri Lanka. The SIPRI Yearbook 2009 states that 'Between mid-2002 and mid-2007 Sri Lanka received at least $140 million worth of military equipment from China. A large part of this was probably for ammunition stockpiles, but it is also likely to have included small arms for the expanded Sri Lankan forces.'[37]

A report dated 2 June 2007, citing Britain's renowned *Jane's Defence Weekly*, which claimed exclusive access to an internal Sri Lankan Cabinet document, reported that Sri Lanka had placed, what it called, 'the largest single order' with Poly Technologies for 120 mm mortar shells for the army, of which 70,000 rounds are priced at $10.4 million.[38] Additional imports include 68,000 rounds of varied 152 mm artillery shells worth nearly $20 million besides 50,000 81 mm high-explosive mortar bombs for $3.7 million.

The navy's requirement valued at $2.7 million included a varied range of ammunition like 100,000 14.5 mm cartridges, 2,000 RPG-7 rockets and 500 81 mm airburst mortar shells. There are also fifty Type 82 14.5 mm twin-barrel naval guns, 200 Type 85 12.7 mm heavy machine guns, 200 Type 80 7.62 mm multipurpose machine guns, 1,000 Type 56–2 7.62 mm submachine guns and 1,000 Type 56 7.62 mm submachine guns, as per the reports by *Jane's Defence Weekly*.

China, meanwhile, was also helping Sri Lanka augment its air defence capability following four strikes in 2009 by the fledgling Tamil Tiger Air Force. *Jane's Defence Weekly* declared that the China National Electronics Import Export Corp is to provide Sri Lanka a JY 11 3D radar for $5 million over the next few weeks once the site for its location near Colombo was ready. The purchase of a JY 11 3D radar raised some protests from India on the grounds that 'the system would "over arch" into its air space'.

A report in the *Time Magazine* dated 2 May 2009 states the following: 'China gave Sri Lanka — apparently free of charge — six F7 jet fighters last year, according to the Stockholm International Peace Research Institute, after a daring raid by the Tigers' air wing destroyed ten military aircraft in 2007. One of the Chinese fighters shot down one of the Tigers' aircraft a year later.'[39] According to a report from Pakistan defence sources Beijing was to provide Sri Lanka with twelve F7G fighter jets, in addition to the six F7G jets earlier delivered.[40]

The SIPRI Arms Transfers data base gives the following statistics shown in Table 9.4 for Trend Indicator Values (TIVs) of arms imports to Sri Lanka between 2007 and 2008.

TABLE 9.4: Trend Indicator Values (TIVs) of arms imports to Sri Lanka (2007–8)

(Figures are SIPRI Trend Indicator Values expressed in US$ m. at constant [1990] prices. Figures may not add up due to the conventions of rounding. A '0' indicates that the value of deliveries is less than US$ 0.5 m.)

Country	2007	2008	Total
China	8	53	60
India	21	11	32
Israel	1	0	1
USA	2	0	2
Total	31	64	95

Source: Sipri Arms Transfers Database, http://armstrade.sipri.org/arms_trade/values.php (accessed 27 August 2011).

Energy

With increasing energy requirements, finding new sources of petroleum is an important goal of China, which is already engaged in petroleum exploration in several countries in Africa. Sri Lanka has allocated an exploration block in the Mannar Basin to China for exploration of petroleum resources. China National Petroleum Corporation (CNPC) has begun oil exploration work in Sri Lanka.

Tourism

With the opening up of China's economy, the striking economic advances achieved and the increasing number of Chinese travelling overseas as tourists, Sri Lanka pursued several methods to tap the Chinese tourism market.

Sri Lanka and China signed an agreement on Accredited Destination Status (ADS) in November 2002. Sri Lanka, thereby, gets on to the list of approved destinations for Chinese tourists. Since then, a steady rise in the number of Chinese travelers to Sri Lanka has been noted and the number of Chinese tourists visiting Sri Lanka has increased by 25 per cent in 2004 in comparison to 2003.

- An MOU on tourism cooperation between the China National Tourism Administration (CNTA) and the Sri Lanka Tourist Board (SLTB) was signed on 30 August 2005, during President Kumaratunga's state visit to China, under which, among others: the two sides would promote joint ventures in the tourism industry, in particular the hotel industry.[41]

Sri Lanka was to offer training programmes in the Hotel School for Chinese nationals involved with the industry.

According to the Sri Lanka Tourism Authority, the number of Chinese nationals arriving in Sri Lanka has increased from 4,350 in 2002 to 10,015 in 2008. The highest number of arrivals, that is, 16,364 was recorded in 2006.[42] The drop in arrivals is probably due to the unfavourable travel advisories issued against Sri Lanka towards the tail end of the Sri Lankan government's battle with the Tamil Tigers which ended in May 2009.

Education

There has always been a regular number of scholarships that the Chinese government used to offer to Sri Lanka. However, the number of such scholarships used to be limited at institutions where foreign students were accepted, and in a somewhat limited range of disciplines. But after 2008, the Chinese government awards approximately twenty-three scholarships to Sri Lanka annually. These are offered in subjects such as medicine, agriculture, telecommunication, cinema and fine arts. Courses in naval, aeronautic, nuclear, telecommunication and civil engineering, are also on offer. With the limited opportunities for education in the more advanced scientific field, there is a growing interest in the higher education opportunities.

Future Scenarios

Future scenarios are projections that are plausible constructions addressing the most critical issues that a decision-maker needs to face. They are usually envisaged for a period of ten–twenty years and exclude wild card predictions. Thus the future trajectory of China–Sri Lanka relations is likely to continue as at present unless there is a dramatic shift in even one of the following three areas. The variables would be:

(a) the domestic situation in China and consequent changes in foreign policy:

(b) the domestic situation in Sri Lanka and consequent changes in foreign policy and

(c) major changes in global alliances.

Of course the developments in one of these areas can also spill over into the other and influence the shift.

With regard to the first variable, after the Cultural Revolution convulsed China the steady hand of Chou En-lai and the subsequent reforms of Deng Xiao-ping not only restored stability but also by 1978 placed China on the road to being a 'socialist country with a market economy'.[43] This has resulted in a dramatic surge in China's economy developing at double-digit growth rates over three decades to raise some 300 million people above the poverty line and become the world's third largest economy. The global international financial meltdown of 2008–9 triggered by the US secondary mortgage crisis has imperiled China's considerable US dollar investment and slowed her growth to less than the average 10 per cent per annum.[44] Nevertheless, with signs of the global economy recovering it seems likely that China's economic prosperity and growth will continue perhaps at a less dramatic rate than before. There seems little doubt that the next generation of China's leaders will want to continue the economic policies of the recent past, if at all, fine tuning them to respond to periodic changes in global trends. The pressures will come more from those who feel excluded from the economic boom in the rural under-developed areas in the West of the country. China's leaders are aware of this soft underbelly and are moving towards developing these regions.

A crucial factor is the degree to which China deals with internal pressures for the self-determination of Tibet and other predominantly non-Han areas like Xinjiang. Additionally, pressures for democracy and for human rights will determine its future political stability. Will there be, for instance, another Tiananmen Square incident? Another Cultural Revolution with violent repercussions in the foreign policy of China can be ruled out because the Cultural Revolution began as a clash between two perceptions of the future course of the Chinese revolution with a power struggle between Mao on the one side and Liu Shao-chi and Deng Xiao-ping on the other. There is no evidence of a similar ideological polarisation within the Chinese Communist

Party or outside it. Moreover, the spread of the material benefits of China's economic growth have created too many vested interests. At the same time the desire for more political power by the economically empowered groups of Chinese will demand changes faster than China's leaders and her communist party would like to concede. That may cause strains and some turbulence but the strong autocratic nature of the Chinese state will prevent any major turbulence. Strong national pride in a united and rising China after the humiliation of the 19th and early 20th centuries remains a glue bonding the Chinese people together against perceived national threats. Thus nationalist demonstrations are quickly assembled whether against alleged Japanese militarism or US 'aggression'.

Autonomous regions like Tibet and the Muslim-dominated Xinjiang pose other threats of secession. China's policies here too are sufficiently managed so as to allow a major change. The eventual passing away of the Dalai Lama may reduce the vigour of the Tibetan independence movement. An implosion such as that which occurred in the former USSR is unlikely in China. This is of course closely connected to the Taiwan issue and China's jealous safeguarding of her territorial integrity. The one possible cause for China to launch a war against the West is if there is a deliberate attempt to create an independent Taiwan supported by the West.

Natural disasters are another scenario that must be considered, especially in a vast country like China where earthquakes have caused great damage throughout history. Here too, the careful attention paid to the prediction of earthquakes and the advances in disaster preparedness and disaster recovery will ensure that total chaos will not result following a natural disaster in China. Past experience has led to greater controls on standards regarding buildings while flood control measures have resulted in rivers to be no longer viewed as the 'sorrow of China'. We must also consider the possible outbreak of pandemics and the ability of the Chinese authorities to control them safeguarding the health of its population and preventing panic. If past experience is any guide China has learnt from recent outbreaks of avian flu and SARS and is better equipped to cope, especially with the help of the WHO and the international community.

The Geneva-based World Economic Forum (WEF) in its 'China and the World: Scenarios to 2025' published in 2006 identified two critical questions:[45]

(a) Can China implement internal reforms to further its development?
(b) How will China's relationship with the rest of the world affect its development and shape the global context?

The first question is relevant to our discussion. The WEF response is that this depends on the following factors:

- The intent and ability of China's leaders to sustain the implementation of decisions made,
- The economic policy choices made including the degree of liberalisation and openness,
- The extent to which social stability can be maintained and popular expectations managed,
- The reaction of other global actors to China's rise and the broader geopolitical situation.

On this basis, the assessment is that three scenarios will emerge –

(1) Regional Ties: Where China's export-led growth is hampered by protectionism in the West, China will turn to the Asian region to provide the motor for its trade and investment and to support it on a path of reform and economic development. While economic growth will not be dramatic, this Asian orientation will help overcome historical enmities and lead to the eventual creation of an Asian Economic Region. Sri Lanka will obviously stand to benefit from this. Domestically, it will lead to strong one-party leadership and maintenance of social stability and cohesion within China

(2) Unfulfilled Promises: Where promises made to the Chinese people in terms of inclusive economic development are not met and reforms are not pushed forward because of corruption, vested interests and for fear of social unrest. This will undermine economic growth, increase disparities, heighten security concerns, curtail innovation and lead to tighter controls. This is the worst scenario of the three but even under these conditions there can be no deterioration

of Sino-Sri Lankan relations except that China's propensity to trade with and provide aid to Sri Lanka will decline. The other variable of Sri Lanka's own domestic situation will depend on the success of the government in eliminating any vestiges of the LTTE separatist terrorist group that may still exist supported by the Tamil diaspora and elements in South India and in ushering in a political solution to assuage minority demands for power sharing and equal rights and opportunities. This will determine political, economic and social stability of Sri Lanka. If the government fails in this critical policy area, relations with India will deteriorate mainly because of South Indian influence and could lead to increased dependence on China for trade and security assistance. Stakeholders in Sri Lanka's relations with China will be driven by chauvinist reactions to Indian moves to intervene in Sri Lanka on behalf of the Tamils and will look to China. A Sri Lanka with its ethnic problem resolved or even papered over could be a more confident player in international relations with a healthy balance in its relations with the two giant Asian countries — China and India.

(3) New Silk Road: The best scenario with China flourishing economically and culturally and a peaceful integration of the country geopolitically. Exports expand, foreign investment flows help create jobs and a confident government presses ahead with reforms addressing problems with State-owned Enterprises (SOEs), the environment and the rule of law. Engagement with the world is closer with participation in peacekeeping and conflict resolution. The middle class grows, and democracy and civil liberties being to improve.

Finally there is the global scenario where today's sole surviving superpower, the USA, may have to yield its position to a more multipolar world with the EU, Russia, China, India, Brazil, Japan and South Africa emerging as important great powers economically and politically. This could be consistent with China's 'peaceful rise' as it is integrated into the global system. On the other hand, if the USA's support for Taiwan's independence or Tibetan secession becomes assertive, China's hostile reaction will almost certainly result in conflict, which will be long drawn-out and could escalate into nuclear war. This latter scenario is probably a wild card unless an extreme right-wing president takes power in the US and/or a fierce nationalist leadership is in charge of a China that is contracting economically under protectionist pressures from the West.

Conclusion

Commenting on the Sri Lanka president's June 2010 visit to India, *The Hindu* editorialised on 12 June stating

With the Liberation Tigers of Tamil Eelam eliminated as a military entity, the Sri Lankan leader clearly wants to reformulate the bilateral relationship. That he is prepared to go the extra mile for this is evident from his agreement to an Indian consulate in the southern city of Hambantota where China is assisting in building a modern port, in addition to the already agreed diplomatic outpost in Jaffna.[46]

The Sri Lanka president returned from his visit to India in time to host China's vice premier Zhang Dejiang for breakfast at the conclusion of a Chinese visit which saw the signature of six agreements between the two countries.

The juxtaposition of these two important bilateral visits is symbolic of the co-existence of Sri Lanka's two important sets of bilateral relationships in a transparent, business-like and complementary style of diplomacy.

The preceding narrative is then about a bilateral relationship free of complexity or tension which is likely to continue. The geographical distance, absence of ethnic minorities in either of the two countries with links to the other, absence of any disputes that could sour the relationship and a maturity that excludes the arrogance of a big country towards a smaller nation or a fear complex of a small country — all contribute in their own way towards Sri Lanka's perception of a rising China. The Sri Lanka–China relationship stands alone and is not viewed in relation to other sets of bilateral relations.

Thus Sri Lanka policy makers of the major political parties view China through a non-partisan lens as a friendly country whose economic growth and defence modernisation is to be admired as a model for a developing country helping to achieve a multipolar world. No contradictions exist within the stakeholders of

Sri Lanka's China policy especially with the growing normalisation of Sino-Indian relations. The problem of the Dalai Lama and Tibetan Buddhists does not impact on Sri Lanka's Theravada Buddhist groups. A small Taiwan lobby in the past influenced by commercial considerations has had very weak political influence in the face of an overwhelming commitment to a 'One China Policy'. Barring violent political upheavals in both countries or a serious deterioration in Sino-western or Sino-Indian relations the present trends will continue for the foreseeable future.

✷

Notes

1. K. M. De Silva, *A History of Sri Lanka*, Colombo: Vijitha Yapa Publications, 2nd edition, 2008, p. 68.
2. Senake Bandaranayake, Yuneskō Jātika Maṇḍalaya, Madhyama Saṃskrtika Aramudala (Sri Lanka National Commission for UNESCO and the Cultural Fund), Colombo, 2003, Sri Lanka and the Silk Road of the Sea, Colombo: Sri Lanka Institute of International Relations, 2nd edition, pp. 9–10.
3. De Silva, *A History of Sri Lanka*, p. 115.
4. Shelton U. Kodikara, *Foreign Policy of Sri Lanka, A Third World Perspective*, Delhi: Chanakya Publications, 2nd edition, 1992, p. 109.
5. Ibid., p. 78.
6. Amal Jayawardane (ed.), *Documents on Sri Lanka's Foreign Policy 1947–1965*, Colombo: RCSS, 2005, pp. 176–81.
7. Kodikara, *Foreign Policy of Sri Lanka*, p. 83. Ibid., pp. 122–23.
8. Ibid., p. 86.
9. Ibid., p. 91. See also, Jayantha Dhanapala, *China and the Third World, India*, New Delhi: Vikas Publishing House Pvt Ltd, 2005, pp. 66–81.
10. W. Howard Wriggins, *Ceylon: Dilemmas of a New Nation*, Princeton, New Jersey: Princeton University Press, pp. 403–11.
11. Swaran Singh, *China–South Asia: Issues, Equations, Politics*, New Delhi: Lancer Books, 2003, p. 234.
12. Ibid., p. 238.
13. Ibid., p. 245.
14. 'China—Sri Lanka's Top Lender in 2009', *Sunday Observer*, 18 April 2010, available at http://www.sundayobserver.lk/2010/04/18/fea01.asp (accessed 24 August 2011).
15. The details of the phases and the work done so far have been identified by Sri Lanka's Ministry of Transport, available at http://www.transport.gov.

lk/web/index.php?option=com_content&view=article&id=122%3Acon
struction-of-matara-kataragama-railway-line&catid=63%3Aongoing-
projects&Itemid=111&lang=en (accessed 26 August 2011).

16. Teresita C. Schaffer, 'India and the United States in the 21st Century:
Reinventing Partnership', Washington DC: CSIS — Center for
Strategic and International Studies, 2009, p. 119.

17. Lakshman Kadirgamar, 'The Peaceful Ascendancy of China: A South
Asian Perspective', Daily News, 15 January 2009, available at http://
www.dailynews.lk/2005/01/15/fea01.html (accessed 4 August 2009).

18. Ibid.

19. Jayawardane, *Documents on Sri Lanka's Foreign Policy,* pp. 200–207

20. Ibid.

21. Ibid.

22. Kodikara, *Foreign Policy of Sri Lanka,* p. 119.

23. Jayawardane, *Documents on Sri Lanka's Foreign Policy,* pp. 200–207.

24. Ibid.

25. Douglas Jayasekera and Thusitha Tennekoon (eds), *Conference on
China-Sri Lanka Relations to Mark the 50th Anniversary of Diplomatic
Relations, Colombo, Sri Lanka 21–22 October,* Colombo: BCIS, 2007,
pp. 45–53.

26. Ibid., p. 46.

27. Ibid.

28. Ibid.

29. Ibid., p. 51.

30. 'China — Sri Lanka's Top Lender in 2009', *Sunday Observer.*

31. See Table 10.2.

32. T. K. Premadasa, 'A Glimpse of Trade between Sri Lanka and China',
Sri Lanka Guardian, Colombo, 1 October 2009, available at http://www.
srilankaguardian.org/2009/10/glimpse-of-trade-between-sri-lanka-and.
html (accessed 4 August 2011).

33. Jeremy Page, 'Chinese Billions in Sri Lanka Fund Battle against Tamil
Tigers', *The Timesonline,* available at http://www.timesonline.co.uk/tol/
news/world/asia/article6207487.ece (accessed 3 May 2009).

34. Ibid.

35. Jyoti Thottam, 'The Man Who Tamed the Tigers', *Time,* 13 July 2009,
available at http://www.time.com/time/world/article/0,8599,1910095,0
0.html, (accessed 5 August 2009).

36. *The SIPRI Year Book 2009: Armaments, Disarmament and International Security* (Stockholm, Solna, Sweden: Stockholm International
Peace Research Institute, 2009), sourcing *Jane's Defence Weekly* in
footnote 85 of page 316 states that 'Since 1993 the Chinese company
NORINCO has operated a warehouse in Sri Lanka from which it can
supply weapons on short notice. Sri Lanka was reportedly $60 million
behind in payments to NORINCO in mid-2002. By mid-2007, when

Sri Lanka replaced its agreement with NORINCO with an agreement with its Chinese competitor Poly Technologies, this debt had increased to $200 million.'

37. *SIPRI Yearbook 2009*, p. 316.
38. 'Sri Lanka Turns to Pakistan, China for Military Needs', *Lanka Newspapers.com*, 2 June 2007, available at http://www.lankanewspapers.com/news/2007/6/15520_space.html (accessed 20 May 2009).
39. Page, 'Chinese Billions in Sri Lanka'.
40. 'Sri Lanka to Get Chinese Jets', Pakistan Defence, available at www/defence.pk/forums/china-defence/22925-Sri-Lanka-get-chinese-jets.html (accessed 20 May 2009).
41. 'China-Sri Lanka Tourism Pact', 8 July 2005, available at www.asiatribune.com/oldsite/show_news php ?id=14983 (accessed 20 May 2009).
42. Sri Lanka Tourism Development Authority, *Annual Statistical Report 2008*, available at http://datastore.sltda.gov.lk/SLTDA/Reports/Annual_Report_2008.pdf (accessed 28 August 2011).
43. *Xinhua News Agency*, 'Deng Xiaoping: Leading Thinker in China's Market Economy', August 12, 2004, available at http://www.china.org.cn/english/features/dengxiaoping/103785.htm (accessed 20 May 2009).
44. The Economist Intelligence Unit ViewsWire 'How Much Worse Will it Get?', *Economist.com*, 3.2.2009, available at http://www.economist.com/agenda/displaystory.cfm?story_id=13053205 (accessed 20 May 2009).
45. World Economic Forum, 'China and the World: Scenarios to 2025', 2006, available at http://www.weforum.org/pdf/Asia/China_Scen.pdf (accessed 20 May 2009).
46. *The Hindu*, 'Productive Visit', 12 June 2010, available at http://www.thehindu.com/opinion/editorial/article453209.ece. (accessed 26 August 2011).

10

An Overview
Positive Perceptions, Anxious Undercurrents

S. D. MUNI

Three decades of sustained and very impressive economic growth, a determined effort to modernise militarily, an assertive confidence to participate in multilateral institutions and organisations as also to contribute to the international community's efforts to resolve conflicts and, above all, an ever increasing capability and willingness to engage people across the borders socially, culturally and also politically, are the signs of China's rise. This has been acknowledged and admired all over the world and South Asia is not, and cannot be an exception in this respect. South Asia is among the closest geographical regions of China, and has been heavily impacted by the rise of China. It is of interest and relevance to understand how the South Asian countries are looking at China's rise.

Mutual perceptions of the countries, as among the individuals, though based on reality are not always identical with it. Perceptions are essentially interest driven, where aspects of reality, incompatible and uncomfortable to interests, are often screened out, marginalised or treated with a spin. Perceptions are shaped and showcased by many other factors: experience, exposure and the nature of engagement. Ideology also plays a role in it but this role is not often decisive. Of course there are communist parties in South Asia and elsewhere that take a benign view of whatever China does or does not do. But then, communist parties of South Asia also got divided between admiration and endorsement of China and the then Soviet Union during the years and decades of the Sino-Soviet split. The dominance of interests in shaping perceptions is underlined by the fact that the military regimes, monarchies as also democratic governments and leaders in South Asia have not hesitated in perceiving a communist, even a radically turbulent (during the Cultural Revolution) China in a positive light.

Evolving interests and experiences also make perceptions change, from positive to negative, or negative to positive. Recall Nehru's India which, within the period of a decade, swung from the rhetoric of *Bhai-Bhai* and 'Peaceful Co-existence' to hostile and adversarial mutual images. The change in the perception of China is also a fact in the case of other South Asian countries. The constituencies and stakeholders that cluster around interests define, nurse, reinforce and even change perceptions. The way to understand perceptions therefore is a cautious and careful attempt at an understanding of the dynamics of these constituencies and stakeholders built around the interests of a given country in relation to the other. For all the constituencies and stakeholders do not have identical interests, nor is there a harmony in the perceptions they have of a given country. We are dealing here primarily with the state-centric perceptions which are a sum-total of all the negative and positive perceptions of the critical constituencies and stakeholders put together.

Two Categories

In terms of looking at China and its rise, South Asian countries clearly fall into two broad categories. India stands by a category of itself for having sharply defined positive as well as negative perceptions of China's rise, as compared to its other South Asian neighbours who are generally comfortable with the rising China. A case can be made of taking Pakistan out of the group of 'other South Asian neighbours' of India in this respect as Sino-Pakistan relationship is described as an 'all-weather friendship'. In some ways, Bangladesh's relationship with China has also been described as that of an 'all-weather friendship'. But the quality and substance of Bangladesh's relationship with China does not match that of the Sino-Pak relationship. Bangladesh has no direct border with China, nor does it have the nuclear weapon's technology component in its relations with China like that of Pakistan. It is also useful to bear in mind that Bangladesh emerged as a sovereign, independent country by breaking away from Pakistan in 1971 in the teeth of opposition of China, which took almost four years to accord recognition to the new South Asian nation and establish diplomatic relations with it. Even before the breakaway of Bangladesh, China's engagement with the western wing of Pakistan in economic, political and security sectors had a far greater scope and depth than with the eastern wing which subsequently emerged as Bangladesh. Therefore, if Pakistan is also treated as a category by itself due to the nature of its relations with China, we may have three categories. However, though the quality of their relations with China vary, in some cases drastically (like Bhutan does not even have formal diplomatic relations with China), there is a strong similarity in the perceptions of Pakistan and other South Asian countries towards China, as we shall discuss later.

An extended definition of South Asia must also include Afghanistan and Myanmar. While Afghanistan has become a full member of the South Asian Association of Regional Cooperation (SAARC), Myanmar has been included in this association as an 'observer', since 2007. Both Myanmar and Afghanistan also look towards China as a friendly and cooperative neighbour and both these countries have welcomed China's rise as a powerful Asian and global player. Differences between these two countries and the rest of India's South Asian neighbours, with regard to their perception of China, lie in the role of the India factor. Afghanistan does not look towards China primarily as a balancer of India as other smaller South Asian countries do. If at all, Afghanistan would be happy to see China exercising a moderating influence on its assertive southern neighbour, Pakistan. Myanmar looks towards India and other countries like ASEAN, to balance the burden of the Chinese neighbourhood. This is notwithstanding its substantial dependence on China in economic and defence sectors. The other South Asian countries of the second category look towards China as a cushion against the burden of India's neighbourhood. Let us now underline various aspects of these countries' perception of a rising China.

China generally, and its rise in particular, has been viewed positively by the South Asian countries as mentioned earlier. The two major dimensions of China's rise are phenomenal economic growth and a faster military modernisation. On both these counts, the South Asian countries relate themselves to China as a source of support and comfort in various ways.

Positive Perceptions

An Economic Opportunity

China's rise is seen as an economic opportunity. Smaller South Asian economies always looked towards China for economic support, trade and investment opportunities. China has not only been providing occasional budgetary support but also developmental assistance to undertake industrial and infra-structural projects since the 1950s. However, until its rise, Chinese capacity to respond to the needs and expectations of the South Asian and other developing countries was limited. Now, for the past decade of the 21st century, the fact is not only that the developing countries need China but China also needs them for their markets and primary products to sustain the momentum of its growth and manufacturing. As a result, the trade of South Asian countries with China has been registering a steady growth. With India, for instance, the trade targets set for 2010 were crossed a year earlier, when the two-way trade touched the figure of $50 billion, making China India's largest trading partner. Chinese investments have grown in South Asian countries with an increasing number of Chinese companies operating in the region, creating opportunities for joint ventures.

China has shown particular interest in infrastructure, energy exploration and mineral extraction projects. Such projects also have a bearing on China's own requirements besides being of advantage to the targeted country. China's financial support for high visibility infrastructure projects like the development of ports in Pakistan (Gwadar), Bangladesh (Chittagong), Sri Lanka (Hambantota) and Myanmar (Sittwe) have been extensively debated for their potential strategic significance. China has also offered to link with Pakistan, Nepal, Bhutan and Myanmar through rail and road connections, where new links are being undertaken and old ones are being upgraded and reinforced. China is exploring and accessing oil and gas resources in Myanmar and Sri Lanka and has shown keen interest in energy pipelines linking with Myanmar, Bangladesh, Pakistan, Afghanistan, India and Iran. As against this, China has been either slow or reluctant in extending outright financial grants, as it used to do during the 1950s through the 1970s and offering soft credits without getting directly involved in specific projects. China's status as an observer in SAARC will surely facilitate its increasing economic engagement with the region.

A Model of Economic Development

South Asia looks towards China as a model of economic development. During the initial years of reforms in China (1980s), South Asian countries showed a keen interest in the growth of agricultural productivity. Many countries did not have the socio-economic context of land reforms or the ambiance of a political system to streamline rural labour and agricultural productivity but attempts were made to learn from the Chinese best practices. In recent years, China is inspiring South Asians as the factory of the world. China's phenomenal success in mobilising foreign direct investment to build a robust manufacturing sector is a matter of envy for every South Asian country. Attention is also being paid to the high rate of domestic savings, financial and banking reforms to make easy availability of credits for manufacturing and export ventures. There is an admiration for the way China has managed the global liquidity crisis of 2008 and revived the momentum of its economic growth by providing economic bail out programmes worth more than $500 billion during 2008–9. This admiration is enhanced by the fact that the world's largest economy, the US, has to rely upon China for coming out of the economic soup it has slipped into.

A Security Provider

China has emerged as a defence provider to South Asian countries. Pakistan and Bangladesh have traditionally depended upon China for import of arms. Myanmar is also heavily depending upon China for the supply of arms particularly since 1990. Pakistan has received technology transfer and license to produce specific weapon systems (see Annexures). Such weapons that include tanks, aircrafts, missiles, armoured carriers, etc. are for its own use as also for transfer to some of the other developing countries' destinations including in South Asia. China has also been a major source of support for Pakistan's nuclear programme. Its latest example is the Chinese proposal in the Nuclear Suppliers Group (NSG) submitted in June 2010 for the transfer of nuclear technology and material to strengthen Pakistan's civil nuclear programme, on the line of the Indo-US civil-nuclear deal of 2009, ignoring Pakistan's military-nuclear programme and its pathetic record of proliferation.

Bangladesh also depends heavily on China for its arms imports and military training. Now Sri Lanka has also joined the list of Chinese arms importers in South Asia. Sri Lanka proudly boasts that its anti-LTTE war during 2008 and 2009 was won largely with the help of Chinese supplies. Sri Lanka had to resort to arms imports from China, Pakistan and other countries in the face of India's refusal to meet its growing requirements. This gave Sri Lanka freedom from political conditions that were being imposed by India, US and other members of the international community. Nepal has also periodically approached China for the supply of arms in the face of India's refusal to do so.[1] It happened during the 1960s, in 1988 and in 2005. China did not hesitate to strengthen King Gyanendra of Nepal in his fight against the 'Maoist' insurgency. China has therefore been able to emerge as the 'friend in need' and a 'reliable partner' in the defence field in the perceptions of the democratic, military and monarchical regimes of South Asia.

While being a reliable provider of defence needs, China has not been a military protector to the South Asian countries. The only exception may be of Afghanistan where China actively joined hands with the US and Pakistan during the 1980s in building military resistance against the Soviet intervention. Pakistan learnt this to its bitter experience in 1965 and again in 1971. Belying expectations, China did not intervene in Pakistan's bilateral conflict with India. All it did to show its solidarity to the 'all-weather friend' was to make a token move of troops in 1971 and diplomatic protests for the 'stealing of sheep and goats' across the un-demarcated Sino-India border in 1965. Pakistan has expressed public resentment on the US Enterprise Naval Task Force's inability to save its breakup in 1971, though the US flotilla sailed from the Pacific to the Indian Ocean to intervene. However, Pakistan did not express disappointment on China's failure to stop the emergence of Bangladesh. It seems that, rhetorical and undue expectations apart, it is understood in South Asia that countries do not fight wars for others, even when very close friends are involved.

A Protector of Sovereignty and Independence

China has come forward to politically assure the South Asian countries that it stands by their sovereignty and independence. This has been done through the use of both multilateral institutions as well as bilateral engagement. Multilaterally, China has made strategically advantageous use of its veto power and political clout in the UN Security Council. China used its first veto in the UN Security Council on 4 September 1972, against the admission of Bangladesh as a new UN member, to show solidarity with Pakistan and demonstrate that it did not recognise the breakup of Pakistan's territorial integrity. In 2007, 2008 and 2009, veto was used in support of Myanmar.[2] When the West was agitating on Myanmar opposition leader Aung San Suu Kyi's sentence by the Myanmar court on the adventure of an American citizen to breach her security and meet her, China in the UN Security Council urged that the 'world should respect Myanmar's judicial sovereignty'.[3] Similarly, when the West moved against Sri Lanka on the question of humanitarian crisis during the last phase of the war against the LTTE, China, along with India and other countries, mobilised support against the move and helped the Sri Lankan government.[4]

Bilaterally, China has come out with statements to show solidarity with the South Asian countries whenever they felt pressure from outside, particularly India or the West. Recall the then Chinese defence minister Chen Yi's statement on 6 October 1962 to assure Nepal that any attack on Nepal will be treated as an attack on China and would be defended accordingly. Nepal was facing difficulties with India on account of King Mahendra's dismissal of the democratic system on 15 December 1960. The Nepali Congress was fighting against the king's action using Indian support and territory.[5] Such statements pledging support for the sovereignty and independence of the South Asian countries have been issued by China several times, especially in the cases of Pakistan, Bangladesh, Nepal and Sri Lanka, particularly on the occasions of difficulty in their respective relations with India.[6] On many of such occasions, the South Asian countries have approached China for these assurances to cushion the political pressure they have felt from India. China on its part has always kept the issues like Tibet and Xinjiang in mind to ensure that external interference in its internal affairs does not take place.

From the South Asian countries, as also from all others, China has repeatedly sought the reiteration of their 'One China Policy' and the principle of non-interference. This was evident during the Tainnanman Square incidents in 1989 and also during the trouble in Tibet on the eve of the Olympics in 2007 and 2008.

A Mediator to Resolve Conflicts

There have been instances where some South Asian countries have looked upon China as a benign and neutral mediator of their conflicts. In November 2008, Bangladesh approached China with a request to get a Myanmar Oil Rig withdrawn from what it considered as its territorial waters. The Chinese permanent representative in UN intervened through his Bangladeshi and Myanmarese counterparts and the issue was amicably resolved.[7] Myanmar is militarily more powerful than Bangladesh. The two countries have tensions on the border question as also due to the influx of Rohingya Muslims from Southern Myanmar into Bangladesh. There are hopes in Dhaka that China would help deter any inadvertent or unexpected conflict with Myanmar if there was the possibility of one.[8] If Bhutan had diplomatic relations with China, the possibility of Nepal asking China to help it resolve the problem of 'Bhutanese refugees' in Nepal cannot be ruled out as its similar pleas on India have not been responded to.

Pakistan has also sought China's mediation in its dispute with India on Kashmir. This in any case is not acceptable to India. It is however, widely known that since 1998, China has been pleading moderation with Pakistan on the Kashmir issue and has encouraged it to find a peaceful, negotiated resolution through direct talks. The US has been invoking Chinese good offices in moderating Pakistan beginning with the Pakistani intervention in Kargil in 1999. During his visit to China in November 2009, the US President Obama called upon China to help in bringing about peace and stability, including nuclear non-proliferation, in South Asia. The US–China Joint Statement issued in Beijing on 17 November 2009 said: 'The two sides are ready to strengthen communication, dialogue and cooperation on issues related to South Asia and work together to promote stability and development in that region.' India has strongly rejected this proposition but such statements have naturally added to China's profile in intra–South Asian affairs particularly in the context of China's status as an observer in SAARC.

Concerns and Anxieties

The positive perceptions of a rising China in the smaller South Asian countries have not been completely free from concerns and anxieties. While trade and investment prospects have been promisingly enhanced, the thrust and direction of trade and investments have largely been one sided. In trade, China exports more to these countries than it imports from them leaving a yawning trade deficit. There has been unease among the commercial sectors in Pakistan, Bangladesh and Sri Lanka about this negative trade. This issue has been raised at the official levels by these countries with China asking the latter to address it. The character of trade where the South Asian countries export primary products to China and in return import value added manufactures is not very reassuring in the long run. Even India is not free from this kind of imbalance in its trade with China. For instance, 71 per cent of Indian exports to China in 2008 comprised iron ore and this was 12 per cent more than in the previous year 2007.[9] It creates a dependency nexus. Bangladesh and Sri Lanka have also been worried about the adverse effect of aggressive Chinese manufacturing and trade on their respective textile sectors. In response to the concerns raised by Bangladesh, China has assured that it will come up with projects to out-source textile manufacturing to Bangladesh. China has also granted specific tariff concessions to Bangladesh.[10] Such possibilities exist in relation to other South Asian trading partners of China. However, as these concerns have been outweighed by overall economic benefits and political support, they have not become major issues in bilateral relations. Bangladesh has made a huge political issue out of its trade deficit with India, but with China, the same question has been handled through normal diplomatic channels. Responding to the concerns raised by the Pakistani business community about China's large imports affecting Pakistani industry, Prime Minister Shaukat Aziz assured that the Chinese imports were mostly of high-value end products, and did not pose any threat to Pakistani industry.[11]

China's military modernisation is not perceived as any threat in South Asia, except in India. Four of these countries being recipients of the Chinese arms in fact look for newer and better weapons from China. Besides, they have no issue of bilateral potential conflict as their borders with China have been settled. In addition, China has also concluded or been ever willing to conclude treaties of peace and friendship and undertake confidence-building measures with its South Asian neighbours. The only undercurrent of anxiety in South Asia about China's military modernisation is in the context of China becoming more assertive and coercive in its dealing with them after it has fully emerged as a major world power. There are also fears and anxieties, at least in Bangladesh, Nepal, Bhutan and Sri Lanka, regarding China and India getting locked into a military conflict. While competition and moderate level of tensions seem to be welcomed by them, as it enlarges the scope for bargaining and diplomatic manoeuvre for them in the region, none of them would like to see a war-like situation between their two giant neighbours.

All the South Asian countries support the 'One China Policy', but there is not much approval for the way minorities in Tibet and Xinjiang have been dealt with by China. There are sympathetic ethnic and religious constituencies on the Tibet issue in India, Nepal, Bhutan and Sri Lanka that support and respect the Dalai Lama. There are also strong sections of fundamentalists in Pakistan and Bangladesh that sympathise with the Uyghur Muslims of Xinjiang. But these ethnic and religious sections have not been able to mobilise enough support to influence the position of their respective governments towards China. In fact China has been regularly drawing the Pakistani government's attention to the activities of organisations like Jamat-e-Islami and related extremist outfits in this respect since 1989. With the growing strength of jihadi forces in Pakistan, China remains concerned, as was evident during the crisis in Lal Masjid (Red Mosque) in Islamabad in 2007 when the extremists had also taken nine Chinese nationals associated with sex workers and massage parlours as hostages. Chinese nationals were also killed by extremists in Peshawar.[12]

How India Looks at China

Unlike the other South Asian countries, a sharp divide exists between the dimension of economic cooperation and strategic concerns in India's perception of China.[13] India's engagement with China seems to be revolving around four 'C's namely: cooperation, competition, containment and conflict. All these 'C's are operating simultaneously, a combination of them at times becoming dominant and at other times, remaining dormant. While the Indian strategic community takes the conflict and the containment issues seriously, the business leaders, and some of the political parties (like the communist and left parties) and academia emphasise upon cooperation and competition. The policy makers are thus called upon to strike a balance. Delivering a lecture on India's foreign policy, former foreign secretary and present national security adviser, Shiv Shankar Menon said:

> The rise of China is probably the major geopolitical development of our times. . . . We are not the only power affected by the rise of China. Like the others, we have opted to build on cooperative elements in our relationship with China while trying to solve difficult bilateral issues like the boundary and the trans-boundary rivers and to embed China in positive international relationships.

> We are dealing today with a new China, a China that has grown by over 10% for over thirty years. The result is a young, assertive and confident China, which is looking to consolidate her position in the international hierarchy. We see this on issues like Tibet, the boundary and Tawang. Dealing with this complex of issues and our relationship with China will be the greatest test of our diplomatic and strategic skill in the immediate future.[14]

India, like other South Asian countries, has welcomed the prospects of greater trade and investments and also seen China as a model of development from which many things can be learnt. The Indian business community has resented China's unfair trade practices, particularly 'dumping' and India has lodged complaints about such practices, both bilaterally as well as in the WTO.[15]

While admiring China's growth, India has also been critical of the methods employed in achieving this growth that do not respect human values. In critical comments on China's growth in his interaction with the US Council on Foreign Relations in Washington on 23 November 2009, India's prime minister Manmohan Singh said that this growth has been achieved by the

writ of the ruling group in an undemocratic set-up. . . . There is no
doubt that the Chinese growth performance is superior to the Indian
performance. But I have always believed there are other values which
are more important than the growth of gross domestic product (GDP)
like respect for fundamental human freedoms, respect for the rule
of law, respect for multi-religious, multi-ethnic rights. . . . Certainly,
I would not like to choose the Chinese path. I would like to stick to
the Indian path.[16]

On the strategic dimension, China was described as a threat and
'potential enemy no. 1' to India, by India's then defence minister
George Fernandes in 1998.[17] The then NDA government had to
make amends for it with the Chinese subsequently by disowning
his statement. But George repeated this in 2008.[18] In recent
years, not only has Prime Minister Manmohan Singh expressed
concern about China's assertiveness on the border dispute which
he said 'I cannot understand', but the former chief of naval
staff as chairman of the Chiefs of Staff Committee, Admiral
Sureesh Mehta described the pace and extent of China's military
modernisation as too fast, admitting that the gap between the two
(India and China) may even widen and India has no capacity, or
intentions to match China 'force for force'.[19] Security implications
of China's military modernisation around South Asia are being
viewed with concern by India's defence and strategic analysts.[20]
There have also been several complaints of China's intrusions
into India along the Line of Control in the Himalayas. India has
also taken serious note of China's military modernisation in the
fields of space and cyber warfare.

India's security apprehensions are also affecting its economic
engagement with China. Some of the investment proposals of
the Chinese companies, particularly Huawei, have been facing
difficulties in clearance by Indian authorities on account of
their security implications.[21] While this issue was hitherto being
raised by the communist parties of India, now it has created
controversy within the Congress party and in the cabinet of
Dr Manmohan Singh. Minister of state in charge of environment,
Jairam Ramesh, while on an official visit of China in May 2010,
asked his own country India to be more relaxed in its approach
to the Chinese investments. He criticised the 'overly alarmist
and defensive approach' in some of the Indian establishments
and said: 'India should get rid of the needless restriction on

Chinese investments. We are imagining demons where there are none.'[22] The prime minister cautioned him 'to exercise maximum restraint while commenting on the functioning of other ministries'. The Congress party also expressed strong resentment of Ramesh's criticism of Indian decisions without knowing all the details of the departments concerned.[23] There was, however, no effort to explain why the investments have been held up. This incident exposed the lack of consensus even at the highest political level in India on how to deal with China.

The difference in the perceptions of India and other South Asian countries on Rising China are accounted by many factors. We noted that all other countries have resolved their respective border issues with China. Bhutan is perhaps an exception but it is largely waiting for a green signal from New Delhi, which still does not seem to be prepared for Chinese diplomatic presence in Thimpu. There are of course questions on the tri-junctions between India, China and Bhutan, spilling into the disputed areas between India and China. India has encountered a military conflict with China in 1962, and there are Indian analysts who project the prospects of another similar conflict imposed on India by China by 2012 or later.[24] Until the 1970s, China's support for India's Maoists and northeast ethnic insurgencies was suspected. Such fears have been revived in the past couple of years.[25] The reported Chinese support for the insurgencies in India is lending credence to the Chinese analysts' projections of 'balkanising India'.[26] China also is going slow on resolving the boundary issue and instead has raised new controversies on Arunachal Pradesh as well as Sikkim. India also strongly resents China's continuing support for Pakistan and its military so as to keep India boxed in 'South Asia'. Both India and China have aspirations to emerge as major powers to play an effective role in Asian and world affairs. In this respect, India feels that China has gone much ahead and seems willing and capable of creating obstacles in India's path. India's apprehensions in this regard are enhanced by the propositions like the emergence of G2 (US and China) formulated by the western experts and strategic observers.

China Cultivates South Asian Constituencies

The constituencies of positive perceptions of rising China in South Asia are carefully and consciously cultivated by China.

It displays its soft power in South Asia and elsewhere through economic generosity and diplomatic accommodation. China's phenomenal growth has enabled it to use its economic resources generously for cultivating goodwill both in the pursuance of its strategic objectives as also for keeping the momentum of growth through the unhindered supply of raw materials and protection and expansion of markets. Through the expansion of trade and investment as well as infrastructure projects, China has been able to expand and consolidate such business constituencies in South Asian countries that profit on continuing engagement with China. China has also been quick in accommodating the concerns of the business interests in these countries through tariff concessions and innovative proposals like outsourcing of selected manufacturing, such as textiles. The efficiency with which China responds to economic requests from South Asia has impressed most of the stakeholders in the region.

China has also been very responsive towards the defence requirements of the South Asian countries, which has helped it to build strategic space. Through supply of arms and defence cooperation, China has cultivated powerful stakeholders in the security establishments. It has pursued an effective policy, particularly since the beginning of the 1980s in supporting the state, irrespective of who is in power. In Nepal, for instance, it supported the king by supplying arms against the Maoists but once the monarchy was eliminated, it quickly established contacts with Maoists and cultivated them when they were in power during 2008–9. In Sri Lanka it could not care less if its military support to the Rajapakse regime made the Tamils and the Sinhala opposition parties unhappy. China's consideration has been to expand its arms market in South Asia and establish links with the armed forces in the countries around India. The fact that China has resolved most of the territorial and political issues with India's neighbours has greatly facilitated its friendly and cooperative image in the region.

China does not have strong socio-cultural constituencies in South Asia. It has been mentioned that its treatment of the Tibetans and the Uyghur Muslims has alienated sections of population in South Asia. There is also not much room for encouraging the Chinese diaspora in these countries due to cultural and racial incompatibilities. There has been an exception in this respect in Myanmar where a large number of Chinese have gone and settled down like in other South East Asian countries.[27] China has, however, cultivated communist parties of South Asia through the exchange of delegations and support. It has also cultivated other ruling political parties and socially active groups. At the popular level, China has tried to reach academics, journalists and common people through cultural exchanges and scholarships as well through the establishment of China Study Centres and Confucius Institutes within and outside the universities in Nepal, Bangladesh, Pakistan and India, for the propagation of Chinese language and culture. In cultivating academics all over the world, China uses both rewards and punishments (like visa denial).[28]

The task of cultivating a positive image has a strong political imperative for China. South Asia borders on China's alienated ethnic periphery in the west and south. Despite massive infusion of developmental activity and demographic alterations through the migration of the Han ethnic majority people, China has not been able to win or deal with the alienation of the Tibetans and the Uyghur Muslims. Cultivating the South Asian states border-ing these Chinese minorities so as to contain their alienation and suppress separatist forces is, in a significant way, an act of self-defence and preventive diplomacy for China. Infusion of massive infrastructural projects like the Gwadar Port and Karakoram Highway link in Pakistan or Sittwe Port and Irrawaddy river navigation link in Myanmar or even Chittagong Port in Bangladesh and Humbantota Port in Sri Lanka also has a defencive dimension for China. These facilities may help keep some of its Indian Ocean-based trade flowing in the unforeseen contingency of difficulties on the South China sea front. It may be recalled here that during the Taiwan Strait missile deployment crisis in 1996, China's blockade on the South China sea front was actually threatened by the US.

In a very important way, India's failure in keeping its regional neighbours in South Asia happy has facilitated China in improving its image and standing in this region. There is no doubt that the challenge of India's policy in the South Asian region is much more complex and tough as compared to that for China. Deep and extensive historical and cultural links as well as political, social and economic contiguities throw formidable issues of identity, security and perpetual day-to-day interests in India's relations with its immediate neighbours. The Chinese mainland is far away and much different for these neighbours with little or no areas of clash and friction. This creates a natural comfort level with a perceivably distant but generous and accommodative power. China also does not suffer from the existential antagonism from any of its South Asian neighbours as is evident between India and Pakistan. But then India has not been able to harness its socio-cultural and economic advantages in the neighbourhood for a variety of reasons, not excluding the failure of its diplomacy and political vision.[29] One recent stark example of such failure is Nepal where India earned tremendous goodwill for its positive role in the 2006 Jan Andolan-II (peoples' struggle). Much of this goodwill has been frittered away in a period of two to three years. In 2009, India stood as one of the most unpopular countries, particularly with the Maoists and the Madheshi (Tarai) people that constitute Nepal's most powerful emerging popular constituencies. China has naturally been quick to cash in on the recurring tensions and irritations between India and any of its neighbours.

Prospects

South Asia is democratising. Its democratic norms and insti-tutions are still in the process of transition and consolidation. When this transition is completed, will South Asia's perceptions of China, a one-party-dominated and -controlled state undergo any reformulation? Perhaps not, because our contention here is that perceptions are driven by interests, not ideologies. So long as the imbalance and political hiatus between India and its neighbours remain, the need of the smaller South Asian countries to seek a balancer in China which is rising as a global power will continue to exist. Only India's success in resolving its contentious issues with countries like Pakistan and build-ing strong people-based economic, political and strategic con-stituencies in the neighbouring region will reduce their tendency to look for support and balance from outside.

What can dent China's image in South Asia is a major internal upheaval within China. There are no immediate prospects for such an upheaval, nor the kind of internal turbulence witnessed during the 'cultural revolution' of the late 1960s and early 1970s. A rising China is hopefully expected to experience greater internal consolidation and national cohesion. But China has a major unresolved ethnic problems in Tibet and Xinjiang. Persisting persecution of minorities is not going down well with the South Asian people even if the disapproval and resentment is not being articulated and politicised at the state level. An authoritarian state devoid of humanitarian values may generate awe and fear but cannot invoke respect and goodwill, either from within or outside.

The tendency of the South Asian countries to look towards China can also suffer a setback if China's rise eventually transforms it from a peaceful and accommodating neighbour to an assertive and encroaching one. A rise in China's tensions and conflict prospects with India or any other neighbour would also deter India's neighbours, perhaps with the exception of Pakistan, from playing a balancing game with China. Greater harmony and cooperation between India and China in the aftermath of the resolution of their border dispute may also reduce the utility and propensity of this balancing game. For India, such harmony and cooperation will open new prospects for Asian stability and security.

✹

Notes

1. In November 2005, Nepal received 4.2 million rounds of ammunition for 7.62 mm rifles and 80,000 high explosive grenades from China. It also received 12,000 AK series rifles. There were also two MA-60 military aircrafts on the inventory which are still to be received. The Nepalese side is asking for a different military aircraft, perhaps Y-12. The total amount of the deal has been estimated to be more than US$ 1 million. *Indian Express*, New Delhi, 30 November 2005; *The Telegraph Nepal*, Kathmandu, 4 December 2009.
2. Danial Soloman, 'In Myanmar, UN Irrelevant Without China', available at http://www.thehoya.com/opinion/Myanmar-un-irrelevant-without-china/ (accessed 5 December 2009). Also 'China Failing on Myanmar: US', *StraitTimes*, 19 August 2009.
3. *China Digital Times*, 12 August 2009, available at http://chinadigitaltimes.net/2009/08 (accessed 5 December 2009).
4. 'A Disgraceful Vote Which Discredits the UN Human Rights Council', *Times Online*, 28 May 2008, available at http://www.timesonline.co.uk/to/news/world.asia/article6382331.ece (accessed 5 December 2009).

5. For details see S. D. Muni, *India and Nepal: A Changing Relationship*, New Delhi: Konark Publishers, 1992.

6. See Bhaskar Roy, 'China: Back to Containing India', *South Asia Analysis Group*, Paper No. 3296, 7 July 2009, available at http://www. southasiaanalysis.org/%5Cpapers33%5Cpapers3296.html (accessed 28 July 2011). Also, Tarique Niazi, 'China's Foot in India's Door', *Asia Times*, 24 August 2005, available at www.asiatimes.com (accessed 5 December 2009).

7. See Iftekhar Chowdhury's chapter in this volume.

8. 'Dispute Resolution, Strategic Partnership to Better Serve Bangladesh and Myanmar', *The Financial Express*, Dhaka, vol. 18, no. 374, 5 December 2009, available at http://www.thefinancialexpress-bd.com/ more.php?news_id=84283 (accessed 5 December 2009).

9. Ranjit Gupta, 'Prospects of China — India Partnership', a paper presented at ICWA-AAS Conference on 'Emerging China: Prospects for Partnership in Asia', 21–23 November 2009, New Delhi.

10. See C. M. Shafi Sami's chapter in this volume.

11. See chapters of S. Javed Burki and Iftikhar Lodhi in this volume.

12. Howard W. French, 'Letter from China: Mosque Siege Reveals the Chinese Connection', *The New York Times*, 12 July 2007.

13. See the chapters of Srikant Kondapalli and Bibek Debroy and Amitendu Palit in this volume.

14. Text of the speech delivered at Thiruvananthapuram, 14 November 2009. This was the Sree Chitra Thirunal memorial lecture (unpublished).

15. 'China Faces Indian Dumping Allegations', BBC News, available at http://news.bbc.co.uk/2/hi/business/5224370.stm (accessed 6 December 2009), also see Pallavi Aiyar, 'Hindi Chini Buy Buy', *Business Line* (The Hindu Group of Publications), 20 February 2009, available at http://www.blonnet.com/2009/02/20/stories/2009022050200900.htm.

16. Zee news report on 25 November 2009, available at http://www.zeenews. com/printstory.aspx?id=581658.

17. Sunil Narula, 'George in the China Shop', *Outlook India*, 18 May 1998, available at http://www.outlookindia.com/article.aspx?205518 (accessed 6 December 2009).

18. *The Indian Express*, 30 March 2008.

19. *The Indian Express*, 10 August 2008.

20. See, for instance, Vijay Sakhuja, 'Military Buildup Across the Himalayas: A Shaky Balance', The Jamestown Foundation, 'China Brief', vol. 9, no. 18, 10 September 2009, available at http://www.jamestown.org/ single/?no_cache=1&tx-ttxnews%5btt_news%5D=35469 (accessed 28 July 2011).

21. See the contributions of CPI leader A. B. Bardhan and the CPM leader Nilotpal Basu in S. D. Muni and Suranjan Das (eds), *India and China: The Next Decade*, New Delhi: Rupa & Co., 2009, pp. 8–13, 113–18.

22. *DNA*, Mumbai, 9 May 2010.

23. *The Economic Times*, New Delhi, 11 May 2010.

24. Bharat Verma, 'Unmasking China', *Indian Defence Review*, vol. 24, no. 3, October–December 2009, available at http://www.indiandefencereview. com/2009/08/unmasking-china.html (accessed 28 July 2011).

25. The recently arrested Arabinda Rajkhowa, chairman of the United Liberation Front of Asom (ULFA) and Raju Barua, deputy commander of the insurgent outfit have admitted that their organisation received arms and training in China. *The Hindustan Times*, New Delhi, 5 December 2009.

26. Zhong Guo Zhan Lue Gang published an article to this effect on the website of one of China's Beijing-based think-tanks, The International Institute of Strategic Studies, on 8 August 2009. As cited in D. S. Rajan, 'China Should Break-up India: Chinese Strategist', on Rediff.com, 10 August 2009, available at http://news.rediff.com/special/2009/aug/10/ china-should-break-up-india-suggest-chinese-strategist.htm (accessed 7 December 2009).

27. Parama Sinha Palit, 'Cultural Diplomacy for Engaging Southeast Asia: Indian and Chinese Experiences', *The IcfaiUniversity Journal of International Relations*, vol. 3, nos 3 and 4, 2009, pp. 32–48.

28. Gary Schmitt, 'Kowtowing to China: A New Report Details How Beijing Influences American Academics", *The Weekly Standard*, 1 December 2009, available at http://www.weeklystandard.com/Content/Public/ Articles/000/000/017/282kdzck.asp.

29. For some discussion of the issues involved see S. D. Muni, 'India and Its Neighbours: Persisting Dilemmas and New Opportunities', *International Studies*, vol. 30, no. 2, 1993, pp. 189–206; also his 'Problem Areas in India's Neighbourhood Policy', *South Asian Survey*, vol. 10, no. 2, 2003, pp. 185–96; and 'Coping with the Contentious Issues in South Asia', in L. L. Mehrotra (ed.), *SAARC 2000 and Beyond*, New Delhi: Omega Publishers, 1995.

Annexure 1

China's High-level Political Visits to South Asia,
South Asian Political Visits to China (2000–2009)

South Asian Visits to China

India

Date	Delegation Head	Agreements Signed	Remarks
May 2000	K. R. Narayanan (President)		
June 2003	Atal Bihari Vajpayee (Prime Minister)	(1) Joint Declaration on Principles for Relations and Comprehensive Cooperation between India and China. (2) Memorandum on enhancing border trade.	The Indian Prime Minister made it clear that India recognises that the Tibet Autonomous Region is an integral part of the People's Republic of China.
January 2006	Mani Shankar Aiyar (Petroleum Minister)	(1) MOUs on Hydrocarbon Cooperation (2) MOUs between Indian and Chinese petroleum organisations	
June 2006	Pranab Mukherjee (Defence Minister)	None	China raised the issue of Tibet and their concerns about the activities of Tibetan refugees.

Date	Delegation Head	Agreements Signed	Remarks
January 2008	Manmohan Singh (Prime Minister)	Joint Document 'A Shared Vision for the 21st Century of the People's Republic of China and the Republic of India'.	The Indian Prime Minister spoke about the pivotal role of both China and India in Asia and the world
June 2008	Pranab Mukherjee (External Affairs Minister)		

Pakistan

Year of Visit	Delegation Head	Agreements Signed	Remarks
January 2000	Pervez Musharraf (President)		
December 2001	Pervez Musharraf (President)		
March 2003	Mir Zafarullah Khan Jamali (Prime Minister)	Decision to set up bilateral friendship forum.	
November 2003	Pervez Musharraf (President)		
February 2006	Pervez Musharraf (President)	(1) MOUs signed under which China would provide Pakistan $300 million in soft loan to assist reconstruction in the earthquake-hit areas (2) Framework Agreement on cooperation in defence (3) Framework Agreement on bolstering cooperation in energy	
June 2006	Pervez Musharraf (President)		
April 2007	Shaukat Aziz (Prime Minister)		
April 2008	Yousaf Raza Gilani (Prime Minister)		
August 2008	Yousaf Raza Gilani (Prime Minister)		

Year of Visit	Delegation Head	Agreements Signed	Remarks
October 2008	Asif Ali Zardari (President)	China Great Wall Industry Corporation (CGWIC), a space industry service provider, was contracted to launch a telecommunications satellite for Pakistan in the first half of 2011 from the Xichang Satellite Launch Center in Sichuan.	
February 2009	Asif Ali Zardari (President)		
August 2009	Asif Ali Zardari (President)	MoU signed on building a 7,000 MW hydro power project in Bunji in the Northern Areas.	
October 2009	Yousaf Raza Gilani (Prime Minister)	Government Concessional Loan Agreement for Paksat–1R Satellite System Project between Ministry of Economic Affairs and Statistics (Economic Affairs Division) Government of Pakistan as borrower and the Export-Import Bank of China as lender.	

Nepal

Year of Visit	Delegation Head	Agreements Signed	Remarks
August 2006	K. P. Sharma Oli (Deputy Prime Minister and Minister for Foreign Affairs)		
August 2008	Pushpa Kamal Dahal Prachanda (Prime Minister)		
September 2009	Sujata Koirala (Deputy Prime Minister)		

Bangladesh

Year of Visit	Delegation Head	Agreements Signed	Remarks
December 2002	Begum Khaleda Zia (Prime Minister)		
September 2008	Fakhruddin Ahmed (Chief Adviser, caretaker Government)		

Sri Lanka

Year of Visit	Delegation Head	Agreements Signed	Remarks
2004	Lakshman Kadirgamar (Foreign Minister)		
August 2005	Chandrika Bandaranaike (President)	MOU on tourism cooperation between the China National Tourism Administration (CNTA) and Sri Lanka Tourist Board (SLTB).	
February 2007	Mahinda Rajapaksa (President)		The SL President said that Sri Lanka adhered to the 'One China Policy' and resolutely supported the policy of the Chinese government on Taiwan and Tibet issues.
December 2007	Rohitha Bogollagma (Minister for Foreign Affairs)		
July 2009	Rohitha Bogollagma (Minister for Foreign Affairs)		

Chinese Delegations to South Asia

India

Year of Visit	Delegation Head	Agreements Signed	Remarks
January 2002	Zhu Rongji (Prime Minister)		
April 2005	Wen Jiabao (Prime Minister)	(1) Agreement on the Political Parameters and Guiding Principles for the Settlement of the India–China Boundary Question	

Year of Visit	Delegation Head	Agreements Signed	Remarks
		(2) Protocol on Modalities for the Implementation of CBMs in the Military Field Along the Line of Actual Control in the India–China Border Areas; Agreement on Mutual Administrative Assistance and Co-Operation in Customs Matters between India and China	
		(3) Memorandum of Understanding on Cooperation between the Indian Council of World Affairs, India and the Chinese People's Institute of Foreign Affairs, China	
November 2006	Hu Jintao (President)		
September 2008	Yang Jiechi (Foreign Minister)		The visiting foreign minister denied attempting to block an exemption for India at the Nuclear Suppliers Group (NSG) meeting in Vienna.

Pakistan

Year of Visit	Delegation Head	Agreements Signed	Remarks
May 2001	Zhu Rongji (Prime Minister)		
April 2005	Wen Jiabao (Prime Minister)	Treaty of Good-Neighbourliness and Friendly Cooperation between China and Pakistan.	

Year of Visit	Delegation Head	Agreements Signed	Remarks
November 2006	Hu Jintao (President)	Free Trade Agreement signed between China and Pakistan.	China appreciated Pakistan's valuable support on such issues as Taiwan, Tibet and human rights.

Sri Lanka

Year of Visit	Delegation Head	Agreements Signed	Remarks
April 2005	Wen Jiabao (Prime Minister)		
September 2008	Yang Jiechi (Foreign Minister)	Agreement on Economic and technological cooperation	

Bangladesh

Year of Visit	Delegation Head	Agreements Signed	Remarks
April 2005	Wen Jiabao (Prime Minister)		
April 2008	Yang Jiechi (Foreign Minister)		The Chinese foreign minister appreciated Bangladesh's support on the issue of Tibet.

Nepal

Year of Visit	Delegation Head	Agreements Signed	Remarks
July 2006	Wu Dawei (Vice Foreign Minister)	An agreement on Economic and Technical Cooperation was signed. Grant assistance of 100 Million RMB (approximately US $ 12,400,000/-) was given by China to Nepal.	
2008	Yang Jiechi (Foreign Minister)	Agreement on economic and technological cooperation.	

Source: Compiled by Tridivesh Singh Maini.

Annexure 2

Chinese Investments in South Asia (2003–2006)*

	2003	2004	2005	2006
Afghanistan	0.30	0.76	0.18	0.25
Bangladesh	1.41	0.35	11.16	5.31
India	0.15	1.68	1.35	5.61
Nepal				0.32
Pakistan	9.63	1.42	4.34	−62.07
Sri Lanka	0.23	0.25	0.03	0.25
Asia	1505.03	3013.99	4484.17	7663.25
World	2854.65	5497.99	12261.17	17633.97

Source: Statistical Bulletin of China's Outward Foreign Direct Investment 2006. Compiled by Sasidaran Gopalan.
Note: *The figures mentioned here are in US$ million and refer to outward stocks of Foreign Direct Investment.

Annexure 3.1

China's Arms Trade with South Asian Countries

South Asian Arms Imports from China, 1990–2008 (US$ million at 1990 constant prices)

	1990	1991	1992	1993	1994	1995	1996	1997	1998	1999	2000	2001	2002	2003	2004	2005	2006	2007	2008	Total
Bangladesh	95	81	89	7	17	8	5			27	9	2			6	1	184	54	10	**595**
Nepal																1				**1**
Pakistan	313	283	214	710	364	262	133	101	100	83	64	295	282	256	78	79	99	137	164	**4,017**
Sri Lanka		101	20		23	10	39	17	17	18	32	14	2		10	17	10		75	**388**
Total	408	465	323	717	404	280	177	101	117	128	105	311	284	256	94	98	293	191	249	**5,001**

Source: Stockholm International Peace Research Institute (SIPRI), November 2009. Compiled by Iftikhar A. Lodhi.

Annexure 3.2

China's Arms Trade and Defence Agreements in the Region

**Transfers of major conventional weapons from China to South Asia:
Deals with deliveries or orders made for years ranging from 1990 to 2008**

Recipient (R) or Licenser (L)	Number(s) Ordered	Weapon Designation	Weapon Description	Year of Order/ Licence	Year(s) of Deliveries	Delivered/ Produced	Comments
R: Bangladesh	(12)	A-5C Fantan	FGA aircraft	(1989)	1989–1990	(12)	No. could be 20
	(20)	F-7M Airguard	Fighter aircraft	(1989)	1989–1990	(20)	No. could be 21; F-7MB version; incl 4 FT-7B version
	(250)	PL-2A	SRAAM	(1989)	1989–1990	(250)	For A-5C and F-7M combat aircraft
	(50)	YW-531/ Type-63	APC	(1989)	1989–1990	(50)	Status uncertain
	(50)	HN-5A	Portable SAM	(1990)	1991–1992	(50)	Designation uncertain; possibly Type-54-1 version
	42	M-30 122 mm	Towed gun	(1991)	1992	42	
	(50)	WZ-121/Type-69	Tank	(1991)	1991	(50)	Type-69-I and Type-69-II version
	1	Hegu/Type-024	FAC(M)	(1992)	1992	1	Bangladeshi designation Burbar

(Annexure 3.2 continued)

(Annexure 3.2 continued)

Recipient (R) or Licenser (L)	Number(s) Ordered	Weapon Designation	Weapon Description	Year of Order/Licence	Year(s) of Deliveries	Delivered/Produced	Comments
	1	Huangfen/Type-021	FAC(M)	1992	1992	1	Bangladeshi designation Durdharsha
	(8)	HY-1/SY-1/CSS-N-1	Anti-ship missile	(1992)	1992	(8)	For Huangfen (Durdharsha) FAC
	(4)	HY-2/SY-1A/CSS-N-2	Anti-ship missile	(1992)	1992	(4)	For Hegu (Durbar) FAC; SY-1A (CSS-N-2) version
	1	T-43/Type-010	Minesweeper	1993	1994	1	Bangladeshi designation Sagar
	(5)	W-653/Type-653	ARV	(1993)	1993	(5)	
	1	Haizhui/Type-062-1	Patrol craft	(1995)	1995	1	Shanghai-3 version; Bangladeshi designation Barkat
	(18)	Type-59-1 130 mm	Towed gun	(1995)	1996	18	Designation uncertain; possibly ex-Chinese
	4	F-7A	Fighter aircraft	(1996)	1999–2000	4	FT-7 version
	(21)	HN-5A	Portable SAM	(2000)	2001	21	HN-5JA1 version
	(114)	Red Arrow-8	Anti-tank missile	(2000)	2001	114	
	20	Type-83 122 mm	Towed gun	(2003)	2004	20	
	1	Crotale	SAM system	(2004)	2007	(1)	FM-90 version; for DW-2000 frigate
	(250)	QW-2	Portable SAM	2004	2007	(250)	
	(10)	C-802/CSS-N-8	Anti-ship missile	(2005)	2008	(10)	For 1 Jianghu (Type-510) frigate
	(54)	D-30 122 mm	Towed gun	(2005)	2006–2007	(54)	Type-96 version
	(100)	PL-7	SRAAM	(2005)	2005–2007	(100)	For F-7MG combat aircraft
	(10)	PL-9	SRAAM	(2005)	2006	10	For F-7MG combat aircraft

No.	Designation	Description	Year of order	Year of deliveries	No. delivered	Comments
Nepal						
(20)	R-440 Crotale	SAM	(2005)	2007	(20)	FM-90 version; for DW-2000 (Bangabandhu) frigate
Pakistan						
16	F-7MG	Fighter aircraft	(2006)	2006	16	$44-118 m deal; F-7BG version
(5)	WZ-551	APC	2005	2005	(5)	$225 m deal; F-7P (F-7MP) version; incl 15 FT-7P version
75	F-7M Airguard	Fighter aircraft	1988	1989–1991	(75)	Pakistani designation Barkat; for coast guard
4	P-58A	Patrol craft	(1988)	1989–1990	4	
(250)	WZ-121/Type-69	Tank	(1990)	1993–1999	(250)	Type-69-IIP or Type-69-IIMP version; incl assembly and probably production in Pakistan
40	F-7M Airguard	Fighter aircraft	1992	1993	40	F-7P (F-7MP) version
(87)	Type-59-1 130 mm	Towed gun	(1992)	1998–2000	87	
3	LL-1	Fire control radar	(1994)	1996–1997	(3)	For modernisation of 3 Tariq (Amazon or Type-21) Class frigates; for use with LY-60N SAMs
(36)	LY-60	SAM	(1994)	1996–1997	(36)	For 3 modernised Tariq (Amazon) Class frigates
2	Type-76 37 mm	Naval gun turret	(1995)	1997–1999	2	For 2 Jalalat FAC produced in Pakistan
(6)	Y-12	Transport aircraft	1995	1996–1997	(6)	For 2 Jalalat FAC produced in Pakistan
2	Type-347G	Fire control radar	(1996)	1997–1999	2	For Jalalat FAC
(20)	C-802/CSS-N-8	Anti-ship missile	1997	1997–1999	(20)	For Jalalat FAC
46	F-7MG	Fighter aircraft	(2001)	2001–2003	(46)	F-7PG version; incl 6 or 9 FT-7PG version

(Annexure 3.2 continued)

(*Annexure 3.2 continued*)

Recipient (R) or Licenser (L)	Number(s) Ordered	Weapon Designation	Weapon Description	Year of Order/ Licence	Year(s) of Deliveries	Delivered/ Produced	Comments
	11	F-7MG	Fighter aircraft	(2002)	2003	11	F-7PG version
	(6)	A-5C Fantan	FGA aircraft	(2003)	2003	6	For Jalalat FAC
	(20)	C-802/CSS-N-8	Anti-ship missile	(2003)	2006	(20)	
	(143)	D-30 122 mm	Towed gun	(2003)	2003–2004	143	
	2	Type-347G	Fire control radar	(2003)	2006	2	For 2 Jalalat FAC produced in Pakistan
	1	YLC-2	Air surv. radar	(2003)	2003	1	
	10	YLC-6	Air surv. radar	(2003)	2005–2006	(10)	
Sri Lanka	5	F-7A	Fighter aircraft	1990	1991	5	F-7B version; incl 1FT-7 mainly for use against LTTE rebels
	2	FT-5	Trainer aircraft	1990	1991	2	
	(12)	Type-59-1 130mm	Towed gun	(1990)	1991	12	
	3	Y-12	Transport aircraft	1990	1991	3	Incl for use as bomber aircraft against LTTE rebels
	(35)	YW-531H/Type-85	APC	(1990)	1991–1992	(35)	Designation uncertain (possibly YW-531/Type-63)
	3	Type-062/Shanghai	Patrol craft	1991	1991–1992	3	Modified Shanghai-2 version; Sri Lankan designation Rana
	(10)	WZ-551	IFV	(1991)	1991	(10)	
	(10)	YW-309/Type-85	IFV	1991	1991	(10)	
	(1)	Y-8	Transport aircraft	1992	1994	1	Possibly second-hand; possibly incl for use as combat aircraft against LTTE rebels
	1	Haiqing/Type-037-1	Patrol craft	1994	1996	1	Sri Lankese designation Parakramabahu
	3	Haizhui/Type-062-1	Patrol craft	1994	1996	3	Sri Lankese designation Ranajaya

			1994	1995	1	
1	Yuhai/Type-074	Landing ship			1	Sri Lankan designation Shakthi
3	Type-062/Shanghai	Patrol craft	(1996)	2000	3	Shanghai-2 version; Sri Lankan designation Rana
2	Lushun	Patrol craft	(1997)	1998	2	Sri Lankese designation Prathpa
36	D-20 152 mm	Towed gun	1998	1999	(36)	Type-66 version
10	BT-6/CJ-6	Trainer aircraft	2000	2000	10	BT-6A version
6	K-8 Karakorum-8	Trainer/combat ac	(2000)	2001	6	
(10)	WZ-551	APC	(2001)	2002	(10)	
(3)	CEIEC-408C	Air surv radar	2004	2004–2006	(3)	Designation uncertain; incl for civilian air traffic control
L. Pakistan						
3	K-8 Karakorum-8	Trainer/combat ac	(2004)	2005	3	
6	F-7MG	Fighter aircraft	(2007)	2008	6	Possibly aid; F-7GS version
6	K-8 Karakorum-8	Trainer/combat ac	1987	1994	6	Incl some components produced in Pakistan and some assembled in Pakistan
(1000)	HN-5A	Portable SAM	(1988)	1989–1998	(1000)	Pakistani designation Anza-1
(55)	M-11/CSS-7	SSM	(1988)	1992–1994	(55)	Incl assembly in Pakistan
..	Red Arrow-8	Anti-tank missile	1989	1990–2008	(15100)	Pakistani designation Baktar Shikan
(268)	Type-85-IIM	Tank	1990	1992–1996	268	Type-85-IIAP version; incl assembly from kits and production in Pakistan
..	QW-1 Vanguard	Portable SAM	(1993)	1994–2008	(1250)	Pakistani designation Anza-2
(65)	W-653/Type-653	ARV	(1994)	1995–2000	(65)	Incl assembly/production in Pakistan; Pakistani designation ARV-W653

(Annexure 3.2 continued)

(Annexure 3.2 continued)

Recipient (R) or Licenser (L)	Number(s) Ordered	Weapon Designation	Weapon Description	Year of Order/ Licence	Year(s) of Deliveries	Delivered/ Produced	Comments
	(300)	Type-90-2/MB T-2000	Tank	(1998)	2001–2008	(81)	MBT-2000 (Al Khalid or P-90) version
	(250)	JF-17 Thunder/FC-1	FGA aircraft	1999	2007–2008	(8)	Developed for Pakistan; incl production of components and assembly in Pakistan
	6	K-8 Karakorum-8	Trainer/combat ac	(2001)	2003	6	Incl production of components and assembly in Pakistan
	(27)	K-8 Karakorum-8	Trainer/combat ac	2005	2007	12	Incl production of components and assembly in Pakistan

Source: SIPRI Arms Transfers Database, 30 November 2009. Compiled by Iftikhar A. Lodhi.

Note: Deals have only been included if a delivery took place during the time period specified. The 'Number(s) Delivered/Produced' and the 'Year(s) of Deliveries' columns refer to all deliveries since the beginning of the contract. Deals in which the recipient was involved in the production of the weapon system are listed separately under 'L'. The 'Comments' column includes publicly reported information on the value of the deal. Information on the sources and methods used in the collection of the data, and explanations of the conventions, abbreviations and acronyms, can be found at URL http://www.sipri.org/contents/armstrad/at_data.html. The SIPRI Arms Transfers Database is continuously updated as new information becomes available.

Bibliography

ADB, 'Key Indicators for Asia and the Pacific 2008', Manila: Asian Development Bank, 2008.

'A Bengali's Grandstand View', *Far Eastern Economic Review*, 11 October 1974.

'A Disgraceful Vote Which Discredits the UN Human Rights Council', *Times Online*, 28 May 2008, available at http://www.timesonline.co.uk/to/news/world.asia/article6382331.ece (accessed 5 December 2009).

Acharya, Shankar, 'Rising India Labors in the Shadow of Asia's Real Giant', *Financial Times*, 29 July 2009, p. 7.

'Address by Secretary (ER) at CII Conference on "India–China: Drivers of the Asian Century in a Post-Crisis World', 4 March 2009, available at http://meaindia.nic.in/speech/2009/03/04ss01.htm (accessed 8 July 2009).

Agarwal, Ajay B., *India, Tibet and China: The Role Nehru Played*, Mumbai: NA Books International, 2003.

Ahmed, Ishtiaq, 'Forthcoming Pakistan Elections: A Profile on Benazir Bhutto', ISAS Brief No. 37, 19 December 2007, available at http://www.isasnus.org/events/backgroundbriefs/38.pdf (accessed 2 May 2010).

Ahsan, Nazmul, 'China Interested to Finance Five Large Projects', *Financial Express*, 4 August 2009.

Aiyar, Pallavi, *Smoke and Mirrors: An Experience in China*, New Delhi: The Fourth Estate, 2008.

———, 'Hindi Chini Buy Buy', *Business Line* (The Hindu Group of Publications), 20 February 2009, available at http://www.blonnet.com/2009/02/20/stories/2009022050200900.htm.

Akhtar, Shahzad, 'Sino-Pakistan Relations: An Assessment', *Strategic Studies*, vol. 29, no. 2 and 3, 2009, pp. 65–89.

Al-Rfouh, Faisal O., 'Sino-Indian Relations: From Confrontation to Accommodation (1998–2001)', *China Report*, vol. 39, no. 1, January–March 2003, pp. 25–28.

Albright, Madeline, *Memo to the President: How We Can Restore America's Reputation and Leadership*, New York: Harper Perennial, 2001.

Ali, Ghulam, 'China's Kashmir Policy: Back to Neutrality, *IPRI Journal*, vol. 5, no. 2, Summer 2005, pp. 48–61.

Ali, Imran, 'Political Economy of Pakistan', in Rajshree Jetly (ed.), *Pakistan in Regional and Global Politics*, New Delhi: Routledge, 2009.

Ali, Tariq, 'Pakistan and Bangladesh: Results and Prospects', in Robin Blackburn (ed.), *Explosion in a Subcontinent*, London: Penguin, 1975.

Alvi, Hamza, 'The Army and the Bureaucracy in Pakistan Politics', in A. Abdel Malek (ed.), *Armee et Nations dans les Trios Continints*, Alger 1975 (original paper in English, mimeographed).

Aneja, Urvashi, 'China-Bangladesh Relations: An Emerging Strategic Partnership?' IPCS Special Report 3, Institute of Peace and Conflict Studies, New Delhi, India.

Annual Report, 2005–06, Directorate General of Anti-dumping and Allied Duties, available at http://commerce.nic.in/traderemedies/ANNUAL_ REPORT_2005_2006.pdf?id=1.

Arif, K., *Pakistan's Foreign Policy*, Lahore: Vanguard Publishers, 1984.

Ash, Robert, David Shambaugh and Seiichiro Takagi (eds), *China Watching: Perspectives from Europe, Japan and United States*, London: Routledge, 2007.

Ashraff, Fahmida, 'India-Afghanistan Relations: Post 9/11', *Strategic Studies*, vol. 27, no. 2, 2007.

'Asia in the "Catch-up" Game' II, ISAS Working Paper, 107, 10 May 2010.

Ayoob, Mohammed, 'Pakistan's Alliance with the United States, 1954–1965', Thesis (Ph.D.), University of Hawaii, 1966, available at http://scholarspace.manoa.hawaii.edu/handle/10125/11839 (accessed 2 May 2010).

———, 'India Matters', *The Washington Quarterly*, vol. 23, no.1, 2000, pp. 27–39.

Bagchi, Indrani, 'India, China at Loggerheads', *The Times of India*, 27 August 2005, available at http://timesofindia.indiatimes.com/ articleshow/1211953.cms (accessed 2 September 2005).

Bajpai, Kanti and Amitabh Mattoo, *The Peacock and the Dragon*, New Delhi: Har Anand Publications, 2001.

Bandaranayake, Senake, Yunesko Jatika Maṇḍalaya, Madhyama Saṃskrtika Aramudala (Sri Lanka National Commission for UNESCO and the Cultural Fund), 2003, *Sri Lanka and the Silk Road of the Sea*, Colombo: Sri Lanka Institute of International Relations, 2nd edition, *Bangladesh*, vol. 2, no. 4, Dacca, Ministry of Information and Broadcasting, 15 January 1977.

Bandow, Doug, 'China Rising: The Next Global Superpower', available at http://original.antiwar.com/doug-bandow/2007/01/26/china-rising-the-next-global-superpower, www.Antiwar.com, 26 January 2007 (accessed 16 May 2009).

———, 'Turning China into the Next Big Enemy, Foreign Follies', available at www.antiwar.com/bandow/?articleid (accessed 18 May 2009).

Basrur, Rajesh, 'South Asia's Persistent Cold War', ACDIS Occasional Paper, November 1996, pp. 2–3, available at https://www.ideals.illinois. edu/bitstream/handle/2142/15/Basrur%2520OP.pdf?sequence=1 (accessed 2 May 2010).

Basu, Gautam Kumar, 'Bhutan's Foreign Economic Relations Integration with Global Capitalism or Dependency-Reversal', in G. K. Basu, *Bhutan: The Political Economy of Development*, New Delhi: South Asian Publishers, 1996.

'Between Rising Naval Powers: Implications for Southeast Asia of the Rise of Chinese and Indian Naval Power', S. Rajaratnam School of International Studies, 18–19 November 2008.

Bhattacharjea, Mira Sinha, 'New Equations, Hard Decisions', in Verinder Grover (ed.), *China, Japan and India's Foreign Policy*, New Delhi: Deep and Deep Publications, 1992.

———, 'India-China-Pakistan: Beyond Kargil-Changing Equations', *China Report*, vol. 35, no. 4, Oct.–Dec. 1999, pp. 493–99.

Bhattacharya, Abanti, 'China's Foreign Policy Challenges and Evolving Strategy', *Strategic Analysis*, vol. 30, no. 1, Jan.–Mar. 2006, pp. 182–86.

Bhatty, Maqbool Ahmad, 'China's Peaceful Rise and South Asia', IPRI Paper 13, Islamabad: Asia Printers, August 2008.

Bijian, Zheng, 'China's "Peaceful Rise" to Great-Power Status', *Foreign Affairs*, vol. 84, no. 5, Sep./Oct. 2005, pp. 18–24.

Bisht, Medha, 'Bhutan in 2009: A Retrospective View', New Delhi: Institute for Defence Studies and Analyses, 2010.

Bitzinger, Richard A., 'China's Naval Ambitions: Aircraft Carriers will Make Waves', *Straits Times*, 10 April 2009.

——— 'China's Reemergence as an Arms Dealer: The Return of the King?' *China Brief*, Jamestown Foundation, vol. 9, no. 14, 9 July 2009.

Bottelier, Pieter, 'India's Growth from China's Perspective', *Margin: The Journal of Applied Economic Research*, vol. 1, no. 1, 2007, pp. 119–38.

Bradsher, Keith, 'China is Taking Steps to Free its Currency', *International Herald Tribune*, 6 July 2009.

Brobst, Peter, *The Future of the Great Game*, Ohio: The University of Akron Press, 2005.

Brown, Gordon, 'All Together Now', *The New York Times*, 23 September 2009, p. A35.

Burki, Shahid Javed, *The Rise of China: How It Will Impact The World*, Institute of South Asian Studies, Insight No. 80, 6 August 2009.

———, 'China's Second Rise', *The Business Times*, Singapore, 11 August 2009.

———, 'Asia in the "Catch-up" Game' I, ISAS Working paper 106, 9 April 2010.

Byron, Rejaul Karim, 'China Offers $1 billion for 5 Projects', available at http://www.thefinancialexpress-bd.com/2009/08/04/75246.html (accessed 6 September 2009).

CII, 'Country Briefing: China', 2003, available at http://www.ciionline.org/ (accessed 8 April 2007).

Cabestan, Jean-Pierre, 'The China Factor: China between Multipolarity and Bipolarity', in Gilles Bouquerat and Frederic Grare (eds), *India, China and Russia; Intricacies of an Asian Triangle*, Singapore: Marshall Cavendish International Private Ltd., 2004.

Caroe, Olaf, *Wells of Power: The Oilfields of South-Western Asia: A Regional and Global Study*, London: Macmillan, 1951.

'Central and South Asia Caribbean and Latin America', *The Military Balance 2009*, vol. 109, no. 1, pp. 329–62.

Chang, John K., 'Striving Toward the Chinese Century', available at www.chsource.org/ Striving.htm (accessed 6 April 2009).

Chaudhri, Mohammad Ahsen, 'Strategic and Military Dimensions in Pakistan China Relations', in Mehrunnisa Ali (ed.), *Readings in Pakistan Foreign Policy 1971–98*, Karachi: Oxford University Press, 2001, pp. 317–29.

Cheema, Pervaiz Iqbal, 'The China Threat: A View from Pakistan', in Herbert Yee and Ian Storey (ed.), *The China Threat: Perceptions, Myths and Reality*, New York: Routledge Curzon, 2002.

Chellaney, Brahma, *Securing India's Future in the New Millennium*, New Delhi: Orient Longman Limited, 1999.

———, *Asian Juggernaut: The Rise of China, India and Japan*, New Delhi, HarperCollins Publishers, 2006.

———, 'Sino-Indian Water Divide', *Lhasa Post*, 25 August 2009.

Chicago Council on Global Affairs, 'The United States and the Rise of China and India: Results of a 2006 Multination Survey of Public Opinion', Chicago: The Chicago Council on Global Affairs, 2006, pp. 37–38, available at http://www.thechicagocouncil.org (accessed 2 June 2008).

'Chin ko Nepal Najar' (China's Nepal View), *Nepal National Weekly*, Kantipur Publications, Sunday, 10 Jestha 2066 (16 May 2009).

'China Bigger Threat than Pakistan, Says IAF Chief', *The Times of India*, 24 May 2009.

'China's Strategic Nuclear Weapons', available at http://www.fas.org/nuke/ guide/china/doctrine/huan.htm (accessed 4 May 2009).

'China Disputes Indian Media Report of Political Interference in Nepal', *Xinhua*, 12 May 2009, available at http://english.people.com.cn/9000 1/90776/90883/6656326.html (accessed 4 July 2009).

'China Faces Indian Dumping Allegations', BBC News, available at http://news.bbc.co.uk/2/hi/business/5224370.stm (accessed 6 December 2009).

'China Failing on Myanmar: US', *StraitTimes*, 19 August 2009.

'China, India Discuss Trade Disputes, Call for Regular Communication and Coordination', *Xinhua*, 20 March 2009, available at http://english. people.com.cn/90001/90776/90883/6618131.html (accessed 4 April 2009).

'China Mounts Cyber Attacks on Indian Sites', *The Times of India*, 5 May 2008, available at http://timesofindia.indiatimes.com/India/File_China_mounts_cyber_attacks_on_Indian_sites/articleshow/3010288.cms (accessed 4 July 2008).

'China—Sri Lanka Tourism Pact', 8 July 2005, available at www.asiatribune.com/oldsite/show_news php ?id=14983 (accessed 20 May 2009).

'China—Sri Lanka's Top Lender in 2009', *Sunday Observer*, 18 April 2010, available at http://www.sundayobserver.lk/2010/04/18/fea01.asp.

'China Refutes Reports of Helping Anti-govt Groups in India', *Xinhua*, 3 November 2008, available at http://english.people.com.cn/90001/907 76/90883/6525740.html (accessed 2 December 2008).

'China's Industrial Association Strongly Dissatisfied by Indian Toy Ban', *Xinhua*, 11 February 2009, available at http://english.people.com. cn/90001/90776/90883/6590610.html (accessed 4 April 2009).

'China's Peaceful Development Road', Information Office of the State Council of the People's Republic of China, December 2005, available at http://www.china.org.cn/english/features/book/152684.htm (accessed 2 May 2010).

'China's Position Paper on the New Security Concept', Ministry of Foreign Affairs, Peoples Republic of China, July 2002, available at http://www. mfa.gov.cn/eng/wjb/zzjg/gjs/gjzzyhy/2612/2614/t15319.htm (accessed 2 May 2010).

'China–India Financial Dialogue Discusses Co-op on Fight against Crisis', *People's Daily*, 23 January 2009, available at http://english.people.com. cn/90001/90776/90883/6580338.html (accessed 4 February 2009).

'China–India Strategic Dialogue Manifests Partnership', *People's Daily*, 12 January 2006, World News Connection File Number 985, Accession Number 219700118.

'Chinese Checkers', *The Times of India*, 22 May 2009.

'Chiniya Paisako Ohiro (Flood of Chinese Money)', *Nepal National Weekly*, Kantipur Publications, Sunday, 32 Saun, 2066, 16 August 2009.

Choudhury, G. W., *The Last Days of Pakistan*, London: C. Hurst & Co., 1974.

Chowdhury, Iftekhar Ahmed, *The Roots of Bangladeshi National Identity*, ISAS Working Paper No. 63, 10 June 2009.

———, 'A Method in the Dragon's Moods: Why China Behaves as it Does', ISAS Working Paper No. 75.

———, 'Bangladesh–China: An Emerging Equation in the Asian Diplomatic Calculations', ISAS Working Paper 105, 31 March 2010.

The Chronicles of Pakistan, 8 March 1958, available at http://www. therepublicofrumi.com/chronicle/1956.htm (accessed 2 May 2010).

Chuan, Lin, 'South Asia Becomes a Target That China and the US Compete to Woo', Zhongguo Tongxun She, 10 April 2005, World News Connection File Number 985, Accession Number 205850293.

Cloughley, Brian, *A History of the Pakistan Army*, Karachi: Oxford University Press, 2000.

———, *War, Coups and Terror: Pakistan's Army in Years of Turmoil*, New York: Skyhorse Publishing, 2009.

'Communist Parties of China, India Eye Stronger Ties', *Xinhua*, 2 December 2009, available at http://english.people.com.cn/90001/90 776/90883/6544776.html (accessed 8 January 2010).

Conboy, Kenneth and James Morrison, *The CIA's Secret War in Tibet*, Lawrence: University Press of Kansas, 2002.

'Crisis Focus: A Leg Up for China', *Beijing Review*, 15 April 2009.

Crisis in Bangladesh Movement, Bangladesh Foreign Ministry, Mujibnagar, 25 September 1971.

Daftari, Maryam, 'Sino-Indian Relations and "Encounters": Challenges and Opportunities in the Nineties', *China Report*, vol. 30, no. 3, 1994, pp. 283–93.

Dahal, Dev Raj, 'Legislators' Attitude on Foreign Policy', in *Political Parties and the Parliamentary Process in Nepal: A Study of the Transitional Phase*, Kathmandu: POLSAN, 1992.

De, Anjali, 'Soviet Strategy in Bangladesh', *Holiday*, 21 January 1973.

Deepak, B. R., 'Sino-Pak Entente Cordiale and India', *China Report*, vol. 42, no. 2, 2006, pp. 129–51.

Deshingkar, Giri, 'The PRC at Forty: The Security Dimension', *China Report*, vol. 26, no. 4, 1990, pp. 351–64.

De Silva, K. M., *A History of Sri Lanka*, Colombo: Vijitha Yapa Publications, 2nd edition, 2008.

Dhanapala, Jayantha, *China and the Third World, India*, New Delhi: Vikas Publishing House Pvt Ltd, 2005.

'Dispute Resolution, Strategic Partnership to Better Serve Bangladesh and Myanmar', *The Financial Express*, Dhaka, vol. 18, no. 374, 5 December 2009, available at http://www.thefinancialexpress-bd.com/more. php?news_id=84283 (accessed 5 December 2009).

Dixit, J. N., *Indian Foreign Policy and Its Neighbours*, New Delhi: Gyan Publishing House, 2001.

———, *Makers of India's Foreign Policy: Raja Ram Mohan Roy to Yashwant Sinha*, New Delhi: HarperCollins, 2004.

Dobell, W. M., 'Ramifications of the China–Pakistan Border Treaty', *Pacific Affairs*, vol. 37, no. 3, Autumn 1964, pp. 283–95.

Dubey, Muchkund, 'The United Nations as a Foreign Policy Arena for India and China', in Surjit Mansingh, *Indian and Chinese Foreign Policies in Comparative Perspective*, New Delhi: Radiant Publishers, 1998, pp. 187–96.

Dumbaugh, Kerry, 'China's Foreign Policy: What Does It Mean for U.S. Global Interests?' CRS Report for Congress, 18 July 2008, RL34588.

Dutt, Srikant, 'China and the Hill Peoples of South-east Asia and North-east India', *China Report*, vol. 17, no. 3, 1981, pp. 3–16.

'East Pakistan: Poor Relations', *Times Magazine*, 14 July 1958.

Economic Survey, Ministry of Finance, Government of India, available at http://indiabudget.nic.in.

The Economist Intelligence Unit ViewsWire, 'How Much Worse Will it Get?' *Economist.com*, 3.2.2009, available at http://www.economist.com/agenda/displaystory.cfm?story_id=13053205 (accessed 20 May 2009).

Economy, Elizabeth C. and Adam Segal, 'The G-2 Mirage, Why the United States and China Are Not Ready to Upgrade Ties', *Foreign Affairs*, vol. 88, no. 3, May/June 2009, pp. 14–23.

Eleventh Five Year Plan (2007–2012), Inclusive Growth, vol. 1, Planning Commission, Government of India, Oxford University Press, 2008.

Emmott, Bill, *Rivals: How the Power Struggle Between China, India and Japan will Shape Our Next Decade*, London: Allen Lane, 2008.

Faruqui, Ahmed, 'The Complex Dynamics of Pakistan's Relationship with China', *IPRI Journal*, vol. 1, no. 1, Sep.–Nov. 2001, pp. 1–17.

Fei-Ling, Wang, 'Preservation, Prosperity, and Power: What motivates China's Foreign Policy', *Journal of Contemporary China*, vol. 14, no. 45, pp. 669–94.

Frankel, Francine R. and Harry Harding (eds), *The India–China Relationship: Rivalry and Engagement*, New Delhi: Oxford University Press, 2004.

French, Howard W., 'Letter from China: Mosque Siege Reveals the Chinese Connection', *The New York Times*, 12 July 2007.

Frey, Karsten, *India's Nuclear Bomb and National Security*, London: Routledge, 2006.

'From Poor Areas to Poor People: China's Evolving Poverty Reduction Agenda', An assessment of poverty and inequality in China, report of the Poverty Reduction and Economic Management Department, East Asia and Pacific Region, The World Bank, Washington DC, March 2009.

Gandhi, P. Jagdish, *India and China in the Asian Century: Global Economic Power Dynamics*, New Delhi: Deep and Deep Publications, 2007.

Ganguly, Sumit, 'India's Pathway to Pokhran II: The Prospects and Sources of India's Nuclear Weapons Program', *International Security*, vol. 23, no. 4, Spring 1998, pp. 148–77.

———, 'Assessing India's Responses to the Rise of China: Fears and Misgivings', in Carolyn W. Pumphrey (ed.), *The Rise of China in Asia: Security Implications*, Carlisle Barracks: The Strategic Studies Institute, 2002, pp. 95–104, available at http://www.strategicstudiesinstitute.army.mil/pdffiles/PUB61.pdf.

Garver, John W. 'Sino-Indian Rapprochement and the Sino-Pakistan Entente', *Political Science Quarterly*, vol. 111, no. 2, Summer 1996, pp. 323–47.

Garver, John W. *Protracted Contest: Sino-Indian Rivalry in the Twentieth Century*, New Delhi: Oxford University Press, 2001.

———, 'The Future of the Sino-Pakistani Entente Cordiale', in Michael Chambers (ed.), *South Asia in 2020: Future Strategic Balances and Alliances*, Strategic Studies Institute, USA, 2002, pp. 385–448.

———, 'Asymmetrical Indian and Chinese Threat Perceptions', in Sumit Ganguly (ed.), *India as an Emerging Power*, London: Frank Cass, 2003.

———, 'China's Influence in Central and South Asia', in David Shambaugh (ed.), *Power Shift: China and Asia's New Dynamics*, California: University of California, 2006.

———, 'China's Decision for War with India in 1962', 2004, available at http://www.people.fas.harvard.edu/~johnston/garver.pdf (accessed 2 May 2010).

Genchu, Xu, 'China's Peaceful Development and Rising Military Strength', *Chinese Foreign Affairs Journal*, vol. 83, December 2008.

George, T. J. S., 'Peking's Pre-war Message to Bhutto', *Far Eastern Economic Review*, February 1978.

Gerschenkron, Alexander, *Economic Backwardness in Historical Perspective: A Book of Essays*, Cambridge, Mass.: Belknap Press of Harvard University Press, 1962.

The Globalist, Globalist Factsheet, 'Global History. China in History — From 2000 to 2005', available at http://www.theglobalist.com/Search. aspx?txtSearch=China%20History (accessed 15 June 2009).

Gordon, Sandy, 'South Asia After the Cold War: Winners and Losers', *Asian Survey*, vol. 35, no. 10, October 1995, pp. 879–95.

Government of India, *The Ministry of Defence Annual Report*, 2007–8.

———, *The Ministry of Defence Annual Report 2006–7.*

———, *The Ministry of Home Affairs Annual Report* (various years).

Guihong, Zhang, 'U.S. Security Policy toward South Asia after September 11th and Its Implications for China: A Chinese Perspective', January 2003, Washington: Henry L. Stimson Centre, Briefings, available at http://www.stimson.org/regions/south-asia/essays (accessed 2 May 2010).

———, 'China's Peaceful Rise and Sino-Indian Relations', *China Report*, vol. 41, no. 2, 2005, pp. 159–71.

———, 'The Rise of China: India's Perceptions and Responses', *South Asian Survey*, vol. 13, no. 1, 2006, pp. 93–102.

Gungwu, Wang, *Ideas Won't Keep: the Struggle for China's Future*, Singapore: Eastern University Press, 2003.

Gupta, Ranjit, 'Prospects of China–India Partnership', a paper presented at ICWA-AAS Conference on 'Emerging China: Prospects for Partnership in Asia', 21–23 November 2009, New Delhi.

Guruswamy, Mohan and Zorawar Daulet Singh, *India China Relations: The Border Issue and Beyond*, New Delhi: Viva Books, 2009.

Hachhethhu, Krishna, 'State of Democracy in Nepal: Survey Report', Kathmandu: SDSA/N and International IDEA, 2004.

Haider, Zaglul, *The Changing Pattern of Bangladesh Foreign Policy*, Dhaka: University Press Limited, 2006.

Haider, Zaid, 'The China Factor in Pakistan', *Far Eastern Economic Review*, October 2009, full version available at http://64.151.79.128/?p=131 (accessed 2 May 2010).

'Hands Off Projects in PoK, India Tells China', 14 October 2009, available at http://news.rediff.com/report/2009/oct/14/hands-off-projects-in-pok-india-tells-china.htm (accessed 18 April 2010).

Haqqani, Husain, 'Pakistan's Endgame in Kashmir', *India Review*, vol. 2, no. 3, July 2003, pp. 34–54.

Hariharan, Col R (retd), 'China's Influence in India's Neighbourhood', Paper No. 2084, South Asia Analysis Group, available at www.southasiaanalysis.org (accessed 16 June 2009).

Hill, John E., *Through the Jade Gate to Rome: A Study of the Silk Routes during the Later Han Dynasty, First to Second Centuries CE*, South Carolina: BookSurge, 2009.

The Hindu, 'Productive Visit', 12 June 2010, available at http://www.thehindu.com/2010/06/12/stories/2010061253891200.htm.

Holz, Carsten A., 'China's Economic Growth 1978–2025: What We Know Today about China's Economic Growth Tomorrow', available at ideas.repec.org/p/wpa/wuwpdc/0512002.html (accessed 27 March 2009).

Horta, Loro, 'China Takes to the Sea', *Pacnet Newsletter*, no. 63, 18 September 2009.

Huntington, Samuel, *The Clash of Civilizations and the Remaking of World Order*, London: The Free Press, Simon & Schuster UK Ltd, 2002.

Husain, Javid, 'The Process of Foreign Policy Formulation in Pakistan', Briefing Paper No. 12, PILDAT (April 2004), available at http://www.pildat.org/Publications/publication/FP/The%20Process%20of%20Foreign%20Policy%20Formulation%20in%20Pakistan.pdf (accessed 2 May 2010).

Hussain, Arif, *Pakistan: Its Ideology and Foreign Policy*, London: Frank Cass & Co., 1966.

'In Anguish, Not Anger', *Times Magazine*, 30 November 1962.

'India's Unwise Military Moves', *Global Times*, 11 June 2009, available at http://english.people.com.cn/90001/90777/90851/6676088.html (accessed 22 July 2009).

'India Wants No Confrontation with China: Antony', *The Indian Express*, 10 June 2008.

'Indian Army Looks to "Catch Up with China" in Space Warfare', PTI News Agency, 22 October 2007.

'India-China Relations in the New Era', *ORF Discourse*, vol. 1, no. 4, December 2006, available at http://www.orfonline.org (accessed 8 June 2005).

'India's Drill Report "Surprises" Chinese Govt', *China Daily*, 1 April 2009, available at http://english.people.com.cn/90001/90776/90883/6626802.html (accessed 4 July 2009).

Issacson, Walter, *Kissinger: A Biography*, New York: Simon and Schuster, 2005.

Jacques, Martin, *When China Rules the World: The Rise of The Middle Kingdom and the End of the Western World*, London: Allen Lane, 2009.

Jahan, Rounaq, 'Bangladesh in 1972: Nation Building in a New State', *Asian Survey*, February 1973.

James, Harold, *The Creation and Destruction of Values: The Globalization Cycle*, Cambridge, MA: Harvard University Press, 2009.

Jayasekera, Douglas and Thusitha Tennekoon (eds), *Conference on China–Sri Lanka Relations to Mark the 50th Anniversary of Diplomatic Relations, Colombo, Sri Lanka 21–22 October*, Colombo: BCIS, 2007.

Jayawardane, Amal (ed.), *Documents on Sri Lanka's Foreign Policy 1947–1965*, Colombo: RCSS, 2005.

Jetley, Nancy, *India–China Relations, 1947–1977: A Study of Parliament's Role in the Making of Foreign Policy*, New Delhi: Radiant Publishers, 1979.

Jetly, Rajshree, 'Forthcoming Pakistan Elections: A profile on Benazir Bhutto', ISAS Brief No. 36, 13 December 2007, available at http://www.isasnus.org/events/backgroundbriefs/37.pdf (accessed 2 May 2010).

Jing-dong, Yuan, 'Sizing up the Elephant: Beijing's Perspectives on a Rising India', *East Asian Policy*, vol. 1, no. 4 (Oct.–Dec.), pp. 25–33.

———, 'The Dragon and the Elephant: Chinese-Indian Relations in the 21st Century', *Washington Quarterly*, Summer, 2007.

Jisi, Wang, 'China's Changing Role in Asia', in Kokubun Ryosei and Wang Jisi (eds), *The Rise of China and a Changing East Asian Order*, Tokyo: Japan Center for International Exchange, 2004.

———, 'China's Road to Peaceful Development and the USA', text of a lecture given at a meeting organised by Casa Asia and the Elcano Royal Institute on 18 July 2007 in Madrid, available at www.realinstitutoelcano.org/wps/ (accessed 10 May 2009).

Kadirgamar, Lakshman, 'The Peaceful Ascendancy of China: A South Asian Perspective', *Daily News*, 15 January 2009, available at http://www.dailynews.lk/2005/01/15/fea01.html (accessed 4 August 2009).

Kagan, Robert and Dan Blumenthal, '"Strategic Reassurance" that Isn't', *The Washington Post*, 10 November 2010, p. A15.

Kapila, Subhash, 'China-India Strategic Alliance — Should Not be Unthinkable: An Analysis', *South Asia Analysis Group*, May 2005, available at http://www.saag.org (accessed 8 June 2005).

Kapila, Subhash 'Bangladesh-China Defence Cooperation Agreement's Strategic Implications: An Analysis', Paper no. 582, South Asia Analysis Group, available at www.southasiaanalysis.org/papers6/paper582.html (accessed 6 April 2009).

Kaplan, Robert D., 'The Revenge of Geography', *Foreign Policy*, May/June 2009.

Kapur, Harish, *Foreign Policies of India's Prime Ministers*, New Delhi: Lancer International, 2009.

Keidel Albert, 'Assessing China's Economic Rise: Strengths, 2007, Weaknesses and Implications', available at www.carnegieendowment. org (accessed 8 April 2009).

———, 'China's Economic Rise — Fact and Fiction', Policy Brief 61, July 2008, Carnegie Endowment for International Peace.

Kennedy, Paul, *The Rise and Fall of the Great Powers: Economic Change and Military Conflict from 1500 to 2000*, London: Fontana Press, Collins Publishing Group, 1989.

Khan, Humayoun, 'A Historical View of China's Foreign Policy towards Great Powers', *Strategic Studies*, vol. 26, no. 2, 2006, available at http://www.issi.org.pk/old-site/ss_Detail.php?dataId=391 (accessed 2 May 2010).

Khan, M. Shamsur Rabb, 'China's Cyber Warfare', Article No. 2597, 18 June 2008, available at http://www.ipcs.org/whatsNewArticle1. jsp?action=showView&kValue=2613&status=article&mod=b (accessed 4 July 2008).

Khan, Mohammad Ayub, *Friends Not Masters*, Karachi: Oxford University Press, 1967.

Khan, Tanvir A. 'New Developments in Pakistan–China Relations', *Arab News*, 20 April 2007, available at http://www.arabnews.com/ ?page=7&section=0&article=95216&d=20&m=4&y=2007.

Kharat, Rajesh S., *Foreign Policy of Bhutan*, New Delhi: Manak Publications, 2005.

Khurana, Gurpreet S., 'China's "String of Pearls" in the Indian Ocean and Its Security Implications', *Strategic Analysis*, vol. 32, no. 1, 2008, pp. 1–39.

Kissinger, Henry, *The White House Years*, Boston: Little Brown and Company, 1979.

———, *Years of Upheaval*, Canada: Little Brown and Co., 1982.

———, *Diplomacy*, New York: Simon & Schuster, 1994.

Knoor, Klaus (ed.), *Power, Strategy and Security*, New Delhi: Asian, Books, 2nd Reprint, 1987.

Kodikara, Shelton U., *Foreign Policy of Sri Lanka, A Third World Perspective*, Delhi: Chanakya Publications, 2nd edition, 1992.

Kondapalli, Srikanth, 'India–China Border Perspectives', in *A Presentation Collection for Conference on India in 21st Century: External Relations*, Shanghai: Shanghai Institute of International Studies, 2002, pp. 129–49.

———, 'Chinese Military Eyes Southern Asia', in Andrew Scobell and Larry Wortzel (eds), *The PLA Shapes the Future Security Environment*, Carlisle Barracks, PA: US Army War College & The Heritage Foundation, 2006, pp. 197–282, available at http://www.strategicstudiesinstitute. army.mil/pdffiles/PUB709.pdf (accessed 8 April 2008).

———, 'Policy Perspectives on India–China Interaction', *Indian Foreign Affairs Journal*, New Delhi, vol. 2, no. 1, January–March 2007, pp. 75–87.

Kuan-I, Chen and Joginder S. Uppal, *India and China: Studies in Comparative Development*, New York: The Free Press, 1971.

The Kuensel Online, 'Round 18 and Counting . . .', posted 31 December 2008, available at http://www.kuenselonline.com/modules.php?name= News&file=article&sid=11725 (accessed 9 March 2009).

———, 'Joint Field Survey Next on Agenda', posted 14 January 2010, available at http://www.kuenselonline.com/modules.php?name=New s&file=article&sid=14485 (accessed 18 June 2010).

The Kuensel, 'GNH Takes Centre Stage', 19 January 2008.

Kuhn, Anthony, 'China's Growing Influence', NPR.org., 31 March 2008 (accessed 19 June 2009).

———, 'China Tries to Export Culture as Influence Increases', China and the World, available at www.npr.org (accessed 7 April 2009).

Kumar, Anand, 'Changing Dynamics of Sino-Bangladesh Relations', available at www.saag.org/common/uploaded_files/paper1345.html (accessed 12 June 2009).

Kundi, Mansoor A., 'Politics of American Aid: The Case of Pakistan', *Asian Affairs*, vol. 29, no. 2, April–June 2007, pp. 22–39.

Kurian, Nimmi, *Emerging China and India's Policy Options*, New Delhi: Lancer Publications, 2001.

Kwan, Clarence and Karl P. Sauvant, Ph.D., 'Chinese Direct Investment in the United States — The Challenges Ahead', available at http://www. cpii.columbia.edu (accessed 10 May 2009).

Lall, John, 'The Sino-Indian Border Problem as a Leftover of History', in Surjit Mansingh, *Indian and Chinese Foreign Policies in Comparative Perspective*, New Delhi: Radiant Publishers, 1998.

'Lee Kuan Yew Reflects', *Time Asia*, 5 December 2005.

Lodhi, Iftikhar, 'Forthcoming Pakistan Elections: A Profile on the Islamic Parties', ISAS Brief No. 39, 26 December 2007, available at http://www. isasnus.org/events/backgroundbriefs/40.pdf (accessed 2 May 2010).

Lodhi, Iftikhar, 'IPI or TAPI?', in Marie Lall (ed.), *The Geopolitics of Energy Security in South Asia*, Singapore: ISEAS Publications, 2008.

Lodhi, Iftikhar and Rajshree Jetly, 'Sino-Pak Relations: Retrospect and Prospect', in Tan Tai Yong (ed.), *South Asian Perspectives: Societies in Transition*, Delhi: Macmillan Publications, 2010, pp. 153–86.

'Looking from India at the Spy Plane', May 2001, available at http://www.fpif.org (accessed 2 July 2001).

Madhok, Bal Raj, *Kashmir: The Storm Centre of the World*, Houston, Texas: A. Ghosh Publishers, 2002.

Mahbubani, Kishore, *The New Asian Hemisphere: The Irresistible Shift of Global Power to the East*, New York: Public Affairs, 2008.

Mahmud, Khalid, 'Sino-Pak Ties: India Factor', *Dawn*, 14 April 2001.

Malik, Mohan, 'India-China Relations', Brief Analytical Report, Asia-Pacific Centre for Security Studies, available at http://www.apcss.org/core/BIOS/malik/India-China_Relations.pdf (accessed 20 September 2009).

Manandhar, V. K., *Cultural and Political Aspects of Nepal-China Relations*, New Delhi: Adroit Publishers, 1999.

Maniruzzaman, Talukder, *Radical Politics and the Emergence of Bangladesh*, Dacca: Bangladesh Books International, 1978.

——, *The Bangladesh Revolution and its Aftermath*, Dhaka: Bangladesh Books International Limited, 1980.

'Maritime Security: The Case of Bangladesh', Bangladesh Institute of Peace and Security Studies, Dhaka, Issue Brief No. 4, January 2009.

The McKinsey Quarterly, 'China's Track Record in M&A', no. 3, June 2008.

Memon, Marvi, 'Reorientation of Pakistan's Foreign Policy after the Cold War', in Mehrunnisa Ali (ed.), *Readings in Pakistan Foreign Policy 1971–98*, Karachi: Oxford University Press.

Maxwell, Neville, *India's China War*, New York: Anchor Books, 1972.

——, 'Henderson Brooks Report: An Introduction', *Economic and Political Weekly*, vol. 36, no. 14/15, Apr. 14–20, 2001, pp. 1189–193.

Millitary Balance 2009, IISS, available at http://www.iiss.org/publications/military-balance/the-military-balance-2009 (accessed 2 May 2010)

'Mirwaiz Seeks China's Help to Resolve Kashmir Dispute', 24 March 2010, available at http://soskashmir.wordpress.com/2010/03/ (accessed 18 April 2010).

Mishra, Keshav, *Rapprochement across the Himalayas: Emerging India–China Relations in the Post Cold War Period (1947–2003)*, New Delhi: Kalpaz Publications, 2004, available at http://www.thedailystar.net/story.php?nid=17802.

Mitchell, Derek J. and Chietigj Bajpaee, 'China and India', available at www.csis.org/media/csis/pubs/090212 (accessed 16 June 2009).

Mohan, Raja C., 'Kashmir: Remaking the Bridge Linking India, Pakistan and China', IDSS Commentaries, 22 August 2005, available at http://www.idss.edu.sg (accessed 18 September 2005).

———, 'Maritime Power: India and China Turn to Mahan', ISAS Working Paper No. 71, 7 July 2009.

Moore, Frank W., 'China's Military Capabilities', Cambridge MA: Institute for Defense and Disarmament Studies, June 2000, available at http://www.comw.org/cmp/fulltext/iddschina.html- (accessed 4 May 2009).

Mowlana Abdul Hamid Khan Bhashani's Appeal to World Leaders, Dacca: Public Relations Department of the Government of the People's Republic of Bangladesh, pp. 2–3, undated.

Muni, S. D., *India and Nepal: A Changing Relationship*, New Delhi: Konark Publishers, 1992.

———, 'India and Its Neighbours: Persisting Dilemmas and New Opportunities', *International Studies*, vol. 30, no. 2, 1993, pp. 189–206.

———, 'Coping with the Contentious Issues in South Asia', in L. L. Mehrotra (ed.), *SAARC 2000 and Beyond*, New Delhi: Omega Publishers, 1995.

———, Problem Areas in India's Neighbourhood Policy', *South Asian Survey*, vol. 10, no. 2, 2003, pp. 185–96.

Muni, S. D. and Suranjan Das (eds), *India and China: The Next Decade*, New Delhi: Observer Research Foundation & Rupa, 2009.

Musharraf, Pervez, *In the Line of Fire*, New York: Free Press, 2006.

Mustafa, Malik Qasim, 'Pakistan Defence Production: Prospects for Defence Export', *Strategic Studies*, vol. 24, no. 4, 2004, available at http://www.issi.org.pk/journal/2004_...article/5a.htm (accessed 2 May 2010).

'NSG Waiver: India Issues Demarche to China', *The Times of India*, 7 September 2008.

Naik, J. A., *India, Russia, China, and Bangladesh*, New Delhi: S. Chand and Co., 1972.

Nair, V. K., 'Armed Forces, Nuclear Weapons and China's Foreign Policy', in Surjit Mansingh, *Indian and Chinese Foreign Policies in Comparative Perspective*, New Delhi: Radiant Publishers, 1998, pp. 176–86.

Narula, Sunil, 'George in the China Shop', *Outlook India*, 18 May 1998, available at http://www.outlookindia.com/article.aspx?205518 (accessed 6 December 2009).

National Strategy for Manufacturing, National Manufacturing Competitiveness Council, Government of India, 2006, available at http://nmcc.nic.in/pdf/strategy_paper_0306.pdf (accessed 3 August 2011).

Nawaz, Shuja, *Crossed Swords: Pakistan, Its Army and the Wars Within*, Karachi: Oxford University Press, 2008.

Niazi, Tarique. 'China's Foot in India's Door', *Asia Times*, 24 August 2005, available at www.asiatimes.com (accessed 5 December 2009).

Nixon, Richard, *The Memoirs of Richard Nixon*, New York: Grosset and Dunlap, 1978.

Nizami, Taufiq Ahmad, *The Communist Party and India's Foreign Policy*, New York: Barnes & Noble, Inc., 1971.

'Now, Space Cell to Keep an Eye on China's Plans', *The Times of India*, 11 June 2008, available at http://timesofindia.indiatimes.com/India/File_Now_space_cell_to_keep_an_eye_on_Chinas_plans/articleshow/3118491.cms (accessed 22 June 2008).

'Official Claims Big Rise in Arms Exports', *Dawn*, 18 July 2008.

Opinion, 'Economic Strength Sees Miraculous Changes in New China', *The People's Daily*, 19 June 2001, available at http://English.peopledaily.com.cm (accessed 31 March 2009).

'PM's Reply to the Debate in the Lok Sabha on the President's Address', available at http://pmindia.nic.in/speech/content.asp?id=787 (accessed 22 July 2009).

'PM Calls for Increased Economic Engagement between India and China', 13 January 2008, available at http://pmindia.nic.in/pressrel.htm (accessed 28 January 2008).

Page, Jeremy, 'Chinese Billions in Sri Lanka Fund Battle against Tamil Tigers', *The Timesonline*, available at http://www.timesonline.co.uk/tol/news/world/asia/article6207487.ece (accessed 3 May 2009).

'Pakistan', Country Studies Series by Federal Research Division, Library of Congress, United States, available at http://www.country-data.com/cgi-bin/query/r-9896.html (accessed 2 May 2010).

'Pakistan: Courtship in the Air', *Time Magazine*, 6 September 1963.

'Pakistan and China: A Fraying Friendship?' *Time Magazine*, 19 February 2009.

'Pakistan Saved China from Embarrassment on Xinjiang Violence: Chinese Ambassador', *Daily Times*, 5 September 2009.

Palit, Amitendu, 'Why Fear Cheap Chinese Imports?' *Financial Express*, 13 November 2009, available at http://www.financialexpress.com/news/whyfearcheapchineseimports/544836/ (accessed 4 April 2010).

Palit, Amitendu and Shounkie Nawani, 'India–China Trade : Explaining the Imbalance', Institute of South Asian Studies (ISAS), National University of Singapore (NUS), Working Paper no. 95, October 2009, available at http://www.isasnus.org/events/workingpapers/94.pdf (accessed 26 December 2009).

Palit, Parama Sinha, 'Cultural Diplomacy for Engaging Southeast Asia: Indian and Chinese Experiences', *The IcfaiUniversity Journal of International Relations*, vol. 3, nos 3 and 4, 2009, pp. 32–48.

Pan, Esther, 'China and Pakistan: A Deepening Bond', available at http://www.cfr.org/publication/10070 (accessed 11 August 2009).

Pandey, Ramesh Nath, 'Ke Dakshin Asia Ko Manchitra Pherindaichha' (Is the Map of South Asia Changing?), *The Kantipur daily*, Kathmandu, Monday, 16 February 2009.

'Parliamentary Committees', available at http://www.parliamentofindia.nic. in/ls/intro/p21.htm (accessed 22 July 2009).

Pehrson, Christopher J., *String of Pearls: Meeting the Challenge of China's Rising Power Across the Asian Littoral*, Strategic Studies Institute, United States Army War College, available at http:// www.strategicstudiesinsti tute.army.mil/pubs?display.cfm?Pubid=721 (accessed 5 July 2009).

Pelden, Sonam, 'Will Bhutan Really Get 250,000 Tourists?' *Business Bhutan*, vol. 1, no. 6 (4 November 2009), available at http://www. businessbhutan.bt/?p=304 (accessed 17 June 2010).

Penjore, Dorji, 'Security of Bhutan: Walking Between the Giants', *Journal of Bhutan Studies*, vol. 10, Summer 2004, pp. 108–31, available at http://www.bhutanstudies.org.bt/pubFiles/v10-9.pdf (accessed 20 July 2011).

Perkovich, George, 'The Nuclear and Security Balance' in Francine R. Frankel and Harry Harding (ed.), *The India-China Relationship: Rivalry and Engagement*, New Delhi: Oxford University Press, 2004, pp. 178–218.

Phillips, Nicola, 'China: Is Development Space Disappearing for Latin America and the Caribbean?' Working Paper No. 14, January 2007, available at www.cigionline.org (accessed 26 January 2007).

Pillsbury, Michael, *China Debates the Future Security Environment*, Washington DC: National Defense University Press, January 2000.

Prasad, Eswar S., 'How to Sustain China's Growth Miracle', in Dali Y. Yang and Litao Zhao, *China's Reforms at 30: Challenges and Prospects*, Singapore: World Scientific, 2009, pp. 1–18.

Premadasa, T. K., 'A Glimpse of Trade between Sri Lanka and China', *Colombo Today*, 1 October 2009, available at http://www.colombotoday. com/english/articles/Lite/A-glimpse-trade-Sri-Lanka—China/6571. htm.

Puah, Chin-Hong, Jerome Swee-Hui Kueh and Evan Lau, 'The Implications of Emergence of China towards ASEAN-5: FDI-GDP Perspective', available at http://mpra.ub.uni-muenchen.de/4550/, Munich Personal RePEc Archive MPRA Paper No. 4550, posted 4 November 2007 (accessed 18 February 2009).

'Public Announcement of the Ministry of Commerce on Preliminary Adjudication of Anti-dumping Case Concerning Imported Nonyl Phenol Originating from India and Taiwan Region', China's Ministry of Commerce, 10 July 2006, available at http://www.isinolaw.com/ isinolaw/english/detail.jsp (accessed 24 July 2006).

Qazi, Shehzad H., 'United States' Attempts to Balance the Rise of China in Asia', *IPRI Journal*, vol. 9, no. 2, Summer 2009, pp. 32–48.

Qingguo, Jia, 'Learning to Live with the Hegemon: Evolution of China's Policy Toward the United States since the End of the Cold War', *Journal of Contemporary China*, vol. 14, no. 44, 2005, pp. 395–410.

RMA, 'Royal Monetary Authority Report 2006–2007', Thimphu: Royal Monetary Authority, 2008.
———, Selected Economic Indicators, Royal Monetary Authority, Thimphu, Bhutan, 2009.
Raghavan, V. R., *India–China Relations: A Military Perspective*, New Delhi: Gyan Publishing House, 1998.
Rahman, Rita Dulci and Jose Miguel Andreu, *China and India: Towards Global Economic Supremacy?* New Delhi: Academic Foundation, 2006.
Fazal-ur-Rahman, 'Pakistan's Relations with China', *Strategic Studies* (Winter 1998), pp. 55–87.
Rajamony, Venu, 'India-China-U.S. Triangle: A "Soft" Balance of Power System in the Making', *Center for Strategic and International Studies*, available at http://www.csis.org/saprog/venu.pdf (accessed 15 March 2002).
Rajan, D. S., 'China Adjusts Fast to the Situation in Nepal — Implications', C3S Paper No. 202, 14 August 2008, available at http://www.c3sindia.org/india/309 (accessed 18 August 2008).
———, 'China Should Break-up India: Chinese Strategist', on Rediff.com, 10 August 2009, available at http://news.rediff.com/special/2009/aug/10/china-should-break-up-india-suggest-chinese-strategist.htm (accessed 7 December 2009).
Rajan, Ramkishen, 'What does the Economic Ascendancy of China Imply for ASEAN?' available at http://www.freewebs.com/rrajan01/PRCASEAN-1.pdf (accessed 18 February 2009).
Ramo, Joshua Cooper, *The Age of the Unthinkable*, New York: Little Brown and Company, 2009.
Ranganathan, C. V., 'The China Threat: A View from India', in Herbert Yee and Ian Storey (eds), *The China Threat: Perceptions, Myths, and Reality*, London: Routledge Curzon, 2002.
Ranganathan, C. V. and Vinod C. Khanna, *India and China: The Way Ahead After 'Mao's India War'*, New Delhi: Har Anand Publications, 2003.
Rashid, Harun Ur, 'Bangladesh Foreign Policy: Realities & Challenges', *The Daily Star*, 5 January 2008.
———, 'India's Water Diversion Policy May Turn on Itself', *Daily Star*, 11 July 2009.
'Renewing American Leadership', *Foreign Affairs*, Special Edition, Davos, 2008.
Report on Wilton Park Conference WP843, China's Growing International Security and Diplomatic Role, Thursday 15–Monday 19 March 2007.
Roach, Stephen, 'I've Been an Optimist on China. But I'm Starting to Worry', *Financial Times*, 29 July 2009.

Rosenfield, John M., *The Dynastic Art of the Kushans*, New Delhi: Munshiram Manoharlal, 1993.

Roy, Bhaskar, 'China: Back to Containing India', *South Asia Analysis Group*, Paper No. 3296, 7 July 2009, available at http://www.southasiaanalysis. org/%5Cpapers33%5Cpapers3296.html (accessed 28 July 2011).

Royal Government of Bhutan, 'Bhutan 2020: A Vision for Peace, Prosperity and Happiness', Thimphu: Royal Government of Bhutan, 1999.

———, 'Economic Development Policy of the Kingdom of Bhutan, 2010', available at http://www.mti.gov.bt/Tender/edp-2010.pdf (accessed 18 July 2010).

Rubin, Barnett R. and Ahmed Rashid, 'From Great Game to Grand Bargain: Ending Chaos in Afghanistan and Pakistan', *Foreign Affairs*, vol. 87, no. 6, November/December 2008, pp. 30–45.

Rudolph, Lloyd and Susanne H. Rudolph, 'The Making of US Foreign Policy for South Asia', Economic and Political Weekly, vol. 41, no. 8, 25 February 25–3 March 2006, pp. 703–9.

SIPRI Year Book 2009, Armaments, Disarmament and International Security, Stockholm International Peace Research Institute, Stockholm, Solna, Sweden, 2009.

Safire, William, *New Political Dictionary*, New York: Random House, 1993.

Sakhuja, Vijay, 'Maritime Multilateralism: China's Strategy for the Indian Ocean', at the Institute of Southeast Asian Studies, Singapore, seminar presentation, 14 November 2009.

———, 'Military Buildup Across the Himalayas: A Shaky Balance', The Jamestown Foundation, 'China Brief', vol. 9, no. 18, 10 September 2009, available at http://www.jamestown.org/single/?no_cache=1&tx-ttxnews%5btt_news%5D=35469 (accessed 28 July 2011).

———, 'China Bangladesh Relations and Potential for Regional Tensions', *China Brief*, vol. 9, no. 15, 23 July 2009, available at www.defence.pk (accessed 21 June 2010).

Samantha, Pranab Dhal, 'Breaking 10-year Silence, China Reveals its Now No. 1 Arms Supplier to Bangladesh', available at http:// www. indianexpress.com/news/breaking-10year-silence-china-reveals-its/215320/ Posted online Sunday, September 2007 (accessed 8 September 2009).

Sami, C. M. Shafi, 'Growth of SAARC and Prospects of SAARC-China Collaboration', paper presented at an international conference on China and SAARC: Towards a Partnership of Common Prosperity, organised by China Institute of International Studies (CIIS) and Bandaranaike Centre for International Studies (BCIS), 19–20 April 2008, Beijing, China.

Santhanam, K. and Srikanth Kondapalli (eds), *Asian Security and China 2000–2010*, New Delhi: Shipra Publications, 2003.

Sarkar, Sudeshna, 'China Steps Up Military Ties with Nepal', *The Hindustan Times*, 6 December 2008.

Sattar, Abdul, *Pakistan Foreign Policy: 1947–2005*, Karachi: Oxford University Press, 2007.

Schaffer, Teresita C., 'India and the United States in the 21st Century: Reinventing Partnership', Washington DC: CSIS — Center for Strategic and International Studies, 2009.

Schmitt, Gary, 'Kowtowing to China: A New Report Details How Beijing Influences American Academics", *The Weekly Standard*, 1 December 2009, available at http://www.weeklystandard.com/Content/Public/Articles/000/000/017/282kdzck.asp.

Scissors, Derek, 'Deng Undone The Costs of Halting Market Reforms in China', *Foreign Affairs*, vol. 88, no. 3, May/June 2009, pp. 24–39.

'Security and Opportunity for the Twenty-first Century', *Foreign Affairs*, Special Edition, Davos, 2008.

'Security, Defence and Foreign Policy', available at http://aicc.org.in/new/security-agenda.php (accessed 26 June 2010).

Shafqat, Sahar and Kanishkan Sathasivam, 'In India's Shadow: The Evolution of Pakistan's Security Policy', in Uk Heo and Shale Asher Horowitz (ed.), *Conflict in Asia: Korea, China-Taiwan, and India-Pakistan*, London: Praeger, 2003, pp. 119–38.

Shambaugh, David, 'China Engages Asia: Reshaping the Regional Order', *International Security*, vol. 29, no. 3, 2004/2005, pp. 64–99.

———, 'Rising Dragon and the American Eagle — Part I', online at YaleGlobal, 20 April 2005, Yale Centre for the Study on Globalization, available at http://yaleglobal.yale.edu/content/rising-dragon-and-american-eagle-%E2%80%93-part-i (accessed 8 April 2009).

———, 'Return to the Middle Kingdom? China and Asia in the Early Twenty First Century', in David Shambaugh (ed.), *Power Shift — China and Asia's New Dynamics*, Berkley: University of California Press, 2006.

Sheridan, Greg, 'Asian Democracy and Australia', in *The Asialink Essays*, August 2009, No. 6, University of Melbourne.

Shesheng, Hu, 'Role of SAARC Observers: China's Perspective', in S. D. Muni (ed.), *The Emerging Dimensions of SAARC*, New Delhi: Cambridge University Press, 2010.

Siddiqui, Kalim, *Conflict, Crisis, and War in Pakistan*, London: Macmillan, 1972.

Sidhu, W. P. S. and Yuan Jingdong, *China and India: Cooperation or Conflict?* Boulder: Lynne Rienner Publishers, 2003.

Sikdar, B. K. and A. Sikdar, *India and China: Strategic Energy Management and Security*, New Delhi: Manas Publications, 2004, pp. 311–31.

Sikri, Rajiv, *Challenge and Strategy: Rethinking India's Foreign Policy*, New Delhi: Sage Publications, 2009.

'Silk Road', in Encyclopædia *Britannica*, from Encyclopædia Britannica Online, available at http://www.britannica.com/EBchecked/ topic/544491/Silk-Road (accessed 2 May 2010).

Simkhada, Shambhu Ram, 'Global Human Rights Agenda: Emerging Issues' in Ajit M. Banerjee and Murari Raj Sharma (eds), *Reinventing the United Nations*, India: Prentice Hall, 2007.

———, 'Complexities of Nepal's Foreign Policy', paper presented at the seminar organised by the Institute of Foreign Affairs, Ministry of Foreign Affairs, Kathmandu, December 2008.

Simon, Sheldon W., 'The Kashmir Dispute in Sino-Soviet Perspective', *Asian Survey*, vol. 7, no. 3, March 1967, pp. 176–87.

Singh, Amar Jasbir, 'The Tibetan Problem and China's Foreign Relations' in Surjit Mansingh, *Indian and Chinese Foreign Policies in Comparative Perspective*, New Delhi: Radiant Publishers, 1998, pp. 243–79.

Singh, Baljit, 'Pundits and Panchsheela: Indian Intellectuals and Their Foreign Policy', *Background*, vol. 9, no. 2, August 1965, pp. 127–36.

Singh, Jasjit, 'India's Strategic and Security Perspectives', *Strategic Analysis*, vol. 13, no. 5, August 1990, pp. 479–81.

———, *India's Defence Spending: Assessing Future Needs*, New Delhi: Knowledge World, 2000.

Singh, Jaswant, *Defending India*, New Delhi: Macmillan Publishers, 1999.

Singh, Manmohan, 'PM's Address to IFS Probationary Officers', 11 June 2008, available at http://pmindia.nic.in/lspeech.asp?id=689 (accessed 2 June 2009).

Singh, K. Natwar, *My China Diary, 1956–88*, New Delhi: Rupa & Co, 2009.

Singh, Rahul, 'Indian Army Fears China Attack by 2017', *The Hindustan Times*, 26 March 2009.

Singh, S. K. et al., *External Affairs: Cross Border Relations*, New Delhi: Roli Books, 2003.

Singh, Swaran, *China–South Asia: Issues, Equations, Policies*, New Delhi: Lancer's Books, 2003.

Smith, Jeffrey and Joby Warrick, 'A Nuclear Power's Act of Proliferation', *The Washington Post*, 13 November 2009, pp. A1 and A13.

Sobhan, Farooq, 'South Asia, American Role in Asia: Asian Views', The Asia Foundation, California, USA.

Sobhan, Rehman, *Transforming Eastern South Asia, Building Growth Zones for Economic Cooperation*, Dhaka: The University Press Limited, 1999, available at http://www.sydneybashi-bangla.com/Articles/Harun_Bang ladesh%20Foreign%20Policy%201.pdf.

Soloman, Danial, 'In Myanmar, UN Irrelevant Without China', available at http://www.thehoya.com/opinion/Myanmar-un-irrelevant-without-china (accessed 5 December 2009).

'Sri Lanka to Get Chinese Jets', Pakistan Defence, available at www/defence.
pk/forums/china-defence/22925-Sri-Lanka-get-chinese-jets.html
(accessed 20 May 2009).

'Sri Lanka Turns to Pakistan, China for Military Needs', *Lanka Newspapers.
com*, 2 June 2007, available at http://www.lankanewspapers.com/
news/2007/6/15520_space.html (accessed 20 May 2009).

Sri Lanka Tourism Development Authority, *Annual Statistical Report 2008*,
available at http://datastore.sltda.gov.lk/SLTDA/Reports/Annual_
Report_2008.pdf.

Sridharan, Kripa, *Indo-US Strategic Engagement*, New Delhi: MacMillan,
2009.

Srivastava, Siddharta, 'China Warms to Indo-US Nuclear Deal', *World
Security Network*, 3 April 2006.

Standing Committee on Defence (1995–96) Tenth Lok Sabha Sixth Report,
Defence Policy, Planning and Management, New Delhi: Lok Sabha
Secretariat, March 1996.

Standing Committee on Defence (1998–99) Twelfth Lok Sabha First
Report, New Delhi: Lok Sabha Secretariat, July 1998.

Standing Committee on Defence (1999–2000) Thirteenth Lok Sabha
Seventh Report, 'Modernisation of the Indian Air Force', New Delhi:
Lok Sabha Secretariat, December 2000.

Standing Committee on Defence (2006–7) Fourteenth Lok Sabha Twenty
Second Report, *Review of Implementation Status of Group of Ministers*,
New Delhi: Lok Sabha Secretariat, July 2007.

Stiglitz, Joseph E., *Globalization and its Discontents*, New York: W. W. Norton
and Company, 2002.

Subrahmanyam, K., 'Don't Get Fooled by China', *The Times of India*, 28
August 2007.

Sutter, Robert G., *China's Rise in Asia: Promises and Perils*, Maryland:
Rowman & Littlefield Publishers, 2005.

Swaine, Michael D. and Ashley J. Tellis, *Interpreting China's Grand Strategy:
Past, Present, and Future*, Washington: RAND Corporation, 2000.

Swaminathan, R., 'India-China Relations in the Emerging Era', South Asia
Analysis Group, available at www.saag.org/common/uploaded_files/
paper2019.html (accessed on 12 August 2009).

Swamy, Subramanian, *Financial Architecture and Economic Development
in China and India: A Comparative Perspective*, New Delhi: Konark
Publishers, 2006.

Syed, Anwar, *China and Pakistan: Diplomacy of an Entente Cordiale*, Amherst:
University of Massachusetts Press, 1974.

Tabuchi, Hiroko, 'China's Day Arriving Sooner than Japan Expected', *The
New York Times*, 2 October 2009, pp. B1 and B2.

Tahir-Kheli, Shirin, 'The Foreign Policy of "New" Pakistan', *Orbis*, vol. 20, no. 3, Fall 1976.

Thacik, John J., Jr , 'China's Rise at Stake in Power Struggle', *Asian Times*, September 2004.

Tibetan Review, '19th Bhutan-China Border Talk Held', available at http://www.tibetanreview.net/news.php?cat=2&&id=5333 (accessed 18 June 2010).

Thottam, Jyoti, 'The Man Who Tamed the Tigers', *Time*, 13 July 2009, available at http://www.time.com/time/world/article/0,8599,1910095, 00.html (accessed 5 August 2009).

'US–China Seek Role in South Asia, Irked India Says No', 19 November 2009, Zee News, available at http://www.zeenews.com/news580042. html (accessed 2 May 2010).

Verma, Bharat, 'Unmasking China', *Indian Defence Review*, vol. 24, no. 3, October–December 2009, available at http://www.indiandefencereview. com/2009/08/unmasking-china.html (accessed 28 July 2011).

Vogel, Ezra F., *Japan as Number One: Lessons for America*, New York: Universe, 1999.

Walker, Christopher and Sarah Cook, 'The Dark Side of China Aid', *International Herald Tribune*, 25 March 2010.

Waseem, Mohammed, 'Civil-Military Relations in Pakistan', in Rajshree Jetly (ed.), *Pakistan in Regional and Global Politics*, New Delhi: Routledge, 2009.

'Washington Draws India in Against China', *People's Daily*, 8 July 2005, World News Connection File Number 985, Accession Number 210300049.

'What are the Indian Expansionists Trying to Do?', *Peking Review*, vol. 14, no. 16, 16 April 1971.

'White Paper on China's National Defence', December 2000, available at http://www.china.org.cn/e-white/2000/index.htm (accessed 2 May 2010).

White Paper on National Defense, 2008, available at http://english.gov. cn/official/2009-01/20/content_1210227.htm.

White Paper on Peaceful Development Road, The State Council of China, December 2005, available at http://www.china.org.cn/english/2005/ Dec/152669.htm (accessed 2 May 2010).

Wilson, Dominic and Roopa Purushothaman, 'Dreaming with BRICs: The Path to 2050', Goldman Sachs, Global Economic Paper No. 99, October 2003, available at http:// www2. Goldman. Sachs .com?insight?research/reports/99 pdf.

Wirsing, Robert, 'Pakistan's Strategic Options: From the Cold War to the War on Terrorism', in Saeed Shafqat (ed.), *New Perspectives on Pakistan*, Karachi: Oxford University Press, 2007.

Woo, Wing Thye, 'The Economic Impact of China's Emergence as a Major Trading Nation', available at www.econ.ucdavis.edu/ (accessed 10 May 2009).

The World Bank, *The East Asian Miracle: Economic Growth and Public Policy*, New York: Oxford University Press, 1973.

World Economic Forum, 'China and the World: Scenarios to 2025', 2006, available at http://www.weforum.org/pdf/Asia/China_Scen.pdf (accessed 20 May 2009).

Wriggins, W. Howard, *Ceylon: Dilemmas of a New Nation*, Princeton, New Jersey: Princeton University Press.

Xinhua News Agency, 'Deng Xiaoping: Leading Thinker in China's Market Economy', August 12, 2004, available at http://www.china.org.cn/english/features/dengxiaoping/103785.htm (accessed 20 May 2009).

Yang, Xiao, 'Children Lead the Way into the Meeting', *China Daily*, 7 July 2010, p. 1.

———, 'Zardari Visit Cements All-weather Friendship', *China Daily*, 9 July 2010, p. 4.

Yew, Lee Kuan, *The Fundamentals of Singapore's Foreign Policy: Then and Now*, S. Rajaratnam Lecture 2009, Singapore: MFA Diplomatic Academy, 2009.

Zakaria, Fareed, *The Post American World*, New York: W. W. Norton & Company, 2008.

Zedong, Mao, 'Theory on the Division of the Three Worlds and the Strategy of Forming an Alliance Against an Opponent', available at http://www.fmprc.gov.cn? Eng? Ziliao/ 3602/3604/ t 18008. htm (accessed 29 June 2009).

Zhang, Guihong, 'India's Perceptions of a Rising China; An Assessment', *South Asian Survey*, vol. 13, no. 1, 2006, pp. 93–102.

Zhang, Yunling and Shiping Tang, 'China's Regional Strategy', in David Shambaugh (ed.), *Power Shift: China and Asia's New Dynamics*, California: University of California, 2006, pp. 48–70.

About the Editors

S. D. Muni is Visiting Research Professor at the Institute of South Asian Studies, National University of Singapore. He has served as India's Ambassador to Laos and Special Envoy, and was Professor at the School of International Studies, Jawaharlal Nehru University, New Delhi, from 1974 to 2006. His publications include *India and China: The Next Decade* (2008, co-edited with Suranjan Das; *India's Foreign Policy: The Democracy Dimension* (2009) and *The Emerging Dimensions of SAARC* (2010)

Tan Tai Yong is Director of the Institute of South Asian Studies, National University of Singapore. Professor Tan, a historian, is concurrently Vice Provost (Student Life) at the National University of Singapore. Some of his publications include *Socio-political and Economic Changes in South Asia* (2009); *From Classical Emporium to World City: A 700 Year History of Singapore* (2009), co-authored with C. G. Kwa and Derek Heng and *South Asia: Societies in Political and Economic Transition* (2010).

Notes on Contributors

Caroline Brassard is Assistant Professor of Economics at the Lee Kuan Yew School of Public Policy, National University of Singapore.

Shahid Javed Burki is Visiting Senior Research Fellow at the Institute of South Asian Studies, National University of Singapore. He is also the former vice president of the World Bank and former finance minister of Pakistan.

Iftekhar Ahmed Chowdhury is Senior Research Fellow at the Institute of South Asian Studies, National University of Singapore. He is former foreign advisor (foreign minister) of Bangladesh.

Bibek Debroy is Research Professor at the Centre for Policy Research in New Delhi. He was Visiting Senior Research Fellow at the Institute of South Asian Studies, National University of Singapore. He is also Professor at the International Management Institute, New Delhi.

Jayantha Dhanapala is former Under-Secretary-General for Disarmament Affairs, United Nations and served in that capacity from 1998 to 2003. From December 2005 to December 2007 he was Senior Advisor to the president of Sri Lanka.

John Gooneratne is former Sri Lanka Foreign Service Officer and Ambassador to Iraq. He was Associate Director at the Regional Centre for Strategic Studies (1993–99). He also worked at the Government Peace Secretariat from 2002 to 2006.

Sasidaran Gopalan was a research associate with the Institute of South Asian Studies, National University of Singapore. He is currently pursuing his Ph.D. at the George Mason University, Arlington, Virginia, USA.

Srikanth Kondapalli is Chairman, Centre for East Asian Studies, School of International Studies, Jawaharlal Nehru University, New Delhi.

Iftikhar A. Lodhi is a research associate at the Institute of South Asian Studies, National University of Singapore. He has written and published on energy security, geopolitics, economic development, Pakistan's political economy and foreign relations.

Tridivesh Singh Maini was a research associate at the Institute of South Asian Studies, National University of Singapore. He is currently Associate Fellow at the Observer Research Foundation, New Delhi.

Amitendu Palit is Head (Development and Programme) and Visiting Senior Research Fellow at the Institute of South Asian Studies, National University of Singapore. He is also a member of the Indian Economic Service which he joined in 1992.

C. M. Shafi Sami is former Adviser to the Government of Bangladesh. Sami, a former diplomat, also served as Foreign Secretary of Bangladesh.

Shambhu Ram Simkhada is former Member of the Peace and Conflict Management Committee, Government of Nepal, and former Ambassador.

Index

For Product Safety Concerns and Information please contact our EU
representative GPSR@taylorandfrancis.com
Taylor & Francis Verlag GmbH, Kaufingerstraße 24, 80331 München, Germany